Ontology

T0325328

Central Problems of Philosophy
Series Editor: John Shand

This series of books presents concise, clear, and rigorous analyses of the core problems that preoccupy philosophers across all approaches to the discipline. Each book encapsulates the essential arguments and debates, providing an authoritative guide to the subject while also introducing original perspectives. This series of books by an international team of authors aims to cover those fundamental topics that, taken together, constitute the full breadth of philosophy.

Published titles

Free Will
Graham McFee

Knowledge
Michael Welbourne

Ontology
Dale Jacquette

Relativism
Paul O'Grady

Scepticism
Neil Gascoigne

Truth
Pascal Engel

Universals
J. P. Moreland

Forthcoming titles

Action
Rowland Stout

Analysis
Michael Beaney

Artificial Intelligence
Matthew Elton & Michael Wheeler

Causation and Explanation
Stathis Psillos

Meaning
David Cooper

Mind and Body
Robert Kirk

Modality
Joseph Melia

Paradox
Doris Olin

Perception
Barry Maund

Rights
Jonathan Gorman

Self
Stephen Burwood

Value
Chris Cherry

Ontology

Dale Jacquette

McGill-Queen's University Press
Montreal & Kingston • Ithaca

ISBN 0-7735-2463-0 (bound)
ISBN 0-7735-2464-9 (paper)

Published simultaneously outside North America
by Acumen Publishing Limited

McGill-Queen's University Press acknowledges the financial support of the
Government of Canada through the Book Publishing Development
Program (BPIDP) for its activities.

National Library of Canada Cataloguing in Publication

Jacquette, Dale
    Ontology / Dale Jacquette.

(Central problems of philosophy)
Includes bibliographical references and index.
ISBN 0-7735-2463-0 (bound).—ISBN 0-7735-2464-9 (pbk.)

                1. Ontology. I. Title. II. Series.

BD311.J36 2002   111   C2002-904418-9

Designed and typeset by Kate Williams, Abergavenny.
Printed and bound by Biddles Ltd., Guildford and King's Lynn.

For Tina

an existent entity if ever there was one

There is a science which investigates being as being and the attributes which belong to this in virtue of its own nature. Now this is not the same as any of the so-called special sciences; for none of these others deals generally with being as being.

Aristotle, *Metaphysics* Γ 1003a20–25

Contents

Preface

This book investigates and proposes a theory to solve the most fundamental problems of being. I know how that sounds. But trying to understand the meaning, the undeniable but non-self-explanatory fact and nature of existence, is indispensable to philosophy. Accordingly, we must not shrink from the task, whatever difficulties are entailed.

I distinguish between *pure philosophical* and *applied scientific ontology*. Pure philosophical ontology deals with such questions as what is meant by the concept of being, why there exists something rather than nothing, and why there exists exactly one logically contingent actual world. Applied scientific ontology advances a preferred existence domain consisting of three categories of existent entities, including existent (we can also say actual) objects, existent states of affairs, and the actual world. The actual world is itself an entity, one that contains all other entities; it contains all and only actual states of affairs, involving all and only existent objects. The entities included in a theoretical ontology are those minimally required for an adequate philosophical semantics, the things to which we must be able to refer in order to make sense of meaningful thought and discourse, especially in the sciences. These are the objects that we say exist, to which we are ontologically committed.

The problems of pure philosophical ontology have seemed so deep or confused that philosophers who concentrate primarily on the concept of being as such have acquired an occasionally deserved reputation for obscurity and even incoherence. On the other hand, philosophers who turn away from the problems of pure philosophical ontology as beyond reach, focusing exclusively on what appear superficially to be technically more manageable problems of applied ontology in the special disciplines, face a serious but usually unacknowledged methodological difficulty. For it is only by answering the questions of pure philosophical ontology that we can come to understand the nature of being, what it means for something to exist, without which applied scientific ontology lacks a sound theoretical foundation.

If we do not know what it means for something to exist, how can we intelligently argue that quarks and electrons exist but Euclidean points or universals do not exist? In lieu of an adequate applied scientific ontology, metaphysics defaults on its responsibility to explain all of existence, to justify a choice of what things and kinds of things exist. Without a satisfactory pure philosophical ontology to answer the question of being, to explain what it means for something to exist, applied scientific ontology cannot competently identify existent objects, or decide which putative entities actually exist and which do not exist, which should be included in and which should be excluded from a preferred existence domain.

Philosophers who confine their work to applied scientific ontology sometimes argue that it is pointless to investigate the supposedly profound but ultimately incomprehensible questions of pure philosophical ontology. They maintain it is enough to know from immediate experience that there exists something rather than nothing. They are often prepared from this empirical starting place to proceed immediately to arguments for or against the inclusion of this or that particular entity or category of entities in the existence domain. They may then delve without further ado into considering the best reasons for admitting numbers but not sets, or sets but not numbers, particulars versus universals and instances, parts and wholes, and the like, into the existence domain. Others may try again without preliminary philosophical analysis to dismiss the problems of pure philosophical ontology as altogether meaningless according to a favored criterion, methodology or ideology; or, they may enter the fray polemically at a higher level of abstraction, casting scorn on the pretensions of speculative metaphysics in an age of modern science. How can we waste our time, they wonder, asking what it means to be and why there exists something rather than nothing?

I think, on the contrary, that we are stuck with ontology's toughest questions. Mathematics and science enjoy the luxury of advancing systematically by taking the metaphysics of their respective existence domains for granted. Philosophy, by contrast, as a study in part of the deepest presuppositions of truth, cannot avoid the challenge of understanding the nature of existence. I am unimpressed with efforts to set aside the problems of ontology as unintelligible or otherwise outside our grasp. I am persuaded that we cannot build much of interest in philosophy unless we have first thought through the fundamental problems of being. Finally, I am optimistic about the possibility of shedding light on the first principles of ontology, because the answers I find most attractive dovetail perfectly with the assumptions of classical logic. My thesis is that the problems of pure philosophical ontology can be satisfactorily answered from the implicit conceptual resources of elementary logic. The questions that have baffled ontologists in trying to explain the nature of being are inextricably intertwined with the requirements of standard formal symbolic logic. All we have to do is look closely at what logic expresses in order to see why there must exist something rather than nothing, and why there is only one logically contingent actual world. When we have done so, we will have explained what it means for something to exist, and thereby demystified the metaphysics of being. Logic, furthermore, provides the only possible answers to the fundamental problems of pure philosophical ontology. The concept of being is so basic to all our thinking that there is nowhere else to turn for explanation. The principles of pure philosophical ontology are indistinguishable in this sense from the conceptual foundations of logic. The situation could not be otherwise. If logic were unable to answer the fundamental problems of pure philosophical ontology, if these difficult questions were not already answered by logic, then they could not be answered at all, and there could be no hope for pure philosophical or applied scientific ontology. As we shall see, logic does not let ontology down.

Pure philosophical ontology, indispensable as groundwork, is only the first major step toward a complete fully integrated ontology. When we know what it means for something to exist, we can then proceed to the details of applied scientific ontology, defending the choice of a particular domain of existent entities. It is in this branch of ontology that we explain the concepts and clarify the existence conditions of physical entities and declare ourselves in favour of or opposed to the existence of numbers, sets, universals, relations, propositions, and abstract objects generally, minds and persons, God as a divine supernatural mind, language, art and other cultural artefacts. The traditional controversies of descriptive and speculative metaphysics are located here, where the stakes are higher than in pure philosophical ontology, in arguments for the existence or nonexistence of specific contested entities.

The two components, pure philosophical and applied scientific ontology, complement one another. No metaphysics of being can claim to be complete if it does not keep each separate and in its proper place while providing satisfactory answers to both specialized sets of problems. It is as much a mistake to investigate only the more tractable problems of applied scientific ontology, say, of whether or not numbers or universals exist, while giving up on pure philosophical ontology, as it would be to devote attention exclusively to the fundamental problems of pure philosophical ontology to the neglect of making substantive commitments to the existence of real entities in applied scientific ontology. We should not try to establish a domain of existent entities that is not guided by a prior clarification of the concept of being; but having addressed the problems of pure philosophical ontology, we must then move on to fill in the details of a preferred existence domain as a contribution to applied scientific ontology.

Dale Jacquette
23 March 2001
Essaouira, Morocco

Acknowledgements

I am grateful to John Shand for inviting me to contribute to Acumen's series on the Central Problems of Philosophy. John Divers and Jack Macintosh offered insightful criticisms of an earlier draft of the book. I further benefited from the opportunity to present my ideas in a series of seminar lectures on "Logik und Ontologie" at the Bayerische-Julius-Maximilians-Universität, Würzburg, Germany, during my 2000–2001 sabbatical from The Pennsylvania State University. I thank my friend Wilhelm Baumgartner for hosting my research visit in Würzburg and providing access to the facilities of the Franz Brentano Forschung. Above all, I am indebted to the Alexander von Humboldt-Stiftung for continuing support of my work in philosophy.

Introduction: Being as such

A metaphysical question

The concept of being is so fundamental to philosophy that we usually take the idea of existence for granted rather than try to analyse its meaning. Philosophical confusions nevertheless lie in wait for thinkers in any branch of philosophy who have not first clarified what it means for something to exist. When the dust settles in these most basic of reflections in pure philosophical ontology, it appears that the definition of existence is transparently simple, although its implications are easily misinterpreted.

What exists? This is what we really want to know: whether and in what sense spatiotemporal physical entities, numbers and sets, propositions and universals, persons and minds and God, among other things, are real. Before we can address questions of what specific things or kinds of things exist, we need to understand the concept of existence, of being as such, or what Aristotle in the motto from *Metaphysics* Γ quoted in the epigraph refers to as being *qua* being or being *as* being, ον η ον. What is it, what does it mean, to *be*? This is the ultimate question for pure philosophical ontology. We cannot meaningfully assert the existence or nonexistence of physical entities, of numbers, sets, universals or anything else, unless or until we comprehend what it means for something to exist in the most general sense. The fact that the actual world exists is not generally in doubt, and perhaps cannot sanely be questioned. The mere presumptive fact of the world's existence nevertheless offers no philosophical insight as we try to fathom what it *means* for the world to exist as a problem in pure philosophical ontology, and try on the basis of a good analysis of the concept of being to rigorously justify belief in the existence of the world.

The question of being asks what it means for something to exist. Alternatively, but equivalently, it enquires into the precise meaning of the words "being", "to be", "exist", "existence", to be "real", "actual", "present", "manifest", and like cognates. It is tempting in light of the hazards of defining a concept as fundamental as being to try to explain what it means for something to exist by spooning up synonyms. To *exist* is then to *be*, to be *real*, *actual* or *present*. The trouble is that all these expressions and others that might be introduced equally stand in need of explanation, and by themselves only add to the stock of concepts that require clarification. Nor is it particularly helpful to plunge in and begin drawing distinctions between different kinds or categories of being, as though we already know perfectly well what it means for something to exist and are prepared to start carving up the field. We cannot hope to explain the concept of being by pointing triumphantly to any given choice or subdivision of types of existent things. We remain equally in the dark in that case as to what it means for any of these things to have being.

If we want to know what it means for something to be, we must try to understand the concept in more familiar terms. We might appeal to even simpler properties, if there are any; or we might be driven in desperation to clarify the meaning of being by resorting to metaphor and analogy. The history of ontology offers a useful methodological inroad to the meaning of being. The connection between these questions is not immediately obvious, and has not always been appreciated. An analysis of being, of what it means for something to exist, can be discerned in efforts to answer the problem of why there exists something rather than nothing, and of whether, and if so why, there exists only one logically contingent actual world. Conceptual analysis rarely succeeds in a vacuum, and we must take our insights where we can, often by addressing the practical applied problems in which the concepts are found working at their day jobs. The analysis of a concept as it relates to the solution of the conceptual difficulties from which it emerges and to which it contributes, when things go well, all fit together in a satisfying way. By tackling the above problems we approach the concept of being indirectly. We discover the only theory of being that makes headway with these long-standing metaphysical puzzles in the only place where it could possibly be found – in logic, the only philosophical study more basic than ontology.

Pure and applied ontology, as discipline or domain

The word "ontology" has four established meanings in philosophy. There are two intersecting sets of distinctions. Pure philosophical ontology is different from applied scientific ontology, and ontology in the applied scientific sense can be understood either as a *discipline* or a *domain*.

Ontology as discipline is a method or activity of enquiry into philosophical problems about the concept or facts of existence. Ontology as a domain is the outcome or subject matter of ontology as a discipline. Applied scientific ontology construed as an existence domain can be further subdivided as the theoretical commitment to a preferred choice of existent entities, or to the real existent entities themselves, including the actual world considered as a whole, also known as the *extant* domain. Ontology as a *theoretical* domain is thus a description or inventory of the things that are supposed to exist according to a particular theory, which might but need not be true. Ontology as the extant domain, in contrast, is the actual world of all real existent entities, whatever these turn out to be, identified by a true complete applied ontological theory. As a result, we must be careful in reading philosophical works on ontology, when an author speaks of "ontology" without qualification, not to confuse the intended sense of the word with any of the alternatives. The distinctions are collected in Figure 1.

The distinction between ontology as discipline and domain cuts unevenly across the distinction between pure philosophical and applied scientific ontology. Pure philosophical ontology is concerned with the

Type	Use		
	As discipline	**As domain**	
Pure philosophical ontology (Prior foundational study)	Most general branch of metaphysics (1)	No ontological commitment – cannot be interpreted as preferred existence domain	
Applied scientific ontology (Secondary ontological superstructure)	Metaphysics of specific fields of thought and discourse (2)	*Theoretical* Ontological commitment to preferred existence domain (3)	*Extant* Actual world of all real or existent entities described by a complete true theoretical ontology (4)

Figure 1 Four meanings of "ontology"

meaning of the concept of being, with the question why there is something rather than nothing, and the modal ontological status of the actual world. Applied scientific ontology builds on the conceptual analysis of what it means for something to exist in order to recommend a preferred existence domain, thereby committing itself to the existence of a particular choice of entities. Applied ontology, as discipline or domain, is scientific in that it applies the definition of being to determine the ontological commitments of other disciplines, notably but not exclusively in the natural sciences, in much the same way that applied mathematics in engineering is related to pure mathematics.

A major source of confusion in ontology results from the failure to distinguish questions and answers that are appropriate to pure philosophical as opposed to applied scientific ontology, and between the questions and answers that are proper to ontology in the sense of a discipline versus those pertaining to ontology in the sense of a theoretical or extant existence domain. An illustration of such cross-categorical mayhem can be anticipated for the thesis developed in the first part of the book: that ontology is "reducible" to logic. This is a breezy but not necessarily inaccurate way of describing a particular answer to the question of what it means for something to exist. The obvious criticism to raise at the first whisper of a reduction of ontology to logic is that logic is a system of purely formal relations, and that from pure logical form we can never validly derive the real existence of any contingently existent entity.

The objection has a point, but not the one it is usually thought to have. It would, admittedly, be hopeless, even meaningless, to try to derive an applied scientific ontology in the sense of a preferred existence domain from logic alone. Theoretically, but even more certainly in the sense of an extant domain consisting of existent entities themselves, we cannot squeeze ontology out of pure logic in the sense of validly deducing the contents of a preferred theoretical existence domain. The logical principle, "If p, then p" neither proves that there are camels, nor that there are not. The present thesis, fortunately, is not that we can derive the existence of any particular entity or specific kind of entity from logic in applied scientific ontology, but that pure logic suitably interpreted provides correct answers to such problems of pure philosophical ontology as why there exists something rather than nothing and why there exists exactly one logically contingent actual world. In the process, logical analysis in pure philosophical ontology implicitly explains what it means for something to exist.

Pure ontology does not promote and cannot be associated with any preferred existence domain. It is indifferent to whether or not there are physical objects, or whether or not there are numbers and sets, or numbers but no sets, or sets but no numbers, or universals, or propositions, or minds, or God. The questions of pure philosophical ontology, ultimately about the meaning of the concept of being, are much more rudimentary.

Applied scientific ontology, in contrast, can be understood both as discipline and domain. As a discipline, applied scientific ontology is a method of enquiry dedicated to identifying a system of categories for a preferred domain of existent entities. As a domain, applied scientific ontology is divided in its responsibilities to identify the ontology of specific areas of thought and discourse whose meaning requires the positing of a particular choice of entities. The ontology of Aristotle's science, in contrast with Darwin's or Einstein's, gives a sense of the possibilities. Each of these theories has a theoretical ontology, in which the putative entities to which it is ontologically committed are listed or described. The ontology in the sense of a scientific theory's existence domain must be adequate for its individual purposes and capable of being integrated with the ontologies of other true theories in other fields and disciplines. None of these need be *the* ontology in big letters that correctly explains the way things really are, in the second, stronger sense of the term existence "domain". The one and only correct ontology in this sense is the extant realm of actually existent entities – all, and only, the actually existent objects and states of affairs that constitute the actual world.

Applied scientific ontology is supposed to recommend a unified ontology, a preferred existence domain of entities for all true thought and expression. Applied ontology is tasked with explicating a system of categories of existent entities. Some applied ontologies strive for uniformity throughout a single domain by adhering to a higher metaphysical principle, letting the chips fall where they may with respect to the existence or nonexistence of abstract entities, minds, persons or God. They may try to do so, for example, by insisting that only individuals exist, or only those entities that are absolutely required in order to make sense of mathematics or science or religion exist, or the like, often disagreeing along the way about what should count as mathematics or science or religion, what counts as, or is absolutely needed for, a correct explanation of their respective subject matters. Other applied ontologies with equal legitimacy piece together their conclusions about what kinds of things must exist from the best available arguments in each area of application, often trying to preserve consistency in the resulting package, and sometimes deriving metaphysical morals as they emerge in a synthesis of otherwise independent domains. As a rule, the more interesting an applied ontology, the more interesting the principle by which its ontological commitments are justified. A preferred existence domain is usually upheld by or lends distinct intuitive appeal to a general metaphysical principle in support of the existence or nonexistence of particular disputed entities.

Applied ontology has little choice in accommodating motley existence requirements. It is the nature of applied ontology in both the discipline and domain sense to be precisely as fragmented as all the distinctive types of discourse for whose meaning it provides a domain. In the end, there may be no unifying overarching principle by which physical objects, sets and numbers exist, qualities but not relations exist, minds and persons exist, but God does or alternatively does not exist, if that should turn out to be the preferred existence domain endorsed by an applied ontology. The separate results of arguments for and against the inclusion of any of these entities or kinds of entities in the preferred existence domain recommended by applied scientific ontology as a discipline must then be gathered together as putative entities, and, to whatever extent possible, reconciled to one another's presence in the domain.

Similar problems plague applied ontology in choosing between incompatible existence claims. If a particular science disagrees with a particular religion about the existence of God, the origin of the universe, or the evolution of species, for example, then that particular science and that particular religion are committed to significantly different applied ontologies in the sense that each accepts a different preferred existence domain. Their differences, whether or not the scientists or religious followers in question are aware of it, will then come down to disputes about applied ontology in the domain sense. If they do not happen also to be ontologists, they will not ordinarily disagree about applied ontology as a discipline. The interesting problem, whether the theoretical applied ontology of religion is correct as against that of science, or the opposite, can only be answered if we know which if either side is committed in its preferred theoretical existence domain to the extant domain of real existent entities. This is precious knowledge; but many thinkers involved in ontic conflicts have not hesitated to offer opinions.

To resolve an ontological dispute, religion and science must either come to share a single preferred existence domain that includes or excludes the existence of God, or their disagreements must be brought to applied ontology as discipline for arbitration. Their differences need not be fixed in stone. Scientists and religious followers can modify the ontological situation significantly if they move toward a universal God-less religion (of which there are numerous models, Zen and Taoism, among others) or if they adopt a universal God-ly science (of which historically there are many more models, especially prior to the nineteenth century). Unless or until that point is reached, the respective theoretical existence domains of science and religion remain at least somewhat apart. Applied ontology, if it is to have any role in the dispute, must ascend to a higher plane from which vantage point it can identify each disputant's commitments to distinct theoretical existence domains. The domains of ontically conflicting theories must remain at least partially outside one another, even if in other ways they overlap. They can only be unified, collapsed into one or completely absorbed one into the other, if the theories themselves eventually coalesce, or if applied ontology as a discipline concludes that one is right and the other wrong, in the course of articulating its own preferred existence domain, thereby eliminating all rival theoretical ontologies. Applied ontology as discipline and domain can affect to resolve ground-level disagreements between theists and atheists by superimposing its own preferred existence domain, potentially as a pox on both their houses, in which God or the Big Bang or natural selection either exists or does not, as correctly describing the actual world.

Nor need philosophical interaction end there. It remains open indefinitely to other ontologists to challenge previous findings and launch an opposing applied ontology that might reflect very different conclusions, favouring the other or neither side of the dispute. When this happens, conflicting applied ontologies must minimally disagree in the sense that each by hypothesis offers a different preferred existence domain. Interestingly, applied ontologies can also disagree in the discipline sense, if their conclusions issue, as they are likely to do, from a sufficiently divergent methodological conception of what it means for something to exist, the criteria of ontological commitment, or the standards of comparative preferability for competing existence domains. The refinement of applied ontology as a discipline is often motivated by precisely this adversarial dynamic between opposed applied ontologies positing incompatible preferred existence domains. It is a worthwhile endeavour in such circumstances to explore the possibilities of obtaining leverage at a methodological plane for resolving incompatible existence claims. What passes for applied ontology as discipline or domain in such cases is often quite legitimately a partisan effort to resolve lower-level ontological conflicts in the service of philosophical enquiry.

Toward an integrated philosophical–scientific ontology
The applied ontology presented in Part II need not be accepted in any or all of its specific details. If I reduce numbers to sets, or prefer sets to numbers, if I include or exclude universals, propositions, minds, God or any other putative existent entity, and a critic is persuaded of the opposite, then we disagree on the exact contents of the preferred existence domain. It happens that some ontologists prefer an existence domain that includes universals or God, while others favour an existence domain that excludes universals or God or both.

Applied scientific ontology can only offer good reasons for advocating a particular existence domain, and leave it to others to agree or disagree. We trust that a carefully managed theory will have sufficient intuitive appeal to be counted a serious contender to be recommended as the preferred existence domain. Ontology, like other areas of philosophical investigation, is a battleground for internecine disputes, in pure philosophical ontology, when the subject is taken up, but more especially in applied scientific ontology. Whether universals exist or fail to exist is an interesting question; whether God exists or fails to exist is arguably even more interesting. Ontologists disagree, sometimes quite profoundly, about matters of pure philosophical ontology, and they fill in the details of applied scientific ontology, as we should expect, in radically different ways.

It is the overall design of the ontological framework that I am primarily advocating. Although I stand by the analysis of problems and the specific contents of the preferred existence domain that finally emerges, it is the perception of the issues and the structure for a complete and correct ontology that I hope will appear to many to be headed philosophically in the right direction. I maintain that questions of pure philosophical ontology precede those of applied scientific ontology, but that a philosophically correct and complete ontology must adequately address both. A correct pure philosophical ontology, moreover, must aspire to objectivity while remaining open-minded about the existence of subjective phenomena. The mind may have its place in the world, but its place is surely not wilfully to determine all the actual facts of the actual world. We can accomplish many things by thinking, planning and undertaking action. We are nevertheless not free to create or destroy the world as a whole by simply willing its objects and facts into existence or nonexistence. Thought itself is among the existent objects and facts that constitute the actual world, to which it must also be subordinate. The existence of objective and subjective objects and facts also cannot be taken for granted, but must be upheld by sound argument against serious opposition. It cannot, in any case, legitimately be assumed as part of a solution to the problems of pure philosophical ontology if its properties remain to be discovered only afterwards in applied scientific ontology.

The ontological literature, as we have warned, is replete with concepts of pure philosophical ontology mistaken for concepts of applied scientific ontology. The converse is also true, with references to ontology as a discipline sometimes further confused with ontology in the sense of an existence domain. It is enlightening, if disconcerting, to see how many ontologists confine their contributions to ontology to one side of these distinctions, while neglecting if not completely excluding the other. Martin Heidegger is a good example of an ontologist who claims to be fully engaged in what he calls the *question of being* as a problem of pure philosophical ontology, and who officially merely gestures towards the problems of applied scientific ontology, for which he seems to have little patience. What Heidegger presents as pure ontology aimed at answering the question of being, however, turns out actually to be what Heidegger himself should recognize instead as a contribution to the ontic sciences. W. V. O. Quine is a good example of an ontologist of the opposite sort, who devotes extraordinary attention exclusively to matters of applied scientific ontology, particularly to *criteria of ontological commitment*, and to the problem of identifying the minimal existence domain needed for logic, mathematics and science. Quine pursues these questions, remarkably, without deigning to address the question of being, of what it means for something to exist, why there is something rather than nothing, or why there is only one logically contingent actual world.

We will take our bearings as we proceed from Heidegger's and Quine's ontological enterprises, without allying ourselves too closely with either. We will have much to say, first about Heidegger in relation to the problems of pure philosophical ontology, and later about Quine when we turn to issues of applied scientific ontology, as we navigate between their opposing standpoints toward our final destination – a fully integrated scientific–philosophical ontology that explains the nature of being as such and such as it is.

I Pure philosophical ontology

1 | What it is to be (on Heidegger)

The question of being

What is it for something to be? It is for that thing to have being, to exist, to be present, real, actual, manifest. If true at all, these equations are either trivial or viciously circular, and hence not much help in understanding the concept of being. They are trivially true if they merely pair together synonyms without explaining the concept of what it means to exist. They are circular if to *be* in the ontic or actual *existence sense* is not definable independently of whatever it means to actually "be" in the *predication sense* – to actually be red, for example, or non-red.

A circularity threatens if all that we can say about the meaning of any of these existence terms is to invoke a synonym. An even more bothersome circularity occurs if we try to say that to *be* is to *be* existent or to *be* present or the like. The only way to avoid circularity is to understand being in the predication sense as conceptually independent of being in the existence sense. If we are to avoid circularity in the concept of being, then we must begin by defining the concept of being in the predication sense and use it to explain the meaning of being in the existence sense. If we are going to understand and hope to answer the question of being, and if we require of our ontology as discipline that it explain in a non-circular way what it means for something to exist, then we must begin with the subject-predicate copula "is" ("is red") or with the infinitive "to be" ("to be joyful"), that comes before the explanation of what it means simply to be, to have being or exist, in any of its equivalent terms.[1]

The question of being is the question of what it means for something to have being, to exist. We can think of the fundamental conceptual problem of pure philosophical ontology as the question of the meaning of the words "exist" or "being", or of what it means for something to exist or to be, to have being as an existent entity in the actual world. We use such expressions even in everyday contexts, as when we say that the old clubhouse no longer exists; while in science, mathematics and philosophy we frequently discover battles for the existence or non-existence of this or that putative actually existent entity. If we want to speak intelligibly about the existence or nonexistence, being or non-being, of putative entities, or of objects more generally, as it seems we must even in pure philosophical ontology, then we must provide a non-circular analysis of the concept of being that will in turn underwrite a non-circular answer to the question of being.

When, and only when, the concept of being is correctly analysed, it can be used as a yardstick for deciding what specific things and kinds of things actually exist. This is probably the best way to understand the sense in which applied scientific ontology depends on pure philosophical ontology. We cannot say that genes exist and ghosts do not exist, let alone make up our minds about numbers, sets, universals, propositions and God, if we do not know exactly what we mean when we affirm, withhold or deny being or existence claims. We do not insist that a complete analysis of the concept of being precede the recognition of existent things. On the contrary, we assume that an intuitive grasp of clear-cut uncontroversial cases of being and non-being provide the basis whereby we can advance a correct definition of what it means for something to exist, on the strength of which an answer to the question of being can be tested and refined. When the definition is firmly in place, we can use it to decide initially more difficult grey area cases and draw philosophical implications from our understanding of the concept, keeping always before us the possibility of further corrections and fine adjustments to the necessary and sufficient conditions that define the concepts of existence and nonexistence. We require a good philosophical answer to the question of being, of what it means for something to exist, conceptually, explanatorily in the abstract, and epistemically also in concrete efforts to justify our beliefs about what exists before we can venture philosophically to say what particular things and kinds of things actually exist.

Manifold senses of "being"

It is important to distinguish between multiple senses of "being", not all of which are relevant in the same way to the problems of pure philosophical ontology. Aristotle, especially in *Metaphysics*, Book Γ, comments on these systematically ambiguous meanings. His study provides the inspiration for Franz Brentano's doctoral dissertation, later published in 1862 as his first book, *On the Several Senses of Being in Aristotle* (*Von der mannigfachen Bedeutung des Seienden nach Aristoteles*) (Brentano 1975). Heidegger claims to have been greatly influenced in his early reflections on metaphysics by Brentano's treatise, which he says was the most important philosophical text he worked through again and again from the time of his first interest in philosophy.[2]

Brentano considers Aristotle's four-part division between different meanings of ov, the Greek equivalent of the word "being" ("*Sein*" in Brentano's German). These include what Aristotle speaks of as *accidental being*, being in the sense of *being true*, which we can also refer to as the predication sense, the *being of categories*, and *potential and actual being*, the latter of which we have distinguished as the existence sense. We shall accordingly collapse three of Aristotle's senses into being in the existence sense, whether of accidental beings, abstract categories or potential or actual beings, all of which we distinguish from being in the predication sense. The rough and ready sense in which "being" is used to attribute existence to an entity, including an object, state of affairs or the actual world, is clear enough. It is the sense in which we say that the number π exists or does not exist, that oxygen exists but phlogiston does not exist, that God exists or does not exist. The predication sense of "being" is equally familiar, but is not always adequately distinguished from the existence sense. We use the predication sense of "being" in grammatically explicit ways when we say for example that π has the property of being an irrational real number, or simply that π is an irrational real number. We can equally say in the same family of expressions for the existence sense of being that π simply is (or is not), or in attributing any property to any object, including, as we have seen, the predication of the property of being in the existence sense, as when we say that π has the property of being existent, and even of the being of an object's being. The difference is apparent when we consider the distinct but similar-sounding questions posed when we ask "What is it for an apple to be?", as opposed to "What is it for an apple to be red or sweet or tart?"

As far as everyday language is concerned, it is a fallacy to infer the being of an object in the existence sense from the attribution of a property to the object involving being only in the predication sense. Thus, it is invalid, a logical howler, in attempts to prove the existence of God, to argue that God *is* (really exists, in the existence sense of "being") from the assumption that God *is* (defined in the predication sense as being) omnipotent. We shall consider "being" primarily in the existence sense, and the question of being accordingly as the question of what it means for something to exist, rather than what it means for something regardless of its ontological status to possess a property. By defining objects in terms of properties, rather than interpreting predicates in terms of the sets of existent objects that possess the corresponding properties, the logic and ontology we develop is *intensional* rather than *extensional*.[3] We do not assume, in other words, that an object must have being in the existence sense in order to be related by being in the predication sense of the copula to a property it can be said to possess or not possess – including the property of having being in the existence sense.[4]

Thus, we avoid Plato's Parmenidean problem about whether something must in some sense exist in order for it even to be true of the object that the object has the property of *being* nonexistent. We consider this to be a logical–grammatical–philosophical confusion that arises from a conflation of the existence and predication senses of being that were not systematically disambiguated until the time of Aristotle, but that need not cause insuperable difficulties today, provided that we do not encourage the elision from being in the predication sense to being in the existence sense.[5]

Subcategories of being

The question "What is it to be?" or "What does it mean for something to exist?" cannot be answered by any enumeration of entities or even of the most general ontological categories of entities. We are as much in the dark about what it means for something to exist when we are told that physical objects and abstract objects exist as if we had never heard of that distinction. We might fix the reference of terms like "being" and "existence" by calling attention to things that obviously fit the bill. What we cannot reasonably hope to do is arrive at an understanding of the concept of being simply by taking inventory of all the things and many kinds of things that happen to exist.

That task, in the first place, is the business of applied scientific ontology, which presupposes rather than provides a good answer to the question of what it means for something to exist. Pure philosophical ontology has no empirical data to work with, not even as a meagre starting place for commitment to the existence of physical objects in a complete applied ontology. Pure philosophical ontology cannot assume the things or kinds of things that are subsequently to be posited by a correct applied scientific ontology. Neither, however, does pure philosophical ontology have the responsibility to recommend a preferred existence domain, or to commit itself philosophically to any specific applied ontology as discipline or domain. It is, instead, supposed to be in every way a purely conceptual analysis of what it means for something to exist, of being as such or being *qua* being.

Why not try, in view of these obstacles, to answer the question of being by saying that to be is to be a physical object or an abstract object, and elaborating on these distinctions to make room for anything else that we want to be able to say exists? The suggestion is tempting, especially for anyone independently inclined to think that we can explain a concept by exhibiting its position in a network of related concepts, or by offering a taxonomy that shows a tree-like division of concepts arranged into all known or categorically possible instances or types. To simplify, we allow ourselves to say that to exist means to be a physical object or an abstract object, and then explain what we take each of these terms to mean. We may want to say that physical and abstract objects both exist, but that physical objects exist in one way and abstract objects exist in another way. Each "mode of being" then requires different types of credentials for admission to an existence domain. The existence of actual physical objects is usually not contested, although we shall later examine arguments that cast doubt even on the ontic status of ordinary physical entities. More lively and interesting are conventional metaphysical debates about the existence of abstract entities.

Regardless of how these issues of applied scientific ontology are settled, we do not advance a single step in understanding the concept of being by deciding that to exist means to be a physical object or an abstract object, or by any variation of any choice of categories of existent entities. Without fully understanding the concept, we cannot hope correctly to sort out real from merely putatively existent entities. In lieu of a good answer to the question of being, we do not even know what it means to say that physical let alone abstract objects exist. No system of subcategories of being, even if perfectly justified as a conclusion of applied ontology, can explain what it means for something to exist, any more than we can explain the concept of colour by listing all the names of individual colours. How, then, can we appeal to the existence of physical and abstract objects in order to answer the question of being? To maintain that to exist is to be a physical or abstract object reverses the priority of understanding a concept before applying it to relevant cases, and as such does nothing to explain the concept of existence. This is an instance of the kind of circularity we need to avoid in answering the question of being. If there is not a better way of understanding the concept of being, then we should simply give up the project of pure philosophical ontology. We can nevertheless take heart in the thought that the concepts of ontology might turn out to be relatively simple, if only we can identify the right ones and put them together in the right way. It can nevertheless be philosophically useful to distinguish between physical or spatiotemporal being and abstract spaceless, timeless, and in every other way physically dimensionless being. In what follows, we shall frequently do so. It is artificial, on the other hand, to distinguish between physical or spatiotemporal and abstract existence, if both are supposed to be modes (or whatever) of being. It does not paint a complete enough picture in trying to understand the meaning and nature of being merely to be told that being, whatever it is, comes in two flavours. Such an approach does not answer the most basic question of ontology, as a problem for philosophical definition, by providing an analysis of the concept of being. We further use the terms "being" and "existence" interchangeably, distinguishing when necessary between physical and abstract being or existence. We say equivalently of entities in both categories of concrete and abstract existents that they exist or have being. In equating the use of "being" and "existence", we do not imagine that the synonymy contributes in any way to understanding the concept under either name. The point is that entering into open-ended enquiry about the concept of being in pure philosophical ontology makes it important to minimize if we cannot altogether eliminate any conceptual baggage we may have assumed from ontological commitments in applied ontology. We should try to distance ourselves from or otherwise take into account and make appropriate adjustments to avoid ontological prejudices we might have taken on from the specific scientific, philosophical, historical, religious and other kinds of beliefs we accept when we are not fully immersed in investigating the concept of being.[6]

Heidegger's fundamental ontology

As a way to begin thinking about the most challenging problems of pure philosophical ontology, we shall critically consider a famous exposition of the metaphysics of being. Martin Heidegger's theory in *Being and Time* (originally published in 1927 as *Sein und Zeit*) (Heidegger 1996) offers to answer the question of being. Although we reject Heidegger's conclusions and his methodology on their own terms and as antithetical to the analytic philosophical perspective we develop and on which we rely, it is worthwhile to examine closely Heidegger's ontology for the sake of the questions he raises and the general terms in which he proposes to seek answers. We need not enter deeply into this thorny text to see that Heidegger's understanding of ontology is similar in its divisions of subject matter to the distinctions among two of the four meanings of "ontology" that we have drawn. Heidegger distinguishes much as we have proposed between pure and applied ontology, which he refers to as ontology and the ontic sciences.

The extent to which it may be necessary to disagree with Heidegger's methods and conclusions in ontology will become clear as we proceed. The main problem turns out to be Heidegger's betrayal of his own conditions for a pure philosophical ontology, and his confusion of its requirements with those of applied scientific ontology or the ontic sciences, condemning Heidegger's ontology in *Being and Time* and the related writings into committing what we shall call "Heidegger's circle". Despite these difficulties, Heidegger's statement of what he calls the question of being seems perfectly correct. We have adopted and shall continue to use the same phrase, which is meant in the same sense as in Heidegger. We further concur with Heidegger's distinction between ontology as the study of the question of being and the ontic sciences, described in related terms as the distinction between pure philosophical and applied scientific ontology. We can explain the proposed approach to the problems of pure philosophical ontology by contrasting them with Heidegger's. This makes it useful to examine what Heidegger seems to be saying, and his overall design for investigating the concept of being.

First, Heidegger is right not only to distinguish between ontology and the ontic sciences, but more importantly to insist that the question of being take philosophical precedence over the deliberations of the ontic sciences. Heidegger's subordination of the ontic sciences to ontology corresponds exactly to what should be urged as the foundational priority of pure philosophical ontology over applied scientific ontology. The relevant passages appear in the Introduction to *Being and Time*, "The Exposition of the Question of the Meaning of Being", where Heidegger in an exact if long-winded manner keynotes the deepest questions of pure philosophical ontology. Under Part I, "The Necessity, Structure, and Priority of the Question of Being", in Section 3, "The Ontic Priority of the Question of Being", Heidegger identifies the object of his enquiry:

> The question of being thus aims at an *a priori* condition of the possibility not only of the sciences which investigate beings of such and such a type – and are thereby already involved in an

understanding of being; but it aims also at the condition of the possibility of the ontologies which precede the ontic sciences and found them. *All ontology, no matter how rich and tightly knit a system of categories it has at its disposal, remains fundamentally blind and perverts its innermost intent if it has not previously clarified the meaning of being sufficiently and grasped this clarification as its fundamental task.*[7]

An interesting feature of Heidegger's thesis is his support for an ontology that fully integrates an answer to the question of being with the ontic sciences, based on the priority of the question of being. This is an appealing ideal for ontology as a discipline, which sees the project of ontology as complete only when the question of being is answered and the ontic sciences are in place. It is roughly the same model that we shall adopt as an archetype for a fully integrated pure philosophical and applied scientific ontology.

What Heidegger maintains generally about the appropriate method for answering the question of being seems correct. We have no choice but to proceed a priori, with methods that can be assured of attaining an a priori answer to the question of being. We cannot turn to the ontic sciences in order to understand the meaning of being because, as Heidegger graphically puts it, the ontic sciences are "blind" without having first clarified what it means for something to have being. Applied ontology considered only in itself literally does not know what it is talking about and does not know what to look for or whether or not to recognize it as being or even as a being. The "tightly knit system of categories" that the best applied scientific ontology is supposed to provide – that there are or are not numbers or sets or universals or minds or God – is no better than tunnelling randomly for a treasure with no prior understanding of the concept of being.

Thus far, we have no quarrel with Heidegger's parameters for philosophical reflection on the nature of being. Where things begin to go awry, and where we find it necessary to part company with Heidegger's ontology most sharply, is almost immediately thereafter, when Heidegger declares that phenomenology alone is the proper a priori method for understanding the meaning of being. We have already indicated that we intend to go in a very different direction, trying to answer the problems of pure philosophical ontology, including Heidegger's question of the meaning of being, by means of logic rather than phenomenology. Up to this point, with only minor terminological differences, we are almost entirely in agreement with

Heidegger's distinction between the question of being and the ontic sciences as comprising the two major components of ontology, with his thesis of the priority of the question of being over the ontic sciences, and with his requirement that the proper philosophical investigation of the question of being must be a priori, using a priori methods and resulting in a priori conclusions. The only difference, although one of overwhelming significance, is that in the approach to the question of being that we favour it is logic rather than phenomenology that holds the key.

Heidegger dramatizes his commitment to phenomenology as the a priori method of answering the question of being when he declares:

> Phenomenology is the way of access to, and the demonstrative manner of determination of, what is to become the theme of ontology. *Ontology is possible only as phenomenology.* The phenomenological concept of phenomenon, as self-showing, means the being of beings – its meaning, modifications, and derivatives. This self-showing is nothing arbitrary, nor is it something like an appearing. The being of beings can least of all be something "behind which" something else stands, something that "does not appear".[8]

> Ontology and phenomenology are not two different disciplines which among others belong to philosophy. Both terms characterize philosophy itself, its object and procedure. Philosophy is universal phenomenological ontology, taking its departure from the hermeneutic of Da-Sein, which, as an analysis of *existence*, has fastened the end of the guideline of all philosophical inquiry at the point from which it *arises* and to which it *returns*.[9]

Heidegger lays down a breathtaking series of heavily philosophically loaded methodological assumptions. It is astonishing aplomb, but once we catch our wind these fundamental moves in Heidegger's ontology do not stand up to careful scrutiny, and we still need to know why anyone should suppose that phenomenology is the only method of ontology. That Edmund Husserl, the founder of scientific phenomenology remotely in Heidegger's sense, was Heidegger's teacher is possibly a good biographical reason, but not a good philosophical reason, for following his lead. No matter how convinced Heidegger was that phenomenology is the only way to go, he still owes the reader a justification, and, indeed, a better explanation, of why he believes that ontology is possible only as phenomenology.[10]

Heidegger gives no reason why we should accept the momentous thesis that identifies ontology with phenomenology, and that leads inexorably, as we shall see, to Heidegger's *existentialist* ontology. Heidegger merely puts the sentence in italics or, using the equivalent German typographical convention at the time, separates the letters of the phrase with spaces. We read such passages with rapt attention, as though the author were speaking slowly and enunciating each syllable for special emphasis, and we must catch every nuance. No argument is offered, however, why any reader who is not easily cowed by that sort of table pounding should possibly want to agree that "*Ontology is possible only as phenomenology.*" If we do not already share the insight that a scientific phenomenology is not only a preferred a priori method, but at some level indistinguishable from ontology as an investigation of the question of being, then nothing that Heidegger says can persuade us that ontology is identical with or possible methodologically only as phenomenology. The only hope for Heidegger is that we become so enamoured of his system as a whole that we no longer require Heidegger to support his phenomenological starting place with good independent reasoning.

The fiat that ontology is possible only as phenomenology and the phenomenological characterization of *Da-sein* as specifically human being-in-the-world supports an existentialist ontology of being, which Heidegger construes as "disclosedness" and "care". Throughout, in making *Da-sein* the basis for his phenomenology, Heidegger invokes the situatedness of the human subject in what he calls the "analysis" of existence. The question of being is answered when we discover in a phenomenological enquiry that existence can only be understood from the standpoint of *Da-sein*, and that *Da-sein* is revealed phenomenologically as successive series of time horizons, extending into branching future dimensions of possible actions and their outcomes, about which the subject is intentionally directed in attitudes of concern. Heidegger's unsupported assumption that ontology is possible only as phenomenology makes existentialist ontology inevitable, which in the end can perhaps only be attained by identifying phenomenology with ontology, as Heidegger does, appointing it the indispensable method of answering the question of being.[11]

We must critically scrutinize this essential premise in Heidegger's methodological metaphilosophical précis to *Being and Time*. As we prepare the way for an alternative approach to the question of being as a problem for logic rather than phenomenology, we nevertheless remain within Heidegger's framework of distinctions between and priority of the question of being over the ontic sciences, the need for an a priori method of explaining what it means for something to exist, and the demand for an integrated ontology that develops an applied scientific ontology on the foundations of a correct answer to the question of being in pure philosophical ontology. The proposed a priori methodology, based in logic rather than phenomenology, the answer to Heidegger's fundamental question of being, and the applied scientific ontology that results, despite these similarities, will be radically non-Heideggerean.

Aprioristic phenomenology

An insuperable philosophical difficulty arises for Heidegger's method. How is a phenomenology validated only by a particular conscious animal's experience of being in the world, granted all its salient intentionalities and time horizons of action, attitudes towards things around it and the like, supposed to be a priori?

For Heidegger, *Da-sein* is the foundation of ontology. We arrive at the concept via phenomenology as an a priori method of answering the question of being. There is no special problem in recognizing phenomenology as Heidegger intends it, as a refinement of Husserl's transcendental phenomenology, as, in one sense, an a priori method capable of sustaining eidetic intuitions in support of apodictic a priori conclusions. It is not as clear that the sense in which Heidegger's phenomenology = ontology is a priori is the sense required by the project of pure philosophical ontology or by what Heidegger demands of a philosophically correct answer to the question of being.

The sense in which Heidegger's Husserlian phenomenology is a priori is that, in the phenomenological *epoché*, thought brackets the existence of objects that come before the mind, and sets aside the question of the ontological status of whatever intended objects are given as data for phenomenological reflection. Phenomenology is a priori in the sense that its conclusions do not presuppose the being or actual properties of any real existent entities, but it applies to the contents of consciousness generally and independently of the deliverances of the ontic sciences, as Heidegger frequently says it should. We need not dispute that this is a legitimate sense in which phenomenology can be a priori in its methods and conclusions. What is less certain is whether it is the same sense, and, worse, whether it is the appropriate sense, needed to satisfy the requirements Heidegger himself stipulates for a proper investigation of and answer to the question of being.

It is not true, in the first place, but even if it were it would be of no help to Heidegger, that pure philosophical ontologists probing into these concepts have no other choice but to try to understand the concept of being a priori through phenomenology, in the introspective experience of *Da-sein*. If logic offers another a priori channel by which to answer the question of being, then it is unavailing because in that case it is simply false to maintain that ontology is possible *only* as phenomenology. Perhaps there is no other choice but to study ontology as we must study everything else, through reflection on our experience. Since in addressing conspecifics our experience is specifically human, however, and the phenomenology of *Da-sein* affords Heidegger's only source of insight into the nature of being, there is another equally obvious sense in which phenomenology is anything but a priori. It is not a priori, in particular, in the relevant sense that it presupposes the existence and psychology of contingently existent human beings, human modes of thinking, humanly experienced time horizons, and other trappings of Heidegger's phenomenology of *Da-sein*. The problem is that we have no good reasons to expect a priori justification for any of these concepts, but only the real-time human empirical experience of the Heideggerean phenomenological ontologist.

If phenomenology offers the only conceivable access to the concept of being, then the a priori status of any insights to which we might appeal in trying to answer the question of being are problematic in a way Heidegger does not explicitly anticipate, but by which his position is substantially compromised. Heidegger, notably, nowhere tries to argue that the conclusions of ontology addressed to the question of being must transcend human being-in-the-world. On the contrary, this is precisely the existentialist conclusion he wants most eagerly to embrace. There seems as a result to be no possible relief from the a posteriori situatedness of *Da-sein* as a specifically human way of understanding being. Heidegger runs together the question of being with the question of the specifically human phenomenology of being. The a priori status of phenomenology in relation to the ontically bracketed sources of the contents of phenomenological consciousness does nothing to offset the a posteriori status of *Da-sein* itself, and hence of any use to which it might be put in trying to understand the nature of being.

A truly transcendent phenomenology applied to Heidegger's question of being ought instead to arrive at its fundamental concepts without presupposing the historically accidental existence of any particular species of thinkers. This, ironically, is precisely what cannot be done if phenomenology under some rubric is made an a priori method of pure philosophical ontology. To his credit, Heidegger makes the right inference in proceeding from phenomenology to existentialist ontology. The way is nonetheless free for him to pass in this direction only because his phenomenology begins empirically in inner perception with the real-time situations of human experience, phenomenologically described, abstracted, and analysed. It is not much of a surprise, then, once the circle is complete, to find Heidegger emerging with the concept of *Da-sein* as a series of humanly enframed time horizons. The programme throughout, from phenomenology to existential ontology by way of *Da-sein* as (human) being-in-the-world, is thoroughly anthropocentric. The persistent question, of which Heidegger maddeningly seems unaware, is how such an account can be a priori in the sense of avoiding all reference to empirical experience of contingently existent entities, and especially of the phenomenologist's real-time-horizoned lived-through experience or human being-in-the-world that Heidegger calls *Da-sein*.

The genius in Heidegger's existentialist ontology is the remarkable way in which it preserves the order of enquiry he requires between the more fundamental question of being and the applied ontic sciences. He rightly postpones philosophical work on the project of applied scientific ontology until we have satisfactorily answered the question of being. We must accordingly not assume that an actual world exists, even as a source of phenomenological raw data. The beauty of Heidegger's ontology is that phenomenology, as Heidegger understands it, does not presuppose the existence of any corresponding real or actual world entities to be perceived. It is only the content of experience that provides the subject matter for scientific phenomenology, while the existence of a real-world entity that might have occasioned the relevant perception is bracketed from philosophical consideration in the phenomenological *epoché*. Although Heidegger can suspend belief in the existence of intended objects of perception, withholding judgment about their ontic status, he not only recognizes but welcomes the conclusion that he cannot bracket the phenomenologist's humanity and human being-in-the-world as the only revelation of being *per se*. Appropriately, and with unflinching consistency, Heidegger concludes that ontology is identical in an insightful way with phenomenology, and that it can only be understood a priori existentially from a specifically human perspective.

A second major stumbling block in Heidegger's ontology is the problem of why he assumes that phenomenology is the only a priori way of addressing the question of being. Logic is less equivocally an a priori discipline that arguably affords a correspondingly less anthropocentric method of investigating the nature of being, thanks to its greater distance from the contingencies of the actual world. If the question of what it means for something to exist can be answered by interpreting the principles of classical logic, then we might be entitled to suppose that logic by definition is the same for every comparably capable thinker of any species, human or otherwise. Logic in that sense is better able than phenomenology to answer the fundamental question of being.

Heidegger is interested in the alienation of humanity from nature as a result of the characterization of *Da-sein* as technological *Zuhandenheit*. A good Heideggerean parable, and a Marxist one too, goes back to the story of Adam and Eve. When Adam and Eve acquired their peculiarly human knowledge, awakening to the distinction between good and evil by eating the forbidden fruit, they at once, in the words of Genesis 3.7, "knew that they were naked", and immediately established the first light manufacturing industry, setting humankind against nature forever in the simple act of sewing together aprons of leaves to cover their shame. This, in a nutshell, is *Da-sein*, emblematic of our existential situation and our distinctively human way of being in the world.

The influence of Arthur Schopenhauer's *The World as Will and Representation* pervades Heidegger's *Being and Time* in this regard, despite Heidegger's efforts to distance himself from Schopenhauer's philosophical pessimism. It is a commonplace in particular to see Schopenhauerian resonances in Heidegger's concepts of *Zuhandenheit* and *Gelassenheit*. *Zuhandenheit*, an attitude by which objects in the world of experience are conceptualized as available for human use in taking them to hand, is akin to Schopenhauer's concept of the will to life (*die Wille zum Leben*). It is thereby further related to Friedrich Nietzsche's derivative concept of the will to power (*die Wille zur Macht*) or, for that matter, with the ancient Greek concept of *eros* and the political category of the erotic man. Schopenhauerian renunciation of the world of representation as unreal in contrast with the real world or Kantian thing-in-itself (*Ding an sich*) as Will is often compared with Heidegger's notion of *Gelassenheit*. In different ways, each is recommended as offering salvation from the unsatisfiable Schopenhauerian individual will to life, translated into Heidegger's philosophy as the technological condition brought on by our unsatisfiable grasping utilitarian appropriations. Heidegger, much like Schopenhauer, thinks that we can learn to overcome the alienation from authentic existence that occurs as a result of seeing the world primarily as a warehouse of tools, supplies and raw materials to satisfy our needs and wants.

We should, Heidegger maintains, try to just leave things alone, according to his ethics of *Gelassenheit*. Schopenhauer similarly believes that the ascetic saint and aesthetic genius in their suppression of individual will are on a higher path of knowledge opposed to the pursuit of desire. They endeavour to overcome the strivings of empirical will in favour of truth, and ultimately of release from the inner conflicts of the individual will to life. Nietzsche, by contrast, in philosophical poetry and Dionysian revelry, embraces the will to life understood as the will to power, and projects a state of guilt-free spontaneity for the superman or philosopher of the future, whose advanced moral thinking has gone beyond the distinction between good and evil, and so has no need to seek salvation from the erotic implications of the will to life. Where Schopenhauer says "no" to life, as a result, and Nietzsche says "yes", Heidegger, in tempering *Zuhandenheit* with *Gelassenheit*, it is irresistible to conclude, more cautiously says "maybe".

Importantly, Heidegger is also often compared to Schopenhauer on the basis of Schopenhauer's prephenomenological understanding, in many ways similar to that of Maurice Merleau-Ponty in *The Phenomenology of Perception*, concerning the sense of place and interaction with the world that occurs through proprioception, body knowledge, and the range and limits of activity available to a human agent.[12] This concept is much in sympathy with if not actually derivative from Heidegger's concept of *Da-sein* as human being-in-the-world, revealed by phenomenology in terms of time horizons for alternative courses of action. A related methodological epistemic analogy between Heidegger and Schopenhauer should also be emphasized. Schopenhauer argues that experience of desire and other manifestations of the individual will to life is the Trojan horse by which knowledge gains access to the fortress that guards the distinction between the world as it appears and as it is in reality or as Kantian thing-in-itself. The empirical will for Schopenhauer allows metaphysics to peek behind the veil of Maya and discover that the world in reality for want of a better word is Will or blind urging and undirected striving and desire. Heidegger similarly regards phenomenology as offering the only possible glimpse of the nature of being through the eyes of temporally situated experience, and in particular as *Da-sein* or specifically human being-in-the-world.

By making phenomenology the methodological foundation of ontology, rather than the other way around, Heidegger, like Schopenhauer before him, investigates the nature of being from the standpoint of the knower's condition. For Schopenhauer, this is the individual will or will to life, while for Heidegger it is *Da-sein* as human being-in-the-world. The difference, and the reason why Schopenhauer's pre-Husserlian phenomenological starting place in metaphysics is more excusable than Heidegger's, is that Schopenhauer, unlike Heidegger, is clearly involved in an empirical enquiry into introspective clues about the nature of reality, of Will as Kantian thing-in-itself, and not, like Heidegger, attempting rigorously to establish the meaning of a concept a priori before proceeding to its application.[13]

Heidegger on circularity and circularity in Heidegger

We must now consider the problem of circularity in Heidegger's fundamental ontology. Heidegger anticipates circularity objections to his method of ontology as phenomenology, and attempts to forestall criticisms of his phenomenological existentialist ontology on grounds of circular reasoning. There nevertheless remains a damaging circularity in Heidegger's answer to the question of being. Heidegger first extends blanket pardon to circular expositions of concepts in trying to answer the question of being:

> This being which we ourselves in each case are and which includes inquiry among the possibilities of its being we formulate terminologically as Da-sein. The explicit and lucid formulation of the question of the meaning of being requires a prior suitable explication of a being (Da-sein) with regard to its being.[14]

> But does not such an enterprise fall into an obvious circle? To have to determine beings *in their being* beforehand and then on this foundation first pose the question of being – what else is that but going around in circles? In working out the question do we not presuppose something that only the answer can provide? Formal objections such as the argument of "circular reasoning," an argument that is always easily raised in the area of investigation of principles, are always sterile when one is weighing concrete ways of investigating. They do not offer anything to the understanding of the issue and they hinder penetration into the field of investigation.[15]

The passage makes it appear as though Heidegger scoffs permissively at circularity objections generally in order to protect his own theory from that type of complaint. That this is not immediately so is clear when he continues:

But in fact there is no circle at all in the formulation of our question. Beings can be determined in their being without the explicit concept of the meaning of being having to be already available. If this were not so there could not have been as yet any ontological knowledge. And probably no one would deny the factual existence of such knowledge. It is true that "being" is "presupposed" in all previous ontology, but not as an available *concept* – not as the sort of thing we are seeking. "Presupposing" being has the character of taking a preliminary look at being in such a way that on the basis of this look beings that are already given are tentatively articulated in their being. This guiding look at being grows out of the average understanding of being in which we are always already involved *and which ultimately belongs to the essential constitution of Da-sein itself.* Such "presupposing" has nothing to do with positing a principle from which a series of propositions is deduced. A "circle in reasoning" cannot possibly lie in the formulation of the question of the meaning of being, because in answering this question it is not a matter of grounding by deduction but rather of laying bare and exhibiting the ground.[16]

Heidegger's investigation of the question of being risks several types of circularity. The effort to downplay circularity considerations in theory construction generally, but especially in pure philosophical ontology, does nothing to alleviate the logical havoc wreaked by the kind of circularity in which Heidegger's answer to the question of being seems implicated. Logically objectionable circular reasoning need not always take the form of deductive inference in which the truth of an individual assumption explicitly presupposes the truth of the conclusion. This is one, but not the only, common and pernicious type of theoretical circularity. Another type of circularity affects the structural organization of concepts arranged to define technical terms or answer philosophical problems like the question of being, to analyse higher-level concepts in terms of lower-level comparatively more fundamental concepts. Heidegger appears to have involved the ontology of *Being and Time* in several such circularities. The circularity in Heidegger's phenomenological existentialist ontology casts serious doubt on the dialectical integrity of his theory, despite his disclaimer that no interesting circularity can arise in the enterprise of revealing and clarifying the transcendental ground of the metaphysics of being.

If we are engaged in answering the question of being in Heidegger's framework, then we must not allow ourselves to make use of any fact or concept that belongs properly to the ontic sciences, all of which presuppose for their intelligibility a prior understanding of the concept of being. We have already seen that Heidegger describes *Da-sein* as at first distinctively human being-in-the-world, which is only later claimed to transcend human particularity. In its original occurrence in Heidegger's phenomenology, at its starting place, *Da-sein* is essentially temporal, defined by a characteristic succession of time horizons, with all the ontological freight these concepts are supposed to carry. The concept of *Da-sein* as such seems far too rich a conclusion to derive even from the resources of scientific phenomenology. We are right to be suspicious of a theory that so lavishly characterizes the nature of being anthropocentrically, even if only as a stage in a process of phenomenological reflection, and even if they have been partially sanitized by some adaptation of a Husserlian transcendental *epoché*.

Heidegger seems unaccountably to assume, since in phenomenology the existence of perceived entities are bracketed for theoretical purposes, that phenomenology is ontologically presupposition-free. Heidegger's account of *Da-sein* as specifically human being-in-the-world shows that precisely the opposite is true. Where can so much information about being *qua* being as Heidegger discovers possibly come from if it has not been surreptitiously smuggled into the assumption that phenomenology is the only method of ontology? The result is a circular arrangement of concepts in an ultimately question-begging proposal to uncover the transcendental ground of being. The situatedness of the human phenomenological enquirer is already mired in human empirical psychology, and finally comes down to Heidegger's own personal and hence highly particular existential situation as he perceives it phenomenologically. How can any of this be a priori, and how can such vicious circularities in the foundations of metaphysics be tolerated? Do we want to say, as Heidegger is apparently prepared to do, that ontology is such a special discipline that we can ignore the ordinary rules of good definition in trying to answer the question of being by allowing the *definiendum* also to appear in the *definiens*?

Heidegger tries to blunt concerns about circularity in this part of his exposition by designating the structure of his phenomenology of being as involving what has come to be known as a "hermeneutic circle". In a crucial passage, he explains:

> But is not the ontologically clarified idea of being in general first to be attained by developing the understanding of being that belongs to Da-sein? However, that understanding can be grasped

primordially only on the basis of a primordial interpretation of Da-sein guided by the idea of existence. Does it not thus finally become evident that this problem of fundamental ontology that we have set forth is moving in a "circle"?[17]

We already showed, in the structure of understanding in general, that what is faulted with the inappropriate expression "circle" belongs to the essence and the distinctiveness of understanding itself. Still, our inquiry must now return explicitly to this "circular" argument if the problem of fundamental ontology is to have its hermeneutical situation clarified. When it is objected that the existential interpretation is "circular," it is said that the idea of existence and of being in general is "presupposed," and that Da-sein gets interpreted "accordingly" so that the idea of being may be obtained from it. But what does "presupposing" mean? In positing the idea of existence, do we also posit some proposition from which we can deduce further propositions about the being of Da-sein, according to the formal rules of consistency? Or does this pre-supposing have the character of an understanding project in such a way that the interpretation developing this understanding *lets* what is to be interpreted be *put in words for the very first time, so that it may decide of its own accord whether, as this being, it will provide the constitution of being for which it has been disclosed in the projection with regard to its formal aspect?* Is there any other way that beings can put themselves into words with regard to their being at all? In the existential analytic, a "circle" in the proof cannot be "avoided," because that analytic is *not* proving anything according to the rules of consistency *at all*. What common sense wishes to get rid of by avoiding the "circle", thinking that it does justice to the loftiest rigor of scientific investigation, is nothing less than the basic structure of care. Primordially constituted by care, Da-sein is always already ahead of itself. Existing, it has always already projected itself upon definite possibilities of its existence; and in these existentiell projects it has also projected pre-ontologically something like existence and being . . .[18]

Heidegger seems at times to embrace the circle as inevitable, and at times to say that the circle cannot possibly result from the "existential analytic" of the concept of *Da-sein*. He claims that if we concern ourselves or worry about whether or not a circle obtains in the concept of *Da-sein*, then this is further proof that *Da-sein* in its essence is concern or care. It is then as though we were obligated to admit that *Da-sein* is self-disclosedness manifesting itself as concern or care even when we try to deny the thesis, worrying, as we might, about whether the explication of the concept is circular, getting caught up in the very same "circle" ourselves.

Heidegger goes so far as to maintain that an adequate description of a circular phenomenon must itself be circular, and that circularity in an account of a circular phenomenon contributes to the account's being correct. If this is what Heidegger means, then, whatever the merits of his existentialist ontology, he cannot be said to have rescued fundamental ontology as phenomenology from all philosophical objections to its apparent circularities. If Heidegger hopes to domesticate circularity by maintaining that any adequate theory of a circular phenomenon must itself be circular, then his defence is refuted by numerous counter-examples. There is an evident use–mention confusion in the view that the description of a circular definition, inference or explanation must itself be circular. Does Descartes slip into circularity in his dedicatory letter preceding the *Meditations on First Philosophy*, addressed "To the Wisest and Most Distinguished Men, the Dean and Doctors of the Faculty of Sacred Theology of Paris", when he warns that it would be circular to justify belief in the existence of God by appealing to holy scripture if we should also trust holy scripture on the grounds that it is the word of God?[19] We need not get caught in a whirlpool of circular reasoning in order to correctly recognize another thinker's circularity, just as we need not suffer from gout in order to correctly diagnose a patient's symptoms. A critic should be able to maintain logical integrity despite correctly identifying circularity in another thinker's argument, definition or concept, explanation or account.

Heidegger proposes yet another way to learn to love circularity in a phenomenological theory of being. He observes that the same circle inevitably arises for anyone who tries to think through the question of being in the rigorous "scientific" fashion he requires. He argues that if a circle is inevitable in tackling the problems of fundamental ontology, then we can and should accept and even celebrate circularity as revealing something philosophically unobjectionable and phenomenologically interesting about the existentialist concept of being: that it too is unobjectionably circular. Why should we not concern ourselves instead with circularity as a sign not of conceptual confusion, but of the poverty of trying to do ontology as a branch of phenomenology, in which we must at least presuppose the existence of a phenomenological thinker or specifically humanly situated psychological subject? Heidegger adds:

But the "charge of circularity" itself comes from a kind of being of Da-sein. Something like projecting, especially ontologically projecting, necessarily remains foreign for the common sense of our heedful absorption in the theory because common sense barricades itself against it "in principle." Whether "theoretically" or "practically," common sense only takes care of beings that are in view of its circumspection. What is distinctive about common sense is that it thinks it experiences only "factual" beings in order to be able to rid itself of its understanding of being. It fails to recognize that beings can be "factually" experienced only when being has already been understood, although not conceptualized. Common sense misunderstands understanding. And *for this reason* it must also necessarily proclaim as "violent" anything lying beyond the scope of its understanding as well as any move in that direction.[20]

The talk about the "circle" in understanding expresses the failure to recognize two things: (1) That understanding itself constitutes a basic kind of the being of Da-sein. (2) That this being is constituted as care. To deny the circle, to make a secret of it or even to wish to overcome it means to anchor this misunderstanding once and for all. Rather, our attempt must aim at leaping into this "circle" primordially and completely, so that even at the beginning of our analysis of Da-sein we make sure that we have a complete view of the circular being of Da-sein. Not too much, but *too little* is "presupposed" for the ontology of Da-sein, if one "starts out with" a worldless I in order then to provide that I with an object and an ontologically baseless relation to that object.[21]

The quotation marks around selected terms in the passage seem intended to offer Heidegger a measure of ironic distance from what is actually a serious difficulty in his attempts to explain the concept of being. Again, even if being is somehow a circular concept, it by no means follows that an adequate pure philosophical ontology must therefore be circular. If we are committed to a phenomenological exposition of these concepts, drawing the existentialist conclusion that being is essentially temporally horizoned when we are made to begin with phenomenology and its scientific categories, with *Da-sein* as specifically human being-in-the-world, then perhaps a damning vicious circularity in Heidegger's existentialist ontology is finally unavoidable.[22]

Why, then, not reconsider the demand that phenomenology is the only method of ontology? Although the term is much abused, it appears unjustified for Heidegger to accuse common sense as exclusively preoccupied with existent entities in its "circumspection". Common sense is very much interested in – cares about, in the sense Heidegger frequently exploits – nonexistent objects and states of affairs. We encounter unexemplified intended objects in thought every time we plan to undertake an action that will bring about an as yet unrealized state of affairs, particularly in the free exercise of imagination, assumption and hypothesis in art and science. Nor should common sense alone, however polemicized as philosophically naive, be regarded as the chief adversary of Heidegger's circle. There are philosophical reasons for being alarmed even about the circularities that Heidegger himself acknowledges in his existentialist ontology, against which his efforts to blunt circularity objections offer inadequate reassurance.

The circularity in Heidegger's ontology occurs because Heidegger tries to answer the question of being in terms that presuppose the existence of entities that belong only to the ontic sciences. Specifically, Heidegger assumes the existence of human beings, their mental states occurring in real time, and phenomenological time horizons. These factors are given in the data of phenomenological reflection if Heidegger's phenomenology is correct. We must nevertheless ask by what right the question of being as a problem for a priori judgement occurs as something given to phenomenology in the first place. The concept of *Da-sein* is fundamental in Heidegger's ontology, yet it requires prior appeal to very specialized existent entities, entities whose existence conditions Heidegger maintains cannot be understood until the question of being has been answered. We cannot disguise the structure of such reasoning as anything but viciously circular in Heidegger's understanding of the nature of being, nor is it any consolation to conclude that the circularity is unavoidable if we equate ontology with phenomenology.

A related circle arises because according to Heidegger we cannot answer the question of being without presupposing the existence of such specific kinds of entities as time horizons and human beings, which should nevertheless be treated by the ontic sciences only after the question of being has been answered. The circularity deprives us of the understanding of the concept we seek, for which Heidegger says we should turn to the account in the first place, and that in the opening sections of his treatise he encourages us to expect. We cannot know whether specific kinds of entities, including time horizons and human beings, exist, or even what it means for such things to exist, unless or until we have answered the question of being. Heidegger cannot have it both ways. He seems to sense that his account may involve even deeper circularities, and hopes to cut off potential criticisms of any *petitio principii* the theory might contain with both general philosophical considerations about the triviality of circularity objections, and specific mitigating considerations with respect to their applications in the case of ontology.

Heidegger remarks that "A 'circle in reasoning' cannot possibly lie in the formulation of the question of the meaning of being, because in answering this question it is not a matter of grounding by deduction but rather of laying bare and exhibiting the ground".[23] This, in a way, is true. Circularity is avoided in such an exposition, however, only if when we dig down we eventually reach the ground. The trouble in Heidegger's existentialist ontology is that when he has excavated the question of being or of the meaning of being, he only scratches the surface and makes questionable progress by assuming the existence of entities that are supposed to belong only to the higher reaches of the ontic sciences. Time, time horizons and the phenomenological capabilities and limitations of human beings are elements of the applied ontology of physics, biology, anthropology and human psychology and phenomenology. If only Heidegger *could* lay bare and exhibit the ground of the question of being. When he thinks he has hit rock bottom, on the contrary, he has merely gone round in a circle to topics that are supposed to be compassed only when the question of the meaning of being has been independently answered.

"But in fact there is no circle at all in the formulation of our question", Heidegger writes. "Beings can be determined in their being without the explicit concept of the meaning of being having to be already available."[24] This again may well be true; yet it is impossible to see how someone like Heidegger who makes phenomenology the cornerstone of ontology could possibly justify such a conclusion. Heidegger reasons that: (a) we know that the actual world exists – he writes: "If this were not so there could not have been as yet any ontological knowledge. And probably no one would deny the factual existence of such knowledge";[25] (b) the actual world can exist only if being is grounded in the ultimate ontological foundations laid bare by an answer to the question of the meaning of being. Heidegger's consolatory remark, appealing to prior knowledge of the existence of the actual world, which "probably no one would deny", is extraordinarily revealing. We encounter in this frank passage yet another, third, major stumbling block to understanding Heidegger's ontology. Heidegger disastrously fails to recognize that admitting the fact of the existence of the actual world does nothing to prevent philosophical ontology from lapsing into circularity, but makes its circularity inevitable. The existence of the actual world, as in Husserl's *epoché*, is supposed to be bracketed by Heidegger's phenomenological practice from the very outset, especially in investigating the question of being – this is what is supposed to make the method a priori. The reference to and very mention of the existence of the actual world prior to answering the question of being in Heidegger's ontology is an undisguised source of circularity.

It is true that the actual world exists, and that underlying the fact of its existence there is a wealth of concepts to be uncovered in order to understand the meaning of being. Heidegger is right to hold that this is not and should not be a question for pure philosophical ontology. The circularity in Heidegger's ontology arises when we propose to give an account of the existence of the actual world, in which, as Heidegger rightly insists, the question of the meaning of being must be answered first, before we are entitled to make theoretical use of facts about the existence of specific entities, including our knowledge of the existence of the actual world, ourselves as human beings, even in the most general or transcendental terms, real-time horizons, or any other contingently existent entity.

Being in the extant domain sense is whatever it is, and has whatever structures and character it has, independently of being in the discipline sense. We must devise an appropriate ontology in the discipline sense to discover and explain the truths of ontology in the domain sense. The extant existence domain does not need ontology in the discipline sense to help it along. As Heidegger also advises, there is no threat to being itself even in the most viciously circular account of being. The trouble, if trouble there is, lies entirely in the theory, in the metaphysics of being, with how we try to answer the question of the meaning of being. If we want to avoid circularity in this context, then we should not accept any propositions that presuppose a concept or proposition to which we are not entitled until we have drawn further conclusions lower down in the chain. If in the end it appears that we cannot avoid circularity, then we must acknowledge and try to live with it, as Heidegger does. Alternatively, we can try to sidestep circularity in ontology in the first place by developing a different answer to the question of being that, to challenge the most conspicuous source of circularity in Heidegger's existentialist ontology, does not depend on and is not offered as a special exercise in phenomenology.

We are not home free when we have recognized that the world exists and therefore must have some stable foundation that it is the business of ontology to investigate. As ontologists, we inevitably face the task of identifying a correct methodology to uncover the ground of existence, the meaning of being, what it is for something to exist, that does not inevitably set us spinning in explanatory circles. The objection to Heidegger's approach to the question of being is that his choice of phenomenology as the route to discovering the meaning of being is inherently circular. Heidegger requires that we presuppose the actual existence of particular kinds of entities, while at the same time insisting that we first understand what it means for entities of any kind to exist before we are entitled to posit the existence of specific things. The arc of the circle is completed when it becomes clear that we cannot presuppose the existence of an entity unless we already know what it means for something to exist, a matter about which we are supposed to be uninformed unless or until we have first answered the question of being.

Fact and meaning of existence

There is a tendency to appeal to the bare facts of the existence of the actual world as we experience it through sensation as a starting place for philosophical ontology. This is a fatal mistake that confuses much discussion under the heading of fundamental ontology with an inversion of explanatory priority. We should resist the urge to seize hold of something existent within our grasp and firmly shake it about, as though this could help us to understand the fact and meaning of existence. Heidegger, for all his disclaimers and apparent metaphilosophical scruples, falls into this trap in a spectacular way in *Being and Time*. The problem is instructive because it is more general than the form it takes in Heidegger's existentialist ontology. Experience teaches us that there exists an actual world. Who would deny it? Pure philosophical, as opposed to applied scientific ontology, however, cannot rely on the empirical data of sense experience, no matter how impressive, vivid or compelling.

Heidegger tries to forestall similar objections to the apparent subjectivity implied by his existentialist ontology, when he writes "The priority of Da-sein over and above all other beings which emerges here without being ontologically clarified obviously has nothing in common with a vapid subjectivizing of the totality of beings."[26] Merely declaring an account to be free of subjectivity does not make it so, as any defender of non-subjectivity in ontology should appreciate. It is not comforting in Heidegger's case to be handed down yet another lofty pronouncement to join the unsupported claim that ontology is possible only as phenomenology, or that objections to blatant circularity in trying to answer the question of being are futile. If the phenomenology of *Da-sein* is not subjective, or at least not "vapidly" so, it is nonetheless an articulation of specifically human being-in-the-world. This makes Heidegger's existentialist ontology objectionably anthropocentric in so far as it purports to offer through phenomenology a supposedly scientific a priori description of ontological structures as experienced intersubjectively by human beings in human thought. Heidegger writes:

> The answer to the question of who this being actually is (Da-sein) seems to have already been given with the formal indication of the basic characteristics of Da-sein . . . Da-sein is a being which I myself am, its being is in each case mine. This determination *indicates* an *ontological* constitution, but no more than that. At the same time, it contains an *ontic* indication, albeit an undifferentiated one, that an I is always this being, and not others. The who is answered in terms of the I itself, the "subject," the "self." The who is what maintains itself in the changes throughout its modes of behavior and experiences as something identical and is, thus, related to this multiplicity. Ontologically, we understand it as what is always already and constantly objectively present in a closed region and for that region, as that which lies at its basis in an eminent sense, as the *subjectum*. As something self-same in manifold otherness, this subject has the character of the *self*.[27]

If these remarks are meant to allay concerns about the subjectivity of Heidegger's existentialist ontology, they seem to have the opposite effect, especially if we expect pure philosophical ontology to transcend the peculiarities of human experience. Would not some kind of world exist even if human beings had never happened to evolve? Surely the existence of our species is a biological accident, despite being in some sense causally necessitated. We cannot be limited in scientific metaphysics to the anthropocentrism entailed by ontology as phenomenology, and so we are not required to adopt Heidegger's existentialist ontology in the sense either of a discipline or domain. We can and should cast about for an alternative that does not presuppose the existence of entities whose ontic status can only subsequently be validated by enquiry in the ontic sciences.

It is we human beings who are struggling valiantly to attain ontological understanding, as no one need deny. Neither, however, need we admit that our conclusions can only be limited to our specific epistemic and other social and environmental situatedness. Ontology, contrary to Heidegger, must not only account for the world as we perceivers happen to find it, but must also explain the logical possibility of non-actual worlds and non-contemporaneous times within a world, including the actual world, in which worlds or at which times there are no minds, and hence no *Da-sein* or human being-in-the-world. Prior to the logically contingent evolution of minds capable of subjective states of consciousness in our own world, before life of any kind had emerged, we assume that there existed as there exists at this moment an actual world. It is surely, moreover, the same actual world that existed, then as now, modified in its accidental characteristics over time; otherwise, where did we come from and from what did we evolve? We must therefore strive to make ontology theoretically independent of the accidental representation of the world in subjective states of consciousness. We know that the actual world exists, but we cannot use that knowledge in the pursuit of pure philosophical ontology without prejudging the result. We cannot answer Heidegger's question of the meaning of being without vicious circularity if we must refer to our knowledge that the actual world actually exists, even and especially as a sop against the charge of circularity in the ordering of concepts, definitions and explanations, that is supposed to be established by a pure philosophical ontology.

We should not expect a common-sense ontology for this reason to agree with any anthropocentric concept of the world. Nor should we imagine that a pure philosophical as opposed to applied scientific ontology can proceed by assuming that the actual world exists because we experience its actuality. This limitation contradicts efforts to make heavy ontological capital out of Heideggerean considerations about *Da-sein* as human being-in-the-world. Even Heidegger, armoured, like Dürer's knight, with Husserlian transcendental phenomenology, scorning vapid subjectivity in ontology as he tries to answer the question of being a priori, and arguing as he does later in the book for the transcendence of *Da-sein*, appeals, as we have seen, when the chips are down, to "ontological knowledge" that comes before the resolution of the question of being, and to the "factual existence of such knowledge", which "probably no one would deny". Heidegger's frequently discussed concept of *Da-sein* is philosophically sterile, as a result, even as a vocabulary for raising first philosophical questions about the concept of being, existence, the human condition and the ontology of mind through an emphasis on its subjective states of consciousness.

Heidegger offers an interesting and important theory. It is clearly not an *ontology*, as Heidegger professes to define the discipline, but an exercise in phenomenology at the level of the applied "ontic sciences". Heidegger's existentialism is not a system of ontology in the sense that would satisfy Heidegger's own metatheoretical requirements concerning the priority of the question of the meaning of being over any and all questions of applied scientific ontology. *Being and Time*, Heidegger's more elevated characterization of his project notwithstanding, is an existentialist applied ontic science of the human condition, developed unscientifically from an idiosyncratic perspective that does not answer the question of being and is incapable of explaining the nature of existence. Heidegger's existentialism is extraordinarily perceptive in its phenomenological exploration of what constitutes human being-in-the-world, but it is not pure philosophical ontology. By Heidegger's own distinction, *Being and Time* is a contribution to the ontic sciences masquerading as fundamental ontology.

The human psychological limitations of Heidegger's existential ontology are especially evident in his analysis of *Da-sein* as "disclosedness". It appears in his exposition of the experiential ground of *Da-sein* in feelings of guilt, *Angst*, ecstasy and tending (*Sorge*, care in taking care of things), and its extension to social manifestations typified by empathy and other forms of awareness and concern for the "other", which Heidegger calls *Mitda-sein*.[28] How does Heidegger propose to justify these conclusions? Even if we agree to look past the inherent circularity in a phenomenological account of being, justifying Heidegger's central thesis, we may still be puzzled about what phenomenological method he is supposed to be following, and how he arrives phenomenologically at his conclusions about the nature of being. If we are friendly in principle to phenomenology, then if we are candid we must admit that the phenomenological method in Heidegger is too obscure to be considered scientific. How, exactly, does Heidegger propose to justify his central thesis, how is his phenomenology supposed to reveal, that being as such should be understood as *Da-sein* in the sense of human being-in-the-world? How does Heidegger then conclude that human being-in-the-world is care for or attentiveness to things in the phenomenal order, in what he calls the existential analytic of the concept of being? How does he accomplish the remarkable transition from *Da-sein* to *Mitda-sein*?

What, phenomenologically, is supposed to justify any of these moves? These are important questions to ponder as we evaluate some of Heidegger's even more momentous if opaque conclusions about the interpretation of *Da-sein*. Heidegger has many interesting things to say about the human condition. Although he uses phenomenological language to couch his conclusions, he is nonetheless either not

following a disciplined phenomenological method, or his phenomenological investigations are so deeply in the background as to be
inaccessible. Try to work out a phenomenological method other than
"this is what Heidegger says" in the following crucial passages:

> [I]t seems that we have reached the requisite, primordial interpre-
> tation of Da-sein with the clarification of temporality as the
> primordial condition of the possibility of *care*. Temporality was
> set forth with regard to the authentic potentiality-of-being-a-
> whole of Da-sein. The temporal interpretation of care was then
> confirmed by demonstrating the temporality of heedful being-in-
> the-world. Our analysis of the authentic potentiality-of-being-a-
> whole revealed that an equiprimordial connection of death, guilt,
> and conscience is rooted in care. Can Da-sein be understood still
> more primordially than in the project of its authentic existence?[29]

> What seems "more simple" than the nature of the "connection of
> life" between birth and death? It *consists* of a succession of
> experiences "in time". If we pursue this characterization of the
> connection in question and above all of the ontological assump-
> tion behind it in a more penetrating way, something remarkable
> happens. In this succession of experiences only the experience
> that is objectively present "in the actual now" is "really" "real".
> The experiences past and just coming, on the other hand, are no
> longer or not yet "real". Da-sein traverses the time-span allotted
> to it between the two boundaries [birth and death] in such a way
> that it is "real" only in the now and hops, so to speak, through the
> succession of nows of its "time". For this reason one says that
> Da-sein is "temporal". The self maintains itself in a certain same-
> ness throughout this constant change of experiences.[30]

We struggle here and throughout with Heidegger's tortured prose.
If we seek guidance about the nature of being in these writings, we
must come to terms with the fact that Heidegger stylistically is the
Gertrude Stein of philosophy, who may yet have worthwhile things to
say – if only we can determine what they are.

The theory of *Da-sein* as human being-in-the-world can at best and
at most be a contribution to the applied ontology of a scientific
phenomenology. It can at best be so because it is not clear in the first
place that what Heidegger calls phenomenology is scientific. It can at
most be so because it presupposes the contingent existence of the
human mind. If we are pure idealists, and are satisfied to go no further

than the contents of thought, well and good. If, on the other hand, we want to allow for as much as the possibility that there is a world beyond thought that corresponds positively to our cognitive representations, then we cannot escape the Heideggerean circle that occurs when we assume that phenomenology is the only method of ontology, and conclude by accepting an existentialist ontology of *Da-sein* as specifically human being-in-the-world. Pure philosophical ontology, contrary to Heidegger's ultimatum, does not have to be identified with phenomenology. A better alternative is offered by logic, and the formal methods and philosophical interpretation of pure classical logic. We need not learn to love a "hermeneutical" circle in order to answer Heidegger's question of being.

By Heidegger's own criteria, existentialist ontology does not satisfy the metaphilosophical requirements of the ultimate priority of the question of being. We should, and indeed we must, look to logic as a more appropriately a priori discipline than phenomenology for the purposes of pure philosophical ontology. Phenomenology thematizes its own real-time processes of introspection and philosophical reflection, which it imposes on the structures it claims to discover in occurrent conscious thought. Of course, we can only conclude that being is intimately bound up with time if we require the question of being to be answered by phenomenology as a real-time investigation of real-time thought. There is then, unsurprisingly, no other choice. Heidegger's fundamental ontology, and much of his applied ontology, is a foregone conclusion once we grant that phenomenology is the only way to answer the question of being. An existentialist ontology is thereby unavoidable, and Heidegger deserves credit for following an insupportable assumption to its inevitable if unsatisfying conclusion. Heidegger, nevertheless, does not try to argue that phenomenology is the only way to answer the question of being. His insistence that ontology is possible only as phenomenology signals that the proposition with all its weighty methodological implications has an exalted status in Heidegger's philosophy, but provides no reason for regarding the proposition as true.

It is revealing that Heidegger does not consider or try to refute the possibility that logic rather than phenomenology might provide another, potentially even more acceptable a priori answer to the question of being. That is the radically alternative, radically non-Heideggerean approach to Heidegger's question of being in fundamental pure philosophical ontology that we shall now explore as we try in a very different way to understand what it means for something, anything, to exist.

2 Combinatorial ontology

Logic and ontology

The idea of making logic the basis of ontology is not new. This chapter develops a particular choice of logical foundations for a combinatorial pure philosophical ontology.[1] The answer to the question of being that the theory makes possible depends on the totality of logically possible combinations of predications involving all logically possible combinations of logical objects with all logically possible properties. Combinatorial ontology explains what it means for something to exist, why there is something rather than nothing, and why the actual world is uniquely existent and logically contingent. It further requires and provides a rationale for revising the concept of a logically possible world in a reform of conventional model set-theoretical semantics for modal logic.

A combinatorial ontology based on logic stands in sharp contrast with Heidegger's existential ontology based on phenomenology. If we accept Heidegger's thesis of the priority of the question of being over the ontic sciences, then we cannot proceed to the applied ontic sciences unless or until we answer the question of being by explaining what it means for something to exist. Where Heidegger applies a derived Husserlian phenomenology as the a priori method for answering the question of being, we shall consider an a priori logical investigation of the concept of being involving all logically possible combinations of logically possible predications, as required by the principles of pure classical logic. The totality of pure logical possibilities has metaphysical implications for pure philosophical ontology that are different, and, one might argue, methodologically more pristine, than Heidegger's proposal to answer the question of being in terms of *Da-sein*.

The proposal for a combinatorial ontology from purely logical resources provides an alternative to Heidegger's existential ontology.

Moreover, it answers Heidegger's question of being without stepping away from his reasonable requirement that the question of being take precedence over the ontic sciences. Logic is less questionably a pure a priori discipline than even the most transcendental phenomenology. Combinatorial ontology takes advantage of the extensive overlap of concepts shared by logic and ontology. The presuppositions of any logic, of the logically possibilities of combining all logically possible objects with all logically possible properties, support a logical solution to the problems of pure philosophical ontology. Where Heidegger's phenomenological answer to the question of being draws him into an existentialist ontology via *Da-sein* as specifically human being-in-the-world, the resources of classical logic in contrast constitute the basis for a more abstract combinatorial ontology that has nothing immediately to do with human beings or the logically contingent facts of human psychology, sense experience, perception, introspection, emotional attitude, existential situatedness or other phenomenological categories.[2]

Logic as an alternative method of ontology

We begin with the most fundamental assumptions of any logic. Logic depends on logical possibilities, in which logically possible properties are predicated of logically possible objects. Logic describes inferential structures among sentences or propositions expressing the predications of properties to objects.

We can think of logic syntactically as a system of terms and symbols minimally for propositions, but more usefully also for propositional connectives, objects, properties and quantifiers. What is a sentence or a proposition if not a concrete or abstract expression of an object's possession of a property? The same is as true in Aristotelian syllogistic logic as in modern symbolic logic. Logical objects are truly or falsely said to have properties, and the sentences or propositions of logic are expressions of these combinations that logic takes as its building blocks in syllogistic and sentential or propositional logic, the internal logical-predicational structures of which it logically analyses in Boolean algebra, predicate-quantificational logic and related formalisms. Without the logical possibility of predicating properties of objects, without, that is to say, the concept at least of logically possible states of affairs, there is no fund of sentences or propositions for which to define deductively valid inference in even the simplest logic. To develop logic by introducing sentences or propositions is already to presuppose the possibility of predication, which is all we need to get started in pure philosophical ontology. Although at one level logic can be regarded as a theory of signs and formal rules for manipulating strings of signs, we cannot neglect the meanings of logical expressions as they relate to logically possible states of affairs, and thereby to logically possible objects and their logically possible properties. The sentences or propositions of a logic must have truth-values or the possibility of truth-values, which they acquire by virtue of expressing existent or nonexistent states of affairs in which logically possible properties are predicated of logically possible objects.

We shall soon consider ways of collapsing objects into properties and properties into objects. For the time being it may be more intuitive to think of logically possible objects as anything that can possibly have a property, and of logically possible properties as anything that can possibly be true of a logically possible object, or any way in which a logically possible object can possibly be qualified or related to itself or other objects. Logically possible objects and logically possible properties can be combined in astronomical but definite numbers of ways to produce different logically possible objects, states of affairs and worlds. We do not say that all such combinations are or correspond to actually existent entities. The concept of existence is definable instead as a special logical condition on the full range of combinations of logically possible objects with logically possible properties, logically possible states of affairs and logically possible worlds. It would be premature at this point in laying down the foundations of pure philosophical ontology to be driven to any definite metaphysics of logically possible objects or properties, or even to ontological commitment about whether or not objects or properties actually exist. Holding such issues at arm's length, by analogy with the distinction between pure and applied mathematics, is a large part of what helps to keep pure philosophical ontology pure.

Combinatorial pure philosophical ontology at this level is indistinguishable from the principles of pure philosophical logic. The conceptual roots of ontology overlap significantly with those of classical first-order formal symbolic or Aristotelian syllogistic logic, Boolean algebra or other formal logics in which logically possible properties are truly or falsely combined with or predicated of logically possible objects. We expect any and all logical possibilities to derive from logic alone. We uncover the same logical-ontological concepts when, from the resources of pure logic, we try to answer the questions why there is something rather than nothing and why there exists at most exactly one logically contingent actual world. Logic by itself already has built into it a sufficient implicit basis for answering these questions of pure philosophical ontology. To appreciate the ontological implications of logic, we must recognize that existent entities and actual states of affairs, even the actual world as a whole, are included among, although they do not exhaust, the full range of combinatorial possibilities of predicables that a correct applied scientific ontology must explain. The combinatorial predicables of pure classical logic include all logically possible objects of all logically possible predications; collectively, these logically possible combinations of logically possible objects and logically possible properties constitute the only logically possible, and in that sense logically necessary, semantic domain for pure philosophical logic.

What, exactly, is a *combination*, and how does it compare to other more familiar ontological categories? Combinations are intensional devices, in that they are collections of properties, brought together purely nominally under a concept term in an ontically neutral way for a variety of purposes in pure or applied ontology. Combinations are not sets or themselves properties, but logically possible groupings or aggregates of properties or properties and objects. The concept of a combination is schematic for reference to any logically possible selection of logically possible properties, or of objects defined in terms of properties combined with properties. Unlike sets, therefore, which include the possibility of a null set containing no members whatsoever, there can be no null combinations. Nor do combinations considered generally as such, again unlike sets, have any definite applied ontic status, but partake of whatever ontic status the constituents they combine possess, which a combination merely logically gathers together for consideration under a name or description. Finally, combinations generally do not have any definite internal structure whereby relations such as Rab and Rba can be logically and ontologically distinguished. What individuates such relations from one another is their own distinct internal logical structures. Thus, Rab is not supposed to be distinguished from Rba within the undifferentiated combination of R, a and b. Rather, Rab is a different combination of R with a and b than Rba; the two relations represent different ways in which their constituents can be combined. Relation or relational property R has two argument places already built into its internal logical structure. It is, in effect, $R\_\_ \_\_$. Among indefinitely many other distinct combinatorial possibilities, there must therefore be included the combinations, Rab, Rba, Raa, Rbb, Rac, Rca, Rbc, Rcb, Rcc, and so on.

We get an idea of the totality of logically possible states of affairs involving all combinations of all logically possible objects with all logically possible properties by thinking syntactically of the possibilities accruing to an artificially limited set of two logically possible objects, a and b, and two logically possible properties, F and G. The complete set of logically possible states of affairs is determined by the total number of ways in which these terms can be combined, expressed as the total number of propositions or predications that can be constructed out of these elements. We have, in particular, Fa, Ga, Fb and Gb. Things immediately become more complicated if we try to take account of the full number of logically possible objects and logically possible properties needed for all logically possible propositions or predications of logically possible properties to logically possible objects, and include among logically possible properties not only qualities like F and G, but also relation terms, such as R, for relational states of affairs, Rab, Rba, Raa and Rbb, among unlimitedly many others.

To complete the theory of pure philosophical logic, we must further explore the foundations of pure philosophical ontology. The implications of the totality of logical possibilities involved in combining all logically possible objects with all logically possible properties in all logically possible states of affairs expressed by all logically possible propositions in logic turn out to be sufficient to answer Heidegger's question of being, to know what it means for something to exist, and to arrive at a precise definition of these concepts in purely logical-combinatorial terms. Logic is intertwined with pure philosophical ontology in so far as it presupposes a pure philosophical ontology in the existence domain sense; while, in the discipline sense, a combinatorial pure philosophical ontology depends only on a philosophical interpretation of the formal methods of symbolic logic. The methods of pure philosophical ontology in this sense are also purely logical, and ontology is continuous with logic at this level. To such an extent, pure philosophical ontology as a discipline is indistinguishable from the syntax and formal semantics of pure classical logic.

The idea of answering the question of being from the standpoint of logic does not seem to have occurred to Heidegger. He does not explore the possibility and try to refute it or explain why he thinks it a non-starter, but considers the problem exclusively in terms of phenomenology. He does not, for example, declaim against the poverty of logical form for purposes of understanding the concepts of fundamental ontology as a way of defending his preference for the comparative riches of phenomenological content. It is possible, perhaps, that Heidegger finds the idea of explaining existence in terms of logic too preposterous even to mention. If so, if he has thought about the matter at all, it would still be worthwhile to know in what specific form he considers and rejects the reduction of ontology to logic. Heidegger offers no indication that he has even so much as considered the possibility of approaching the question of being as a problem of logic, or compared its advantages and disadvantages with those of phenomenology. To decide whether or not Heidegger is right to begin with phenomenology and conclude by advocating a distinctively humanized existential ontology, we are now prepared to investigate an important alternative that Heidegger does not consider. Why should we agree with Heidegger that ontology is possible only as phenomenology? Why not as logic?

Logical objects and property combinations

We answer the question of being by articulating the concept of existence presupposed by a good solution to the only slightly less fundamental question of pure philosophical ontology: why is there something rather than nothing? The analysis of being is then further tested by its consequences in trying to solve the related conceptual problem: why is there exactly one logically contingent actual world?

The quick answer to the question why there is something rather than nothing is that something exists because logically something, some particular actual world or other, must exist. What we call the actual world, with all its colour and substance, as we ordinarily think of it, is no more and no less than a certain logically possible combination of logically possible properties possessed by logically possible objects, a logically possible structure of logically possible states of affairs.

The meagre resources of logical possibility in pure classical logic entail the logical necessity in combinatorial pure philosophical ontology that something rather than nothing actually exists, and that the uniquely actual world in its existent state is logically contingent. The idea of juicing ontology from logic may seem to extract more from pure logic than it can possibly provide. We should nevertheless recall that we are not trying to derive ontology from pure logic either as a theoretical commitment to a preferred existence domain, or in the sense, whatever this could mean, of trying to deduce from logical principles alone an extant domain of real existent entities. The reduction of pure philosophical ontology to pure logic is not supposed to be a kind of logical Big Bang, in which logic by itself suddenly calls forth the actual world we see and touch. That idea clearly makes no sense. In the realm of pure philosophical ontology, we are thinking of ontology exclusively as a discipline, for which logic, also as a discipline, has sound prospects of explicating the concept of being by specifying the logical requirements of existence. As we shall see, pure classical logic provides a combinatorial pure philosophical ontology that answers the question of being in the course of explaining why there exists something rather than nothing, and why there exists exactly one logically contingent actual world.

Despite these disclaimers, we are, indeed, in a more innocuous sense engaged in a project of deducing the existence of the actual world from the combinatorial possibilities of states of affairs presupposed by pure logic. Logic requires that there be such a possibility, and that it is the one and only such possibility. The important point is that logically we avoid the need to say that the actual world is the world where we happen to live or where we particular kinds of thinkers enjoy our particular type of conscious being, living in a world that we can see and touch or otherwise experience. Moreover, we should, consistently with our programme, avoid saying these things, because any appeal to the experience or situation of the supposedly pure philosophical ontologist slips again into Heidegger's circle. We are not trying to say that logic brings the actual world into existence, but only that the logical concepts we shall define explain why some sort of world must exist.

All logical formalisms express, some more rigorously and precisely than others, a remarkably fundamental concept, without which we cannot undertake the study of ontology. Nothing is meaningful, true or false at all, except by virtue of a property being truly or falsely predicated of an object or objects. We cannot even say that a combinatorial ontology is correct or incorrect without attributing a property to an object. The logical possibility of combining objects with properties, represented in the most articulate logical notations as the combination of object terms with property terms, is the foundation of every formal system of logic. To the extent that logic represents the structure of reasoning, it equally underlies the possibility of thought, and, as we shall see, of reality in so far as it is thinkable. If we are to consider pure philosophical ontology exclusively as a discipline, then this is the explanatory level at which we should expect to discover its most fundamental concepts.

We can think of predication as minimally as possible, as the logical possibility that there could be something that has a property. The presupposition of logic that we can predicate properties to objects makes it intelligible to refer to predication objects and the properties predicated of them, without which there could be no philosophical problem of their ontological status. We assume that we can speak at least provisionally of possible predication objects and the properties predicated of them, as a minimal combinatorial requirement of pure logic. We further assume that when an object, whatever an object is and whether or not objects exist, whether or not it is not something more than a purely logical predication subject, has a property, whatever a property is and whether or not properties exist, then a logically possible object's having a logically possible property is a logically possible state of affairs. A logically possible world, in turn, including the actual world, is constituted by logically possible states of affairs, and ultimately by logically possible objects combining with logically possible properties.

What are objects and what are properties? The question is ambiguous. Its two meanings ask about the ontic status of objects and properties, and about the inventory of objects and properties, the list of objects and properties that might be available for predication in the sentences or propositions of logic. It would be useful to have such a list. Then we could say: these are the objects and these are the properties, and they can enter into any logically possible predications for any logically possible state of affairs in any logically possible combination. The trouble is that the list could only enter theory as an outcome of applied scientific ontology, and not an assumption of pure philosophical ontology. For present purposes, we need only consider the idea in its most logically abstract form involving a logically possible object of predication, whatever it is that can have or fail to have a property. If we prefer, we can speak of all logically possible states of affairs, which logic with equal justice can be said to presuppose, but whose exact ontological status for the time being remains indeterminate.

Do we thereby conclude that objects and properties or states of affairs exist? We defer answering such questions until later, as belonging more properly to applied scientific ontology than pure philosophical ontology. We need only remark that logic speaks and must speak of objects and properties, and of the logically possible predication of properties to objects in logically possible states of affairs. We will merely follow logic's lead, recognizing the possibility of objects having properties as conceptually fundamental to the problems of pure philosophical ontology. We speak accordingly of an object's having certain properties, being red or round, even if the object does not exist. We rely on a distinction between senses of "being" in order to characterize the being or non-being of an object in the existence sense in terms of what we regard as the ontologically neutral predication sense of being, in which logical objects, regardless of their ontological status, have or fail to have certain kinds of properties in the property combinations by which they are defined, identified and individuated.

If we are grappling with problems of pure philosophical ontology, then we are not yet ready to commit ourselves to any particular domain of existent objects, but are trying to answer more fundamental, metaphysically deeper questions about the nature of being. As a result, we need to adopt as ontologically neutral and noncommittal a logical vocabulary as possible, in trying to see what can be learned from logic alone. We speak intensionally of logically possible properties and property combinations, which is to say a choice of logically possible properties considered together, as the logically possible properties of a particular logically possible object. We leave all options open for interpreting the ontology of objects and properties in alternative ways, none of which is excluded by the logical explanation of why there exists something rather than nothing, and why there exists exactly one logically contingent actual world. By presupposing the possibility of predication, pure logic presupposes only logical possibilities, of a logically possible object having or not having a logically possible property. The ontological status of properties and objects, predication subjects, the "something" capable of having a property, is reserved as a topic for applied scientific ontology, in the course of which objects or properties might in principle be eliminated in favour of a radically different concept of predicability.

Ontic neutrality of objects and properties in pure logic

We now address an obvious related objection. Have we not already forged ahead of ourselves in trying to answer the problems of fundamental ontology from the standpoint of supposedly "pure" classical logic? Are we not, in particular, assuming that there are such things as objects and properties? If so, are we not guilty in a different way of the same circular reasoning that we have charged against Heidegger? Do we not suppose by speaking of objects and properties that such things exist at least as logical possibilities before we have said what it means for anything, in any category of applied scientific ontology, to exist or have being? Are we not simply assuming that pure classical logic is inherently ontologically committed to the existence of at least these two kinds of things – properties and objects?

The answer to all of these questions is no. The reason is that while we have adopted this terminology to speak of the basic combinatorial logical possibilities that underlie all logical forms in thought and language, we have not tried to say that they must exist in order to do so. We are free, if we think it might help to avoid confusion with the question of whether properties and objects exist, to adopt a new set of terms to refer to this basic combinatorial relation as the fundamental presupposition of logic. We could, for example, confine our vocabulary instead to logical objects and their putative properties or attributes, or the like, to gain a bit of distance from ontically loaded and grammatically superficially indistinguishable discourse about real existent entities. Logic, generally, as it has developed from Aristotle's day to contemporary formalisms, speaks without ontological prejudice of logically possible objects, without assuming that any particular objects exist, or enquiring into their ontic status. If we think, as some logicians do, that properties are also objects, then we can construe logic's references to properties as enjoying the same ontically neutral status as logical objects. Otherwise, we can adopt the same attitude of principled indifference to the ontic status of logically possible objects as logically possible combinations of logically possible properties.

This is why Ludwig Wittgenstein, in developing another style of combinatorial ontology in his (1922) *Tractatus Logico-Philosophicus*, should not be faulted, as he frequently is, for not explaining precisely what he means by the "simple objects" of his theory, or for failing to give examples of objects or of the analysis of atomic states of affairs into juxtapositions of simple objects. Wittgenstein's simple objects are the ontically neutral logically possible predication subjects of his formal symbolic logic. Every logic must begin with logically possible objects that cannot be further specified within the confines of pure logic or pure philosophical ontology. Wittgenstein seems to have understood that nothing of substance can be said about the nature of simple objects, drawing this conclusion from a more general conception about the requirements of logic. If so, then his reticence to provide examples or detailed information about the nature of *Tractatus* objects is not a quirk of his philosophical personality, or a failure to carry logical analysis far enough in the direction toward which he points, as is sometimes thought, but is necessitated by the abstract level of description at which he characterizes the principles of his logic and metaphysics. The most we can ever say is that logical objects are the objects with which pure as opposed to applied logic is concerned. Objects are whatever logically can have or fail to have a property so as to constitute an existent or nonexistent state of affairs that can be represented by a true or false predication in a sentence of logic.[3]

It may appear that logic is not ontologically indifferent to the existence of objects and properties generally, but only to any particular choice of objects and properties. Logic does not say that apples or camels exist, but that whatever objects truly or can intelligibly be considered to have properties must exist. Does logic also require there to be any substantive truths other than so-called tautologies or logical truths? A tautology is true even if its component object–property predicational sentences are false. Thus, "If p then p" and "Either p or not-p" are true, even if p is not. It is truth-functionally atomic propositions like p in first-order logic, along with categorical propositions of Aristotelian syllogisms, that are basic units of meaning in logic. They are explicated in modern predicate logic as the combination of a property term, F, with an object term, a, in the form Fa. If no substantive predications in pure formal symbolic logic are true, but the notation speaks only in terms of the logically possible combination of objects in general with properties in general, then it is hard to see how logic could be ontologically committed to a theoretical existence domain involving the existence of any particular objects or properties. Logical objects and their properties must be considered merely as logical possibilities in order to preserve the necessary ontic neutrality of a pure philosophical ontology based on logic.

We can further economize on concepts in the foundations of logic and pure philosophical ontology. We can say that logic involves the possibilities of predicating properties of objects in a conceptual scheme wherein objects and properties are included in altogether separate categories, or we can say that objects are reducible to combinations of properties. If objects and properties are distinct, then we may think of objects as something like logically bare particulars that are something like logical pegs on which to hang properties. An object has a property predicated of it in this sense just in case the right property is hung on the right peg. The difficulty in such a view is trying to understand the appropriate identity conditions needed to support reference to multiple objects serving as possible bearers of properties. As logically bare particulars, such objects, unless they are decently clothed with properties, are logically indistinguishable from one another. How, then, can there be more than one? If logical objects are considered instead as property combinations, then the identity problems vanish, since we can identify a unique logical object with each unique combination of properties, in an application of what is sometimes called Leibniz's Law. We also understand a logical object's having a property as the property's belonging to the relevant property combination. The attribution of a property to a logical object is then the true or false proposition that a property belongs to the property combination associated with the object.[4]

The alternatives might be represented as shown below, with the arrow indicating direction of conceptual reduction.

Alternative predication models

Logical bare particulars and properties:
  OBJECTS & PROPERTIES

Reduction of objects to property combinations:
  [objects] → Combination-of (PROPERTIES)

Reduction of properties to objects:
  [properties] → Special-subcategory-of (OBJECTS)

Nor does it matter which choice we make. Logic is indifferent to the actual existence of logically possible objects and logically possible properties. We do not effect an ontological, but at most a conceptual, reduction by eliminating reference to objects in favour of property combinations. Property combinations do not introduce any new elements into the account because property combinations are purely logical: nothing more than logically possible combinations of logically possible properties. The advantages therefore seem to favour an account of logical objects and properties whereby objects are identified intensionally with property combinations. The theory nevertheless allows us for convenience to continue to speak of objects as having properties, according to the principles for reducing properties to property combinations, and for interpreting the attribution to and the logically possible possession of properties by objects.

We say that for logical purposes an object is anything, existent or nonexistent, to which a property can be truly or falsely attributed, and that a property is anything by which the nature or condition of an object is qualified. We can then improve on the first description of the onto-logical neutrality of objects and properties by regarding logically possible properties as themselves logically possible objects that can be possessed by other objects, or by reducing all logically possible objects to all logically possible property combinations. We reduce references to states of affairs to object–property combinations, and we reduce logi-cally possible worlds to logically possible states-of-affairs combinations. The actual world is then a particular logically possible combination of actual states of affairs involving all and only actually existent objects and their actually instantiated properties. We offer a unified answer to the question of being that explains what it means for something to exist in all three of these categories, from existent objects and actual states of affairs to the actual world. As part of the explanation, we identify jointly sufficient general requirements for any logically possible world to be actual, which we speak of as "an" actual world as opposed to "the" actual world, and we do not assume at the outset that an argument for the existence of *an* actual world necessarily implies the unique existence of *the* actual world, which may require special proof.

Finally, we note that the combinatorial theory of logical objects does not have any ontological significance in the domain sense, but at most in the discipline sense. The combinatorial theory has conceptual consequences only, and only within pure logic and pure philosophical ontology, precisely where these disciplines conceptually overlap. The situation is very different in applied scientific ontology, where the ontology of objects is raised as an issue about whether objects like the number 2 and the camel in the courtyard are bare particulars that possess properties added to them as antecedently independently existing entities with individuating identity conditions, or whether 2 and the camel are nothing more than the combination of properties somehow ontologically glued together. At this point, we are seriously engaged in applied ontological disputes, in the depths of metaphysics, trying to understand the nature of numbers and physical entities. In logic, and as far as the principles of logic and fundamental ontology are concerned, we can say either that logical objects are or have properties indifferently, just as we like, without assuming any definite ontological commitments. We shall therefore continue to speak of logically possible predication objects, recognizing these not as bare particulars but as logically possible property combinations.

Ineliminability of object–property combinations

We can reduce talk about objects to properties or properties to objects, but we cannot eliminate both altogether from the informal metatheory of logic without depriving logic of its essential starting place. A reduction in either direction might at most be undertaken for the sake of theory, to be replaced in practice by conventional references to the logical possibilities of objects having properties in an ontically neutral sense. It is natural to think of objects as having or being constituted by combinations of properties, even before we have made up our minds about whether there actually exist such things, and, if so, precisely what kinds of things they are.

A variation of an argument that Aristotle offers to establish the law of non-contradiction, and that Kant later makes the engine of his method of transcendental reasoning, demonstrates the indispensability to logic, and hence to all discursive thought and language, of the logical possibility of objects combining with properties. The principle is that we cannot reject a concept that is required for or presupposed even by our attempt to reject it. If we try, then the metaphor is that we saw off the branch on which we are perched, or are hoist by our own petard, or pull the rug out from under ourselves. To presuppose concept C in an argument that purports to discredit or do away with concept C is defective reasoning. We cannot, in any event, deny that logic is entitled to speak in an ontically neutral and noncommittal way of objects and properties without finding an alternative method of couching the criticism that does not itself presuppose that logic is something, an object of some kind, that fails to have the property of being ontically neutral and noncommittal about the existence of objects and properties.[5]

Thus, a dilemma arises. Either the critic can or cannot provide an alternative way of denying that logic is entitled to speak in an ontically neutral way of objects and properties without making logic into an object that is said not to have this property. If there is no alternative, as the present thesis maintains, then the critic's objection cannot be sustained. If there is yet another choice, what is it supposed to be? What could possibly be more basic than something's having or not having a property? How can we decide whether an entirely new way of doing logic is being proposed, or if it is just a terminological riff on the established object–property terminology? We have yet to find even so much as a suggestion of how logic could proceed without the distinction, or how an objection to logic as presupposing too much by permitting predications as combinations of objects with properties could hope to make sense of the logical possibility of true or false thoughts or sentences without distinguishing between objects and properties, or recognizing the logical possibility of objects having properties.

If we cannot speak of objects even as logical predication subjects that might have properties, then we cannot hope to make progress in ontology. The fact that logic presupposes the possibility of a logical predication object having properties reinforces the assumption that if we are to address the problems of pure philosophical ontology we must do so from the basis of a minimal starting place. We must, naturally, start somewhere, recognizing the logical possibility that logically possible predication objects can have logically possible properties. If not, then we cannot even intelligibly entertain the contrary conclusion that the project of pure philosophical ontology is false, misdirected or confused, since in that case, despite ourselves, we continue to speak of objects and properties, claiming in effect that pure philosophical ontology is an object possessing (theoretically undesirable) properties.

The question whether objects must exist in order to have properties, and whether properties exist in order to be truly or falsely predicated of objects, is finally a question for applied scientific ontology rather than pure philosophical ontology. This division of labour indicates that logic by itself does nothing to decide the question of the ontology of objects and properties. We sense no contradiction in the idea that a nominalist ontology standing on logic's shoulders might conclude, among other conceivable outcomes, that the properties referred to in logic are not abstract entities, but function only as names for collections of similar individual physical entities in the extension of a predicate; that all objects are concrete, physical or spatiotemporal; that none or that all are abstract, or the opposite; that some objects are physical and some are abstract. The same is true for the contrary conclusions reached by platonic realist or conceptualist ontologies about the ontic status of objects and properties. If logic were ontologically committed to the existence of any particular objects and properties or objects and properties of any particular ontological category or subcategory, the fact would appear as a tautology or contradiction as soon as applied ontology tried to raise the issue of their ontic status. Needless to say, none of these imaginable directions for applied scientific ontology is ordinarily perceived as a matter of logical necessity or impossibility. Object and property terms in logic function instead as ontically neutral placeholders for the combinatorial possibilities of constructing true or false sentences.

The debate about what objects and properties or kinds of objects and properties if any actually exist is generally conducted in metaphysical rather than purely logical terms. Why is this so? On the present thesis, it is because all logics at some level presuppose the possibility of constructing sentences that express states of affairs in which properties are truly or falsely predicated of objects. A version of the distinction between logical objects and properties, and for immediate purposes it does not matter which, is thereby required of and recoverable from the expressive capabilities of pure logic. In pure logic and pure philosophical ontology, indeed, precisely where these two disciplines are logically–ontologically intertwined, we engage in discourse about logical possibilities to which we are not yet ontically committed. The purely logical possibilities for objects having properties are prior to the deliberations of applied scientific ontology. There is no specific preferred existence domain for logic any more than there is for pure philosophical ontology. We acknowledge the fact by recognizing that pure philosophical ontology, like pure logic, can only be interpreted in the sense of a discipline, and not as a preferred theoretical existence domain, let alone as the extant domain of real existent entities.

Understanding the implications of the logical possibility of predicating properties of objects, however this is interpreted, is not to introduce nonexistent objects, including nonexistent states of affairs or nonexistent merely logically possible worlds, into a preferred existence domain. To consider the requirements of pure logic, first of all, is not yet to speak of any existence domain at all, theoretical or extant. The effort to support such commitments is the business of applied scientific ontology. We have already argued, in agreement with Heidegger, that applied ontology cannot get off the ground unless or until we first answer the question of being in pure philosophical ontology. When we turn from the rarefied atmosphere of pure logic and pure philosophical ontology to applied logic and applied scientific ontology, we are still free to argue that both some objects and some properties exist; or that only objects exist, and that properties, except in so far as they are reducible to objects, do not exist; or that only properties exist and objects, except in so far as they are reducible to property combinations, do not exist; or that neither objects nor properties exist, but that predicability should be reinterpreted in a radically different way.

We do not tie our hands ontically to any preferred existence domain that specifically includes or excludes objects or properties, provided that we do not try to answer the question of being in such a way that no applied scientific ontology of objects and properties is logically possible. The same is true for any theory that tries to explain what it means generally for something to exist. By paying attention to the requirements of logic, we should, if anything, be better able to stay out of that kind of trouble in pure philosophical logic. Applied logic as always has to make do with whatever conceptual resources applied scientific ontology supplies to an underlying pure logic. If we are not allowed, under any terms, or with any reduction of properties to objects or objects to properties, to speak of objects and properties in logic, then we must have decided that we cannot do logic at all, or that logic in itself is not (logically?) possible. The incoherence of trying to deny that we can speak of objects and properties in an ontically neutral way in pure logic is evident now on several fronts. We have already made a good case, at least for present purposes, that any system of logic must allow for sentences or propositions, which is to say, however it is finally interpreted, a good case for the logical possibility of predicating properties to objects in existent or nonexistent states of affairs. The argument, more accurately but less mellifluously, establishes the logical possibility of all logically possible combinations of ontically neutral logically possible predications involving ontically neutral logically possible attributions of ontically neutral logically possible properties to ontically neutral logically possible objects.

Objects, properties, states of affairs

We begin accordingly with mere logically possible predication objects at some level of discourse independently of their ontic status. We need to do so in order to say that some objects exist and others do not, without which distinction we can mean nothing significant when we say that an object exists.

Objects as mere logically possible predication subjects turn out to exist or not to exist, depending on whether they satisfy the definition of the concept of existence, yet to be provided in a satisfactory answer to the question of being. Some objects pass the test, and so are said to exist, and are admitted to the preferred existence domain in applied ontology; others do not pass the test and are not admitted. What is an object, if anything, over and above or in addition to being (in the predication, not existence sense) the logically possible object or true or false predications of properties? We do not assume that all predication objects exist, but distinguish an existent object more particularly as an *entity*. An object must satisfy the requirements of a correct analysis of the concept of being in order to exist or qualify as an entity. There are no objects that are not predication objects, and any predication subject is an object, whether existent or not. We can think about predication objects in the abstract, but the concept of an object is not inherently subjective or phenomenological or intentional. We comply with common sense in assuming that in the actual world there are actually existent entities that have existed before there existed minds, and others that might continue to exist even if all thought like a snuffed candle ceased to exist.

We can say that an object as a predication subject is identifiable in terms of its true predications, in terms, in other words, of everything that is true of it or the properties it has. To be an object is to be a predication subject, and to be this as opposed to that particular object, whether existent or not, is to have a distinctive combination of properties. The red ball, [red, ball], which, as far as logic is concerned, might exist or not exist, is different from the blue ball, [blue, ball], because the red ball is red and the blue ball is not red, and because the blue ball is blue and the red ball is not blue. The same intensional identity conditions hold with appropriate modifications for states of affairs and logically possible worlds, independently and regardless of their ontic status as existent entities or nonexistent mere predication subjects. The state of affairs which is such that this ball is red is different from the state of affairs which is such that this ball is blue, because this state of affairs involves a red and not a blue ball and the predication of the property red rather than blue, while the second named state of affairs involves a blue and not a red ball and the predication of the property blue rather than red. A logically possible world in which a red ball or the redness of a ball only obtains is different from a logically possible world in which a blue ball or the blueness of a ball only obtains, because the first world includes as its only state of affairs a red ball or the redness of a ball rather than a blue ball or the blueness of a ball. The more painfully obvious these elementary observations, the more secure the logical foundations of pure philosophical ontology.[6]

If we consider objects and their properties, regardless of their ontic status, and even if objects are in some sense reducible to property combinations, we can appreciate the virtually unlimited possibilities for distributions of properties among objects. As logical predication subjects, objects can be identified or associated with any logically possible combination of properties. If we have three properties, F1, F2 and F3, then logically there must be property combinations for objects that include these possibilities: [F1], [F2], [F3], [F1, F2], [F2, F3], [F1, F3], [F1, F2, F3]. We do not include the null combination consisting of no properties, which we do not consider a limiting case of predication but as a non-predication, and we do not suppose that there need be any purely logical ordering of properties in an object's property combination. In general, if we are considering a total of N properties, then the number of combinations of properties will be precisely identical to the number of objects as logical predication subjects, which, excluding the null combination as non-predicational, is the *cardinality* or size of the ontology in the sense of a preferred theoretical or extant existence domain, considered here in the abstract without benefit of the findings of applied scientific ontology, and expressed by the formula: *cardinality* $= 2^N - 1$. This is the total number of logical predication objects, of which only some actually exist, minus the null set. Again, only some, presumably the same existent ones, belong to the actually existent states of affairs that collectively constitute the actually existent world. The equation by itself is not very helpful in establishing more meaningfully the cardinality of pure philosophical ontology, unless we know how many properties there are. In some applications, such as Aristotle's metaphysics of substance, there are only as many properties as actually inhere in existent spatiotemporal particulars. A problem for Aristotle's account of inherent properties as "secondary substances" is that we cannot know in advance of completing the project of applied scientific ontology how many properties there are, and hence of how many objects there could be. We do not want to prejudge the truth of Aristotle's theory of substance and essential and accidental properties as a topic for applied rather than pure philosophical ontology. We shall therefore not try to assign definite values to N or decide how many existent or nonexistent objects could possibly exist.

What do we mean when we say some predication objects can or do or must, or do not or need not or cannot exist or have being? Logically possible predication objects are individuated one from another by virtue of their distinctive true predications, corresponding to the distinctive property combinations by which they are defined. We say that a predication object, existent or nonexistent, has or even is (in the predication sense) a certain property combination, which is to say a combination of true predications of properties, and that these identifying and individuating property combinations belong to several distinctive types, in terms of which we common-sensically characterize the existence or nonexistence of objects, states of affairs and logically possible worlds. A property combination can be either *predicationally complete* or *incomplete, internally consistent* or *inconsistent*. These are purely logical characteristics of mere predication objects that might in principle exist or not exist.

A property combination is predicationally complete when, for any property and property complement, the property combination includes the property or its complement. The red ball, considered only as such, has an incomplete property predication combination that includes the property red and the property of being a ball, but does not include or exclude the property of being ten centimetres in diameter or the complementary property of not being ten centimetres in diameter or being other than ten centimetres in diameter. The object itself, we can say, the red ball, considered only as such, is predicationally undetermined. If, by contrast, we consider an actual ball in the actual world, it will have and be correctly defined only as a complete property combination by which the object is fully predicationally determined. In addition to being red or blue or some other colour, it will either be ten centimetres in diameter or not ten centimetres in diameter; it will either be made of rubber or it will not be made of rubber; and so on. There are no gaps in the total combination of logically possible properties or property complements that hold true of an existent as opposed to a merely logically possible entity.

A unicorn does not exist, although it might; untold numbers must frolic about non-actual merely logically possible worlds. No unicorn exists because there is no actual entity that has among its properties the characteristics associated with being a unicorn: roughly, being equine with a single horn sprouting naturally from its forehead. The property combinations of unicorns relative to the actual world are inevitably missing at least one property or property complement. Completeness and consistency are already taken to be hallmarks for the "existence" of logically possible worlds in modal semantics. Whether they are indeed so depends on whether as putative abstract objects they satisfy the existence requirements for entities generally and abstract entities in particular in applied scientific ontology. It can be argued that the existence of logically possible worlds, even as an abstract set of propositions with a specifiably consistent and complete distribution of truth-values, is logically dependent on the prior existence of objects as maximally consistent property combinations. If even one such object does not exist, then any state of affairs in which it is supposed to be involved and any logically possible world to which it is attributed does not exist.

It is similar with respect to the existence of abstract entities, if the concept of being admits any, and if there are strong reasons for including them in the existence domain. An abstract entity like the number π, supposing it for the moment to exist, or the property red, if properties should turn out to exist, will be predicationally complete in its property combination. In the case of π, it will not be red and it will not be blue, but it will be an irrational real number, and it will be the ratio of the diameter to the circumference of a circle and so on. In principle, a nonexistent object might turn out to be incomplete with respect to only one property and property complement, although in practice the nonexistent objects that are considered in ontology are generally the imaginary concoctions of fiction and myth, which have only an easily surveyable number of predications that excludes all other property and property complement combinations. The objects of fiction are more like the red ball considered only as such than the dynamic predicationally inexhaustible objects that we encounter in sensation or study in logic, mathematics and philosophy. We can only say so much about the properties of a nonexistent predication object even in the longest work of fiction or series of myths.

Property combinations, whether complete or incomplete, can also be consistent or inconsistent. An example of a complete and consistent property combination is that of an actually existent physical or abstract entity, say, the Eiffel Tower. The Eiffel Tower is predicationally complete; the fabled Golden City of Eldorado is not. An incomplete and consistent predication combination belongs to a fictional object like Eldorado. There need be no contradictions in its description, but the most that can be said about it leaves innumerable questions unanswered. Did Eldorado have champagne fountains? Was it paved with 18 or 24 carat gold? Was a monkey ever made its king? We cannot say yes or no. What we know of it may be logically consistent, but the most we can possibly know of it will be logically incomplete with respect to at least one property and property complement. Thus, unlike the Eiffel Tower, Eldorado does not exist; it has no being, even as an abstract entity. The Eiffel Tower qualifies for inclusion in a preferred existence domain, but Eldorado as an incomplete and hence nonexistent object does not. This is as it should be. Difficulties nevertheless arise when we try to generalize an analysis of the concept of being or existence from these data. Shall we say that an object has being if and only if it has a consistent and complete property combination?

A combinatorial ontology holds that existence is nothing more or less than completeness and consistency, or what is also called *maximal consistency*. The definition, properly understood and applied, provides a unified analysis of the concept of being for all entities, including existent objects, actual states of affairs and the actual world.

Maximal consistency and the concept of being

It may be unproblematic to maintain that existent entities, states of affairs and the actual world must all be associated with maximally consistent property combinations. Is it also true that all maximally consistent property combinations necessarily define or constitute existent entities, actual states of affairs and the actual world? Could there not be maximally consistent property combinations for objects that do not exist? Why should we believe that maximal consistency is a sufficient as well as necessary condition for existence?

Think of a logically possible world other than the actual world. Can there be a physical object in such a world that is maximally consistent but does not exist? The answer should be no, because there can be no maximally consistent object in a non-actual world. Why not? The conclusion is not immediately obvious. If there is any incomplete object in a logically possible world or logically impossible model, then every other object will also be incomplete with respect to indefinitely many properties and states of affairs that depend on its relations with the first incomplete object. If we consider a world or model in which the incomplete property combination [F1, F2] defines, constitutes, holds true or is exhaustively predicated of an object, then the object is obviously predicationally incomplete. It follows that every other object in the same world is also predicationally incomplete, by virtue of neither having nor failing to have some logically possible property FN with respect to [F1, F2]. Let [F1, F2], for example, be an incomplete property combination [red, ball], and consider the intrinsically predicationally complete object, reducible to or associated with the property combination [F3, F4, F5, . . .], such as, [steel, tower, four-sided, sloping sides reaching to a pinnacle topped by an observation deck, . . .]. Although the object is intrinsically complete, it is still incomplete by virtue of remaining extrinsically incomplete with respect to at least some relational property FN involving it and the red round object reducible to or associated with property combination [F1, F2]. Is the (non-actual, pseudo-) Eiffel Tower in the same world as the red round object taller or not taller than the red round object? Is the (non-actual, pseudo-) Eiffel Tower older or not older than the red round object?

These questions have no answer, which makes the (non-actual) Eiffel Tower as predicationally incomplete as the red round object, for it is thereby spatiotemporally and in other ways relationally incomplete. If, *per impossibile*, the actual world contained even one predicationally incomplete object like the red round object, then all other objects in the actual world would be just as predicationally incomplete and therefore non-actual, the states of affairs to which they belong would be predicationally incomplete and therefore non-actual, and the actual world would be predicationally incomplete and therefore non-actual. The predicational incompleteness of an object that disqualifies it from existing equally affects all other logically possible objects in the same logically possible world. The actual world must contain all and only actual objects in actual states of affairs, whereas mere possibilities and impossibilities must belong to other logically possible worlds or logically impossible states-of-affairs combinations. It follows that only the actual world is intrinsically and extrinsically predicationally complete, consisting of and constituted by an intrinsically and extrinsically maximally consistent states-of-affairs combination. An existent state of affairs in turn involves an intrinsically and extrinsically maximally consistent predication of properties to or possession of properties by what are thereby the actual objects belonging to what is thereby the actual world.

We can think of maximal consistency in terms of abstract operations. A *Lindenbaum maximal consistency recursion* is an inductive procedure that orders all propositions randomly, takes the first proposition in the list and adds the next listed proposition to whatever propositions have already been collected, provided that it is syntactically consistent with the propositions collected, and otherwise adds its negation, successively through the entire potentially infinite list. The adaptation of the Lindenbaum maximal consistency recursion for combinatorial ontology accomplishes much the same purpose in application to logically possible properties and logically possible objects and logically possible properties in logically possible states of affairs. Imagine, therefore, all the combinations of properties into objects and of objects with properties in predications that might logically be constructed according to a Lindenbaum maximal consistency recursion as an abstract characterization of the intensional property constitution of existent objects, actual states of affairs and the actual world.[7]

Maximal consistency

A property combination *PC* for any logically possible object *O* is *maximally consistent* if and only if, for any logically possible extraontological property *F*, either *F* is in *PC* or non-*F* (the complement of *F*) is in *PC*, but not both.

We need only consider logically possible objects in ontology. An extraontology demanded by a fully general philosophical semantics would also need to include predicationally internally inconsistent property combinations, such as [red, non-red], [round, square], and the like. These objects, unlike their predicationally consistent counterparts, identify intensionally and correspond to metaphysically impossible but still thinkable and linguistically designatable objects. They are the bearers of properties in predications that are true by the very definition of *impossibilia*. The same semantic licence required for logically impossible objects generally must then apply equally to logically impossible states of affairs and logically impossible worlds.

In ontology, as the theory specifically of entities or existent objects, objects of all kinds with being, we limit theory to the intensional characterization of logically possible, including actual, objects, states of affairs and worlds.[8]

> **Combinatorial concept of being (existence) answer to the question of being**
>
> For any object O, O *exists*, has *being* or is an *entity*, if and only if O has a maximally consistent property combination.

The actual world can accordingly be defined equivalently as a maximally consistent combination of actual states of affairs, or maximally consistent states-of-affairs combination. An actual state of affairs is defined as the true predication to or possession of a property by an actual object, where an actual object is defined as an intrinsically and extrinsically predicationally maximally consistent property combination. A particular maximally consistent property combination already determines a maximally consistent states-of-affairs combination, and thereby also determines an actual world complete in all its actual states of affairs involving all and only actually existent entities. We can then say that there exists something rather than nothing because there is certain to be a logically possible combination of all logically possible properties with all logically possible objects in which every object is intrinsically and extrinsically predicationally maximally consistent. Such a combination is logically combinatorially necessitated as only one of indefinitely many logical possibilities. There is thus sure to be at least one combination of properties and objects that satisfies the proposed definition of being as maximal consistency.

Combinatorial ontological concepts

An analysis of the concept of being can be given combinatorially in terms of maximal consistency. What it is to be, to exist or be real or actual or to have being, whether the entity in question is a physical or abstract object, state of affairs or world, is to be predicationally maximally consistent. This condition, although purely logical and purely a matter of logical possibility, is, when properly interpreted, sufficiently strong to guarantee that there is only one actual world consisting of and constituted by all and only actually existent states of affairs, involving all and only actually existent objects.

Let us leave abstract objects out of the picture for a moment, and consider only physical things. That there are physical entities is something we believe ourselves to know from our immediate sense experience of the empirical world. We might reject this assumption in light of a sufficiently high-powered philosophical reason to doubt its truth, but it is generally conceded that the existence of physical entities is philosophically less problematic than the existence of abstract entities. The trouble is that we have no direct experience of abstract entities, but must rely on good arguments to accept or reject them in applied ontology. If there are good arguments for including abstract entities, then we can suppose that as non-spatiotemporal objects they will belong to any logically possible world. If there are good reasons, on the contrary, for excluding abstract objects from the preferred existence domain, then we do not have to take them seriously anyway.

By focusing on physical entities, we concentrate on what is generally regarded as the philosophically least problematic aspect of the real world, a robust grasp of which is presupposed by the natural sciences often in the form of a naive realism about phenomenal appearances as the real properties of real entities encountered in sensation. We can think of physical entities as maximally consistent or predicationally consistent and complete, proceeding now in several standard categories of putative entities that are common to alternative ontologies in positing distinct theoretical existence domains. If applied ontology declares that there are abstract objects, then these can be added to the existence domain only if they are predicationally maximally consistent. Since they are not going to include spatiotemporal properties in their property combinations, they are not going to be predicationally incomplete by virtue of existing in any logically possible world that also contains any predicationally incomplete objects or states of affairs. If there are abstract entities, they are spatiotemporally and in every other way relationally untouched by the predicational completeness or incompleteness of any physical objects belonging to any logically possible world, and so generally by their ontic status.

We summarize the three combinatorial categories of existence in the boxes below, beginning with a general division between logically possible objects, states of affairs and worlds, and then defining the concepts of entities, existent states of affairs and the actual world. We categorize objects and entities intensionally in combinatorial pure philosophical ontology in terms of logically possible property

---

Combinatorial existence candidates

Object
Property combination
Most general category; subsumes all objects, including existent
and merely logically possible non-actual objects, states of
affairs and worlds, including the actual world

State of affairs
Inclusion of property or predication in a property combination
Propertyhood, quality or relation, of an object

(Logically possible) world
Consistent states-of-affairs combination, maximal or
submaximal; ultimately logically possible combination of
logically possible objects with logically possible properties

---

combinations and their predicational maximal or submaximal consistency or inconsistency.

The ontically neutral divisions between objects, logically possible
states of affairs and logically possible worlds are now more precisely
specified to represent a parallel three-part division between actually
existent entities, including actually existent states of affairs and the
actual world. The definitions add the requirement of maximal consistency to objects in each of the three original categories.

We can also collect the conclusions of combinatorial pure philosophical ontology in a system of four principles. We presuppose that
in logic we can speak of all logically possible combinations of logical
objects and properties, and that for convenience we can speak of logical objects as logically possible property combinations. We leave it as
an open question for applied ontology whether logically possible
objects are ontically reducible to their associated property combinations. If necessary, we can reformulate all of the principles in any
other metalogical vocabulary that permits all logically possible combinations of ontically neutral logical states of affairs involving all logically possible combinations of ontically neutral logical objects with all
logically possible combinations of all ontically neutral logically possible properties.

The notation calls for explanation. The plus sign, $+$, in Principle 1
does not mean numerical addition. Since logical objects on the

Combinatorial categories of existence

Entity
Maximally consistent property combination
Most general category, subsumes all existent objects, including
existent objects, existent states of affairs and the actual world

Existent state of affairs
Inclusion of property or predication in a maximally consistent
property combination – where entity $a = [F, . . .]$, Fa is an
existent state of affairs
Propertyhood, quality or relation, of an entity

(The) actual world
Maximally consistent combination of all and only existent
states of affairs; ultimately maximally consistent combination
of all logically possible objects with all logically possible
properties
Total reality

Basic principles of combinatorial ontology

Principle 1:   combo (object + property) = state of affairs

Principle 2:   maximally consistent property combination =
               existent entity

Principle 3:   maximally consistent states-of-affairs
               combination involving all and only existent
               entities = actual world

Principle 4:   submaximally consistent states-of-affairs
               combination involving only nonexistent
               nonentities = (merely) logically possible
               non-actual world

---

present account are only intensionally defined as combinations of
properties, we mean by this abbreviation that a state of affairs is (the
fact that) a logical object appropriately combined with a property (as
represented linguistically by a logical object term predicationally
combined with a property term); or, equivalently, that a state of

affairs is (the fact that) a property is included in the property combination associated with a logical object. The equals sign, =, is also not intended as arithmetical, but indicates equivalence in concept or meaning.

Principle 1 makes a terminological stipulation. What we mean by a state of affairs is a logical object's having a property or a property's belonging to an associated property combination. The remaining principles are more contentious. Principle 2 states that a logical object exists just in case its associated property combination is maximally consistent. To be maximally consistent for any property, the combination either contains the property or its complement (red, non-red; round, non-round), and never contains both a property and its complement. A maximally consistent property combination in other words harbours no predicational inconsistencies, and is complete in the sense that there are no gaps among the property and property complement pairs included in the combination.

These conditions are unlikely to excite controversy as necessary requirements for the existence of an object. Why, on the other hand, as we have already asked in another context, should anyone suppose that they are also sufficient? If an object has an inconsistent set of predications, then of course it does not exist. It is similar if the object has predicational gaps, if it is neither human nor non-human, or neither positively charged nor non-positively-charged. How can we be sure that the existence of a logical object is guaranteed by the purely logical character of its associated property combination as maximally consistent? The answer requires first a look ahead to Principles 3 and 4, and then a defence of Principle 2 against interesting but ultimately unsuccessful counterexamples.

We are to think of a world, according to Principles 3 and 4, as a combination of facts or states of affairs. These states of affairs, says Principle 1, are themselves nothing more than the possession of a logically possible property by a logically possible object, or of the inclusion of a property in a property combination associated with a logical object, which are also known as facts about the object or relevant property combination. Principle 4 states that a logically possible world exists or is actual just in case it is associated with a maximally consistent states-of-affairs combination. The idea in different form involving maximally consistent proposition sets is standardly invoked to describe the concept of a logically possible world in the informal semantics of alethic modal logic, the formal theory of logical possibility and necessity, with which both pure logic and pure philosophical ontology are inextricably connected. By such a convention, a merely logically possible but not actual world is usually said to be a maximally consistent set of propositions. We are saying something stronger, namely that only the actual world is a maximally consistent states-of-affairs combination to be completely described by a maximally consistent proposition set. It follows that merely logically possible but not actual worlds are predicationally consistent but submaximal states-of-affairs combinations. It is incumbent, then, to say why we are breaking tradition in this way with the established definition of a merely logically possible world. In doing so, we provide all the necessary background to defend Principle 2 against the objection that it offers only necessary but not jointly sufficient conditions for a logical object to exist as an entity, to have being in the actual world.

Modalities of maximal and submaximal consistency

The definition of a logically possible world defined as or as represented by a maximally consistent set of propositions benefits from the successful reception of conventional model set-theoretical semantics for modal logic. It is easy in retrospect to understand why. The first modal syntax and axiom systems developed by C. I. Lewis in 1918 were formally uninterpreted until Saul A. Kripke and Jaakko Hintikka independently worked out model set-theoretical semantics for modal logics and quantified modal logics in the mid-1960s.[9] Building on the firmly established mathematical foundation of Zermelo-Fraenkel set theory, Kripke and Hintikka provide an exact formal interpretation of these logical languages, valuable in the analysis and formal modelling of a significant part of philosophical, scientific and everyday discourse.[10]

The emergence of a powerful mathematical method for interpreting modal logic made a deep impression on the analytic philosophical imagination in the second half of the twentieth century. It quickly became a favourite tool for formal modelling of many difficult logical concepts. The idea that a logically possible world is a maximally consistent proposition set has been so integral to standard model set-theoretical semantics that it has been accepted as part of the same remarkable package, without much philosophical objection, and, indeed, without much philosophical question or scruple. The brilliance and usefulness of these semantic models and the unified interpretation of the variety of modal logics that they afford made model set-theoretical semantics an immediate paradigm of analytic philosophy, comparable in its impact, and deservedly so, only to Bertrand Russell's theory of definite descriptions.

The defects of standard model set-theoretical semantics are less immediately appreciated, partly, no doubt, because proponents are thoroughly convinced of its usefulness and committed to its truth. The concept of a logically possible world as a maximally consistent proposition set is nevertheless philosophically disastrous, once we look beyond the pragmatics of formal analysis. There is no way to sugar-coat the fact that if sets exist, as mathematical realism classically implies, then any logically possible world as a maximally consistent proposition set exists, even in the case of a non-actual world consisting entirely of nonexistent objects and nonexistent states of affairs. The idea that non-actual merely logically possible worlds are maximally consistent proposition sets combined with a default Platonist or realist ontology of mathematical entities according to which proposition sets exist is profoundly confused.

Among all the logically possible worlds, there is only one that actually exists, the one and only actual world in which we actually existent entities happen to reside. The actual world alone exists, and it includes all and only the genuine entities, all existent individuals, states of affairs and whatever else actually exists as constituting the actual world, while merely logically possible worlds do not exist. If to insist that the actual world is uniquely existent is unobjectionable, then it is impossible to see how we can tolerate the definition of a logically possible world according to which all logically possible worlds exist, including all non-actual merely logically possible worlds. That, regrettably, is the inescapable conclusion if logically possible worlds are defined as maximally consistent proposition sets, and if sets as abstract mathematical entities exist. If sets exist, then the conventional concept of a logically possible world as a proposition set requires a counterintuitive distinction between existence and actuality, between what exists and what is actual, or perhaps between what exists and what actually exists.

Nor does it help to retreat to a redefinition whereby logically possible worlds are only described or represented rather than constituted by maximally consistent proposition sets. The problem in that case is just the opposite of the one that plagues the interpretation of logically possible worlds as maximally consistent proposition sets. If all logically possible worlds are described alike by maximally consistent proposition sets, then we face the equally difficult question of what it is, as far as the conventional semantics of modal logic is concerned, that is supposed to single out the actual world as having special ontic status from all other non-actual merely logically possible worlds.

To this pertinent ontological query, there is no satisfactory answer in a conventional modal model set-theoretical framework. While modal logicians have formalized appropriate model set-theoretical relations among logically possible worlds, they have not looked into or tried in any meaningful way to characterize the metaphysics of being, or to establish the principles of pure philosophical ontology for actually existent entities. It is clear, in reading any standard work of formal modal semantics, that the definition of a logically possible world in set-theoretical terms offers no answer at all to the question of what it means for something to exist, or in particular of what it means for a logically possible world to be correctly identified as the uniquely existent actual world. The usual practice is for a model set-theoretical semantics to define an enormous number of combinatorially generated logically possible worlds, typically by the equivalent of a Lindenbaum maximal consistency recursion, each as a distinct maximally consistent proposition set, and then simply to declare that one of these sets is to be "distinguished" as the actual world. Notations differ, but it is common practice to adopt the mnemonic symbol *alpha*, "α", or the *at* sign, "@", to designate the actual world in modal semantics as "$w_@$".[11] The urgent philosophical question that remains in light of these devices is by virtue of what features a logically possible world, if universally defined as a maximally consistent proposition set, is correctly identified as the actual world?

It is possible for many things in the actual world to be other than they are. Life need not have evolved, the Third Reich might have won World War II, or I might have gone to Mexico to snorkel instead of Austria to ski. The actual world is only one possibility among limitlessly many others. Of all the logically possible worlds, only one is actual. We might not yet know exactly what this means, or why it should be so, if we have not yet grasped what makes the actual world actual, and what distinguishes it from all non-actual merely logically possible worlds. To that extent, also, we do not yet fully and accurately understand what is meant by the concept of a logically possible world. This is precisely what is missing from the definition of a logically possible world in conventional model set-theoretical modal semantics. We transgress the limits of pure logic if we try to say that the actual world is the one that we logicians psychologically experience, or that has the objects or states of affairs that we encounter in sensation. Yet it appears that efforts to single out the actual world in conventional modal semantics never amounts to anything more than this kind of implicit appeal to extralogical empirical facts.

It is astonishing, once we consider the alternatives, to comprehend the extent to which such problems are swept under the carpet in philosophical discussions of contemporary model set-theoretical modal semantics.

We can say, for example, that the actual world is the world consisting of all and only existent states of affairs involving all and only existent objects, and we can say that an existent object is an object that belongs to the actual world, as opposed to a merely logically possible world. We do not know from this alone what either of these statements is supposed to mean in the absence of a unified account of the existence of entities, including actually existent logically possible objects, states of affairs and the actual world. It is only if we come into possession of such an ontology or metaphysics of being that we can hope to explain precisely what it means for a logically possible world to be actual, and why there exists precisely one world, which we recognize as the actual world. We need to know why or with what justification a particular logically possible world is rightly designated as the actual world, and distinguished thereby from all non-actual merely logically possible worlds.

In his lectures on *Naming and Necessity*, Kripke reminds us that logically possible worlds are not viewed through high-powered telescopes to discover what objects they contain.[12] We similarly need to understand that the actual world is not selected from a beauty pageant line-up of all logically possible world hopefuls to be "designated" as actual. We need to break ourselves of certain misleading ways of imagining the semantics of modal logic, and the existence requirements for logically possible objects, states of affairs and the actual world. The actual world does nothing to earn or deserve its actuality. It is the actual world on the present theory because it is a maximally consistent states-of-affairs combination involving all and only the existent objects, which in turn exist because they are maximally consistent property combinations. The combinatorial analysis of being implies that non-actual merely logically possible worlds are not maximally consistent states-of-affairs combinations, contrary to the widely accepted semantics for modal logic. If the principles listed above are to succeed, it is necessary to explain why the conventional wisdom in modal semantics is wrong, and why the alternative conception offered here is preferable.

A defender of conventional modal semantics must challenge the idea that an object exists just in case its property combination is maximally consistent. The concept that has informed model set-theoretical modal semantics from its outset is that all of the property combinations of nonexistent objects in merely logically possible but non-actual worlds are also maximally consistent, in the same way and by the same reasoning that inspires conventional modal logic to suppose that merely logically possible non-actual worlds are maximally consistent proposition sets or structures of facts or states of affairs. Some modal logicians, recognizing the difficulty, and desperate to find a way to resolve conflicting intuitions, go so far as to relativize existence to particular logically possible worlds. They say, for example, that the Statue of Liberty exists in the actual world, but that in other logically possible worlds there exist objects like the Fountain of Youth or city of Eldorado that do not exist in "our" world. The concept of being in combinatorial pure philosophical ontology entails a *modal actualism* that is incompatible with the *modal realism* of conventional model set-theoretical modal semantics and the standard definition of a logically possible world as a maximally consistent proposition set.[13] Conventional modal semantics thus entails that there are objects that truly exist in worlds that truly do not exist. Such a position appears to be logically incoherent, if all and only the entities and states of affairs in the actual world exist.[14]

Why does conventional modal semantic theory insist that all logically possible worlds are, or are completely and correctly describable only as, maximally consistent proposition sets? Perhaps it is because these logicians perceive that the actual world is maximally consistent, and that it is, after all, a logically possible world. The more important question that is not usually asked is, rather, what if it is maximal consistency that makes the actual world actual, a property shared by no merely logically possible non-actual world? It may be less objectionable in trying to work out the formal semantic structures for interpreting the propositions of modal logic not to become embroiled in the metaphysics of being for the actual world or the states of affairs by which it is constituted or the entities it contains. In ontology, on the other hand, and especially in pure philosophical ontology's enquiry into the question of being, we cannot afford to set the problem aside. It appears that conventional model set-theoretical semantics for modal logic, in ignoring the problem of what it means for the actual world to be designated or distinguished as actual from among all other merely logically possible worlds, fails to recognize drastically counterintuitive results, even within its limited project of trying to provide an adequate formal semantics for modal logic. Conventional modal logic does not care about the question of being – but it should.[15]

By adopting Principles 1–4, we explain what it means for the actual world to exist, and we recover consistency in maintaining that only the objects and states of affairs in the actual world exist with the assumption that only the actual world exists. Then we can say that for the actual world to exist, to be designated or distinguished as actual, means for it to be a maximally consistent states-of-affairs combination, involving all and only existent objects, which in turn are maximally consistent property combinations. The account is unified, economical and comprehensive. Is it also true? The sticking point for most contemporary modal logicians is the idea that non-actual merely logically possible worlds are submaximally consistent states-of-affairs combinations: possible, because they are at least internally consistent in their constitutive states of affairs by which properties are attributed to objects; submaximal, in that they are incomplete in the sense of containing property and property complement gaps in their underlying predicational relations, projected into their associated gappy incomplete property combinations. The ethos of mathematical studies in modal semantics is typically Platonistically realistic. Modal logicians have a tendency to suppose that the maximally consistent proposition sets that are invoked in interpreting the sentences of different systems of modal logic exist as abstract entities, and that as such they are freely available like other mathematical structures for use in formal semantics. This seems partly right and partly wrong. We do not want to make premature commitments to the existence of abstract entities while engaged in trying to understand the nature of being, or to answer the question of being, of what it means for something to exist, as a task for pure philosophical ontology.[16]

Maximal consistency of the actual world

We shall, accordingly, consider three different arguments to support the conclusion that non-actual merely logically possible worlds should not be interpreted semantically as maximally consistent, but as at most only submaximally consistent proposition sets or states-of-affairs combinations. As against the assumptions of conventional modal semantics, we conclude that only the actual world is maximally consistent.

If the arguments are correct, then they pave the way to a solution to the question of being in which, working backwards now:

- A logically possible world fails to exist or is merely logically possible if and only if it is a submaximally consistent states-of-affairs combination (Principle 4)
- A logically possible world exists or is an actual world if and only if it is a maximally consistent states-of-affairs combination (Principle 3)

- An object is an existent entity if and only if it is or is associated with a maximally consistent property combination (Principle 2)
- A state of affairs (terminologically) is the possession of an object by a property or the inclusion of a property in an associated property combination (Principle 1)

The question of being is answered in terms of maximal consistency. To be, to be an entity at any ontological level, from existent object to existent state of affairs (an existent object's actually having a property) to the entire actual world, is then to be maximally consistent. Being is maximal consistency, and what it means for something to exist is for it in the appropriate sense to be maximally consistent. If all of these concepts fit together as we have argued, then we can answer Heidegger's question of being. We can do so, moreover, from the standpoint of pure logic in a combinatorial ontology rather than by means of an anthropocentric ontically-freighted phenomenology or existential ontology. We will then have arrived at a pure philosophical ontology that respects rather than flaunts Heidegger's methodological constraints on an answer to the question of being, the priority of the question of being over the ontic sciences, and of pure philosophical ontology over applied scientific ontology.

The difficulty is that we can describe maximally consistent proposition sets, as in conventional model set-theoretical semantics for modal logic, if we can describe any mathematical entities. Nothing prevents a conventional modal logician from adapting the Lindenbaum recursion to project all distinct complete and consistent proposition sets. The method is to consider each proposition in turn and add it to a given set if and only if it is logically consistent with the propositions already collected in the set until there are none left, otherwise adding its negation, following the process in the case of every logically distinct combination of propositions until every proposition or its negation is incorporated. A similar recursive procedure is followed for the original application of Lindenbaum's Lemma in consistency and completeness proofs in standard logical metatheory, which no doubt played a part in the standard concept of a logically possible world as a maximally consistent proposition set. If we are Platonic realists in the applied scientific ontology of mathematics, then we may be strongly inclined, if not irrevocably committed, to regarding such sets as themselves existent mathematical entities to which we can appeal *ad libitum* in theory construction, especially in designing a model set-theoretical semantics for modal logic.[17]

The combinatorial analysis of the concept of being as maximal consistency does not cast doubt on the possibility of such a procedure. On the contrary, we assume that maximally consistent proposition sets, regardless of how they are later classified ontologically in applied scientific ontology, can be thought of as being compiled combinatorially in just this way. The problem now is whether the resulting maximally consistent proposition sets deserve to be called, or considered as describing, non-actual logically possible worlds. The conclusion is rather that the identification or description of a logically possible world as a maximally consistent set of propositions or maximally consistent states-of-affairs combination is warranted only in the unique case of the actual world. Non-actual merely logically possible worlds, by comparison, are fictional creatures of conventional modal semantics, and as such inherently predicationally incomplete. We argue that there are good reasons for adopting this unconventional concept of a logically possible world as required by the combinatorial analysis of the concept of being in a reformed semantics of modal logic.[18]

Objection 1: Kripkean stipulation in the transworld identity problem is always submaximal

The first objection to considering maximally consistent proposition sets as non-actual merely logically possible worlds depends on Kripke's answer to the transworld identity problem. The objects we find in the actual world might have been so different than they actually are that it appears impossible even in theory and certainly in practice to identify the same objects from world to world.

Kripke sidesteps the problem by maintaining that transworld identity is not a matter of discovery, but of decision. We stipulate, in Kripke's terminology, that there is a non-actual logically possible world in which Richard Nixon's chromosomal endowment was so radically altered prior even to his development in the womb that at no time within that world is he recognizable as the Richard Nixon we know from experience of his appearance in the actual world. Kripke's response to transworld identity problems has gained wide acceptance among modal logicians and philosophers of logic. Taken literally, however, although Kripke does not acknowledge the consequence, Kripkean transworld identity stipulation implies a constitutional incompleteness in the proposition sets associated with any non-actual logically possible world, by which they can only be submaximal even if logically consistent. Stipulation involves real-time human decision-making that is incompatible with the possibility of including all the items in a consistent proposition set in order to qualify as *maximally* consistent. We, finite creatures that we are, can only submaximally stipulate so much in describing distinct logically poss-ible worlds in the limited time we can devote to such theorizing, in which this or that is said to be different from the actual world, and leave the rest unspecified.[19]

Stipulation involves real-time human decision-making and the vicissitudes of theory construction, which are incompatible with the possibility of including the required number of propositions in a consistent set of propositions in order to qualify it as *maximally* consistent. If we do not follow Kripke's recommendation, on the other hand, then we may have no plausible solution to the problem of transworld identity. The conclusion might then be that Kripke-style stipulation of logically possible worlds amounts only to a selection from among eternally pre-existent maximally consistent proposition sets identified with or corresponding to every non-actual logically possible world, or to the simple logically consistent replacement of one propo-sition by another, say, that Nixon in another world looks exactly like, and even, if this is a possibility that does not violate Kripke's essential-ist constraints, has all of the genetic structure of Marilyn Monroe, within a different maximally consistent proposition set.

The problem that remains is whether any such alteration, no matter how slight it may appear, is actually consistency-preserving in a maximally consistent propositions set. If it is not, then of course we are no longer assuming that non-actual logically possible worlds are, or are described by, maximally consistent proposition sets. How are we to tell? If Kripke-style stipulation is supposed to amount just to a selection from the wide range of eternally pre-existent maximally consistent proposition sets, how is the choice to be managed? Which set are we supposed to select in order to know that we are dealing with Nixon as a blonde bombshell rather than Marilyn herself? With-out a good answer to that question, we fall back into the problem of transworld identity.

Objection 2: Submaximal consistency is adequate for the modal semantics of non-actual worlds

Secondly, it is significant that submaximally consistent proposition sets are adequate for the formal semantics of modal logic in the case of all non-actual logically possible worlds. It is good enough for the purposes of formalizing a general semantics of modal logic to recognize maximal consistency only in the case of the actual world. There is nothing we can practically do with maximally consistent sets in understanding the truth conditions for sentences in modal logic that we cannot do with submaximally consistent sets or submaximally consistent states-of-affairs combinations.

As a further theoretical advantage, submaximally consistent proposition sets do not incur the difficulties of conventional modal semantics. They encourage an answer to the question of being with respect to worlds, explaining the actual world as uniquely maximally consistent in its fully consistent complement of actually existent states of affairs as determined by the actually instantiated properties of actually existent entities. They further avoid the need to relativize existence to specific logically possible worlds, dispensing with the confusing assertion that the Fountain of Youth exists *in* a particular world, whatever this is supposed to mean, when we assume on the contrary without qualification that the Fountain of Youth does not exist or does not actually exist. The very idea of "existence *in* a (non-actual) world" ought to be avoided if at all possible, because it saddles modal logic with an extremely problematic way of distinguishing the actual world from alternative logically possible worlds. The actual world in that case cannot be identified as the world containing all and only existent states of affairs involving all and only existent entities. All worlds, paradoxically, then, each have their own world-indexed existent entities. We are further obliged in that case to index actually existent entities to the predesignated actual world, whose facts and objects are existent-$w_@$, rather than existent-w_1, -w_2, -w_3, and so on, where $@ \neq 1, 2, 3, \ldots$

What makes our world, in which there is no Fountain of Youth or Golden City of Eldorado, the actual world? Conventional modal semantics, in which all logically possible worlds, including non-actual worlds, are defined in terms of maximally consistent proposition sets, has no choice except to allow that the actual world is the world we experience in sensation, or the world we knowers happen to inhabit. This is not necessarily a bad thing from the standpoint of modal semantics's efforts to describe the formal structures needed to make sense of the modally qualified sentences in a given system of modal logic. The semantics relies on a distinction that we have also adopted between pure and applied modal logic. The practice nevertheless presents a serious obstacle in considering the distinction between non-actual merely logically possible worlds and the actual world in the context of understanding the concept of existence generally, of addressing the question of being, as we are trying to do here in pure philosophical ontology, unpacking what it means for something to exist.

Ironically, modal logicians and semanticists are almost exclusively analytically trained or analytic in philosophical outlook. By forcing the designation of the actual world as the one among all logically possible worlds to get the bouquet on the basis of the presence of the knower, ourselves, within the actual world, or in terms of our experience in thought and sensation as identifying the actual world as the one we are in and happen to inhabit, conventional modal logic tumbles headlong into Heidegger's circle of trying to understand the nature of being from the phenomenological standpoint of *Da-sein* or human being-in-the-world. This is as much a theoretical scandal for the collaboration of pure modal logic with pure philosophical ontology in analytic philosophy as it is in Heidegger's investigation of the question of being in existential ontology.

If it is true that we do not need maximally consistent proposition sets to do modal semantics, and there is no obvious reason why we should, but we can get by perfectly well with submaximally consistent proposition sets or states-of-affairs combinations instead, except in the unique case of the actual world, then there is an argument from the standpoint of theoretical economy and simplicity to favour a non-conventional modal semantics in which only the actual world is understood as a maximally consistent proposition set or states-of-affairs combination, and all non-actual merely logically possible worlds are recognized as submaximally consistent. The distinction is simpler overall, and offers a good basis in logic rather than phenomenology or immediate sense experience for distinguishing the actual world from merely logically possible worlds. We are not limited in that case to identifying the actual world as the one that we as existent human beings inhabit, with reference to our peculiarly human being-in-the-world, or whose actuality we are privileged to experience. We should not appeal to such facts in the context of pure philosophical ontology in answering the question of being anyway, if we agree that we must answer the question of being before proceeding to the nitty-gritty details of applied scientific ontology, in which alone experience of the world and the facts of human existence and psychology find their proper place.

What, then, could possibly justify conventional modal logic's demand that non-actual merely logically possible worlds are maximally consistent rather than submaximally consistent proposition sets? Why go maximal except in the unique case of the actual world? The only imaginable reason has to do with an intuition about the meaning of the word "world", according to which submaximal consistency does not deserve to be called or associated with a *world*, or that a world in the true sense of the word, even if it is non-actual and merely logically possible, must be maximal. Such reasoning can easily be shown to be unfounded and any such counter-objection inconclusive.

There is, in the first place, an undertone of disgruntlement among formal semanticists in modal logic about the concept of logically possible *worlds*. Many modal logicians in their philosophical moments have raised doubts about whether structures of propositions not associated with the actual world deserve to be called worlds at all. A nonexistent world is arguably not a world in the strict and proper philosophical sense. We must wonder, for those theorists who set store by the idea that a world in the true sense of the word must be maximally consistent, whether any advantages of conventional model set-theoretical semantics would be forfeited by referring in the case of submaximally consistent proposition sets as "near worlds", or "world-like structures" in the formal interpretation of modal logics. It is hard to see that anything whatsoever would be sacrificed from the programme of formal modal semantics if the word "world" were restricted to the unique maximally consistent proposition set associated with the actual world, in which case "world" turns out to mean *the* world, and all non-actual merely logically possible "worlds" are renamed as something world-related, but as not themselves genuine worlds. The whole idea of pluralizing "world" as "worlds" might then be reconsidered as misguided, where a definitive lexical remedy could be so simple and painless for an unconventional combinatorial model set-theoretical modal semantics.

The suggestion is predicated on the assumption that some modal logicians will balk at the idea that a world could be merely submaximally rather than maximally consistent. If we have no such linguistic scruples, as a combinatorial theory certainly does not, then there should be no problem in allowing or requiring non-actual merely logically possible worlds in the technical sense of the word in the model set-theoretical semantics of modal logic to be submaximally consistent, reserving maximal consistency only in the unique case of the actual world of real existent states of affairs involving the actually instantiated properties of real existent entities.

Objection 3: Non-actual worlds by definition are submaximally consistent

A third reason for distinguishing the actual world as the only maximally consistent proposition set or states-of-affairs combination, by contrast with the submaximal consistency of non-actual merely logically possible worlds, is based on a trilemma. The argument suggests a deeper reason why non-actual merely logically possible worlds must be submaximally consistent. A maximally consistent set of propositions, even on the weakest accessibility relations between logically possible worlds in model set-theoretical semantics, must include true or false propositions about the actual states of affairs obtaining in the actual world. Non-actual worlds must look over their shoulders at what is happening in the actual world, and make some statement about the situation there, in order to be maximal. Otherwise, there will be propositions entirely left out of their proposition sets, which by definition are thereby submaximal.

The proposition set of a non-actual merely logically possible world as a result has a conflicting set of responsibilities if it is to be maximally consistent. It must pretend, so to speak, in certain cases, that the Fountain of Youth "actually" exists, or exists in its associated world, and must include a proposition to this effect, while at the same time declaring that the Fountain of Youth does not exist, or does not actually exist or exist in the actual world. We have already seen that indexing the truth of propositions to particular logically possible worlds within proposition sets associated with worlds is a philosophically questionable practice in modal semantics. Now we are fated to see worse problems arise, whether or not world-indexing of propositions is tolerated. Consider a proposition set, S, for a non-actual merely logically possible world, w_j, that is striving for maximal consistency in the grain of conventional model set-theoretical modal semantics. Set S either includes or does not include the proposition that the Fountain of Youth does not exist, and either does so indexically by making reference to the truth of the proposition in the actual world, or non-indexically.

Thus, there are three possibilities:

1. If S does not include any proposition expressing the fact that the Fountain of Youth does not exist (in actual world $w_@$), then S is submaximal, even if it is logically consistent.
2. If S includes a proposition expressing the fact that the Fountain of Youth does not exist indexically by referring to the proposition's truth in or with reference to the actual world $w_@$, "The Fountain of Youth does not exist (in $w_@$)", then it must also assert the existence of the Fountain of Youth in or with reference to w_j, "The Fountain of Youth exists in w_j" ($i \neq @$). Then, problems of indexicality for an extensionalist model set-theoretical logic aside

(and they are considerable, including the danger of outright logical paradox), S contains propositions that acknowledge by their explicit indexing that the Fountain of Youth does not actually exist; in effect declaring its own falsehood, a false description of the world, thereby rendering S unfit as a description of w_i.

3. If S includes a proposition non-indexically expressing the fact that the Fountain of Youth does not exist (in $w_@$) and non-indexically expressing the fact that the Fountain of Youth exists (in w_i, $i \neq @$, as before), then, without benefit of the indices indicated in parentheses, S is inconsistent, even if maximal. Set S as a result is inconsistent if it avoids indexicality, submaximal if it ignores the facts of the actual world, and inadequate as a description of w_i if it embraces indexicality in order consistently to include the fact that the Fountain of Youth does not actually exist.

We want to know what it means for the actual world to be distinguished as actual, by comparison with all non-actual merely logically possible worlds. We also want to be able to say that only the actual world exists, that all and only the objects and states of affairs in the actual world exist, that existence is not to be relativized to worlds, but that "existence" means real existence or actuality. Thus, it seems we have no choice but to rethink the conventional wisdom of standard model set-theoretical semantics for modal logic.

If we reject the semantic theory that non-actual merely logically possible worlds are or are describable as maximally consistent proposition sets, as I have argued we should, and opt instead for an unconventional view by which all non-actual merely logically possible worlds are submaximally consistent, and only the actual world is uniquely maximally consistent, then we avoid the problems inherent in conventional modal semantics, and we answer the question of being in a unified way for individual entities, existent states of affairs and the actual world, in terms of maximal consistency. We explain being as maximal consistency, a purely logical concept that does not require sensation or other experience or the revelations of phenomenology about specifically human being-in-the-world in order to designate and distinguish the actual world from non-actual, nonexistent, merely logically possible worlds.

Revisionary modal semantics

It may appear as somewhat of a relief to consider that, even if non-actual merely logically possible worlds are defined combinatorially rather than set-theoretically, all the standard set-theoretical machinery of conventional model set-theoretical modal semantics on which we have come to rely can remain in place, leaving the formal semantics of modal logic untouched.

We can preserve set-theoretical relations among sets of worlds just as before, even if worlds are not themselves sets, and in particular even if they are not maximally consistent proposition sets. A logically necessary proposition, if there are any, is still one that is true in every logically possible world, involving the stipulation-exempt properties of abstract entities exclusively; a logically possible proposition is still one that is true in at least one logically possible world; and we can still invoke differential accessibility relations between logically possible worlds to interpret iterated and especially quantified iterated alethic modalities.

All non-actual merely logically possible worlds are not rightly identified with sets, let alone maximally consistent proposition sets, but with appropriately submaximally consistent states-of-affairs combinations that are not associated with any existent entity. The worlds to which they correspond are fictional, not only in the loose sense of characterizing nonexistent incomplete objects, but in the more accurately delimited sense of being described in a work of discourse. The fictions in which non-actual merely logically possible worlds are presented might be stories, novels, poetry and other forms of entertainment literature, scientific writings, including theories of natural phenomena that happen to be false, and Kripke-style stipulative but intensionally combinatorially interpreted modal semantic constructions. This is reasonable if we assume that the actual world is uniquely existent and that non-actual merely logical possible worlds do not exist even and especially as abstract mathematical or propositional structures. When we produce a formal semantics for alethic modal logic, on the present account, we refer to the uniquely existent maximally consistent actual world, and we also engage in fiction, creating an imaginary order of non-actual merely logically possible submaximally consistent worlds that are different from the actual world in their nonexistent constituent facts and usually also in their nonexistent constituent objects.

Accordingly, we need an intensional theory of submaximally consistent non-actual merely logically possible worlds rather than an extensional mathematical theory of sets for the semantics of modal logic. The reason is that non-actual merely logically possible worlds are the imaginative creatures of formal logical theoretical fictions. Logically possible worlds other than the actual world are not real things, but modal theoretical fictions. What Kripke and others do not seem to have fully appreciated, in the grip of the model set-theoretical apparatus for interpreting modal logic, is that to stipulate a logically possible world is to fictionalize, to tell a partial, inevitably incomplete story about places and times that do not in any sense exist. It might be wondered why we could not similarly dissociate maximally consistent proposition sets from logically possible worlds in conventional model set-theoretical semantics. What final advantage is gained by invoking property combinations in place of sets in combinatorial modal semantics? The trouble is that if we try to separate worlds from maximally consistent proposition sets, then, conventionally, what is a logically possible world if it is not an existent set? If worlds are only remotely associated or correlated with proposition sets, then they cannot be referred to or have constitutive properties truly predicated of them in a conventional extensionalist semantic framework. When we hear a philosopher say, "It is logically possible that pigs fly *means* that there is at least one logically possible world inhabited by airborne swine", we are to understand this as equivalent to a logician's tale, beginning with the preamble, "Once upon a time . . .".

Completeness itself is not a feature of logically possible worlds that can be freely stipulated. If we try to stipulate the completeness of a non-actual merely logically possible world, by declaring and thereby making it true that there is a maximally consistent state of affairs combination in which pigs fly, then when A stipulates a complete world in which pigs fly and B stipulates a complete world in which pigs fly, then, other things being equal, A and B presumably stipulatively identify the same world. If that in turn were true, however, then there should be no further questions, as there obviously are, about whether in the supposedly complete world A stipulates, as in the supposedly complete world B stipulates, donkeys as well as pigs fly, since either possibility could hold true in a complete world in which pigs fly. So, which is it? When A and B stipulate a complete maximally consistent world in which pigs fly, are they stipulating a world in which donkeys fly or one in which donkeys do not fly? The stipulated worlds are clearly indeterminate in this respect; they are and should be understood, in the absence of further specification, as the same constitutionally incomplete stipulated non-actual merely logically possible worlds – otherwise we are committed to the possibility of distinct but logically indistinguishable worlds. This is precisely why an intensionalist property combinatorial semantics is offered as an alternative to traditional model set-theoretical semantics for modal logic. It is also why we are forced to adopt a logic of fiction in order to do justice to the non-actual merely logically possible worlds by which logical possibilities relative to the actual facts or actually existent states of affairs of the uniquely existent actual world are interpreted.

Can we continue as standardly to consider logical necessity as truth in all logically possible worlds if non-actual merely logically possible worlds are submaximal? This is no problem, because all such worlds, despite being submaximal, must include all logically necessary truths (including those, say, about abstract entities, if there are any), while otherwise there simply are no logically necessary truths. Logical necessity in that case is predicated on the possibility of truth in every logically possible world supported ontologically only on the assumption that there exist abstract entities that exist in every logically possible world where they have all the same properties and relations and are identically constituted by the same maximally consistent property combinations. A putative physical entity, a pure logical object with physical properties in its property combination, is predicationally incomplete if it is part of a logically possible world in which any other physical objects are predicationally incomplete. It lacks in that case a complete complement of relations to all other physical objects in the same world. We cannot have a non-actual merely logically possible world that includes some existent and some nonexistent physical objects together. Either *all* of the physical objects in a logically possible world exist – in which case it is the actual world – or *none* exist. We assume throughout that either abstract objects do not exist at all in any logically possible world because they are somehow logically impossible, or else that they exist alike in every logically possible world as necessarily existent entities.

Abstract entities provide no basis for distinguishing one logically possible world from another, but are either absent from every world or uniformly distributed across all worlds. If we discount abstract objects, then, in identifying and individuating distinct logically possible worlds, if a predicationally incomplete object like Pegasus is included in a logically possible world w_i, then all physical objects in w_i are also predicationally incomplete by virtue of gaps in at least some of their relational properties involving Pegasus, and hence non-actual or non-existent. If Pegasus is neither green-eyed nor non-green-eyed, because the myths about Pegasus do not specify the creature's eye colour, then Napoleon in the same logically possible world w_i, if Napoleon is supposed to be one of w_i's inhabitants, equally cannot exist in w_i. Whatever else we might be able to say about Napoleon's properties in w_i, Napoleon in w_i will neither have nor fail to have the same eye colour as Pegasus. Nor can we make up for such predicational deficiencies generally by sweeping stipulations. Although Napoleon exists in the actual world $w_@$, where his property combination is complete, Napoleon does not exist in any non-actual merely logically possible world, such as those associated with Leo Tolstoy's historical novel, *War and Peace*, in which the character of Napoleon appears. As a contingently existent entity, we thus account for Napoleon's variant transworld existence and nonexistence.

If predicational incompleteness cannot be confined to any single contingently nonexistent object relative to any particular logically possible world, how can it be confined to all contingently existent or nonexistent objects relative to every logically possible world? Why, in other words, am I not predicationally incomplete and hence nonexistent according to the combinatorial analysis of being as maximal consistency by virtue of neither having the same nor not having the same eye colour as Pegasus, given that Pegasus does not belong to the actual world that I inhabit, but only to non-actual merely logically possible worlds? The difference is that we must define predicational completeness or incompleteness relative to the specific logically possible worlds a putative entity inhabits. If we do not observe such a restriction, then there are no logically possible worlds, but only logically impossible states-of-affairs combinations. In that case, we face the otherwise insurmountable problem that, for example, an object o in world w_i, with a logically contingent nonessential property F (and there *must* be such if there are to be any logical distinctions between alternative logically possible worlds) in w_i, both has property F and does not have property F, if there is another accessible logically possible world w_k ($i \neq k$, as by hypothesis for the same reason from what we have said there *must* be), in which o does not have property F. Confusion and contradiction ripple through modal logic if the possession or failure of objects to possess properties, including relational properties, is not relativized to specific logically possible worlds.

The restriction must be maintained in order to avoid logical inconsistency and unintelligibility in logic, modal logic, reference and predication theory and the philosophy of language generally. With the restriction firmly in place, we easily get the desired combinatorial conclusion that a logically possible world either contains only existent entities in the sense of maximally consistent constitutive property combinations, or the world contains no contingently existent entities. We can put the result equivalently by saying that if any logically possible world contains at least one contingently non-actual object, then none of the contingent objects belonging to that world exist. This, again, is to say, as we shall argue in a slightly different way more systematically below, that logically combinatorially there can be at most only one actual world.[20]

Being as a logically possible combination of logically possible objects and logically possible properties

We have now presented, but not yet tried to prove, the thesis that being or existence is maximal consistency. The position, if it can be sustained, provides a logical rather than anthropocentric phenomenological answer to the question of being, in contrast with Heidegger's existentialist ontology.

The claim is that for something to exist, regardless of whether it is an entity, existent state of affairs or the actual world, is for it in its respective category to have a maximally consistent property combination. We have further defended the proposal against an objection that might be raised from the conventional semantics of modal logic. If our analysis is correct, then non-actual merely logically possible worlds are not maximally consistent proposition sets, but always predicationally submaximal. None of this yet amounts to a good positive reason for accepting the analysis of existence as maximal consistency in Principles 1–4. The argument is given in the following chapters, in which the combinatorial ontology is recommended by virtue of its solution to the problem of why there exists something rather than nothing and why there exists exactly one logically contingent actual world.

In the process of solving these problems, we answer the question of being. We thereby complete the project of pure philosophical ontology, explaining the nature of being as such or being *qua* being, interpreted combinatorially as maximal consistency. A pure philosophical ontology must fulfil its promise to provide an analysis of what it means for any thing to exist, without which we cannot proceed to the topics of applied scientific ontology. There is no deeper problem for ontology, metaphysics or philosophy, because so much of what we need to say in science and everyday life is predicated on the assumption that there exists only one logically contingent actual world. If we can solve these problems, then we can begin to ask what particular things and kinds of things actually exist.

Why there is something rather than nothing

3

An actual world

What, if anything, can be built on the bare assumption that in logic properties are considered in logically possible combinations with objects? Properly interpreted, we can, for starters, derive from the assumption an explanation in pure philosophical ontology of why there exists something rather than nothing. To the extent that the explanation is successful it reflects positively on the analysis of being as maximal consistency.

The historical honour of having first raised the question "Why is there something rather than nothing?" is usually attributed to G. W. Leibniz, in his 1697 essay, "On the Ultimate Origination of Things".[1] Leibniz's theophilosophical solution of the problem, appealing to God's goodness and creative will, does not satisfy everyone, particularly those who would include God, if God exists, in the category of "something rather than nothing" whose existence needs to be explained.[2] Heidegger takes up the question in his 1935 lectures at the University of Freiburg in Breisgau, updated in 1953, and published as *An Introduction to Metaphysics*, as an instalment in his preoccupation with all aspects of the question of being.[3] Heidegger refers to the question of why there is something rather than nothing as the "Fundamental Question of Metaphysics", and refines the problem in such a way as to return to his phenomenological existentialist ontology and solution to the question of being in terms of *Da-sein*.[4]

The questions Heidegger raises considered in themselves are undoubtedly the right questions to ask; it is Heidegger's methodology and answers to the questions that we have disputed. The problem of Heidegger's circle and the unsuitability of phenomenology as a method of pure philosophical ontology motivates an alternative non-existentialist answer to Heidegger's question of being, and therefore to

Heidegger's fundamental question of metaphysics. Accordingly, we shall approach the question of why there is something rather than nothing as a problem for combinatorial pure philosophical ontology. We begin by considering only the logical possibilities of objects combining with properties. If we prefer, if this way of putting things already sounds too ontologically committal, we can make the same point linguistically in terms of the logical possibilities of object terms combining with property terms to create logically possible meaningful sentences. The truth-conditions of such sentences then take us back to corresponding states of affairs, objects combining with properties, in the extant domain of actually existent entities, whatever these should turn out to be.

The idea of logical objects as property combinations carries over straightforwardly also into this linguistic idiom. It is worth reflecting on the multiplicity of logical possibilities for states of affairs in which objects have or are constituted by properties. Mathematically speaking, the range of possibilities is overwhelming. In logical metatheory it is a problem to assign a definite cardinality to the set of all such possibilities. To do so meaningfully requires that we know first of all how many logically possible objects need to be considered, for which purpose it is standard to take the largest logically possible cardinality in set theory as the minimum number of logical objects. One way of expressing the number of existent or nonexistent states of affairs, where ω is the smallest infinite cardinal and ω^{ω} is the largest transfinite cardinal obtainable combinatorially from a set of elements of cardinality ω, specifies the minimal number of logical objects or predicables as: $(2^{\omega^{\omega}})^{\omega^{\omega}}$. As there are controversies about precisely how these values should be fixed, we will avoid exact specification of the number of possible combinations of states of affairs involving every logically possible combination of every logically possible object with every logically possible property, and merely note that the total number of combinations is enormously large.

The reduction of logical objects to property combinations offers an informal way of thinking about the range of possible combinations. We can describe all of the logical possibilities combinatorially as the total number of logical possibilities of logically possible property combinations. It does not prove or disprove anything in pure philosophical ontology to do so, but we can get a sense of the number of property combinations available as distinct groupings from among the sum of properties and alert our imaginations to the magnitude of possibilities involved by considering the size, diversity and complexity of the actual world. Another sobering realization comes when we reflect on the fact that the actual world is only one logically possible world, and that there must be indefinitely many more complicated, albeit predicationally incomplete, possibilities as well as simpler worlds. There are still indefinitely more possibilities of property combinations that do not belong to any logically possible world, let alone the actual world, because they involve logically inconsistent descriptions of the necessarily nonexistent objects or states of affairs. We can refer to these as logically impossible worlds, as some logicians have proposed, or identify them more generically as logically impossible models or property and states-of-affairs combinations.

Hempel's objection to the question

It may be worthwhile before we enter further into the problem to consider Carl G. Hempel's objection that the question why there exists something rather than nothing is meaningless. Hempel's naysaying provides another kind of solution to the problem, which, if correct, shows that the problem does not intelligibly arise in the first place. We avoid the problem by dissolving it, if Hempel is right, and answer the question by arguing that the question does not need to be answered because it makes no sense. Hempel writes:

> Why is there anything at all, rather than nothing? . . . But what kind of answer could be appropriate? What seems to be wanted is an explanatory account which does not assume the existence of something or other. But such an account, I would submit, is a logical impossibility. For generally, when the question "Why is it the case that *A*?" is answered by "Because *B* is the case" . . . [A]n answer to our riddle which made no assumptions about the existence of anything cannot possibly provide adequate grounds . . . The riddle has been constructed in a manner that makes an answer logically impossible.[5]

The criticism is similar to other attempts to set aside the question of why there exists something rather than nothing as logically impossible to answer. It is very much in the spirit of logical positivism to turn aside difficult metaphysical problems in this way. Hempel's objection to any effort to answer the question raises an interesting challenge for combinatorial ontology. Far from admitting that the question is meaningless because no answer is logically possible, we have argued that logic alone can answer the question why there exists something rather than nothing. We should therefore try to decide whether or not Hempel's argument succeeds on its own terms, before proceeding to answer the question combinatorially.

Ironically, Hempel is on the right track when he says first that the question seems to call for an explanation that does not assume the existence of "something or other". This is clearly true, since to assume the existence of anything in particular can never help to explain why anything at all exists. Whatever existents we try to introduce to answer the question will equally stand in need of having their existence explained. If Hempel is right about the kind of answer required by the question, then he is surely also right to conclude that the question is logically unanswerable, on the grounds and in the sense that an answer to the question in terms of the existence of another entity or kind of entity is impossible. We must therefore enquire more deeply into Hempel's characterization of the question as requiring an explanation of the existence of all entities by appeal to the existence of some entities. The problem is important because the combinatorial solution to the question that we offer does not introduce or presuppose the existence of any entities, but bases its answer on the purely logical possibilities of all logically possible objects combining with all logically possible properties, none of which is said to exist until the conditions of the combinatorial analysis of being for the existence of a logically possible entity are satisfied.

We can also agree with Hempel that ordinarily when we ask for an explanation of the existence of some particular entity other than the actual world in its entirety, we generally require an answer in terms of the existence of another particular entity. An example is when we explain the existence of oak trees as a result of other oak trees, or the existence of acorns, water, soil, sunlight and carbon dioxide. The requirements for explaining the existence of the actual world in its entirety are presumably not the same as in the case of particular existents, as Hempel comes close to acknowledging. Instead of exploring another category of explanation for existence as a whole, Hempel concludes without argument that only the method of explaining particular circumscribed existences is available to metaphysics. In effect, like Heidegger, although obviously in a different way, Hempel mistakenly collapses pure philosophical ontology into applied scientific ontology, with the predictable result we have already seen.

We notice that Hempel's argument does nothing to limit a solution to the problem of why there exists something rather than nothing that does not involve the existence of particular entities. He does not consider the possibility of a combinatorial analysis of the concept of being. The solution defines being in such a way that the concept must be satisfied by at least some among the totality of logically possible property–object or states-of-affairs combinations. A combinatorial solution answers Leibniz's and Heidegger's fundamental question of metaphysics without presupposing that any purely logical logically possible objects and properties involved in the explanation actually exist. Since Hempel's objection does not anticipate or address this type of answer to the question of why there exists something rather than nothing, we might wonder whether a combinatorial solution avoids the problem Hempel poses for other admittedly hopeless but excessively simple-minded solutions.

Hempel does not disprove and does not even consider a combinatorial solution. A combinatorial solution offers the kind of answer to the question why there exists something rather than nothing that Hempel ought to welcome as involving only concepts of pure logic. Hempel does not convincingly argue that the question is logically meaningless or unanswerable. At most, Hempel inadvertently shows that we cannot satisfactorily answer the question of why there exists something rather than nothing as a problem of applied scientific ontology. We grant the point, while maintaining the possibility, and even the necessity, of a satisfactory solution in combinatorial pure philosophical ontology. There is thus no obstacle in Hempel's argument to the combinatorial answer we now begin to explain.

Logical possibility and actuality

We already have all the concepts we need to answer the question why there exists something rather than nothing. We first offer a rough sketch of the solution, and then defend its assumptions in detail. The argument is that the logical possibilities of predication in logic, combinations of logically possible objects with logically possible properties in the abstract, imply that there must exist *at least one* maximally consistent states-of-affairs combination satisfying the definition of the concept of *an* actual world presented as Principle 3. There exists *an* actual world, therefore, we can say, at least one, and hence something rather than nothing, because combinatorially there must be a maximally consistent object–property or states-of-affairs combination among all the logically possible combinations of all logically possible states of affairs involving all logically possible objects combined with all logically possible properties. We do not appeal to Principle 3 as an established truth, but offer the fact of its having this consequence as partial justification for the principle, in light of its purely logical solution to the question why there exists something rather than nothing. The argument has the structure shown overleaf.

Why there is something rather than nothing

1. It is logically combinatorially necessary that the totality of combinations of all logically possible combinations of all logically possible states of affairs include at least one maximally consistent combination.

(Combinatorial necessity)

2. An actual world is and is nothing more than a maximally consistent states-of-affairs combination. (Principle 3)

---

3. An actual world is logically combinatorially necessary; it is logically combinatorially necessary that there be or exist an actual world, that an actual world exist. (1,2)

4. Logically necessarily, there must exist an actual world. The reason why there exists something rather than nothing is that logic combinatorially necessitates a maximally consistent states-of-affairs combination, satisfying the definition of the concept of an actual world. (3)

The deductive necessity and a priori truth of the argument's assumptions are essential in maintaining an a priori answer to the question of being. We can know, without relying on any experience of the world, that out of all the logically possible states-of-affairs combinations, and of all the logically possible combinations of all the logically possible objects with all logically possible properties, there must be at least one that is maximally consistent.

How do we know this? It is simply a consequence of the idea of the totality of combinations of states of affairs or of objects and properties, together with the fact that there is no reason to exclude a maximally consistent combination from the totality of all logically possible combinations. By definition, a maximally consistent states-of-affairs combination is logically consistent, and so cannot be ruled out on what are surely the only relevant purely logical grounds. As we have defined the concept of an actual world, it follows immediately then that a maximally consistent states-of-affairs combination just is an actual world.

There is no special need to prove that logically there must be a maximally consistent combination of states of affairs involving maximally consistent logical object–property combinations. We need

only suppose that a maximally consistent states-of-affairs combination is logically possible. The only obstacle to the possibility of a
maximally consistent states-of-affairs combination would be if it were
somehow logically inconsistent, which is evidently not a problem for
anything that by hypothesis is supposed to be predicationally
maximally consistent. Among all the imaginable combinations of
objects with properties, whether existent or nonexistent, constituting
all imaginable states of affairs, whether existent or nonexistent, and
among all the imaginable combinations of states of affairs, worlds or
models, there logically must be at least one that is maximally consistent. We know this a priori from the logical requirements for object–
property combinations and from the fact that there can be no logical
inconsistency in a combination designated not only as logically consistent, but predicationally maximally consistent. We can therefore
conclude as a matter of logical combinatorial necessity that there must
be such a logically possible maximally consistent states-of-affairs
combination, implied by the underlying presuppositions of pure
classical logic as occurring among all the possibilities of combining all
logically possible objects with all logically possible properties.

Although it may seem paradoxical or even modally invalid to put
the point this way, we can equally say that, since it is logically necessary that it is logically possible for the totality of all logically possible
combinations of all logically possible states of affairs to include a
maximally consistent combination, then it is logically necessary for an
actual world to exist. The logical necessity of the logical possibility of
a maximally consistent states-of-affairs combination logically guarantees that at least one actual world exists, and therefore that something
rather than nothing exists. Later, we consider the modality of the inference in greater detail. There we shall conclude that it is logically
correct, given the definitions of concepts of combinatorial pure philosophical ontology articulated in Principles 1–4, to deduce the actuality of a logically possible world or existence of an actual world from
the logical necessity of the logical possibility that the full range of all
logically possible combinations of objects and properties include a
maximally consistent states-of-affairs combination, which we have
also defined as an actual world.

What remains to be shown is that the logical necessity of there
occurring a logically possible maximally consistent combination of
states of affairs or objects with properties should be defined as an
actual world, an actually existing world consisting exclusively of all
and only existent states of affairs involving all and only existent
entities. If we accept the definition of an actual world as a maximally

consistent states-of-affairs combination, then we can answer a priori
the question why there exists something rather than nothing without
introducing the undisputed fact that an actual world exists, and without referring to our experience of the world, or place or role within it
encountered phenomenologically as existentially situated human
being-in-the-world. Is the definition plausible on its own terms?
When we say that an actual world exists, do we in fact mean nothing
more than that a certain states-of-affairs combination is maximally
consistent?

Maximal consistency = actuality

It might be objected that in defining the concept of an actual world in
terms of a maximally consistent states-of-affairs combination we are
only specifying a necessary but not sufficient condition for actuality.
An actual world must undoubtedly be maximally consistent; otherwise its contradictions or predicational gaps would logically preclude
its existence. Why suppose, on the other hand, that a world is actual
by virtue of satisfying the purely logical condition of maximal consistency alone? Why should maximal consistency be enough for the being
of an actually existent world?

Consider the construction of a randomly chosen maximally
consistent states-of-affairs combination. We begin with an internally
logically consistent state of affairs, and, following a version of the
Lindenbaum recursion, we add another to it, and another, and so on,
making sure each time that the states of affairs we contribute to the
expanding combination are internally consistent and introduce no
logical inconsistencies with any of the other states of affairs that have
already been admitted to the combination. We continue the process
until we have reached maximal consistency. Since we have been
combining states of affairs in a chance way, provided only that we
satisfy the requirements of logical consistency until we arrive at a
maximally consistent combination, we have no reason to suppose in
the first place that the resulting entity bears any resemblance to the
actual world. It might seem as though this should be the end of the
matter, but for a very interesting reason it is not.

We do not say that *the* world is just any old maximally consistent
states-of-affairs combination. We maintain that what it means for *an*
actual world to exist is for it to be a maximally consistent states-of-
affairs combination. If the procedure we have just described for
assembling a maximally consistent states-of-affairs combination is
logically possible, then, according to the proposed definition, we will

in effect have described an existent actual world that is as likely as not to be distinct from the actual world. It is tempting to conclude as a consequence that there must be something additional to be added into the mix, such as a non-Heideggerean *Dasein* (being there, in the ordinary meaning of the German, as opposed to Heidegger's technical appropriation of the terms as *Da-sein*), or *das Modalmoment* (as another phenomenological tradition centring around the work of the early-twentieth-century Austrian philosopher Alexius Meinong refers to much the same concept), or Being as a Platonic Form to be *blended* with other Forms (as Plato in his dialogue the *Sophist* is sometimes interpreted as holding), in order to constitute an actually existent entity.[6] The mere maximal consistency of any choice of states of affairs by itself may not seem strong enough to constitute actuality, for which, the objection continues, we need something more.

The criticism is flawed in several ways. In the first place, by beginning with the substantive conclusion that we need to add a further ingredient in order to coax actual existence out of thin lifeless purely logical conditions like maximal consistency, the proposal is viciously circular. If our purpose is to explain what it means for a world to be actual rather than merely possible, then we cannot sensibly imagine that we can add in Being like a spice to a soup in order to explain the being of the world. Whether we capitalize the word or not, or draw on the impressive-sounding philosophical vocabulary of a foreign language, if we are trying to understand what it means for the actual world to *be*, we cannot hope to do so by saying that in addition to satisfying a necessary logical requirement of maximal consistency the actual world must also have being or Being. This is hardly informative, if, as appears, it amounts to saying only that the actual world must be in order to be, or that it must exist in order to exist. If there is no better way to enhance the maximal consistency of an actual world or entity or state of affairs in the actual world than by saying that its properties also include being or existence, then not only are we no better off than if we had adhered to the definition of an actual world in terms of maximal consistency alone, but we have taken a disastrous plunge into logical and explanatory circularity. We are no more enlightened in that case about the meaning of being in any of these cognate terminologies than if we had allowed from the outset that being is a primitive unanalysable concept. There can then be no further answer to the question of being, and we can do no more than reassure ourselves of the fact that an actual world exists in unclouded moments of lucid sensation, unable to inquire intelligibly into what it means for something to exist or for the actual world to be actual.

There is, furthermore, a kind of confusion in the way the objection is posed. We are first invited to imagine a maximally consistent states-of-affairs combination being assembled over time, following a recursive procedure from random elements and checking at each stage only to make sure that the resulting accretion of states of affairs preserves logical consistency until it reaches the limit of maximal consistency. This is a standard heuristic way of explaining the operation of a recursive function in logic and mathematics, to work up maximally consistent proposition sets, as constituting alternative logically possible worlds, as maximally consistent sets of propositions. It should not be taken literally, for in the present context it has misleading implications. If we imagine a maximally consistent states-of-affairs combination being constructed successively, individual state of affairs by individual state of affairs, then, for one thing, we are not supposing the constitution of all logically possible combinations of states-of-affairs combinations to be a purely logical condition, but as transpiring in real time.

The problem is not that we thereby countenance the possibility of multiple actual worlds. At this stage of the argument we have not yet tried to argue against such an occurrence. That is rather the topic of Chapter 4, concerning the actual world's uniqueness and logical contingency. For the moment, we will be satisfied even if we can only show that there are many actual worlds that actually exist, provided that we can answer the question why there exists something rather than nothing; indeed, rather more than should be thought to exist, if an actual world or worlds logically must exist. We could then consider a plethora of actually existing actual worlds an ontological superfluity.

The challenge posed by the objection nevertheless remains. Why should we suppose, as Principle 3 has it, that maximal consistency is both necessary and sufficient for an actual world to exist? The criticism involves a failure of imagination, and an improper conclusion drawn from a misplaced projection of imagination. When we consider that a logical object could have a maximally consistent property combination but only possibly and not actually exist, we are evidently not imagining each and every one of the object's properties. There are far too many of them for us to be able to do that. As an alternative we do the next best thing, which is simply to assume that we can correctly describe the world in question more or less stipulatively as consisting of a maximally consistent property combination. We declare that the object in question is maximally consistent in its possession of properties and property complements. Such a projection is nevertheless methodologically faulty. The difficulty is not merely that consistency cannot be stipulated imaginatively in this way, but that to try to stipulate maximal completeness in particular ignores an enormous number of properties and property complements that are certain to be missing from a logical object's property combination if the object does not actually exist. These are all the properties and property complements that an actually existent entity has to all other actually existent entities in the same actually existent logically possible world. It is the same problem that arises in trying to stipulate the completeness of a non-actual merely logically possible world that we considered in Chapter 2.

To illustrate the point, we cannot simply declare with respect to an alternative logically possible world where Napoleon won the Battle of Waterloo that there is a red round rubber ball whose property combination is maximally consistent. The ball's property combination, despite our protests, will necessarily be incomplete with respect to its relations to any of the more obviously incomplete objects like Napoleon that inhabit the same world. From the minimal information we have so far, the ball is neither bigger nor smaller than the Napoleon who won at Waterloo. If we specify an exact size for Napoleon and the ball, then we will be referring to different objects in a different world, for which we can quickly find other unspecified relations between the ball and a merely possible non-actual Napoleon. Does the ball weigh as much or not as much as the victorious Napoleon? We do not know, because there is no answer unless we fill in the blanks in our imagination. The only remaining strategy is to take shelter in the idea of simply declaring, again by fiat, that the property combinations of all objects are maximally consistent in the logically possible world in question inhabited by the Napoleon who won, rather than was defeated, at Waterloo. All of the objects in that world will then have maximally consistent property combinations, and so will not suffer any incompleteness in relation to objects with intrinsically incomplete property combinations.

If we are to avoid vicious circularity in trying to understand why there exists something rather than nothing, then we cannot supplement the logical requirements of maximal consistency for actuality simply by adding in Being or *Dasein* or any of the other equivalents for existence. In that case, we will be saying no more than that the actual world exists because it exists, or that it has being because it has being. If there is another possibility, what could it be? We have not tried to say that maximal consistency magically confers existence on the actual world, but that maximal consistency explains logically why it is that the actual world exists. We do not need to imagine a maximally consistent states-of-affairs combination being supplemented item by item until maximality is attained and the actual world suddenly explodes into being. The suggestion is rather that when we analyse the concept of the existence of an actual world, we find it necessary and sufficient to refer only to the purely logical requirements of a states-of-affairs combination's being maximally consistent.

The proposal will seem more or less plausible depending on what we understand to be included in and entailed by the concept of *maximal* consistency. We have argued that when the concept of maximal consistency is fully unpacked, the only thing that satisfies the requirement of maximal consistency is an actually existent entity, either as an existent object, an existent state of affairs, or *an* (not yet *the*) actual world. Anything that fails to exist on the other hand is bound intuitively to be either inconsistent or submaximal somewhere down the line in its total complement of constitutive properties.

Problem of the physically empty universe

Is it logically possible for there to be a physically empty universe? What can such a question even mean? It can only refer to something like a submaximal world that logically could be completed so as to become maximally consistent, in which there are no spatiotemporal objects or events, but at most only existent abstract entities. We try mentally to visualize an empty space, of vast or dimensionless nothingness, and we ask: why not this instead of the existence of the actual world?

Some people claim to be able to imagine that nothing whatsoever exists. Heidegger is nevertheless right when he says that they cannot do so except as a projection of thought from which their own existence is not altogether eliminated as the real-time source of a phenomenological horizon of imaginability. The idea is to imagine at best a space containing no physical entities and no perceivers to be seen, while overlooking the fact that the empty space is imagined *as* seen, even if only as unrelenting blackness, and seen moreover from the perspective of the thinker's subjective situation. No such projection adequately represents a completely physically empty universe, because it does not exclude the thinker's actual world, which remains as the shell within which the world's empty blackness is projected by the imagination. The objection also unwarrantedly assumes that blackness is not a something, a state of consciousness at the very least, in so far as it is imagined, or the emptiness of something, an imagined space or receptacle.

There exists something rather than nothing. What exists, on the other hand, is not necessarily of such a kind that thinkers, or thinkers anything like ourselves, could possibly have evolved. We might not have been here, and need not be here, and will not always be here; although we can say without risk of contradiction that we are here now. That such a world exists in which we happen to flourish and have the strange compulsion to consider the question of being is logically a matter of pure chance. The actual world as a further requirement of the concept of maximal consistency attains logical closure among its physical properties by virtue of implying a particular set of natural law constraints that have the effect of causal determinism among purely physical phenomena. What we evidently have no philosophical obligation to try to do is justify the world we see around us as maximally consistent. The problem is rather, first, to prove that there logically must exist an actual world, then that there can be only one, and finally that the actual world is logically contingent. The actual world must contain at least some physical states of affairs if it is to be even a logically possible world in a nontrivial sense. These physical states of affairs must be different from world to world, including the uniquely actual world. Thus, we cannot conceive of a physically empty universe as one among numerous logically possible worlds consisting of no spatiotemporal physical phenomena.

Why are we thinkers here? That is an excellent question, but not one for pure philosophical ontology. Phenomenology, as Heidegger maintains, might instead be the method by which to confront the question of the meaning of human life. Much of what existentialism has to say about the human condition is philosophically compelling. The point is that these are questions for what Heidegger calls the ontic sciences, for applied scientific ontology. Existentialism fares badly as a pure philosophical ontology in attempts to answer the question of being. It is simply too loaded with ontological commitments to have any role to play in pure ontology. As an applied ontology, by contrast, existentialism offers interesting conclusions about the human situation and cognitive situatedness in understanding many aspects of human experience. What is strange from the present standpoint is why Heidegger in *Being and Time*, Jean-Paul Sartre in *Being and Nothingness*, and other phenomenological existentialists, mislocate their own projects within the same basic pure–applied scheme. Why do they feel entitled to address the question of being phenomenologically rather than logically? Why are they not satisfied to advance the project of applied phenomenological existentialist ontology, and why must they claim to do more than they actually do, which is to describe the phenomenology of the human condition? Who would not welcome the insights of a sincerely committed but ontologically unpresupposing existentialist, without imagining that phenomenology could possibly answer the question of being?

Descartes's *Cogito, sum* might be construed by comparison as providing the basis for another phenomenological answer to fundamental problems of ontology. Whatever its philosophical value, Descartes's conditionally necessary existence does not help to explain *why* there exists something rather nothing. The *Cogito*, or rather the *sum*, at most singles out an epistemically interesting fact about the actual world. It is a fact, if Descartes is right, whose existence cannot be doubted even on the assumption that there exists a malicious spirit that deceives the thinker about everything else. Aside from that, it is obvious, just as in Heidegger's ontology, that to begin as Descartes does with the experience of thinking as a real-time occurrence is to adopt at best an impurely a priori method that is inappropriate for the purposes of pure philosophical ontology. Another problem that is not peculiar to Descartes's approach is whether the reasoning that is supposed to prove the existence of the thinker is correct, and, in particular, as we have also seen in Heidegger's exposition, whether it does not slip into some sort of vicious circularity. In Descartes, a vicious circularity is explicit in his assumption that *I* think is part of the reasoning by which *I* exist.[7]

Descartes, like Heidegger, nevertheless raises crucially important questions for applied ontology. *Why* are *we* here? A good answer, and one that we should not imagine infringes on our dignity in any way, is that we are here as a result of pure chance. As Descartes rightly emphasizes, even if he promptly runs the idea off the rails, we, given what we are, as the kind of entities we are, happen to be here by virtue of thinking. Only mind knows existence, and only mind can think about existence. And we are here now, thinking.

Being and actuality

As a dividend for our labours in the vineyards of logic and predication, we clarify the meaning of being as we consider the concept of existence in purely logical terms. We define an actual world as a predicationally maximally consistent states-of-affairs or object–property combination. There is certain to be included at least one such combination among all the logically possible combinations of logically possible states of affairs. A maximally consistent states-of-affairs combination logically must exist; but since that is what we mean by the existence of an actual world, logically there must exist an actual world. Something rather than nothing exists because it is logically combinatorially necessary for at least one maximally consistent states-of-affairs combination to be included among all logically possible object–property combinations, and hence for something, at least one actual world, to exist.

We may need to remind ourselves at this juncture that pure philosophical ontology is a discipline only, and not a domain. We are not trying to use logic to deduce the particular predications that are true of the actual world, but only to understand that there must exist an actual world, if what we mean by that term is a maximally consistent states-of-affairs combination. As such, we contribute to pure philosophical ontology by explaining why there exists something rather than nothing. There must exist something, because the maximally consistent combination of predications that constitutes an actual world is logically possible; there is logically certain to be at least one such combination of predications in the full range of all logical possibilities. What it means for something other than an actual world in its entirety to exist is then for it to be in some sense a part of or entity within an actual world, as or as a constitutive part of an actually existent state of affairs.

The argument thus far does not show that there is only one actual world. Such a conclusion cannot be taken for granted, because the obvious rejoinder to the proposal outlined above is that a maximally consistent states-of-affairs combination is still only a possibility, and not a real entity. Again, we must remember that we are investigating the question of being as a problem of pure philosophical ontology. We are only trying to explain what it means for something to exist. This we have now accomplished, at least in the sense that we have explained what it means for *an* actual world to exist. *The* actual world by contrast is a certain maximally consistent combination of states of affairs, constituted as a maximally consistent combination of all logically possible objects with all logically possible properties. It is the world that we suppose ourselves privileged to inhabit. We can even limit reference to the physical states or physical states of affairs that constitute the actual world, which, logically, are the only differences that could possibly distinguish alternative logically possible worlds.

We explain why there is something rather than nothing, because for there to be something is for a particular type of states-of-affairs or object–property combination to be logically possible. The actual world with no phenomenological baggage exists as the direct implication of pure logic involving a maximally consistent logically possible states-of-affairs or object–property combination. We can summarize the main proposals for answering the problem why there is something rather than nothing in the tree diagram in Figure 2.

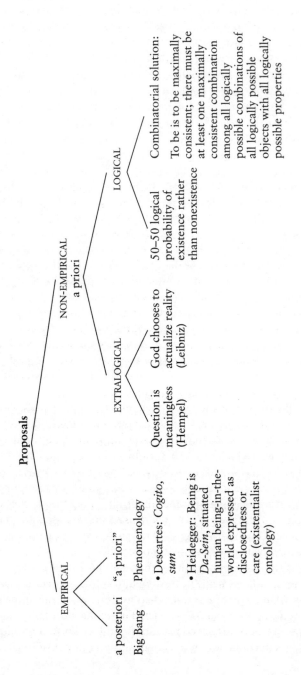

Figure 2   Alternative explanations of why there exists something rather than nothing

We have already criticized Descartes's *Cogito, sum* and Heidegger's existentialist phenomenology of *Da-sein* or human being-in-the-world as inadequate methods of pure philosophical ontology. We withhold discussion until later of the Big Bang, God's decision to actualize the world, and the 50–50 random logical probability of the existence rather than nonexistence of an actual world. As explanations of why there exists something rather than nothing, we shall see that these alternative proposals in one way or another are explanatorily inadequate. Thus, we are left with only the combinatorial theory.

Combinatorial answer to the question of being

We have asked: what makes an object as a mere subject of predication existent or nonexistent? What makes a state of affairs existent or nonexistent? What makes a logically possible world existent or nonexistent? The answers, we have argued, must all depend on the same logical foundation in a combinatorial pure philosophical ontology.

When we spin out all the combinations of all the logically possible predication objects with all the logically possible properties, we can be sure that there must be at least one maximally consistent combination. That combination, or combinations if there is more than one, on the present definition, satisfy the requirements for actual existence, or, more simply, are actual, real, exist or have being. Mere logically possible worlds, mere logically possible states of affairs, and mere logically possible objects, are not actual or real, and do not exist or have being, in the real world or in any non-actual merely logically possible world. As mere *possibilia*, they are sure to be internally predicationally consistent but submaximal. We have argued that, contrary to conventional modal semantics, we can and should interpret non-actual merely logically possible worlds as at most submaximally consistent. Nonexistent worlds, nonexistent states of affairs and nonexistent objects must therefore be missing something that real entities have. On the present account, they do not lack *Dasein* or *das Modalmoment* or Plato's special Form of Being; they fail to exist because they are either predicationally inconsistent or submaximal.

Why is there something rather than nothing? We have argued that an actual world is logically necessitated; it is logically combinatorially necessary that something rather than nothing exist, given the definition of being as maximal consistency. The actual world is a maximally consistent states-of-affairs combination; and we know, logically, since there is no contradiction in the concept, without consulting any data of the actual world or our experience or phenomenological analysis of our experience of it, that there exists at least one maximally consistent combinatorial possibility of objects with properties. Logically, therefore, there must exist a world; the existence of an actual world is logically combinatorially necessary.

Again, this answer to the question of being concerns the meaning of the concept of being, of what it means for something to exist. We assume that pure philosophical ontology is only a discipline, and cannot be construed as a domain, and that since logic is also a discipline, there is no special logical or metaphysical reason why pure logic as opposed to phenomenology or some other discipline could not be invoked to answer the question of being or the fundamental problem of metaphysics. The thesis that to be is to be maximally consistent offers a unified account of the meaning of existence assertions for any existents, since the reduction of ontology to logic is conducted entirely in terms of logically possible objects and logically possible properties. We do not suppose that pure logic can be used to deduce the content of an ontology in the sense of uniquely specifying a preferred existence domain, either in theory or as the extant domain of real existents.

Nor have we tied our hands in other ways with respect to the deliverances of applied scientific ontology. We have not tried to say what kinds of things objects and properties are, whether one is reducible to the other or not, whether properties are just a special kind of object or objects are constituted by and in that sense reducible to property combinations. For the purposes of combinatorial ontology it has not really mattered, because the objects are only logical, considered to be merely logically possible predication subjects. We explain why there exists something rather than nothing as a logical necessity. It is logically necessary that something exist rather than nothing, but we have not excluded the further conclusion that the actual world is logically contingent, or that the actual world as one particular logically possible world happens to exist.

Something rather than nothing exists because "something" is a logically general way of designating *an* actual world that is not necessarily *the* actual world in all its particularity. It by no means follows that human beings with their grabby *Da-seins* exist to experience the actual world, whatever character it chances to have. The possibilities inherent in pure logic offer a less anthropocentric way of understanding the question of being in a combinatorial ontology than phenomenology does in Heidegger's existentialist ontology, with its emphasis on the concept of specifically human being-in-the-world. There is something rather than nothing because:

1. To be means to be maximally consistent, which is a purely logical qualification, whether we are speaking of the being or existence of an individual object, a state of affairs or an entire actual world, including *the* actual world in all its particularity.
2. We know combinatorially that there is certain to be at least one maximally consistent states-of-affairs or object–property combination that constitutes and is linguistically representable as an actual world, a world all of whose states of affairs actually exist, involving all and only actually existent objects. There must be such a combination because there is no contradiction in the idea of there being such a combination.

It is from the logical possibilities for combinations of properties, the distribution of all logically possible properties over all logically possible objects understood as logical predication subjects, that we deduce the logical necessity of the existence of an actual world. There must be a maximally consistent logically possible combination of just the properties that constitute a world of maximally consistent actual objects in maximally consistent actual states of affairs. What it is to be (existence sense) is therefore in a sense to be (predication sense) one of these so-defined actual entities, one of these so-defined actual states of affairs or the so-defined actual world.

The analysis of being as maximal consistency applies at each level of the combinatorial ontology. An actual object is a maximally consistent property combination; an actual state of affairs is the possession by any actual entity or entities of any of the properties in their respective maximally consistent property combinations. *An* actual world is a maximally consistent combination of actual states of affairs. *The* actual world is a particular maximally consistent combination of actual states of affairs. From the fact that all actual states of affairs and all actually existent entities can belong at most only to one truly maximally consistent states-of-affairs combination, it follows as a further implication that there uniquely exists only and at most one actual world, so that, as we shall see, *an* actual world must be identical with *the* actual world. To be is to belong to one of these three kinds of entities – existent objects, actual states of affairs or an actual world in its entirety – and hence, ultimately, of logically possible predication objects having predicationally maximally consistent logically possible property combinations.

Logically, there must be just one combination of properties to objects that exactly instantiates the entities and states of affairs that constitute the actual world. In the distribution of all logically possible properties over all logically possible predication objects, there is certain to be at least one maximally consistent combination. Should we call such a combination, or combinations, if there are more than one, an actual world or the actual world or actual worlds? The question is cantilevered. If we are satisfied with the explanation of why there exists something rather than nothing, which the concept affords, then we may also be inclined to accept the definition. The trouble is that we are not yet in a secure position to judge whether the explanation is satisfactory. We can probably agree, no matter what view we take with respect to the relation between logic and ontology, that the explanation is unacceptable if it does not support a further argument to show that there can at most exist one actual world, that it is identical to the world we happen to inhabit, and that the actual world is logically contingent. That is the subject to which we turn next.

Why there is only one logically
4 contingent actual world

Actual existence

It is reassuring to know, in the progress we have made so far, that there must exist something rather than nothing. The two outstanding problems left to be solved in pure philosophical ontology, concerning the uniqueness and logical contingency of the actual world, must also be addressed before we can be said to have satisfactorily answered the question of being.

If we try to answer the question why there exists something rather than nothing combinatorially, by arguing that an actual world must exist, then we leave open at least temporarily the question whether only one actual world exists. We do not commit ourselves thereby to a logical and ontological relation holding between the necessary existence of an actual world and the presumably logically contingent existence of the actual world. Nor have we said enough yet to relate the existence of the actual world and the existence of an actual world by whose necessary existence we answer the question why there exists something rather than nothing. If it is logically combinatorially necessary that all logically possible combinations of all logically possible states of affairs include at least one maximally consistent combination, then it remains at least conceivable that there be more than one maximally consistent combination, of which the actual world that we know through experience might be only one among many distinct actually existent actual worlds. Can we make sense of any of these consequences?

We must satisfy ourselves that the actual world is uniquely existent, that *an* actual world can only be *the* actual world, and that the actual world is logically contingent. If we cannot establish these two further conclusions, then we must reconsider the wisdom of accepting Principle 3 with its implications for the question of being and the question of why there exists something rather than nothing.

The first problem concerns the presumed unique existence of the actual world. Why should there be only one maximally consistent combination of states of affairs or of objects with properties? Why are there not distinct multiple realities or actual worlds, each of which, according to the definition in Principle 3, actually exists? The argument we have already presented for the reform of the conventional semantics of modal logic implies that non-actual merely logically possible worlds are at most submaximally consistent. What we have not yet tried to show is that there is or can be only one maximally consistent states-of-affairs combination corresponding to the one and only actual world. Why, if in fact it is true, are there not many actual worlds, many actualities, just as there are many planets and galaxies within the actual world, of which we happen to inhabit only one? Why should we not suppose that there are parallel simultaneously existent alternative universes?

The second challenge is to reconcile the logical necessity whereby *an* actual world must exist with the assumption that *the* actual world is logically contingent. An actual world, construed as a maximally consistent states-of-affairs combination, exists as a logical necessity. There must be at least one such combination among the totality of all logically possible combinations. It is, therefore, logically necessary, an inescapable consequence dictated by the requirements of pure logic, that an actual world exists. Thus, we know why there exists something rather than nothing. The particular world that actually exists, and, indeed, any actually existent logically possible world, is nevertheless presumably logically contingent in the sense that another world logically might have existed instead and any of the physical states of affairs that constitute the actual world logically might have been otherwise than they happen to be.

What does this mean, and how, if at all, can we account for the unique existence and logical contingency of the actual world within the framework of a combinatory pure philosophical ontology? We first address the uniqueness of the actual world and then the question of its logical contingency.

An actual world = the actual world

What is the relation between the existence of *an* actual world where *something* (or other) must exist, and the existence of *the* actual world that we thinkers inhabit? We shall see that they are identical, and that logic proves the existence of *the* actual world when it proves the existence of *an* actual world. There can exist only one actual world, as we have interpreted the concept, because logically there can exist only one maximally consistent states-of-affairs combination.

The argument relies on the fully explicated meaning of the predicational completeness of an existent entity defined in terms of its *maximally* consistent property combination. Thus far, we have held only that there exists at least one maximally consistent states-of-affairs combination. This is enough, in conjunction with Principle 3's definition of an actual world, to establish that there exists at least one actual world – that something rather than nothing exists. We are strongly predisposed to believe, it may be unnecessary to say, that there is and can be only one actual world, and that this implication is somehow necessitated by the concept of an actual world. The problem is how we are to prove that the actual world is uniquely existent. Is there a combinatorial justification for the proposition that there can be at most one actual world?

The proposed reform of modal semantics implies that all logically possible worlds other than the actual world are predicationally incomplete and hence non-actual, nonexistent. The difficulty is explaining why merely logically possible worlds are non-actual. The thesis follows immediately from our revised modal semantics, in which an actual world is distinguished as a maximally consistent states-of-affairs combination, and in which every non-actual merely logically possible world has predicational gaps – at best a submaximally consistent states-of-affairs combination. The following inference summarizes this line of reasoning, in which the crucial assumption is that on logical grounds there can exist only one maximally consistent states-of-affairs combination. The argument states:

Unique existence of the actual world

1. An actual world exists.
2. An actual world is a maximally consistent states-of-affairs combination.
3. There can exist only one maximally consistent states-of-affairs combination.

4. *An* existent actual world = *the* actual world.

The analysis depends heavily on assumption 3. Why suppose that there can be at most one maximally consistent states-of-affairs combination? There exist multiple existent objects and multiple existent states of affairs, all of which are supposed to be maximally consistent of their kind. Why, then, suppose that there exists exactly one actual world rather than many actual worlds, each of which in different ways is also maximally consistent? Is there something about the concept of maximal consistency that precludes a multiplicity of maximally consistent states-of-affairs combinations, of actual worlds, but encourages the multiplicity of particular existent objects and states of affairs? If the actual world is logically combinatorially identical with an actual world logically necessitated by the logical possibility of that combination of states of affairs, then does not the actual world with all its states of affairs, objects and properties, share equally in the logical combinatorial necessity by which we propose to explain why there exists something rather than nothing?

Ontology of the actual world

So quickly do we go from logical rags to an embarrassment of apparently excessive ontological riches in pure philosophical ontology. The very idea of actual worlds other than the one we inhabit seems confused. But how, precisely? What does a combinatorial answer to the question of being imply about the unique existence of the actual world?

We should not consider the combinatorial pure philosophical ontology outlined in Principles 1–4 to be correct unless we can argue convincingly that there is only one actual world, unique in its actuality. This is what we expect any competent pure philosophical ontology to conclude. It is only a question of whether a good answer can be given from the resources of pure logic, or whether we must turn to another more opulent discipline like phenomenology in order to answer the question of being. We make a case here for a purely logical justification of the uniqueness of the actual world from the standpoint of combinatorial pure philosophical ontology, arguing that logically there can at most exist only one maximally consistent states-of-affairs combination.

We can, and probably should, continue to remain neutral about the existence of abstract entities until we are ready to take on applied scientific ontology with a better idea of what we mean when we ask whether this or that putative entity actually exists. The dilemma we have already considered is that abstract objects either do not exist at all, or, if they do exist, exist alike in every logically possible world, including non-actual merely logically possible worlds. If we leave abstract entities out of account, on the strength of the dilemma, then we are left to contemplate only physical states of affairs involving physical entities, objects and events in real time, that by their differences distinguish one logically possible world from another. The actual world is, of course, a logically possible world; it is just not merely logically possible, but something more. If we do not want to say that it is something more because it also has *Dasein* or *das Modalmoment* of full-strength actuality, or Being blended in with the other Forms of its objects, then we might find it best to say that it does not need to be anything more, but exists or has being by virtue of a property of its distinguishing states-of-affairs combination considered as a whole, such as the property of being maximally consistent.

Thus, we ask again, is the actual world unique, or might there exist other actual worlds? Is it a consequence of the definition of *an* actual world as a maximally consistent states-of-affairs combination that there can be only one actual world, *the* actual world, and therefore the world we inhabit? Or, could (and therefore must) there be, according to the proposed analysis, multiple maximally consistent states-of-affairs combinations or multiple maximally consistent object–property combinations? If these are permitted, which is to say necessitated, by the analysis, then it casts the definition of being as maximal consistency in a bad light. We are no better off than conventional modal semantics in that case, because we are no better able to distinguish the existent actual world that we inhabit from other non-existent merely possible actual worlds than by referring to our empirical experience or phenomenology of human being-in-the-world, or staking out ontological territory indexically, declaring *this* to be the actual world, the one and none other that we experience and ostend and feel its comforting or terrifying resistance.

The reason why there is exactly one actual world rather than a multitude of existing actual worlds has nothing to do with the fact that we cannot imagine or would be unable even in principle to experience multiple actual worlds. There appears to be something logically or conceptually necessary about there existing only one actual world; that to speak of the actual world, no matter how or by what states of affairs it is constituted, is to speak of a uniquely existent thing, the existence of the universe in the sense of a closed single unitary realm of all being. If that is the correct concept, we must continue to ask, how can it be proved? The combinatorial pure philosophical ontology that we have developed implies, with the help of pure logic, that there cannot be more than one actual world.

If there were two or more actual worlds, then there would be two or more maximally consistent states-of-affairs combinations. The actual world as a maximally consistent states-of-affairs combination is ultimately constituted out of all logically possible combinations of all logically possible objects and all logically possible properties. Logically, then, there can be no additional logically possible objects with which to determine another numerically distinct alternative actual world. The actual world as a maximally consistent states-of-affairs combination ontologically underwrites all true propositions. The existent objects in one actual world *per impossibile* would then need to be so related to all existent objects in an alter actual world that they logically coalesce into a single unified actual world, like two beads of mercury touching. Only such a unified uniquely existent actual world is *maximally* consistent. If both actual world *A* and actual world alter-*A* coexist, then their constitutive states of affairs must be jointly logically consistent, and so they must both belong to and only to a maximally consistent states-of-affairs combination. It follows, then, that *A* and alter-*A* can only be two names for the same logically possible world that is actual on the present account by virtue of being maximally consistent.

By this reasoning we justify the common-sense conclusion that there can exist only one actual world. The argument strongly depends on the assumption that there can at most exist only one maximally consistent states-of-affairs combination, but does not preclude the existence of many objects and many states of affairs. We have argued that the concept of maximal consistency literally applied entails that there can exist only one maximally consistent state of affairs combination. Its predicational maximality makes every other states-of-affairs combination predicationally incomplete, and hence by definition nonexistent, non-actual. If we are truly to have a logically possible maximally consistent states-of-affairs combination, it must, by virtue of its maximality, already include in its combination any existent entity, including such large-scale hypothetical entities as additional maximally consistent states-of-affairs combinations. All hypothetically maximally consistent states-of-affairs combinations therefore logically coalesce into one. According to the combinatorial concept of being, there can exist at most only one actual world. We can rest assured that logically not only must there be something rather than nothing, but that there is only one actual world. The universe, as the name implies, is one.

None of this is to deny the logical possibility of widely separated "universes" within a single actual world. These would have to be distinct "worlds" in the sense of vastly separated distinct spacetime regions between which there are no causally possible interrelations or intercommunication beyond what any epistemic agents might mistakenly believe to be the limits of the actual world. We have said nothing whatsoever yet about the applied scientific ontology of space or time or spacetime, whether or not there can be spacetime islands that are totally physically isolated from one another, what the capabilities and limitations of epistemic agents might be, or any of the other specific applied ontological details we would need from a metaphysical standpoint even to begin deciding whether such possibilities ought to be considered. If there are spacetime islands, and we are stranded on one, we could presumably never know it from a practical epistemic standpoint. A combinatorial pure philosophical ontology does not preclude such a possibility, which does not contradict the unique existence of the actual world considered as a whole, even if it happens to include physically insular spacetime regions.

By regarding only the actual world as maximally consistent, we avoid the schizophrenia that attends conventional modal semantic explanations of the ontological status of non-actual merely logically possible worlds. These are supposed to exist as abstract entities because they are defined as abstract sets of abstract propositions, on the realist assumption common in formal symbolic logic and mathematics that abstract mathematical entities necessarily exist. Non-actual merely logically possible worlds exist (as abstract entities) on this account, even though they do not exist (as actual or actualized, or are not identical with the actual world). The combinatorial analysis of the concept of being on the contrary entails that non-actual merely logically possible worlds do not exist in any sense, even as abstract entities, because they are at best submaximally consistent. Other worlds are logically possible only in the sense that, had the facts of the actual world been different, they logically could have existed, in that no logical contradiction results in supposing that they rather than the actual world could instead have turned out to constitute the one and only maximally consistent states-of-affairs combination.

Physical states of affairs

We have already mentioned the need to introduce physical states of affairs as a subcategory in pure philosophical ontology. We must do so if we are to make sense of distinctions between logically possible worlds that cannot be understood in terms of nonexistent or uniformly existent abstract states of affairs alone. It might seem impermissible to draw conclusions about the existence of physical entities from within the project of pure philosophical ontology. The conclusion is nevertheless a necessary consequence of the identity conditions for distinct logically possible worlds.

Physical states are a logical possibility; thus, there is a combination of logically possible physical states that exactly describes the actual world. The argument can also be recast in terms of the difference between spatiotemporal and non-spatiotemporal properties. Assume, as an instance of excluded middle, that all properties of all predicables are either spatiotemporal (physical) or non-spatiotemporal (abstract). If all properties are non-spatiotemporal, then all identically belong to all logically possible worlds, actual or non-actual. In that case, there is no way to distinguish any logically possible world from any other, since all have precisely the same complement of abstract properties, constituting one and the same logically indistinguishable maximally consistent states-of-affairs combination, involving only the properties of abstract non-spatiotemporal properties, which do not vary from world to world. All worlds then collapse into one, and all truths turn out to be logically necessary. The actual world, indistinguishable from logically possible worlds generally, would then be logically necessary.

The explanation of why there exists something rather than nothing is easily answered if there are only abstract entities. It is necessarily true that something rather than nothing exists on the present assumption, because the actual world as the only logically possible world necessarily exists. The answer is disappointing, because it amounts to saying that something rather than nothing exists because the only existents are abstract entities that cannot fail to exist in any logically possible world. The conclusion is further at variance with empirical evidence about the nature of the actual world, however reluctant we may be to include experiential facts about the logically contingent nature of existence into the deliberations of pure philosophical ontology. It is interesting to see that we nevertheless obtain the same answer to the question of being by this route – that to exist is to be maximally consistent.

If, on the other hand, there are differences between logically possible worlds, they cannot involve non-spatiotemporal entities, and must therefore depend exclusively on differences among spatiotemporal, which is to say physical, properties. The same answer to the question of being is sustainable also on the assumption that there are spatiotemporal or physical properties of objects. As a bonus, we further conclude that there are spatiotemporal physical properties as well as non-spatiotemporal abstract properties. We again leave aside the question whether properties themselves are physical or abstract as a topic for applied scientific ontology, and recognize that even here the conclusion that there are spatiotemporal or physical properties is only hypothetical, conditional on the assumption of only one horn of a dilemma. It is heartening nonetheless to see that things can turn out this way for applied scientific ontology as far as pure philosophical ontology is concerned. The result reinforces previous arguments for the submaximal consistency of non-actual merely logically possible worlds. If we have reason later on to believe that there is only one spacetime realm within which spatiotemporal properties can be instantiated, then it follows that non-actual worlds are inherently incomplete or submaximal with respect to all logically possible physical spatiotemporal properties, and hence non-actual.

We argue in what follows that the uniquely existent actual world is logically contingent in all its physical states of affairs. The recognition of physical states of affairs as a distinguished category of logically possible states of affairs does not poach on applied ontology's territory, because pure philosophical ontology must be as neutral about the ontological status of physical states of affairs as it is generally about the ontic status of any other subcategory of states of affairs. The states of affairs in question are purely logical, as far as the argument at this stage is concerned, in that they involve only the logically possible combinations of logically possible objects and logically possible properties, including logically possible physical objects with logically possible physical properties. We consider the division between physical and abstract objects and properties as grounded on a more purely logical distinction if we construe it as a division between spatiotemporal and non-spatiotemporal objects and properties. We have only ontological play-money to spend in pure philosophical ontology anyway. We have argued that *an* actual world exists because logically combinatorially there must be such a possibility that by definition must exist. We have also maintained on the basis of the combinatorial analysis of being that there can be only one uniquely existent actual world, that *the* actual world is correctly so designated in the sense that there can be only one, and that combinatorially the existence if not the condition of the actual world is logically necessary.

Logical contingency of the actual world

If logically there must exist a world, and if the actual world exists, then a careless inference might have it that therefore the actual world with all its particular states of affairs logically must also exist. The actual world, we would nevertheless like to believe, is logically contingent in at least some of its states of affairs, and presumably in all of its physical spatiotemporal states of affairs. If combinatorially there must exist an actual world, how then are we to prove the logical contingency of the actual world?

The problem we must now address is to account for the presumed logical contingency of the actual world. When we ask, indicating the surrounding actual world in which we find ourselves, why is there something rather than nothing, we do not usually mean the actual world as it actually exists. The world could be very different than it is; but a world of some kind with some physical states of affairs or other would still exist.

The logical contingency of the actual world must be due to the fact that it is partly constituted by spatiotemporal objects and states of affairs existing in real spacetime. The events unfolding in the vast causal spatiotemporal matrix include, but are by no means limited to, the tiny part of the universe where we happen to dwell. This is a good non-empirical reason for considering physical states of affairs in addition to abstract objects as possible entities to be accommodated in a later applied scientific ontology. The topic of the logical contingency of the actual world is a delicate one in the context of the foregoing combinatorial argument that there must and therefore does exist something rather than nothing. If the existence of *an* actual world is logically necessary, how can the details of *the* actual world, its facts and events and occurrences, the condition as well as the existence of the actual world, be merely logically contingent? How, in particular, can *the* actual world be logically contingent if the existence of *an* actual world is logically combinatorially necessary, and if there is only one uniquely existent actual world, if *an* actual world = *the* actual world?

It is deductively invalid to infer a proposition with more information content than the inference's assumptions. If we are required by the logical analysis of being as maximal consistency to admit that all the states of affairs of the actual world are logically necessary rather than logically contingent, then we either owe an explanation of how we can survive deductive invalidity in proving the logical contingency of the actual world in pure philosophical ontology, or we must consider withdrawing the analysis.

We have not tried to prove the actual existence of any logically contingent physical spatiotemporal entities, and we have certainly not done so from the standpoint of pure logic. Any such attempt would evidently be deductively invalid. Instead, we have proceeded conditionally. *If* there are physical spatiotemporal entities, we have said, *then* at least whatever complex physical spatiotemporal entities exist are combinatorially guaranteed to vary from logically possible world to logically possible world. Each world, indeed, will comprise and consist of a distinct such combination. This is logically all we need in order to satisfy ourselves that if physical states of affairs enter into the constitution of the actual world, then those states, since they characterize at most some but not all logically possible worlds, as the concept is defined, are logically contingent. By implication, if physical states of affairs enter into the constitution of the actual world, then the condition of the actual world is not logically necessary but contingent.

As preparation for an explanation of the actual world's logical contingency, we examine two different accounts of the actual world's unique existence and logical contingency. One, like Leibniz's metaphysics, invokes the existence and free choice of God to actualize a world from a range of alternative logical possibilities, and the other postulates the Big Bang of physical cosmology to explain the existence and logical contingency of the entire physical universe. The criticisms offered here apply with equal force to the idea that God's choice or the Big Bang might explain, in response to our previous question, why there exists something rather than nothing. Throughout, we refer to the logical contingency of the actual world's physical states of affairs or to the actual world considered from the standpoint of its physical states of affairs. We thereby bracket the ontic status of abstract objects, and remain ontically neutral about their existence or nonexistence until we are ready to recommend a particular preferred existence domain in applied scientific ontology.

God's choice of a world to actualize

We first briefly consider the idea that God chooses a particular world to actualize. Methodologically, we cannot invoke a particular existent entity whose contested existence is recognized only by some applied ontologies as belonging to some but not all theoretical preferred existence domains. If the logical contingency of the actual world is to be explained as a question for pure philosophical ontology, then we cannot appeal even heuristically to the existence of God or God's choice at any point without plunging into another form of Heidegger's circle.

Nor does it help to appeal to God's perfect good will in choosing to actualize a particular world, as Leibniz does in his theomodal theory, "On the Ultimate Origination of Things". Leibniz holds that the existence of the actual world in its actual condition is the result of God's choosing to actualize this particular world from among all logical possibilities. Why an infinitely perfect being should need to go through any sort of process or procedure of projecting and selecting in order to create the world is already puzzling. If we ignore the most obvious embarrassing questions, and think about the choice of one among an array of alternative logically possible worlds as a model or metaphor for the uniqueness and contingency of the actual world, then we are sure to be disappointed. We first need a sound theological or philosophical reason for agreeing that God's perfect infinite good will does not require God on the contrary to actualize multiple actual worlds, none of which is *the* best, but each of which is qualitatively an exact equal among the best of all logically possible worlds. Why suppose without good argument that there is a single best logically possible world? We similarly need a good reason for admitting that God's perfection does not in the end require actualizing a world in which no events are logically contingent. God might, as Leibniz pictures him, array before divine imagination all the alternative logically possible worlds, in order to consider which is or are best, until, as part of the divine decision process, God sees all possibilities dramatically collapse into one, which, by virtue of its overriding logical necessity, there being no other genuine possibilities left, awaits only God's decision about whether or not to actualize any world at all.[1]

For the same reasons it does not help to refer to the existence of God as choosing existence over nonexistence for an actual world or for the actual world in its existent state. Are we sufficiently desperate to argue that it is a consequence of God's perfection that God must actualize some world or other, and that the actual world is *de facto* whatever world God chooses to actualize? God's choice is no philosophical help in trying to understand why the actual world exists. Aside from the dubious picture of God entertaining ideas and making decisions in real time, the existence of which apparently is dispensable as merely heuristic or else requires no explanation, there is also the philosophically questionable existence of God as a suitable starting place for trying to answer the question of being. We would not be the first to advance the dilemma that, if existence is supposed to be explained by the existence of God, then we merely push the question back to why there exists a God rather than no God. If, on the other hand, God's existence is self-explanatory or stands in need of no explanation, then we should in principle be able to say the same for the existence of the actual world with or without God superadded to the ontology.[2]

The real difficulty in the proposal is that it does not contribute to understanding what it means for something to exist to know that it exists because of God's will. Perhaps there exists a God and the existence of the actual world is God's handiwork. Still, what does it *mean* to say that the world exists as a result of God's will? Nor does God's choice explain why there exists something rather than nothing if we do not know why God decided to actualize the world. It does not solve the problem to learn that God necessarily exists, which in any case is a conclusion, if it can be attained at all, that belongs to applied rather than pure philosophical ontology. There are said to be many necessarily existent entities in several different branches of applied scientific ontology, including numbers, sets, propositions, universals, properties, relations and the like, and we do not suppose that the existence conditions for such abstract entities, if indeed they exist, stand in no need of explanation or justification. Why should God's existence, if indeed God exists, be an exception in a methodologically circumspect ontology?

If neither philosophical nor applied scientific ontology is sufficiently enthusiastic about the existence of God, it remains possible for believers to reaffirm the frailty and hubris of human intellect, and to interpret the exclusion of God from a preferred existence domain as a greater opportunity for the expression of personal faith. In philosophical ontology, even if we had a more purely philosophical argument for the existence of God, it does not seem to add anything to our understanding to say that God wills the existence of something rather than nothing. It is not very informative to claim that God is a self-creating, self-sustaining being who wills to break the logical deadlock over the existence versus nonexistence of anything in favour of existence. The existence and will of God cannot explain the existence of all entities, unless God's existence is self-explanatory. It is hard to know how such an assertion is supposed to be interpreted. To the extent that the concept can be clarified, it offers at best an incomplete answer to the fundamental question of pure philosophical ontology that could equally be applied to a self-creating self-sustaining Godless universe. If we say that it is God's will to decide the existence or nonexistence of the actual world, then we are left with what is if anything a more difficult unresolved issue of why God chooses to actualize rather than not to actualize a world. As far as our limited knowledge of God's ways are concerned, it seems that God, who is usually imagined to have unlimited freedom of choice, either will or will not create a world, let alone our world, let alone as a logically contingent world. God's reasons are no doubt inscrutable to mortals, but the idea that the actual world in all its complexity exists because God wills its existence lacks a non-circular application in pure philosophical or applied scientific ontology.

Odds of existing and the Big Bang singularity

If our previous reasoning has been correct, and we can only justifiably approach the problems of pure philosophical ontology with logic, we continue to confront the same two possibilities. An actual world, although not necessarily the actual world in its existent state, either exists or does not exist. Each of the two possibilities, furthermore, as we have assumed, has a precisely equal 50–50 random probability of prevailing over the alternative. That a world exists in fact we know well enough. The mere fact of existence by itself unfortunately does not answer the question of being or explain why there exists something rather than nothing.

What consideration could shift the weight of probability from one side to the other, and help thereby to account for the existence of an actual world? We should pause at precisely this point, because we are already beginning to adopt a misleading model of the logically equal probability of the existence of something versus nothing at all. The existence of a world or of the actual world as it exists does not have to win out even in any sort of logical struggle with nonexistence in order for something rather than nothing to exist. Existence is not earned or brought into being by an act of will, divine or diabolical, nor is it explainable philosophically as a cosmic-mathematical "singularity" in a Big Bang theory of the origin of the universe. Why did God will existence rather than nonexistence? Why did the Big Bang occur rather than not occur?

These stubborn questions remain when religion or scientific cosmology as exercises in applied ontology try to usurp the explanatory jurisdiction of pure philosophical ontology. The Big Bang in particular is powerless to explain why there exists something rather than nothing. What is meant by the Big Bang is merely an observationally and mathematically supported retrodiction about the origins of the physical universe. The Big Bang is the initial event that breaks the 50–50 deadlock between the equal random probability of the world's existence rather than nonexistence. There is no logical or metaphysical necessity to the world's physical existence progressing from a cosmic singularity at the moment of the Big Bang. According to Big Bang cosmology, all spacetime and matter explode forth from a single geometrical point that, paradoxically in relativity physics, is not yet spatiotemporal. As far as pure logic is concerned, or pure philosophical ontology considered independently of the question whether its problems can sensibly be considered by a discipline other than pure logic, there is no sufficient reason why the 50–50 chance of existence or nonexistence for an actual world could not equally be broken in favour of existence without the occurrence of the Big Bang, but, for example, by the instantaneous distribution of matter throughout the physical universe without expansion over unfolding spacetime from a geometrical singularity.

The Big Bang, as a description of the occurrence and material evolution of the actual physical world, is itself precisely the contingent existence that pure philosophical ontology needs to explain. As such, it can hardly be expected to account for why there exists something rather than nothing. If the Big Bang were said to occur within an absolute spacetime receptacle, like that described in Plato's dialogue *Timaeus* as the *choron*, or like the absolute space and time grid of Galileo, Descartes, Newton and Leibniz, which Newton in his *Opticks* refers to picturesquely as God's visual field, then perhaps we could make sense of its occurring at some definite absolute metaphysical place and time.[3] The Big Bang is supposed to spew forth all of spacetime and the total energy convertible into material substance that the actual physical universe will ever contain. The vast material world expands into the space it creates for itself from a single originally locationless point. It appears all at once, in one convulsive go, and everything that happens thereafter is the consequence and development under natural laws of the first great burst of energy, expanding in complicated internally interacting ways, and possibly contracting upon itself again with a rhythm of systole and diastole. The theory by itself does not explain why the Big Bang took place rather than failed to take place, other than as a matter of sheer random probability. If the reason why there is something rather than nothing is the 50–50 probability of physical spatiotemoral existence occurring, then the Big Bang itself is not the answer. The Big Bang describes how the universe may have happened to come into existence, but does not tell us why.

The effort to explain why there is something rather than nothing as a cosmic crapshoot is tempting in some ways because it holds out the promise, unfulfilled in the end, of explaining not only why there exists something rather than nothing, but why the actual world happens contingently to have the exact state and condition in which it exists. It might explain, if it explains anything at all, why the actual world is logically contingent in all its physical states of affairs in roughly the same way that it tries to answer the question why there exists something rather than nothing. If it is a random occurrence that an actual world exists rather than nothing at all exists, then it is surely no stretch to conclude further that the actual world in all its detail with all its particularity of entities, facts, states of affairs, events, laws, history, past, present and future, is logically contingent, equally an outcome of blind undirected chance. The latter part of the explanation, as it relates to the main problem of this chapter, is, we maintain, basically correct. It is also detachable from the fruitless attempt to explain why there is something rather than nothing as a consequence of random 50–50 probability.

If the two problems are separated in this way, an obvious question is why the logical contingency of the actual world is explainable as a chance outcome. How, in particular, can the logical contingency of the actual world be explained in terms of logically random processes when the existence of an actual world, of something rather than nothing, is combinatorially logically necessary? The combinatorial pure philosophical ontology we have developed justifies the distinction in an intuitive way. We do not say that there is something rather than nothing because of chance, but as an implication of logical necessity. A combinatorial ontology implies that logically there must be a logically possible maximally consistent states-of-affairs combination, which is how the theory defines the concept of an actual world.

There is something rather than nothing because there must be something rather than nothing. Logically, there must be exactly one maximally consistent object–property or states-of-affairs combination. The particular logically possible combination that turns out to be maximally consistent, on the other hand, is a function of random probability, with every possibility of maximal consistency sharing equal weight, and none holding advantage over any other. The probability in the combinatorial as opposed to the 50–50 logical probability solution is in one way the same in assigning an equal probability for every possible outcome. The combinatorial theory is preferable because it necessitates and does not merely make possible the actual existence of the actual world, but distributes equal probabilities over all the indefinitely many combinations that might have turned out to be maximally consistent, over all logically possible worlds, the actual world and merely logically possible worlds alike. If Leibniz had appreciated the force of the concept of maximal consistency in answering the question why there is something rather than nothing or the ultimate origin of things, he would not have needed to invoke God to explain why there exists an actual world. Leibniz could then have explained the particularity of the actual world that happens to exist as a pure matter of chance without slipping into the problematic conclusion that the actual world in all its unevenly distributed poverty and pain is theologically the best of all logically possible worlds. Perhaps Leibniz did understand this implication and deliberately avoided its solution in order to make God necessary to his metaphysics. We can continue to speak metaphorically of God's choice of the particular maximally consistent states-of-affairs combination that constitutes the actual world. When pressed, however, the most reasonable explanation we can offer is that the condition of the actual world, the entities and states of affairs by which it is constituted, is entirely a result of chance.

Chance existence of the actual world

To speak of *the* actual world is already to single it out from other worlds or other ways in which the world might have been if a different combination of possibilities had been realized. For a variety of reasons we might prefer a pure philosophical ontology in which necessarily we are uniquely existent entities, with no actually existent duplicates of ourselves having adventures in other actually existent worlds. Intuitively, we cannot easily make sense of the identity conditions that would need to hold for our doppelgängers and ourselves, even if on the present assumptions we and our counterparts inhabit distinct logically possible mutually inaccessible worlds.

Can we limit the logically possible worlds, to select just one, the one that we ontologists happen to occupy, as the actual world? We might appeal to a more general non-Heideggerean notion of *Dasein*, the *Modalmoment* of "full-strength factuality", or Plato's Form of Being, a property among other properties to enter only into some and not into all objects' property combinations, and thereby into the states-of-affairs combination that constitutes the actual world. Why not just include Being as a property to be blended combinatorially into some property combinations with whatever other properties constitute the Blue Mosque, and as missing from other property combinations, like those that constitute the Golden City of Eldorado? It does not enhance our understanding of why something exists rather than fails to exist to be told that an object possesses or participates in *Dasein, das Modalmoment* or Being, for these only give a name to the factor that needs to be explained. That an object or state of affairs or world actually exists is taken for granted when we ask why it actually exists and what it means for it to exist as part of the actual world. A good explanation is not forthcoming unless we can better say what it means for an object to possess or participate in *Dasein* or *das Modalmoment*, or a blending of Forms including Plato's Form of Being. It similarly adds nothing to a thing for it to be; for its total predicational constitution, identifying it as the unique individual it is, either entails its existence or nonexistence. Its property combination, the unique collection of extraontological predications that constitutes the object, is either predicationally consistent and complete, that is to say, maximally consistent, or it is not. If it is maximally consistent, then the object is an existent entity. If not, not.

An extraontological property, as the name implies, is a property that by itself does not entail anything about an object's ontic status, and that is not instantiated unless the relevant property combination is maximally consistent. To maintain that existence does not characterize any object says, in short form, that the object's property combination is maximally consistent with no predicational gaps only if, for any extraontological property or property complement, the combination includes either the extraontological property or its complement, but not both. If Kant's criticism of Anselm's ontological argument for the existence of God is correct, it implies that Being is not a property that can be added into a property combination to make the object qualify as existent, at the risk of never being able intelligibly to say that the very same numerically identical object either exists or does not exist. The objects by hypothesis will be constitutionally different, in that case, because one has while the other does not have the property of Being in its property combination. We cannot adopt Plato's Form of Being as the extra ingredient needed to make the object associated with a property combination actually exist. The concept of existence is primitive in that type of theory, precluding any informative answer to the question of being.

Why is there a material world? How did it come to exist, and why is there not instead of the existent physical world an empty void without a single material entity? Here is one follow-up answer that we may find perfectly correct as far as it goes, but not entirely satisfying. There are just two possibilities to consider: one in which contingently nothing material exists, and another in which, again contingently, there exists something rather than nothing. That there should be physical entities rather than none in these terms has a 50–50 random probability of occurring, as does the opposite possibility that nothing whatsoever exists. With these generous odds, especially if we assume that a logical principle of excluded middle holds, whereby, necessarily, either something or nothing exists, the existence of the material world can be considered a matter of probability. There is then, by sheer chance, a material world rather than nothing, and the material stuff within it has as a matter of fact developed into galaxies and star systems and all the concrete physical entities whatever they are existing generally throughout the universe. There might have been nothing rather than something, at which point it may finally be appropriate for scientific ontology to remind philosophical ontology, as Heidgegger in effect does, that in that event there would be no minds to ask or try to answer the question.

We might think of the imaginary nonexistence of the physical world on the model of a spacetime receptacle that is completely empty of any physical entities. If this way of approaching the problem is accepted, then we might think of the 50–50 random probability of the material universe coming into existence within the spacetime receptacle as the two equally probable logical possibilities of a mate-rial world existing or not existing tried out successively over time, like separate rolls of dice, with nonexistence coming up on every roll until existence through blind chance finally gets its way. Although scientists and philosophers sometimes claim to understand the concept of totally empty, which is to say absolute materially unoccupied, space-time, it is a consequence of modern relativity physics that the spacetime continuum is determined by the distribution and relative motion of physical matter in large gravitational fields. One implica-tion of a relativistic cosmology is that spacetime itself comes into existence only with the existence of the physical substance of the world. If a relativistic scientific ontology seems most correct, it further implies that the physical existence of the world cannot be adequately explained as an occurrence at a particular place or within a particular period of time, and that space and time are themselves existent entities whose contingent existence needs to be explained in a complete scientific ontology.

Combinatorial roulette

As the name alone implies, logical objects are identically distributed or available for combination with logical properties alike in all logically possible worlds, including the actual world. It is part of the concept of a logical object or predicable that it not be specific to any particular logically possible world, but stand as one of the logical building blocks of any logically possible world.

Is it conceivable, then, even if logical objects are the same in every logically possible world, that the stock of simple physical entities, if any should turn out to exist, in addition to the physical states of affairs involving physical entities, might vary from logically possible world to logically possible world? In its atomic and quantum theories, modern science is ontologically committed to the existence of physi-cally atomic entities defined in terms of energy fields from which more complex physical structures are composed, in a cosmic assembly line that takes quarks and atoms to make molecules and macro-physical entities, star systems, galaxies and, finally, the entire physical universe. It does not try to say whether precisely the same atomic units of matter as individual entities or types of entities must exist in the physical states of affairs of every logically possible world.

Some of these questions cannot be competently answered unless or until we have progressed to a sound applied scientific ontology. We can nevertheless relax the conditional framework of these conclusions by remarking that the logical contingency of the actual world is implied by the fact that it is a combinatorial logical possibility for complex physical entities to be combined out of simpler entities, from objects to states of affairs to entire worlds. Whether or not the actual world consists of physically atomic physical entities, combinatorially, at least some logically possible worlds involve a logically possible physical order that is physically constituted by a compositional hierarchy of physical simples and complexes, and at least some other logically possible worlds do not. It does not matter whether the actual world in point of fact belongs to one category or the other, whether it is physically composed of physical simples or not; it is certain as a result to be logically contingent whatever its constitution.

Logically, there must exist an actual world. It need not have been the actual world as it happens to exist. As far as logic is concerned, the fact remains that of all the logically possible worlds that might combinatorially have involved a maximally consistent property combination, of properties predicated of or possessed by logical objects; any could actually have turned out to be maximally consistent. This makes it logically altogether a matter of sheer blind chance what particular logically contingent entities and states of affairs happen to exist in the actual world. Any fact involving any physical spatiotemporal state of the actual world might have been different than it happens to be. The actual world we inhabit, sufficiently hospitable to sustain the existence of thinking creatures such as ourselves, in all its specific details of facts and events, the distribution of matter and natural laws that govern the physical entities and their properties throughout the vast universe, is, logically speaking, purely a function of random probability.

If the nature of the actual world is a result of pure chance, it might be wondered whether the existence of any actual world is also random. We have previously argued that the existence of an actual world, although not the actual world in all its particularity, is logically necessary by virtue of being a combinatorial possibility. If there were an argument to show that the existence of something rather than nothing is merely logically contingent, it would throw all of our previous reflections into doubt, and cut the ground from under our logical combinatorial explanation of why there exists something rather than nothing. Here we consider another purely logical justification for the existence of something, an actual world, rather than nothing. Although the argument, based also on chance or randomness, is ultimately found to be incorrect, it affords a worthwhile opportunity to contrast the logically necessary existence of something rather than nothing with the logical contingency of the actual physical state of the actual world, the existence of an actual world with the condition of the actual world.

We begin by assuming that logically there is a 50–50 random probability for something rather than nothing to exist, and of course for nothing whatsoever to exist rather than something. In many applications of inductive reasoning, a 50–50 chance of something occurring is often considered explanatorily adequate to account for its existence. If the breakdown of a machine is predicted to have a 50–50 chance of occurring, and then in fact subsequently breaks down, many persons will judge that the machine broke down because, after all, it had an even chance of doing so, and things could have gone either way. Indeed, we often regard it as a sufficient explanation of something's occurring for there to be a much smaller probability. We knew that there could be a storm today, the meteorologist said there was a 30 per cent chance, and, behold, it happened. One might conclude that the same type of reason might apply in the case of there existing something rather than nothing. After all, logically and probabilistically speaking, things could go either way. If God tosses a coin – heads a world exists and tails no world exists – then we might end up with a world rather than no world. A world exists on this account purely as a blind chance occurrence or roll of the cosmic dice. Equally, from this pure logical standpoint, a world might not have existed. Then, of course, we would also not be here to think or talk about it; although the fact of personal existence can no more be invoked in this context than in other attempts to answer the question why there exists something rather than nothing. It is a fact that is out of place in pure philosophical ontology, and a consideration that in a different guise circles back again to Heidegger's appeal to the phenomenological concept of specifically human being-in-the-world as a way of answering the question of being.

The 50–50 logical possibility or random probability of the existence of the universe, mapping as it does onto some interpretations of excluded middle or non-contradiction, is altogether an explanatory non-starter that does not help us to understand why something rather than nothing exists. Why, we still want to know, does an actual world actually happen to exist rather than not exist? Why has existence with precisely equal random or logical probability in its favour won out over nonexistence? We should note that in the case of the weather forecast, there is more behind the probabilistic prediction that a storm will occur than random probability, even if the forecast predicts a precisely 50–50 occurrence on the basis of extralogical considerations. There are all the facts about global and local weather patterns, scientific records of past occurrences of storms in similar geographical circumstances and during the same season, satellite monitoring of atmospheric conditions, and all the other data that are used to make predictions about the weather. The same is true to an even greater degree in the case of the machine's breakdown, for which we should in principle be able to provide a rather detailed mechanical explanation. In both the weather and the machine case, we seem to be saying something substantive about the prior causal condition of a system such that at a relevant earlier time we could not have judged from the information available then whether or how the system would change. We might find that the factors on both sides of opposite predictions precisely cancel each other out, so that we say the change has a 50–50 chance of occurrence. If that idea makes sense, then we might try to apply a slightly modified version to the question of whether the universe as a whole, for purely logical reasons, has a precisely 50–50 chance of existence or nonexistence.

The probability statement in the case of the weather forecast or a machine breaking down is in a way a kind of summary of all this information and reasoning, and is not supposed to stand on its own as an explanation of why something occurred rather than failed to occur. This is in sharp disanology with the attempt to explain why there exists something rather than nothing as a result of random probability, for in that application there is naturally no background information or history of similar events on which to rely. We are trying rather pathetically to explain why the universe exists rather than fails to exist purely on a logical basis of equiprobability for an event to occur or not to occur, which in this context is at least as if not more reasonably interpreted as admitting that we simply have no explanation at all. To say that a universe sprang into existence, as in the Big Bang, because probabilistically it could have done so, does not begin to explain why it actually did. We know before we ask the question that the world could have existed, because we know before then that the world in fact exists.

The actual world exists because the physical objects described as belonging to non-actual merely logically possible worlds are constitutionally incomplete, lacking in some physical property or its complement. Were it otherwise, then combinatorial pure philosophical ontology implies that the objects in question would actually exist. Does the random combination of objects with properties preclude the possibility of many complete physical objects in actual physical states of affairs in non-actual merely logically possible worlds? Why do all the complete physical objects wind up in one world? The reason, previously explained, is that *all* physical objects in a world construed as a states-of-affairs combination are constitutionally incomplete if *any* physical object in that same world is constitutionally incomplete. Hence, none of those world's physical states of affairs is actual. It follows that there is at most one world where all the properties and relations fall out combinatorially so as to constitute an actual world consisting of actually existent physical states of affairs involving actually existent physical entities. There are so many ways in which the actual world might have been, but only one that logically happens to be predicationally maximally consistent. The actual world does not earn the right preconditionally to exist. One world must and only one world can actually exist; but which one happens to exist is not a matter of logic or pure philosophical ontology. That is the fundamental question of applied scientific ontology, for which the answer is, from a logical point of view, pure chance.

Philosophical implications of the world's logical contingency

The logical contingency of the actual world, implied by combinatorial pure philosophical ontology, vouchsafes several important conclusions for other areas of philosophy that require a correct ontology as foundation. We assume that the actual world as studied by natural science is logically contingent, and that any of its specific facts, events and natural laws are logically contingent rather than logically necessary. The contingency of the universe is also presupposed as a necessary but not sufficient condition for the freedom of action and the will. The freedom of will is by no means universally accepted by scientists and philosophers, but in some philosophical theories is believed to provide an essential assumption for the possibility of moral responsibility.

Needless to say, the logical contingency of the actual world, and even the logical contingency of the natural laws that govern causal connections of events in the universe, do not entail the causal contingency of human thought and action, which is often regarded as the stronger sense of contingency required for a robust concept of freedom. As we know, not all philosophers accept the idea of moral responsibility anyway, and are just as happy to have it eliminated. Others, committed to the logical necessity of the actual world in all its particularity, face the difficulty of trying philosophically to reconcile the logical necessity of the universe with the possibility of the freedom of will and moral responsibility. This is not a light burden, and philosophers who hope to make room in their systems for freedom and responsibility ought to appreciate the advantages of a combinatorial pure philosophical ontology in upholding at least the logical contingency of the actual world. We do not want to make pure logic the science of the world, although Leibniz, Hegel and, arguably, the early Wittgenstein tried to do so, even if logic should turn out to be an ultimate and in other ways more fundamental discipline than natural science.

Logic is important; but not so important, and not in this way. If we expect science to be logically contingent because we believe that the world is constituted by logically contingent states of affairs, then we should appreciate the explanation of this feature of the actual world entailed by a combinatorial pure philosophical ontology. What we know for certain is that some number will come up in combinatorial roulette for a particular maximally consistent states-of-affairs combination. Unless the game is fixed, however, we do not know which number it will be. It is the same in combinatorial pure philosophical ontology. *Sub specie aeternitatis*, from an imaginary god's-eye point of view outside and surveying the whole of the existent universe, we know that there must be something rather than nothing, that there is certain to be a maximally consistent states-of-affairs combination or object–property combination; but, importantly, we do not know which. The actual world that happens to exist is a function of pure chance on the proposed combinatorial theory the world we happen to tenant, whose secrets we try to discover in natural science, is the logically contingent result, so to speak, of a single turn of the combinatorial wheel.

The logical analysis of being says, in effect, that in this special case, because of the combinatorial possibilities of pure classical logic, if an actual world is logically possible, then an actual world is logically necessary. The modal status of the actual world is logically contingent, from a logical point of view a matter of pure chance. It may nevertheless turn out to be physically determinate, and in that sense physically or causally necessary, and hence a matter once again of physically or causally circumscribed probability. This is partly an issue for scientists to decide. Newton and Leibniz opt for the necessity of the actual world – Leibniz in the very strong sense of his logical-metaphysical concept of necessity and identity, Newton in terms of absolute space and time and deterministic applied mathematical laws of motion, acting on a random distribution of material substances. Later scientists, from Einstein to Stephen Hawking, with Werner Heisenberg, Paul Dirac, Pierre Duhem and others in between, have regarded the universe as logically contingent and physically-causally indeterminate not only in its physical states of affairs, but in the natural laws by which physical phenomena are governed.

It is no more remarkable – and no less – to think that, of all the different logically possible worlds that might have been actualized as maximally consistent states-of-affairs combinations, we happen to exist and are able to consider these abstruse topics of metaphysics, to suffer and enjoy the moments of our lives, than it is to think that of all the possible galaxies and star systems in the actual world we just happen to have been born on planet Earth. It is not that remote from the amazement we can produce by reflecting that of all the many kinds of terrestrial animals, we just happened to evolve as members of the species *homo sapiens sapiens*, or that we happen to be born of one family in one part of the actual world at a certain time in history in our physical world's spacetime. There is no necessity to any of these occurrences, logical, causal or any other type, except the conditional necessity that were it not for the logically contingent pure random chance satisfaction of all of these conditions – being in a hospitable logically possible actual world, on a hospitable planet in all that vast world, being genetically members of the human species and of a certain race and gender and age and biological family – we would not now be entertaining these thoughts. We would not be able to, for we would not be.

Now, look about; it's okay. You exist, and so does everything around you in the actual world. And existence is very important – just try to get along without it! *Something* rather than nothing *must* have existed, but it need not have included you or me. We exist entirely as a gift of chance – it is in every way a fragile thing.

Concepts of existence in philosophical logic and the
5 analysis of being *qua* being

Logic, predication, existence

What can logic teach us about ontology? Symbolic logic in and of itself is not that philosophically interesting, but reveals something important when, appropriately interpreted, it serves to explain why there is something rather than nothing. Logic embodies a set of concepts and philosophical commitments about what it means for something to exist that can be recovered from the expressive capabilities of logic in the predication of properties to objects.

We have argued that logic supports a non-circular a priori answer to the question of being, of why there is something rather than nothing, and why there exists exactly one logically contingent actual world. The rules of formal symbolic logic, concerned primarily with the normative requirements of deductively valid inference, do not entail that any given specimen of actual reasoning conform to its truth-conditions, let alone that any contingently existent entity in the actual world actually exists. Logic seems ontologically impotent in this regard only if we focus exclusively on the inference mechanisms of formal logical systems. For purposes of pure philosophical ontology, there is much more to be learned from the expressive capabilities of classical logic, whether Aristotelian syllogistic, Boolean algebra or modern symbolic first-order predicate logic.

Logic is easily interwoven with pure philosophical ontology because pure philosophical ontology, like logic, is purely formal, and because it is only as a discipline and not as an ontic domain that logic is called upon to answer the Heideggerean question of being. An obvious objection to the combinatorial analysis of the concept of existence is that if Heidegger's phenomenology is too rich for ontology, if it is already so anchored to the existence of contingently existent actual entities like ourselves, our time horizons, and our experience of being in the world, is formal symbolic logic not too impoverished? If the existentialist ontology that results from accepting phenomenology as the method by which to answer the question of being cannot provide a non-circular answer to the question of what it means for something to exist without presupposing the existence of contingently existent things like human beings and times, or their experience of the actual world, then we must worry about the prospects of making logic too thin a basis for an a priori explanation of what it means for something to exist. As a system of pure expressive and inferential forms, logic is devoid of substantive ontic content. It does not offer enough to "deduce" real existence, whatever that could mean. We cannot logically derive the existence of apples or camels, or of any other entities in a preferred existence domain, which is the business of applied ontology. The fact that logical form includes all logically possible combinations of all logically possible objects with all logically possible properties is nevertheless enough to explain the concept of being and answer related questions of pure philosophical ontology.

Ontology by numbers

It will not avail, for this reason, simply to take note of alternative applied scientific ontologies, and try to say that what it means for something to exist depends on which ontology we accept, as though it were a matter of joining a political party. Plato says one thing; David Hume another. Other philosophers, before and after and in between Plato and Hume, have proposed ontologies different from one another yet again. We may decide to enter the dispute, dissatisfied with the available choices, and thrash out our own applied scientific ontology as a further alternative. Even then, if we have not first clarified the concept of being, we can only say, as we point to the items on a list of entities, that *this* is what it means for something to exist – to be included on the list. It should be obvious by now that this way of proceeding is improper methodology, especially if we agree that pure philosophical ontology has logical and explanatory priority over the questions of applied scientific ontology.

We get nowhere with respect to the problems of pure philosophical ontology, in understanding what it means for something to exist, by choosing, say, a Platonic over a Humean ontology, or the reverse, or by advancing our own preferred applied scientific ontology. To maintain with Plato that only abstract entities are real is to declare our agreement with a particular applied scientific ontology, with a preferred existence domain. The same is true if we accept an entirely different austerely empiricist ontology like Hume's, in which to be real is to be experienced in immediate thought, beyond which we have no knowledge of reality. Here too we have only signed on to what we believe is a more attractive applied scientific ontology. We can never address the problems of pure philosophical ontology from an applied scientific standpoint, because we cannot understand what it means for something to exist merely by considering an inventory of existent entities. We can never satisfactorily answer the questions of pure philosophical ontology by invoking solutions that are endemic to the specific preferred existence domains of applied scientific ontology. Nor can we intelligently compile a description of existent entities in the first place if we do not know what it means for something to exist, if we have no principles to guide our choices as we consider what things exist or do not exist.

The sign of these priority inversions is that we stumble immediately over the fact that alternative applied scientific ontologies reflect entirely different, even logically incompatible, concepts of what it means to exist. Why are we Platonists rather than Humeans, or Humeans rather than Platonists? Why do we gravitate toward a realist ontology, or the reverse? We are forced to adjudicate between extreme ontological alternatives because both Plato and Hume cannot both be right while supporting such different conclusions about what kinds of things exist. If we can explain what it means for something to exist by holding up a good-looking list of supposedly existent entities, then it is equally legitimate for an opponent to hold up a different list, and maintain on the contrary that to exist is to be included among its itemization of very different existent entities. This is precisely what happens when philosophers challenge one another's applied ontologies of preferred existence domains without first having answered the question of being. We cannot intelligently say that this exists and that does not exist if we have not first satisfactorily explained what it means for something, anything, to exist.

The point is that we must first answer the most basic questions of pure philosophical ontology, and then, armed with an understanding of what it means in the most general terms for something to exist, proceed to apply the concept of being to work out the details of an applied scientific ontology. If we get to that crossroads, then we have a chance of deciding objectively whether Plato or Hume's applied ontology is more correct, committed to an extant domain of existent entities, and reflecting a considered pure philosophical concept of existence. Otherwise, the most that we can do is salute one applied scientific existence domain or the other on instinctive grounds, with no understanding of what it means for something to exist.[1]

We might find it gratifying to rescue Plato or Hume from the suspicion of having confused pure philosophical with applied scientific ontology. We could try to do so by pleading that they cannot reasonably be charged with inverting these components of ontology if they never recognized the problems of pure philosophical ontology as meaningful or tractable in the first place. Perhaps they made progress instead in the only way they thought possible by spelling out the details of their respective preferred existence domains. If so, neither Plato nor Hume offers an edifying model of how an integrated philosophical–scientific ontology ought to proceed, and we should once again avoid consulting either of their conflicting applied scientific ontologies in order to address what, by hypothesis, we properly regard as a fundamental question of pure philosophical ontology. We must say the same for any other ontologists who try to avoid explaining the concept of being.

Modality of combinatorial ontology

We have proceeded differently, by defining the concept of being in purely logical terms, and arguing on the basis of a combinatorial analysis of existence that there must exist exactly one logically contingent actual world. The inferences we have proposed have been informally presented, relying on an intuitive understanding of the implications of the idea that to exist is to be maximally consistent.

The modal structure of the arguments we have offered to answer the question of being, to explain why there exists something rather than nothing, and why there exists exactly one actual world that is logically contingent in all its physical states, should now be formalized. Doing so provides an opportunity to review all three of the explanations that have been offered in combinatorial pure philosophical ontology, to see precisely how they are related, and to reconsider their conclusions.[2]

A critic might imagine that the inference used to explain why there exists something rather than nothing contains a modal fallacy. The claim that the combinatorial possibilities for a logical object to combine with a logical property in pure classical logic logically necessitate the existence of an actual world that can then be shown to be the uniquely existent logically contingent actual world may seem modally problematic. The uniquely existent actual world is supposed to be logically contingent, despite the fact that its existence is proved by the combinatorially logically necessary existence of an actual world. Is there not something wrong here?

The fallacy seems to be that, for any proposition p, if it is logically necessary that it is logically possible that p, then it is logically necessary that p. Let $w_@$ be substituted for p by virtue of representing a conjunction consisting of all the propositions that are true in and of the actual world. Then it looks as though by claiming that from the fact that it is logically necessary that there be a maximally consistent combination of states of affairs in the totality of all logically possible states-of-affairs combinations we can logically infer that combinatorially an actual world necessarily exists. It is a modal fallacy to permit the deductively invalid inference, $\Box\Diamond p \vdash \Box p$, or the false conditional, $\Box\Diamond p \rightarrow \Box p$, even in the strongest sound systems of iterated modal logic. A counter-example to remind us of how the statement goes astray can be given in modal system S_5. There we are permitted to infer $\Box\Diamond p$ from $\Diamond p$. Let p be the logically possible proposition that pigs fly. Then it follows in S_5 that $\Box\Diamond p$, but not, even in S_5, that $\Box p$, that it is logically necessary that pigs fly. This, fortunately, is *not* the modal structure of the argument we have advanced, which is modally and in other ways logically more complicated.[3]

To explain how the fallacy is avoided, we formalize the underlying modality of the arguments by which we propose to demonstrate combinatorially that logically there must exist something rather than nothing, that an actual world logically must exist, but that the condition of the actual world is not logically necessary. We refer to the actual world as an individual entity, $w_@$, and apply a special modal operator to represent the actuality of any logically possible world. For this purpose, actuality is symbolized by Δ, within a standard alethic modal logic. We assume, as we have throughout, that for a logically possible world to be actual means for it to be a maximally consistent states-of-affairs combination, which we symbolize as the metalogical predicate *MaxCon*. We allow modal operators to attach directly to individual propositions or to any conjunction of propositions, and even to a conjunction of propositions that completely describe a logically possible world. The distinction makes it possible to formalize the proposition that the actual world is actual, which we write as: $\Delta w_@$. We can then more formally consider the logic of the previous inferences used to explain why there exists something rather than nothing, and why there exists exactly one logically contingent actual world. Through much of the logical symbolizations to follow we make intuitive use of the Δ operator, and only near the end propose inference rules supported by the same intuitions for its introduction in standard first-order predicate logic.

We begin by appealing only to the conditional, $\forall w_i[MaxCon.w_i \rightarrow \Delta w_i]$ (or $\forall w_i[MaxCon.w_i \rightarrow \exists w_k[\Delta w_k \wedge w_i = w_k]]$). The converse conditional appears in other arguments involving the biconditional, whereby we more generally formulate the combinatorial answer to the question of being, $\forall x[MaxCon.x \leftrightarrow \Delta x]$. We refer to the conditional or complete biconditional analysis of being respectively as $Df.\Delta \rightarrow$ and $\Delta \leftrightarrow$. Here, in answering the question why there exists something rather than nothing, it is important to see that we can deduce actuality from maximal consistency alone. We note that in deducing the instantiated consequent, $\Delta\alpha$, from the instantiated antecedent, $MaxCon.\alpha$, we *deduce* the *actuality* of α. The universal implies that we can deduce the actuality of *any* α, including any real existent entity, or state of affairs, or combination of states of affairs or the entire actual world, provided only that, according to the principle, α is maximally consistent. We can in principle soundly substitute for "α" anything we can *name* that is maximally consistent, including the actual world, $w_@$. We prove the actuality of *the* actual world as a substitution instance, $\Delta w_@$, *if* we know that the actual world is maximally consistent, $MaxCon.w_@$. We cannot avoid circularity if we invoke the converse conditional, $\Delta w_@ \rightarrow MaxCon.w_@$, at this stage of the argument, in order to conclude that the actual world is maximally consistent, unless we are in a position to assert what is now supposed to be proved – that the actual world is actual. What, then, can we do?

It is tempting to try to establish the maximal consistency of the actual world by means of an argument that we should consider only to reject. We should not assume that only a maximally consistent world can be perceived, and then cite the empirical fact that we do in fact experience a world, whether in sensation or in the experience of the flow of time in reflecting self-consciously on the fact of thinking, in order to conclude that the actual world that we perceive must be maximally consistent. Experiential data cannot count as evidence in non-circular reasoning to show that the actual world is maximally consistent. Thankfully, inspection of the states of affairs we experience is not the only methodology to which we are limited. We are no more required to survey each state of affairs and consider them in all their complex relations in order to know that the actual world is maximally consistent than we are required to go door-to-door with a questionnaire in order to find out if all bachelors are unmarried. A single glimpse of the outside world by any of the senses is sufficient to uphold this argument, if we also hold that only a maximally consistent states-of-affairs combination could possibly or even logically possibly be perceived. It will not do to dig in our heels and declare that existent thought cannot be related to what is nonexistent. That assumption, in the first place, might not even be true; it disguises, in any case, rather than exposes, the interesting conceptual connections that need to be articulated in order to explain why only a maximally consistent world is experienceable. If there is just an eye (and brain), and nothing else outside it, not even a single light-ray, the eye might still be able to perceive by virtue of internal changes of state.

We only make things worse if we proceed to argue that there must be an actual world in order for anything to be perceived, on the assumption that the fact of perception implies a change of state, and that there can be no changes of state except in physical space and time, the lonely eye and brain changing internal states in the impenetrable darkness. The trouble is that with each step we are wandering farther and farther away from pure philosophical ontology into applied scientific ontology. If we simply stipulate that any experienceable world is actual, and then argue as above that the experienced world is the only uniquely existent actual world, then we seem merely to be insisting on the fact of a connection between experience and actuality without analysing its meaning or explaining its conceptual structure. An argument to the effect that we do in fact experience the world and that we could only experience a maximally consistent world is not absurd, but it is also not the best we can do.

Ultimately, we want to be able to maintain that any logically possible world is actual if and only if it is identical with the actual world, and that the actual world is nevertheless logically contingent. We quantify alike over the actual world and non-actual merely logically possible worlds, even though, as a consequence of our reform of modal semantics, only the actual world exists. In doing so, we in effect quantify over one maximally consistent and indefinitely many submaximally consistent states-of-affairs combinations, which is equivalently to quantifying over one actualized and many unactualized logical possibilities.

As might be expected, combinatorial pure philosophical ontology has a non-empirical non-experiential way of proving that the actual world is maximally consistent. We know that there must exist *an* actual world, and we know that there can exist at most one actual world. We do not try to prove that the actual world, in particular the world we experience, is maximally consistent, regardless of whatever conceptual linkages might be adduced. Accordingly, we shall not try to justify the choice of "$w_@$" as a substitution instance for "α" in the definition of actuality, except by arguing that $w_@$ is the one and only actual world, and hence the only logically possible truth-preserving substitution for "α", together with designations for any particular actual states of affairs or existent entities in $w_@$. We require a principle to mediate the application of alethic modalities of necessity, possibility and actuality, from propositions to worlds, particularly because we do not interpret worlds as proposition sets. Accordingly, we offer the following equivalence to justify the modality of a logically possible world in terms of the modality of the propositions true in or of that world, $\forall w_i[\Box w_i \leftrightarrow \forall p[p^{w_i} \rightarrow \Box p]]$. Similarly for the modal qualification of a logically possible world as logically possible or actual, substituting "$\Diamond$" or "Δ" respectively for "$\Box$". It is sufficient for present purposes that it is logically necessary for there to be included in the totality of all states-of-affairs combinations at least one combination that is maximally consistent. This shows, assuming that only the actual world is maximally consistent, that the actual world actually exists, $MaxCon.w_@ \rightarrow \Delta w_@$. We argue that $\Box MaxCon.w_@$, from which, together with the assumption that $\Box\forall x[MaxCon.x \rightarrow \Delta x]$, we deduce the necessary actuality of the actual world, $\Box\Delta w_@$ and $\Box\Delta\exists w_i\Delta w_i$. We can then prove $\forall w_i[MaxCon.w_i \leftrightarrow w_i = w_@]$ and $\forall w_i[w_i \neq w_@ \leftrightarrow \neg MaxCon.w_i]$.[4]

Logical solution to the question of being in combinatorial pure philosophical ontology

We argue that logically necessarily if a maximally consistent states-of-affairs combination possibly exists, then it exists. The combination exists as a logical possibility in the first instance, as a logically possible combination of logically possible objects and logically possible properties. It is then shown to be actual by virtue of satisfying the definition of actuality as maximal consistency.

We are logically guaranteed the logical possibility of every logically consistent states-of-affairs combination. We prove that there must be a maximally consistent logically possible world, and hence an actual world. Then we prove that there can be only one uniquely actual world, from the intermediate conclusion that logically there can be only one maximally consistent states-of-affairs combination. The maximally consistent states-of-affairs combination by virtue of being maximal eats up all the maximal consistency available, depriving other non-actual merely logically possible worlds of the (especially relational) object–property combinations they would need in order to be independently predicationally complete.

For convenience in what follows, we adopt a standard notation involving restricted quantification over worlds. We consider the modal status of individual propositions and logically possible worlds alike, on the grounds that a logically possible world can be construed as a long conjunction of propositions that collectively express all the states of affairs included in a world's states-of-affairs combination. We permit modal qualifications of some of these restrictedly quantified sentences, where, in an obvious sense, to speak of logical possibility is already to speak of truth in at least one logically possible world, and to speak of logical necessity is already to speak of truth in every logically possible world. Such retranslations are naturally possible, but not as illuminating as allowing the iterations of both forms of reference over all or some worlds, to remind us that some of our assumptions and conclusions are supposed to be logically necessary, and that these are interpreted by reference to worlds as maximally consistent states-of-affairs combinations.

We can now further formalize some of these inferences. We add abbreviations for a function of logically possible combinations (*Combo*) of logically possible predication objects (*Object*) and logically possible properties (*Property*), indicating membership in a combination by the inclusion sign ($\in$). We begin by formalizing the argument that logically combinatorially there must exist an actual world – something rather than nothing must exist.

Logically necessarily, there exists a maximally consistent world:

1. $\Box \exists w_i[[MaxCon.w_i \wedge w_i \in \forall x \,|\, Combo(\forall y \,|\, Object.y,$
   $\forall z \,|\, Property.z).x] \leftrightarrow \Diamond \exists w_i[MaxCon.w_i \wedge w_i \in$
   $\forall x \,|\, Combo(\forall y \,|\, Object.y, \forall z \,|\, Property.z).x]]$

   Df. *MaxCon*

2. $\Box \Diamond \exists w_i[MaxCon.w_i \wedge w_i \in \forall x \,|\, Combo(\forall y \,|\, Object.y,$
   $\forall z \,|\, Property.z).x]]$ Combinatorics

3. $\Box \exists w_i[MaxCon.w_i \wedge w_i \in \forall x \,|\, Combo(\forall y \,|\, Object.y,$
   $\forall z \,|\, Property.z).x]]$ (1, 2)

4. $\Box \exists w_i MaxCon.w_i$ (3)

The core of the combinatorial analysis of the concept of being is that it authorizes deducing the necessary existence of a world on the grounds that necessarily it is logically possible for there to be a maximally consistent states-of-affairs or object–property combination. This, the theory maintains, is what it means for a world to exist. We expand the inference from 1–4 above by citing the logical necessity that the mere logical possibility of a maximally consistent states-of-affairs combination implies its existence, together with the proposition that it is logically necessary that it is logically possible that there exist a maximally consistent states-of-affairs combination.[5] The argument states:

5. $\Box[\Diamond \exists w_i MaxCon.w_i \rightarrow \exists w_i MaxCon.w_i]$ Df *MaxCon*

6. $\Box \Diamond \exists w_i MaxCon.w_i$ Combinatorics

---

7. $\Box \exists w_i MaxCon.w_i$ (5, 6 Modal logic)

We note that assumption 5 is not universal, but applies specifically to worlds or maximally or submaximally consistent states-of-affairs combinations. Now we apply either conclusion 4 or 7 above to prove:

Why there is something rather than nothing – logically, there must exist an actual world:

8. $\Box \forall x[MaxCon.x \rightarrow \Delta x]$ Df. $\Delta \rightarrow$

---

9. $\Box \exists w_i \Delta w_i$ (4 or 7, 8 Modal logic)

10. $\exists w_i \Delta w_i$ (9 $\Box p \rightarrow p$, *a fortiori*)

11. $\Delta \exists w_i \Delta w_i$ (10 $p \rightarrow \Delta p$, *a fortiori*)

12. $\Box \Delta \exists w_i \Delta w_i$ (8, 9, 11 Modal logic)

In conclusion 11 we argue somewhat redundantly that an actual world actually exists. In principle, there need be no limit to how many times we iterate the actuality operator. Similarly, there need be no limit to how many times we iterate a possibility operator; in practice, it is not especially helpful to continue beyond statement 11, by deriving, as we could, $\Delta \Delta \exists w_i \Delta w_i$, $\Delta \Delta \Delta \exists w_i \Delta w_i$ and so on. Instead, we prove 12, relying only on the necessary truth of propositions 8 and 9, to derive conclusion 11, which, if the inference is deductively valid, must be as logically necessary as the two assumptions from which it is inferred. Thus, we prove that it is logically necessary that there exists an actual world. Now we formalize the previous argument to establish the unique actuality of the actual world.[6]

Unique existence of the actual world

The proof depends on the assumption that a maximally consistent combination of all logically possible objects and all logically possible properties into all logically possible states of affairs is unique. If there were other states of affairs that could be consistently added to such a combination, it would not after all be maximally consistent, but at best submaximal. We do not propose to prove formally the uniqueness of maximal consistency, but to formalize it as an assumption from which to derive the conclusion that necessarily an actual world is uniquely actual. This is just to say that logically necessarily there is only one actual world.

Above, we demonstrated the necessary existence of an actual world using only the conditional definition, Df. $\Delta \to$, $\Box \forall x[MaxCon.x \to \Delta x]$, and avoided the circularity with which we were concerned. We can therefore avail ourselves now of the full biconditional combinatorial analysis of the concept of being, Df. $\Delta \leftrightarrow$, $\Box \forall x[MaxCon.x \leftrightarrow \Delta x]$, as provided by Principle 3, to prove the uniqueness of the actual world. As a lemma, we thereby establish the principal conclusion of modal actualism in opposition to the modal realism of conventional model set theoretical modal semantics with its definition of all worlds, including the actual world and nonactual merely logically possible world, as maximally consistent proposition sets. The proof is this:

Why there is only one actual world – there can be at most one maximally consistent world:

13. $\Box \forall x[MaxCon.x \leftrightarrow \Delta x]$ (Df. $\Delta \leftrightarrow$)
14. $\Box \forall w_i[MaxCon.w_i \to \neg \exists w_k[MaxCon.w_k \land w_i \neq w_k]]$
                                         (*MaxCon* Unique)
15. $\Box \forall w_i[\Delta w_i \to \forall w_k[\Delta w_k \to w_i = w_k]]$ (13, 14)

Logical contingency of the actual world

It remains to relate the necessary actual existence of an actual world, $\Box \Delta \exists w_i \Delta w_i$, to the modality of the actual world, $w_@$. Can we validly substitute "$w_@$" for "w_i" in conclusion 12 to obtain $\Box \Delta \Delta w_@$ or $\Box \Delta w_@$?

To prove, on the contrary, that the actuality of the actual world is logically contingent, $\Delta w_@ \land \neg \Box \Delta w_@$, we appeal to the multiplicity of logically possible worlds distinct from $w_@$. We can be sure of their multiplicity because combinatorially we cannot collapse all logically possible worlds into one; there are logically possible combinations of objects and properties in nonexistent merely logically possible states of affairs that do not exist in the actual world. If the combinatorial analysis of being is correct, and it is combinatorially logically necessary that a logically contingent actual world uniquely exists, then intuitively we expect to be able to prove the logically necessary propositions:

$\Box\Delta\exists w_i\Delta w_i$
$\Box\exists w_i\Delta w_i$
$\Box\Delta w_@$

As, indeed, we can; but *not*:

$\exists w_i\Delta\Box w_i$
$\exists w_i\Box w_i$
$\Delta\exists w_i\Box w_i$
$\Delta\exists w_i\Delta\Box w_i$
$\Delta\Box w_@$
$\Box w_@$

As another way of arriving at the same conclusion, consider the following argument. We say that a world is maximally consistent when we write $\exists w_i MaxCon.w_i$. This is a shorthand way of saying:

$$\exists x[MaxCon.x \land x = Combo\forall y\,|\,Object.y, \forall z\,|\,Property.z]$$

Or, equivalently, where *SA* denotes a state of affairs:

$$\exists x[MaxCon.x \land x = Combo\forall y\,|\,SA.y]$$

It is a conclusion of combinatorial pure philosophical ontology that:

$$MaxCon.Combo\forall y\,|\,SA.y \leftrightarrow \Delta w_@$$

We are accordingly entitled to make the following inference, deriving the *de dicto* logically necessary existence of something (rather than nothing, an actual world); the *de dicto* logically necessary existence of the actual world; and the *de dicto* logically necessary actuality of the actual world:[7]

1. $\Box\forall x[[MaxCon.x \land x = Combo\forall y\,|\,SA.y] \to [x = w_@ \land \Delta x]]$	Actuality
2. $\Box\exists x[MaxCon.x \land x = Combo\forall y\,|\,SA.y]$	Combinatorics
3. $\Box\exists x\Delta x$	[1, 2]
4. $\Box\exists x[x = w_@ \land \Delta x]$	[1, 2]
5. $\Box\Delta w_@$	[4]

Again, what cannot be proved from any of the assumptions we have considered is the *de re* logical necessity of the actual world. It is true in combinatorial pure philosophical ontology, in other words, that $\neg\exists x\Box[x = w_@ \wedge \Delta x]$ or $\neg\Delta\Box w_@$ or $\neg\Box w_@$. We shall now see how the required restrictions permit the above inferences of the *de dicto* necessary existence of the actual world, and prohibit inferences of the *de re* necessary existence of the actual world, which would collapse logical contingency and freedom of action and will into logical determinacy.

The excluded inferences in the second list contradict the logical contingency of the actual world considered as one among innumerably many logically possible worlds that might have existed instead. We introduce inference rules for the modal actuality opertor, Δ, formally defining the modality. Proof of the antitheorem $\neg[\Box\Delta p \to \Delta\Box p]$ that safeguards the logical contingency of the logically necessarily actual world is then routine but still instructive. Up until this point, we have relied on an intuitive understanding of the laws of logical inference governing the delta modal operator Δ, and have not needed to support any implications involving its logical properties. We now present formal inference rules in support of the subsequent demonstration:

Inference rules for modal actuality operator Δ

$$\frac{p}{\Delta p} \qquad \frac{\Delta p}{p} \qquad \frac{\Delta\neg p}{\neg\Delta p} \qquad \frac{\neg\Delta p}{\Delta\neg p} \qquad \frac{\Delta\exists x p}{\exists x\Delta p} \qquad \frac{\exists x\Delta p}{\Delta\exists x p}$$

Proof of antitheorem: $\neg[\Box\Delta p \to \Delta\Box p]$

1.	$\neg\Box p$	Assumption
2.	$\Box\Delta p$	Hypothesis for *reductio*
3.	$\Box\Delta p \to \Delta\Box p$	Hypothesis for *reductio*
4.	$\Delta\neg\Box p$	[1 Δ Rule]
5.	$\neg\Delta\Box p$	[4 Δ Rule]
6.	$\neg\Box\Delta p$	[3, 5 *Modus tollendo tollens*]
7.	$\neg[\Box\Delta p \to \Delta\Box p]$	[2, 3, 6 *Reductio ad absurdum*]
8.	$\Delta p \to p$	[Δ Rule]
9.	$\Box[\Delta p \to p]$	[8 Necessitation]
10.	$\Box\Delta p \to \Box p$	[9 Modal logic]
11.	$\Box p \to \Delta\Box p$	[Δ Rule]
12.	$\Box\Delta p \to \Delta\Box p$	[10, 11]
13.	$\neg\Box\Delta p$	[2, 7, 12 *Reductio ad absurdum*]
14.	$\neg\Box p \to \neg\Box\Delta p$	[1, 13]

Let p be a contingently true proposition, that pigs wallow. Then we have $\neg\Box p$ in the second assumption, without any argument. It would be circular, even in this elementary proof context, simply to assume that $\neg\Box w_{@}$, even though our immediate purpose is not to prove that $\neg\Box w_{@}$, but only negatively that $\Box w_{@}$ cannot validly be deduced from $\Box\Delta w_{@}$. It is therefore enough to suppose that there is at least one logically non-necessary proposition that is necessarily actual, in order to show that there is no valid deduction from necessary actuality to actual necessity. This is enough to establish the logical contingency of the condition of the actual world, despite the logical necessity of its existence.

What about $\Box\Delta p$? Is it obvious that it is logically necessary that actually pigs wallow? Not in the absence of a combinatorial modal ontological theory perhaps. We recall that we are dealing not only with any random proposition p in the case we are interested in, but with the proposition Δp that in context has been validly derived from two logically necessary assumptions. As long as the proposition that, or state of affairs in which, pigs wallow is true of, or exists, in the actual world, then we are justified in the problem at issue to infer $\Box\Delta p$ from Δp, which we stipulate accordingly above as the first hypothesis. We prove, even on the strength of the first hypothesis, proclaiming the logical necessity of the actuality of p, that we cannot validly derive the logical necessity of p itself, in the form $\Delta\Box p$ or $\Box p$, for any proposition p. Thus, an inference that would threaten the logical contingency of the condition as opposed to the existence of the actual world, in the sense of the particular states of affairs that constitute the actual world, is blocked.

What can we say more positively about the modal status of the actual world's constituent states of affairs? Is the logically necessarily existent uniquely actual world also logically necessary in all of its constituent states of affairs, or is it logically contingent? There are at least some different states of affairs that distinguish the states-of-affairs combinations to which they belong as world-variable states. These are effectively spatiotemporal physical states, which must vary from logically possible world to logically possible world, discounting nonexistent or universally distributed abstract states of affairs as before. The only way for distinct logically possible worlds to collapse into a single logically possible world would be if the one and only logically possible world consisted of nothing but abstract logically necessary states of affairs, such as the truths of logic and mathematics.

It follows in combinatorial ontology that there must be distinct logically possible worlds. Only one among all logically possible worlds, the uniquely actual world, actually exists. All others are only potentially existent, in the sense that they could and would have existed if they had been maximally instead of submaximally consistent. The possibility of logically possible worlds different in the condition of their physical states from the actual world is sufficient to uphold the actual world's logical contingency. This is an important implication, because if there were no worlds distinct from the actual world, then the actual world would be logically necessary in all its constituent states of affairs, including all its physical states of affairs. This would clearly not be a conclusion in which to rejoice. The implication is unsavoury not only because it does not agree with our intuitive interpretation of the contingency of events in the actual world, but more importantly because it involves an intrusion of pure ontology this time on applied ontology's turf. Pure philosophical ontology, aimed at answering the question of being, should not dictate terms to applied scientific ontology concerning the existence of any particular states of affairs. If pure philosophical ontology determines that the physical state of the actual world is logically necessary, then it crosses the line. It implies that the particular states of affairs that exist in the actual world are the only ones that could logically possibly be recognized as existent by any competent applied scientific ontology. In effect, it tries to usurp applied ontology's work in advance of completing its own project of explaining what it means for something to exist.

The physical and mental events with which we are familiar, however we may later sort out their applied ontology, may or may not be causally necessary. It would be straining to interpret such occurrences as anything but logically contingent. I may have baby-blue eyes, but it is logically possible that, like 60 per cent of all human beings, I have brown eyes instead. In another world, we can easily stipulate a states-of-affairs combination in which I have differently pigmented irises. A little logically possible chromosomal cut-and-paste at the right stage of my embryonic development is all it should take. The logically possible brown-eyed me does not actually exist, because that logically possible me is not maximally consistent in all his (or her?) predications. What is my height? What is my gender? What is my native language? Am I friends with Napoleon in that world? Do I learn to fly a helicopter? What are the further genetic and historical ramifications of altering my eye colour in another logically possible world? It is one thing to wave a hand and say, as conventional modal logicians do, that there exists a logically possible world in which I have brown rather than blue eyes. Do we ever thereby manage to refer to a predicationally complete world? Or do we not rather inevitably leave almost all properties of the objects in such a world unspecified? Why in modal logic should we ever feel the need to pretend otherwise?

If the actual world should turn out to be the only logically possible world, if all logical possibility were to collapse into actuality, we would still have a logical answer to the question of being. We could continue even in that extreme case to say that there is something rather than nothing because there must exist an actual world, where the actual world in all its physical states is logically necessary rather than logically contingent. This, we must re-emphasize, is the very opposite conclusion indicated by a combinatorial pure philosophical ontology. In a combinatorial framework, the logical possibility of transworld-variant world-distinguishing physical properties must be taken into account as among the totality of logically possible combinations of all logically possible objects with all logically possible properties in all logically possible states of affairs.

The physical states of affairs that we might know about from our experience of the actual world are real, they happen to exist, but are not logically necessary. If we trace effect to cause back far enough we find more and more contributing events explainable only as an outcome of pure chance. Consider only that your mother happened to meet your father. Almost every couple has a story of sheer coincidence to tell about how they came together or how they produced their offspring. Additional chance occurrences determine whether or not a woman with child survives the kinds of disease or accidents that threaten their destruction. The same is true of all spatiotemporal occurrences involving physical entities and states of affairs in the actual world. We can, in other words, to answer a previous question, and we should, authorize the substitution of "$w_@$" for "w_i" in conclusion 12, on the grounds that "$w_@$" is our name for the actual world, whose reference we are entitled to stipulate once we have proved that there is only one actual world. That the actual world is logically necessarily actual does not entail that the actual world is logically necessary. We can now formalize these inferences concerning the actuality and logical contingency of the actual world.

Why the actual world is logically contingent – there are other actually nonexistent logically possible worlds:

16. $\exists w_i[\Delta w_i \wedge w_i = w_@]$	(10 @-Nominalization)
17. $\forall w_i[\Diamond w_i \rightarrow \Diamond \Delta w_i]$	Possible actuality
18. $\exists w_i[\Diamond w_i \wedge w_i \neq w_@]$	Multiplicity of $\Diamond$ worlds distinct from @
19. $\exists w_i[\Diamond w_i \wedge w_i \neq w_@]$	(17, 18)
20. $\Delta w_@ \wedge \Box \Delta w_@ \wedge \neg \Box w_@$	(12, 15, 16, 19)

It is worth knowing that, even in the strongest standard systems of modal logic, we can validly derive $\Box \exists w_i[\Delta w_i \wedge w_i = w_@]$ and $\Box \Delta w_@$, but not $\Box w_@$. The latter would blatantly contradict the conclusion in 20. Logically necessarily, there exists an actual world; logically necessarily there exists at most one actual world, which is to say *the* actual world, $w_@$. The actual world is nevertheless not logically necessary but logically contingent in all its constituent states of affairs, and in particular in all its transworld-variant physical states of affairs.[8]

Unique actuality of the actual world

We now express the unique actuality of the actual world more directly than by appealing as in 14 to the conclusion of an informal argument to show there can at most be one maximally consistent states-of-affairs combination. We can say more simply, relying on the combinatorial uniqueness of maximal consistency and its implications for the combinatorial uniqueness of the actual world, that, logically necessarily, the actual world is uniquely actual. We now demonstrate that:

The actual world is uniquely actual:

21. $\Box \forall w_i[\Delta w_i \leftrightarrow \Delta w_i]$		Tautology
22. $\Box \forall w_i[\Delta w_i \leftrightarrow \Delta w_@]$		(15, 21 @-Nominalization)
23. $\Box \forall w_i[\Delta w_i \leftrightarrow w_i = w_@]$		(22)

Actuality defined as maximal consistency combinatorially guarantees that logically something must be actual. There is logically certain to be some physical being, something rather than nothing. While necessarily there exists something rather than nothing, what exists is a matter of pure chance, of combinatorial roulette. If a different combination had been maximally consistent, a different logically possible world other than $w_@$ would exist instead of $w_@$, although whatever logically possible world actually happens to exist could still be called $w_@$. The logical possibility that a combination of states of affairs and ultimately of objects and properties other than those that constitute the actual world might have been maximally consistent is enough to assure that the actual world in all its particularity is logically contingent.

Combinatorial pure philosophical ontology

The combinatorial theory of pure philosophical ontology that we have now developed is not intended as a contribution to applied scientific ontology. It makes no ontological commitment to any particular preferred theoretical domain of existent entities, states of affairs or worlds. All such important discoveries are left to applied scientific ontology.

To criticize the reduction of ontology to logic misses the mark if it merely states the obvious but irrelevant fact that logical form lacks sufficient substantive ontological content to derive a domain of existent entities. The questions of pure philosophical ontology for which logic offers insight are conceptual, asking what it means for something to exist, rather than what actually exists. We should not conclude that logic cannot offer the required explanation just because we cannot conjure an actually existent bunny, or even a theoretical commitment to its existence, wriggling out of a logical magician's silk hat. Logic, of course, can do no such thing. The objection misfires by assuming that a reduction of ontology to logical form is supposed to provide answers to problems of applied scientific ontology by deriving a preferred existence domain of actually existent entities. The possibilities of logical form, on the contrary, are intended instead to answer another very different specific question about the nature of being or meaning of existence in pure philosophical ontology considered exclusively as a discipline.

To avoid equivocation, we proceed carefully, distinguishing the questions and answers appropriate to divisions among the four meanings of ontology, avoiding conclusions that stand in cross-categorial purposes to its distinctions. If and when we answer the problems of pure philosophical ontology, we are entitled to move on to the task of identifying a preferred existence domain as the goal of applied scientific ontology. If we do our work well, then the preferred existence domain we recommend on paper as a result of our theoretical deliberations will also be the extant domain consisting of the actual world and all actually existent entities. We produce a system of categories of existent entities adequate to explain the meaning of thought and discourse. We then commit applied scientific ontology as a discipline to a particular applied scientific domain, the theoretical content of which should ideally correspond perfectly to the real extant order of existent entities. Logic assumes a secondary role in applied ontology as a discipline. It is useful in developing a correct criterion of ontological commitment, and as a watchdog supervising the inferences we make in trying to establish a preferred theoretical existence domain, particularly with regard to the cardinality of infinitary and transinfinitary logical domains. Yet it does not decide any more interesting substantive questions of applied scientific ontology.

Why is there something rather than nothing? Why is there only one actual world? If the reason is supposed to be logical rather than experiential, is the actual world itself logically necessary or logically contingent? If abstract objects and relations are indistinguishably the same for every logically possible world, and if we can distinguish logically possible worlds only as distinct totalities of physical states of affairs, are the actual physical states of affairs that characterize the actual world logically necessary or logically contingent? These questions are not purely academic. If events in the actual world are logically necessary, as some philosophers have believed, then it becomes a problem to uphold common-sense belief in free will, freedom of action and moral responsibility.

The presupposition of logic that we can predicate properties to objects makes it intelligible to refer to predication subjects and the properties predicated of them, without which there would be no philosophical problem of their ontological status. We can at least provisionally speak of objects as possible predication subjects and the properties predicated of them, by virtue of which the problem of the ontology of objects and properties makes sense. When an object, whatever an object is and whether or not it exists, whether it is or is not something more than a logical predication subject, has a property, whatever a property is and whether or not properties exist, then the object's having a property is a state of affairs, while a logically possible world, including the actual world, and even a logically impossible model, is constituted by states of affairs, ultimately by objects having properties. We have used this minimalist logical vocabulary to gain footing among the difficult questions of pure philosophical ontology. We reserve until afterwards, when it is appropriate at last to address the problems of applied scientific ontology, to consider the ontic status of objects and specific types of objects and properties, states of affairs and non-actual merely logically possible worlds.

We have argued that to exist is to be maximally consistent. The combinatorial analysis of the concept of being implies that there is something rather than nothing because in the ontically neutral predication sense there must be a maximally consistent combination of logical objects with properties. We have said that combinatorially there must be variations among the physical states in distinct logically possible worlds, and that the actual world is logically contingent because all physical states of the actual world are logically contingent. Pure philosophical ontology has now done its job, and can hand over its analysis of the concept of being for use in applied scientific ontology. The existence of physical states of affairs and the potential convenience of referring to abstract entities, including logical objects and properties, logical states of affairs, and the like, as candidate items to include in a preferred existence domain, provide an obvious bridge to the ontic sciences. We are ready to begin applying the answer to the question of being, to the analysis of the concept of being as maximal consistency which we have proposed, to some of the most interesting specialized fields of applied scientific ontology.

Applied ontology and the
II metaphysics of science

Ontological commitment
6 (on Quine)

A syntactical criterion

To be ontologically committed is to accept the existence of an entity or type or kind or category of entities. As individual thinkers we make ontological commitments to the things we believe exist, while theories in the abstract are ontologically committed to whatever entities would need to exist in order for the theories to be true.

The first task of applied ontology is to establish adequate *criteria of ontological commitment*. Without these we will not be able to certify a preferred existence domain, as an applied ontology must, because we will not be able to distinguish one existence domain from another. We further need such criteria in order to identify the respective ontological commitments of competing scientific theories, especially when theory choice is supposed to be guided by considerations of explanatory economy, and where the search for a preferred existence domain is conditioned at least in part by the choice of a preferred science.

In "On What There Is", W. V. O. Quine offers a *syntactical criterion of ontological commitment*. We are required to translate a theory such as Copernicus's astronomy or Darwin's biology into a canonical notation in first-order predicate logic, and then determine the domain of objects corresponding to each quantifier-bound variable in the translation that must exist in order for the propositions of the theory to be true. The idea of Quine's syntactical criterion is to begin with a theory that says, in effect, there are chromosomes or there are unicorns, whose ontological commitments are to be determined. We first translate these commitment sentences into a canonical notation like that of standard first-order symbolic logic, to obtain, respectively: $\exists x Cx$ and $\exists x Ux$. The theories are then said to be ontologically committed to whatever entities must belong to the extensions of predicates "C" and "U" in order for the sentences of the theories to be true. The syntactical criterion of ontological commitment is summarized in Quine's slogan that "To be is to be the value of a [quantifier-bound] variable" – a formula in which the ambiguity between being in the existence and predication senses is explicit.

A theory like that of chromosomes or unicorns is true or false depending, among other things, on whether or not the ontological commitments of the theory are included in what we have called the extant domain of actually existent entities. (The theory must not only be ontologically committed to actually existent entities, but it must say only true things about, or truly predicate properties of, these entities.) Quine further adopts a metaphilosophical position that he calls *ontological relativism*, according to which we can never attain a perfectly objective theory-independent overview of all ontic choices. He argues that as ontologists we enter a competition in which we try to determine a correct ontology already laden with ontic baggage that can affect even the interpretation and understanding of another theory's ontology, as it influences our judgement about whether this or that ontological commitment is correct, whether a proposed theoretical existence domain is coextensive with the relevant extant subdomain.

This alone, paradoxically, should be enough to discredit the bound-variable criterion of ontological commitment. We are required to check the bound variables of correctly canonically formalized theories and interpret the values of the variables as a theory's ontological commitment. The first step in Quine's syntactical criterion appears easy and obvious. We begin by translating a theory into canonical logical notation. If ontological relativity prevails, however, as Quine admits, then his syntactical criterion encounters serious difficulties right at the outset. We are bound to distort the ontological commitments of a theory that is sufficiently different from our own, especially if the theory has an interestingly different metaphysics that cannot be adequately formalized in a Quinean logic. If a theory whose ontological commitments are to be determined is truly unlike our own, then we will not be able to rightly recognize it as such by Quine's criterion. We cannot decide, in that case, how to translate a radically ontologically different theory into a canonical bound-variable logical notation, because for such a theory we cannot know what is or is not supposed to be a logically possible object and what is or is not supposed to be a logically possible property.[1] If Quine's criterion remains the best that we can do, then we may simply have to live within its limitations, despite knowing in advance that it is sure to be a crude instrument for judging the ontological commitments of ontically remote theories.

Pure and applied ontology in Quine

Quine's oft-quoted opening remarks in "On What There Is" appear irrefutably commonsensical, but actually embody a confusion about the tasks of pure and applied ontology. Quine declares:

> A curious thing about the ontological problem is its simplicity. It can be put in three Anglo-Saxon monosyllables: "What is there?" It can be answered, moreover, in a word – "Everything" – and everyone will accept this answer as true. However, this is merely to say that there is what there is. There remains room for disagreement over cases; and so the issue has stayed alive down the centuries.[2]

Quine's question, "What is there?", seems to require an applied scientific ontological answer. Perhaps there are physical entities; perhaps there are abstract entities of particular sorts. We must be prepared to dispute efforts to specify a preferred existence domain offered from distinct philosophical perspectives. In contrast, the answer Quine half-seriously gives, "Everything", is a more appropriate type of reply to be tendered in pure philosophical ontology. For Quine, the "everything" that exists is understood extensionally as incorporating everything in applied scientific ontology in the sense of the preferred actually extant existence domain of real existent entities. When he answers the ontological question by saying that everything exists, he evidently means something rather uninformative: that every entity, every existent thing, exists. A superficial agreement concerning only the form of the reply is assumed, inviting disagreement over cases as to the details of content in answering questions about what there is.

Quine presents a syntactical criterion of ontological commitment that depends on an extensional interpretation of the quantifiers in the canonical notation of first-order symbolic logic and its natural language equivalents. The essential passages in which Quine articulates the criterion begin with these remarks:

> We commit ourselves to an ontology containing numbers when we say there are prime numbers larger than a million; we commit ourselves to an ontology containing centaurs when we say there are centaurs; and we commit ourselves to an ontology containing Pegasus when we say Pegasus is. But we do not commit ourselves to an ontology containing Pegasus or the author of *Waverly* or the round square cupola on Berkeley College when we say that

Pegasus or the author of *Waverly* or the cupola in question is *not*. We need no longer labor under the delusion that the meaningfulness of a statement containing a singular term presupposes an entity named by the term. A singular term need not name to be significant.[3]

Quine paves the way for the bound-variable criterion of ontological commitment by identifying its equivalent in ordinary language. We commit ourselves ontologically to the existence of a certain entity or type of entity when we say sincerely and assertorically, even if falsely, that such a thing or type of thing exists. There is a large variety of colloquial devices for expressing ontological commitments, which Quine associates with the use of pronouns such as "he", "she" and "it", all of which are formally expressed by means of quantifier bound variables, like the "x" in $(\exists x)Fx$, which is usually informally interpreted as saying, "There *is* or there *exists* an entity x, such that $x - it$, pronomially – has property F". Quine adds:

> To be assumed as an entity is, purely and simply, to be reckoned as the value of a variable. In terms of the categories of traditional grammar, this amounts roughly to saying that to be is to be in the range of reference of a pronoun. Pronouns are the basic media of reference; nouns might better have been named propronouns. The variables of quantification, "something", "nothing", "everything", range over our whole ontology, whatever it may be; and we are convicted of a particular ontological presupposition if, and only if, the alleged presupposition has to be reckoned among the entities over which our variables range in order to render one of our affirmations true.[4]

The syntactical criterion is explicated in terms Quine has widely popularized in philosophical logic and ontology:

> I have argued that the sort of ontology we adopt can be consequential – notably in connection with mathematics, although this is only an example. Now how are we to adjudicate among rival ontologies? Certainly the answer is not provided by the semantical formula "To be is to be the value of a variable"; this formula serves rather, conversely, in testing the conformity of a given remark or doctrine to a prior ontological standard. We look to bound variables in connection with ontology not in order to know what there is, but in order to know what a given remark or

doctrine, ours or someone else's, *says* there is; and this much is quite properly a problem involving language. But what there is is another question.[5]

The bound-variable criterion, Quine is clear, does not determine what actually exists. By itself, it does not provide a factual inventory of the extant domain of actually existent entities, which only a true and complete theory of the world or complete conjunction of all true theories can supply. The syntactical criterion instead provides a way of establishing the ontological commitments of a given theory in the sense of the theoretical existence domain needed for the propositions of the theory to be true. Conditionally, so to speak, *if* the theory in competition with all of the alternatives should turn out to be true, *then* these values of quantifier variables will be among the actually existent entities.

The syntactical criterion of ontological commitment works well enough in many applications, but also suffers from disabling limitations. In his philosophical logic and semantics, Quine is ontologically committed to a metalinguistic extensionalist semantics by which only tautologies and sentences expressing predications of constitutive properties to actually existent entities are true. It might appear that this is not a serious obstacle to the syntactical criterion, since it speaks only to the question of whether a particular theory is actually true, whatever specific ontological commitments the theory happens to make. The problem is deeper, as we shall see, because it affects Quine's interpretation of quantifiers even in assessing the conditional ontological commitments of conditionally true theories.

Although Quine rightly tries to detach his bound-variable criterion of ontological commitment from the issue in our terminology of the extant domain of actually existent entities, he allows the predications of properties to putative entities to be true only by presupposing the possibility of referring to the entities belonging to the extant domain. In contrast, I doubt that we can make much progress in applied scientific ontology without allowing quantifiers to range freely over entities that belong to a preferred existence domain in the theoretical sense, meeting frequently with putative intended entities that do not actually exist and are not actually members of the extant domain. We cannot apply Quine's syntactical bound-variable criterion of ontological commitment to reach correct conclusions about the distinct theoretical preferred existence domains of ontologically incompatible applied scientific ontologies, or of the scientific or other fields of thought or discourse that require or presuppose such domains, if, as

Quine requires, quantifier semantics refer only to the extant domain of real existent entities, whichever ones they are, in the actual world. The fault lies not with Quine's bound-variable criterion considered in itself, but in the criterion taken together with the extensionalist semantics that, for Quine, is inseparable from a correct theory of meaning.

Critique of Quine's criterion

The underlying problem for Quine's criterion is that it conflates the interpretation of quantifier-bound variables in pure logic with those required by an applied logic in formalizing the principles of a science. What is wanted instead is ontic neutrality in the logical representation of scientific theories and philosophical discourse about their respective ontological commitments. The desired ontic neutrality is precisely what cannot be maintained on Quine's bound-variable criterion, given his extensional quantifier semantics.

If the variables bound by existential quantifiers in the formalization of a theory are logical objects with no specific ontological commitments, as we have proposed in combinatorial pure philosophical ontology, then we attain the necessary ontological neutrality to identify the distinct ontological commitments of different theories and can compare them as impartially as possible. Quine's deeply ingrained extensionalism unfortunately prevents him from acknowledging logical objects in the sense we have prescribed. It entails that a logical formula formalizing a proposition of a theory cannot be meaningful unless the objects and states of affairs to which it is ontologically committed happen actually to exist. A Quinean, as a consequence, cannot intelligibly translate the propositions of alternative false theories that ostensibly make false ontological commitments to objects that do not actually exist. The theories themselves can still be distinguished by exercising what Quine calls *semantic ascent*, talking about the language and terminology of the theories rather than about the actually nonexistent objects to which the theories ostensibly refer.[6] If theory T says that there are unicorns and theory T^* says that there are centaurs, then extensionally the theories have indistinguishable ontologies, both alike being ontologically committed to the null or empty domain, on the assumption that neither unicorns nor centaurs happen to exist.[7] That inevitable confusion of distinct ontological commitments in itself is a problem for Quine, but it is only a symptom of worse difficulties. Why, we must ask, should the effectiveness of a criterion of ontological commitment depend on the contingent facts of the actual world that happen only by pure chance to include zebras and giraffes but no mermaids, unicorns or centaurs?

To make the criterion function properly, Quine *contra* Quine would need to trade-in his extensionalist quantifier semantics for an ontologically neutral reference to logical objects and properties. Quine nevertheless understands the project of scientific semantics in much the same way as Gottlob Frege, interpreting reference and true predications of properties exclusively in terms of actually existent entities.[8] This, to put it mildly, makes it awkward, and in the end not very satisfactory, to understand the meaning and ontological commitments of theories that turn out, as a sheer matter of logically contingent fact, to be false by virtue of their ontological commitments to theoretical existence domains that are not included in what we believe to be the extant domain of actually existent entities.

Quine seems to recognize the need for ontic neutrality at some level in applying his criterion. His strategy for disposing metalinguistically of terms in a language that require reference to actually existent entities derives from Russell's three-part extensionalist analysis of definite descriptions.[9] Where Russell breaks down a sentence of the form "The *F* is *G*" into "There exists at least one *F*, there exists at most one *F*, and that thing is or has property *G*", Quine applies the same existence-presuppositional analysis to avoid the necessity of interpreting sentences containing definite descriptions or names as disguised definite descriptions exhibiting "objective reference" to actually existent entities in the extant domain. Quine introduces two imaginary characters, McX, a realist in metaphysics who incautiously accepts the existence of entities in order to make sense even of true pronouncements of their nonexistence, and his phonetically complementary fellow traveller, Wyman, who tries to explain the semantics of non-being without allowing reference to nonexistents by admitting the existence of unactualized possibles. Quine condemns both approaches, and holds that neither strategy is needed in light of an analysis of the meaning of sentences making ostensible reference to beingless objects. Quine maintains:

> The unanalyzed statement "The author of *Waverly* was a poet" contains a part, "the author of *Waverly*", which is wrongly supposed by McX and Wyman to demand objective reference in order to be meaningful at all. But in Russell's translation, "Something wrote *Waverly* and was a poet and nothing else wrote *Waverly*", the burden of objective reference which had been put upon the descriptive phrase is now taken over by words of the

kind that logicians call bound variables, variables of quantification, namely, words like "something", "nothing", "everything". These words, far from purporting to be names specifically of the author of *Waverly*, do not purport to be names at all; they refer to entities generally, with a kind of studied ambiguity peculiar to themselves. These quantificational words or bound variables are, of course a basic part of language, and their meaningfulness, at least in context, is not to be challenged. But their meaningfulness in no way presupposes there being either the author of *Waverly* or the round square cupola on Berkeley College or any other specifically preassigned objects.[10]

It is quantifiers to the rescue, as by now we should expect. Yet things are not as straightforward as Quine suggests. The reason is that quantifiers themselves are interpreted extensionally by Quine as ranging over the extant domain of actually existent entities, thereby making the Russell–Quine-style analysed sentence "Something wrote *Waverly* and was a poet and nothing else wrote *Waverly*", every bit as ontologically loaded as the original unanalysed sentence "The author of *Waverly* was a poet". How, indeed, could the situation be otherwise if the Russell–Quine paraphrase purports to be an *analysis* of the *meaning* of the original sentence? The analysis would be defective if, in substituting the bound-variable formula for the proper name expression, it let this vital determinant of the sentence's meaning slip through its fingers.

The further crucial question that is not settled by Quine's endorsement of Russell's method is whether in the first place the analysis is correct. The omission is clearly problematic, particularly in the context of trying to establish the ontological commitments of competing theories. The chief difficulty is that on Russell's and Quine's extensional theories of meaning, only actually existent entities actually have properties, while nonentities do not. It is infamous, for example, that on Russell's analysis of definite descriptions the sentences "The winged horse is winged" or "The winged horse has wings" and "The winged horse is a horse" are all false, because in the extant domain of actually existent entities there contingently exist no winged horses. Such an unreflectively extensionalist conclusion is inimical to the intensionalist combinatorial analysis of being as maximal consistency. The combinatorial theory entails that nonexistent entities considered only as logical objects as truly have the properties by which they are constituted as do the actually existent entities that happen to populate the actual world.

Nor is this merely a conflict between the combinatorial analysis versus Russell's and Quine's analysis of definite descriptions. Intuitively, it seems correct to say that the winged horse is winged and a horse, even though no winged horse actually exists. That, it might reasonably be said, is precisely why the winged horse does not exist, because the properties it has, that are truly attributed to it, are not manifested by any actually existent winged or equine entity. If the winged horse does not fail to exist because its property combination, although containing at least the properties of being winged and a horse, is otherwise predicationally incomplete despite being consistent, then what is the explanation of its nonexistence? If the nonexistence of the winged horse is merely the fact that the actual world does not happen to contain a horse with wings, then we have only restated the fact of the winged horse's nonexistence, and not taken any steps toward explaining the fact. We have not, in that case, undertaken to clarify what it means for the winged horse not to exist, or for the actual world contingently not to contain a winged horse in the extant domain of actually existent entities.

Quine claims that the descriptive fragment "the author of *Waverly*" in the sentence "The author of *Waverly* was a poet" does not need to carry objective reference in order to be meaningful. This is true only in the limited sense according to which Quine is willing to unpack the meaning of the sentence in terms of Russell's theory of definite descriptions. He rightly observes that the "objective reference" of the term, analysed or unanalysed, does not disappear under analysis, but is instead taken up by an existential quantifier of appropriate scope within the analysis and by the same range of "objective" entities. These are not just the putative entities that are recommended in a preferred theoretical existence domain, but the actually existent entities of the extant domain. It is mystifying, nonetheless, why and by what philosophical considerations Quine should impose this extensionalist requirement on the meaning of sentences in theories whose ontological commitment is to be established by the syntactical bound-variable criterion, when in the present context he does not try to specify a "correct" ontology.[11]

Quine thereby undermines the impression of achieving any degree of neutrality in the syntactical criterion of ontological commitment. He does not go far enough, in the end, when in the passage quoted above he says only that the "meaningfulness [of the quantifiers] in no way presupposes there being either the author of *Waverly* or the round square cupola on Berkeley College or any other specifically preassigned objects". This is true enough, but the meaning of the quantifiers is hardly the issue. Where we require ontic neutrality in a correct criterion of ontological commitment is rather in understanding the existence claims made by false theories involving predications of null extension that are ostensibly ontologically committed to things that do not happen to exist. Quine's qualification is true only because the meaning of quantifiers in his extensionalist semantics is fixed relative to the extant domain of actually existent entities. He does not unpack a sentence about the round square cupola on Berkeley College as having, say, the property of being round and the property of being square, a cupola, located somewhere on or at Berkeley College, and so on. If he did so according to Russell's three-part analysis of definite descriptions, then, assuming there exists and can exist no round square entity, he would obtain only false sentences. The round square cupola is not round, not square and not a cupola, and fails necessarily to adorn Berkeley College.

What, then, are we talking about when we utter the phrase "The round square cupola on Berkeley College"? Are we only jabbering? Do we speak literally of nothing, just because what we believe ourselves to be talking about happens not to exist? Or are we talking only about the words that the sentence contains? Why, then, must the *semantic analysis* of the *meaning* of a sentence that *happens* to be about logically contingently actually existent entities have to be so different? Why does a sentence about actually existent entities turn out to be about the objects it purports to be about and not about the words and phrases by which the sentence is expressed in a Quinean semantic ascent? If Quine's theory of ontological commitment taken together with his extensionalist quantifier semantics has these implications, and must answer so implausibly to these reasonable questions, then surely it does not provide the ontic neutrality required for an adequately impartial interpretation of the ontological commitments of competing theories. Quine, rightly for this purpose, but inadequately, says that the meaningfulness of a quantifier does not presuppose the existence of any "specifically preassigned objects". The meaningfulness of a quantifier for Quine, in spite of this disclaimer, significantly presupposes that only actually existent entities can be the values of bound variables, and that only actually existent entities can possibly be the objects of true predications of constitutive properties.

To say that "The round square cupola is round and square and a cupola" is to utter something irredeemably false for Quine. A theory ontologically committed only to the round square cupola could not then be said to have anything whatsoever in its preferred existence domain. That is, paradoxically, that a theory ostensibly ontologically committed only to the round square cupola does not actually have any ontological commitments, and in particular is not and cannot be ontologically committed to the existence of the round square cupola. If it seems too fanciful to suppose that a theory might be ontologically committed to such an obviously predicationally inconsistent putative entity, then consider as a more historically seditious example the recent putative ontological commitments by many of the most respected logicians, analytic philosophers and mathematicians to the existence, and even necessary existence, of a reduction of infinitary arithmetic to the axioms of logic and naive set theory.[12]

If, by Quine's criterion as it now appears, no theory can be ontologically committed to the existence of the round square cupola, and if no theory, due to the contingent facts of existence and non-existence in the actual world, is actually ontologically committed to the existence of a winged horse or phlogiston or vortices or the æther or the planet Vulcan or the philosopher's stone, then in what sense can the bound-variable criterion be correct? In what sense can Quine's criterion deliver an accurate account of the ontological commitments of theories that are ostensibly ontologically committed to what, from the standpoint of the extant domain of actually existent entities, are actually nonexistent entities? Quine's criterion fails the most basic prerequisite for a method of establishing the ontological commitment of a theory if it only gives correct results in the case of theories ontologically committed to the extant domain. It fails precisely because it is not ontically neutral; its extensionalism does not meet the demand for ontic neutrality in the interpretation of quantifiers and bound variables in formalizations of a theory's presumed ontological commitment sentences. It limits the specific meaningfulness of such sentences exclusively to the general meaningfulness of quantifiers. The specific meaning, however, and not merely the meaningfulness of a theory's ontologically committal sentences, must be nailed down in order to establish fine distinctions of ontological commitment among competing theories.

The result of Quine's extensional semantics of quantifiers being dependent on the extant domain of logically contingent actually existent entities is that the determination of ontological commitment is restricted exclusively to true theories ontologically committed to the existence of existent entities, and falls far short in correctly identifying and representing the ontological commitments of false theories. There is thus a kind of semantic arrogance built into any extensionally interpreted quantifier and bound-variable criterion of ontological commitment that favours not only the pale meaningfulness but the exact explicit meaning of sentences in true theories, and distorts when it is not simply oblivious to the meaning of any false theory.

Understanding ontological disputes

As a consequence of his extensional interpretation of the quantifiers in logic and natural languages, Quine is equally unable to make intuitively correct sense of ontological commitment in the case of numbers and universals. These are the purported entities about which logicians and philosophers have raised the most ruckus in traditional metaphysics, exemplified by the realism–nominalism debate that has dominated applied ontology ever since Plato. Quine wants to represent the distinct ontological commitments of both sides and every subtle intermediate theory in this important ontological dispute. He explains:

> Up to now I have argued that we can use singular terms significantly in sentences without presupposing that there are the entities which those terms purport to name. I have argued further that we can use general terms, for example, predicates, without conceding them to be names of abstract entities. I have argued further that we can view utterances as significant, and as synonymous or heteronymous with one another, without countenancing a realm of entities called meanings. At this point McX begins to wonder whether there is any limit at all to our ontological immunity. Does *nothing* we may say commit us to the assumption of universals or other entities which we may find unwelcome?
>
> I have already suggested a negative answer to this question, in speaking of bound variables, or variables of quantification, in connection with Russell's theory of descriptions. We can very easily involve ourselves in ontological commitments by saying, for example, that *there is something* (bound variable) which red houses and sunsets have in common; or that *there is something* which is a prime number larger than a million. But this is, essentially, the *only* way we can involve ourselves in ontological commitments: by our use of bound variables. The use of alleged names is no criterion, for we can repudiate their namehood at the drop of a hat unless the assumption of a corresponding entity can be spotted in the things we affirm in terms of bound variables. Names are, in fact, altogether immaterial to the ontological issue, for I have shown, in connection with "Pegasus" and "pegasize", that names can be converted to descriptions, and Russell has shown that descriptions can be eliminated.[13]

In this expanded version of his previous argument, Quine imagines an applied ontologist who makes an ontological commitment to the existence of a certain universal, red or redness, and a certain prime number. If the extant domain should turn out not to contain these putative abstract entities, then no theory on Quine's bound-variable criterion of ontological commitment with its extensionalist interpretation of the quantifiers can actually be ontologically committed to red or redness or any prime number. We do not, in fact, contrary to Quine's assertion, ontologically commit ourselves in that case to abstract entities by saying that "*there is something* that red houses and sunsets have in common", or that "*there is something* that is a prime number larger than a million". If there are no universals and no numbers, then no theories on Quine's criterion interpreted extensionally, as Quine requires, are committed to such things because there are no such things, no objects (contrary to McX), even merely logically possible objects (contrary to Wyman), that actually possess the properties in question, to which a theory can be committed.

It is incomprehensible in light of the limitations of an extensional interpretation of quantifiers and bound variables in quantified formulations of ontological commitment sentences to suppose that a syntactical criterion can possibly do justice to the ontological commitments of false theories ostensibly ontologically committed to entities that necessarily or per chance do not happen to belong to the extant domain of actually existent entities. Despite this evident limitation, Quine persists in maintaining the opposite, as though his criterion treated the ontological commitments of all theories fairly and alike, when he adds:

> This, I think, is characteristic of metaphysics, or at least of that part of metaphysics called ontology: one who regards a statement on this subject as true at all must regard it as trivially true. One's ontology is basic to the conceptual scheme by which he interprets all experiences, even the most commonplace ones. Judged within some particular conceptual scheme – and how else is judgment possible? – an ontological statement goes without saying, standing in need of no separate justification at all. Ontological statements follow immediately from all manner of casual statements of commonplace fact, just as – from the point of view, anyway, of McX's conceptual scheme – "There is an attribute" follows from "There are red houses, red roses, red sunsets".[14]

Quine boxes himself in by insisting on the ontological relativity of ontological investigations, reinforced by his thesis of the *indeterminacy of radical translation.* If I cannot know in any meaningful way whether a tribesman I encounter as a field linguist means, by "*Gavagai*", "Lo, a rabbit", or, "Lo, a sequence of undetached rabbit parts", how can I hope to know what a scientist who might not exactly share my ontological commitments means by speaking of "mass", "force", "cause" or "momentum"? If, indeed, I cannot penetrate these referential opacities, how can I possibly hope to formalize such discourse in the canonical logical symbolism of first-order logic in order to ascertain the theory's ontological commitments by applying the bound-variable criterion? What could such a theory's predicates mean to me if the ontology and conceptual scheme that are built into my language are so different? How can I decide whether the theory in question is more correctly formalized in terms of predicates or names or indexicals or descriptions or something altogether unfamiliar to the logic at my disposal?[15]

The syntactical criterion of ontological commitment, by Quine's reasoning, is not a perfectly ontically neutral instrument for discovering a theory's ontological commitments. It works properly in identifying ontological commitments only for theories that can be accurately formalized in an already ontically loaded canonical predicate–quantifier notation, and then only in application to theories that happen to make true ontological commitments. That is to say, ironically, that Quine's criterion is subjectively limited by what a user of the method believes to be the extant domain. There is no reason to think, and, in light of Quine's theory of ontological relativity, substantial reason not to believe, that there cannot be thinkers and language users whose ontic framework is radically unlike that of an extensionalist who agrees with Quine about the contents of the preferred existence domain, implicitly assumed by the criterion to be identical with the extant domain. Quine's criterion either imposes the user's ontic categories and ontological commitments on every theory it attempts to judge, or else it must syncretically include all logical notations indiscriminately, regardless of their syntactical compatibility or incompatibility.

Do we know in advance whether we might ever need to use quantified modal logic to represent the propositions of a theory whose ontological commitments are supposed to be judged by Quine's criterion, but that are opposed in interesting ways to Quine's own ontological commitments? Quine resisted quantified modal logic through much of his career, although he seems later to have softened his philosophical objections. If we exclude quantified modal logic from the syntactical criterion's canonical notation, how can we possibly do justice to the ontological commitments of an alien theory of quantified modal logic? Should we ignore it because we "know" that it is false or unsound or deductively unclosed? How do we know that it suffers from any of these logical defects if we cannot first accurately determine its ontological commitments? A correct criterion of ontological commitment must do equally ontically neutral double duty in evaluating the ontological commitments of true and false theories alike.

Quine's objection to quantified modal logic is independent of its ontological commitments. Quine does not rule quantified modal logic out of the canonical notation because he objects to its ontology. He resists quantified modal logic because he believes such systems are intensional, because they do not permit the intersubstitution of coreferential terms or logically equivalent sentences *salva veritate*, and because he believes that logic and the semantics of logic must be purely extensional. Otherwise, he thinks we risk psychologism that results when we try to make logic into something conceptual and subjective. Quine's reasoning in rejecting quantified modal logic can be disputed at every step. The argument to show that quantified modal logic is intensional is not particularly convincing. Quine considers an inference from the true assumptions that $\Box(9 > 7)$ and the number of planets = 9, to the presumably false conclusion, substituting identicals in the second assumption within the modal context of the first assumption, that $\Box$(the number of planets > 7).[16] The problem is that the substitution is unjustified if the assumption that the number of planets = 9 is paraphrased without loss of meaning as a predication rather than a literal statement of numerical identity. What, after all, does pure mathematics know about planets? The assumption might be more accurately entered into a canonical logical notation, not as an identity statement, but as a predication, in which the planets are said to have the property of being nine-fold in number, from which no identity substitutions within or without modal contexts are deductively authorized.[17]

The point remains that if Quine considers it philosophically permissible to exclude a formalism like quantified modal logic from the canonical notation required by the syntactical criterion of ontological commitment, then the criterion does not apply to and cannot be used accurately to determine the ontological commitments of excluded theories. Quine's reason for discounting quantified modal logic is his belief that it is intensional. Even and especially if his argument is correct, and we have argued the contrary, he thereby excludes all intensional theories from proper determination of their radically different ontological commitments by means of the quantifier bound-variable criterion. Is the syntactical criterion unable to judge correctly the ontological commitments of any intensional theory? To exclude intensional theories from the bound-variable criterion is to exercise subjective choice in establishing the ontological commitments of other theories. By maintaining a tight rein on the syntactical criterion's canonical notation, Quine unnecessarily limits its applicability. If he loosens his grip and allows other notations to be added indiscriminately to the canon, then he can no longer keep ontology in the sense of his philosophically preferred existence domain as austere in its ontological commitments as he would like.

An intensionalist using an intensional but, from an intensionalist perspective, equally legitimate deservedly canonical notation, rather than Quine's extensional notation, is sure to produce a different characterization than Quine's of the ontological commitments of the same theories. All this indicates, not that intensionalism is preferable to extensionalism, although we might finally arrive at this conclusion, but that a good criterion of ontological commitment ought to identify the ontological commitments of even those radically opposed general categories of theories, which, regardless of whether they are correct or incorrect, can only be so judged on the basis of their respective correctly specified ontological commitments. The objection implies that it is mistaken for both intensionalists and extensionalists to apply any criterion like Quine's if it is limited to the syntactical properties of any chosen logic or language for expressing a theory's principles. What is wrongheaded about the syntactical criterion is its idea that an already philosophically privileged syntax can be used fairly and accurately to represent the propositions of any other arbitrary theory. Any notation inevitably imposes a choice of prior ontological commitments on the theories it is used to formalize. The conservative exclusionary attitude towards canonical syntax required by Quine's criterion makes every determination of ontological commitment ontically biased.

It would, on the other hand, be logically chaotic to allow the canonical notation of Quine's criterion syncretically to incorporate all logical notations for the sake of being able more sympathetically to translate the commitment sentences of any theory. There is nothing canonical about a notation if it lets in all the formalisms that would otherwise be excluded from the syntactical criterion. Which logic are we supposed to use in a particular application when the notations are all jumbled together? Are we meant to use only the logical notation of theory T in investigating the ontological commitments of T by Quine's criterion? Or do we also have the option or even the responsibility to test T by translating it into every distinct logical notation indiscriminately brought into the canon? What are we to make of conflicting ontological commitment judgements that must arise if we can apply the bound-variable criterion to the formalization of a theory's commitment sentences in any and every logical notation? If we open the door to additional logical symbolisms, say, the notation and formal semantics of quantified modal logic, including those that Quine regards as non-canonical, then we must presumably let them all in, on pain of landing again on the first dilemma horn. We shall then inevitably lack adequate syntactical resources to formalize or colloquially paraphrase the ontological commitment sentences of all theories so as to be able to apply the bound-variable criterion in trying to identify their ontological commitments.

If these were Quine's only choices, then he might be expected to decide in favour of the logically more manageable alternative. The syntactical criterion with a conservative canonical notation still comes at the heavy price of applying only to those theories whose ontological commitments are accurately expressible in Quine's exclusionary canonical notation. The notation Quine has in mind is undoubtedly meant to be a version of A. N. Whitehead and Russell's predicate syntax in *Principia Mathematica*, supplemented and refined as necessary in response to advances in mathematics, or equivalently perhaps a corrected version of Quine's "New Foundations for Mathematical Logic".[18] Even so, the restriction remains too severe. How is Quine's criterion rightly to evaluate the ontological commitments of theories whose logics are radically different from the extensionalist canon? Nor does Quine try to show that intensional logic must introduce havoc if it merged with a more classical extensional logic. There are intensional logics that are formally as interesting as their extensional counterparts, and that know how to behave themselves in polite extensional company. Although allowing such an exception, as the second part of our dilemma suggests, opens up more possibilities for accurately identifying the ontological commitments of more distinct kinds of theories, it could also be the highly objectionable thin edge of the wedge leading to an unrestricted incoherent accumulation of any and all logical symbolisms in the criterion's expanded "canonical" notation.

Limitations of Ockham's razor in applied ontology

In his preference for austere desert landscapes over lush tropical ontologies, Quine champions the use of Ockham's razor in applied scientific ontology. This fact makes the logic and methodology of his theory of ontological commitment especially problematic. Quine ultimately maintains that, adopting the bound-variable criterion of ontological commitment and working toward our own decisions about what scientific theories and applied ontologies to accept, we are ontologically committed to whatever entities must be assumed to exist as the values of object variables bound by existential quantifiers in the canonical first-order logical formalization of favoured theories in order for the principles of the theory to be true.

Quine prefers minimalist existence domains, the very least we need to get by in mathematics and science. Ultimately, Quine argues that applied scientific ontology needs to include both individual physical entities and abstract classes. Quine believes that numbers in the foundations of mathematics and ostensible references to universals, propositions and other putative abstract entities, in so far as they are needed in mathematics, science and philosophy, can be ontologically reduced to classes, and that, in the absence of classes, we too severely curtail ontology for the purposes of mathematics and science. We need classes as abstract entities in ontology because we cannot do without them, and only for that reason does Quine grudgingly admit that they exist. Were it otherwise, if we could understand mathematics and science without including abstract classes in the ontology, then Quine, having tried the experiment and failed, would conclude they could and therefore should be said not to exist. Quine's ontological minimalism is in many ways attractive, not least because in slinging Ockham's razor to exclude as nonexistent ostensible entities for which there is no demonstrated theoretical need, we restrict the possibilities of inadvisable ontological commitments to *entia suspecta*, in subdivisions of applied ontology that are not subject to verification by empirical observation. Their exclusion notably incorporates the category of ostensible abstract entities to which many less scientific metaphysical systems have sometimes been committed and inclined to accept as real existent entities in a lavishly appointed Platonic heaven.[19]

The trouble is that by applying Ockham's razor in this way we risk slipping into the methodological circle that obtains when we try to choose among alternative theories on the basis of their ontologies, and try to establish their advantages and weigh them against the disadvantages of alternative ontologies on the basis of a preferred choice of theories. We need to know what sciences and kinds of sciences to promote in order to decide what entities are strictly needed or that would be explanatorily superfluous in a preferred applied scientific ontology, and we need to know how to choose among the alternative ontological commitments of distinct theories in order to decide which sciences or kinds of sciences to promote. This is a more serious problem than is generally recognized in Quine's writings or in the secondary literature on Quine's philosophy. The difficulty becomes acute when we try to apply Quine's criterion to a serious dispute of ontological conflict, such as the problem of universals. Quine argues:

> Now let us turn to the ontological problem of universals: the question whether there are such entities as attributes, relations, classes, numbers, functions. McX, characteristically enough, thinks there are. Speaking of attributes, he says: "There are red houses, red roses, red sunsets; this much is prephilosophical common sense in which we must all agree. These houses, roses, and sunsets, then, have something in common; and this which they have in common is all I mean by the attribute of redness."[20]

Similar observations are offered in the case of putative mathematical entities. Quine nowhere acknowledges the difficulty of making sense of ostensible ontological commitments to nonexistent merely putative entities on an extensionalist interpretation of quantifier bound variables. Instead, he reports:

> Classical mathematics, as the example of primes larger than a million clearly illustrates, is up to its neck in commitments to an ontology of abstract entities. Thus it is that the great mediaeval controversy over universals has flared up anew in the modern philosophy of mathematics. The issue is clearer now than of old, because we now have a more explicit standard whereby to decide what ontology a given theory or form of discourse is committed to: a theory is committed to those and only those entities to which the bound variables of the theory must be capable of referring in order that the affirmations made in the theory be true.[21]

A theory of universals, one would think, is ontologically committed to the existence of universals. Likewise for a theory of mathematical entities. If there are no such entities in the extant domain, then for Quine these false theories are not actually ontologically committed to anything at all. A theory is ontologically committed to those and only those entities to which the bound variables of the theory must be capable of referring "in order that the affirmations made in the theory be true", Quine says. But which entities are these in the case of a theory of the winged horse? Not the winged horse, for on an extensionalist reading of the quantifiers there is no such thing. No entity or nonentity truly has the properties of being winged and a horse on Quine's extensionalist interpretation of quantifiers. There is, then, no entity or nonentity to which a theory of the winged horse can be ontologically committed. The same is true of any theory of universals or numbers or other putative mathematical entities *if* they do not actually exist, whereupon the theories themselves disappear or are bleached of meaning, and with them the possibility of making sense of alleged controversies in the history of metaphysics whose conflicting ontological commitments Quine claims to represent.

Quine is not unaware of the problems of relying on principles of theoretical simplicity and economy in moving toward a preferred existence domain. He warns against the uncritical application of these standards without considering a broader conception of explanatory usefulness in deciding what is or is not needed in explanation. Thus, he states:

> But simplicity, as a guiding principle in constructing conceptual schemes, is not a clear and unambiguous idea; and it is quite capable of presenting a double or multiple standard. Imagine, for example, that we have devised the most economical set of concepts adequate to the play-by-play reporting of immediate experience. The entities under this scheme – the values of bound variables – are, let us suppose, individual subjective events of sensation or reflection. We should still find, no doubt, that a physicalistic conceptual scheme, purporting to talk about external objects, offers great advantages in simplifying our over-all reports. By bringing together scattered sense events and treating them as perceptions of one object, we reduce the complexity of our stream of experience to a manageable conceptual simplicity. The rule of simplicity is indeed our guiding maxim in assigning sense data to objects: we associate an earlier and a later round sensum with the same so-called penny, or with two different so-called pennies, in obedience to the demands of maximum simplicity in our total world-picture.[22]

It might be possible to have a phenomenalist ontology of sense impressions only, in the manner of Condillac, Berkeley, Hume or Ernst Mach.[23] Quine thinks that, despite the simplicity of the account, it would still be preferable to admit external entities related somehow to our sensations of them in a more common-sense or naive realist Aristotelian ontology. Where putative abstract entities are concerned, on the other hand, Quine generally wields Ockham's razor to eliminate from his own preferred theoretical existence domain whatever abstract entities are not absolutely necessary to conduct the business of mathematics and science. He finds, in the process, that he cannot do without classes, from which numbers and other mathematical entities can be constructed, and these, he argues, must therefore exist.

To the extent that Quine relies on Ockham's razor, he opens his criterion of ontological commitment to several kinds of objections. He proceeds as though we could conjure entities into or out of existence purely on the grounds of our perceptions of our extracurricular theoretical needs in the sciences. Such a strategy has two unfortunate conflicts in Quine's programme. It snags on the problem of identifying favoured sciences and preferred ontologies, and it runs into the difficulty of establishing fixed needs in determining which ontological commitments do or do not amount to multiplying entities beyond strict theoretical explanatory necessity.

What are the real needs that are to dictate the contents of a preferred existence domain for the sciences – assuming that we can somehow independently decide which among the competing possibilities we need or want to support – in specifying the details of a preferred existence domain in applied scientific ontology? The difficulties we encounter in trying to answer this question satisfactorily reflect on the doubtful utility of applying Ockham's razor to decide sensitive issues about the extant domain. Quine also regards the principle of explanatory economy as equivocal. He nevertheless appeals throughout his work to considerations of minimizing ontological commitment to what is strictly needed for science, without, remarkably, stopping to ask how choice of science affects choice of ontology and choice of ontology influences choice of science. Quine remarks:

> Our acceptance of an ontology is, I think, similar in principle to our acceptance of a scientific theory, say a system of physics: we adopt, at least insofar as we are reasonable, the simplest conceptual scheme into which the disordered fragments of raw experience can be fitted and arranged. Our ontology is determined once we have fixed upon the over-all conceptual scheme which is to accommodate science in the broadest sense; and the considerations which determine a reasonable construction of any part of that conceptual scheme, for example, the biological or the physical part, are not different in kind from the considerations which determine a reasonable construction of the whole. To whatever extent the adoption of any system of scientific theory may be said

to be a matter of language, the same – but no more – may be said of the adoption of an ontology.[24]

The full implications, amounting to a vicious methodological circle, of trying simultaneously to choose a preferred existence domain as that required by a favoured scientific theory and of choosing a favoured scientific theory (bacteria instead of demons as a cause of disease; atmospheric electrical accumulation and discharge of hydrogen ions versus Zeus's wrath) in terms of its philosophically or quasi-aesthetically preferable ontological commitments, seems to be unappreciated by Quine.

Quine cannot presuppose that the domain of existent entities is already known independently of the philosophically justified preference for one existence domain over its competitors. The only way to arrive at a philosophically justified preference for an existence domain over its rivals is to apply a correct criterion of ontological commitment to competing theories in order to decide which to prefer on grounds of simplicity, economy, theoretical fruitfulness or the like. There is thus a deep circularity in Quine's definition of and suggestions for applying his syntactical bound-variable criterion of ontological commitment in the comparative evaluation of competing existence domains. We are supposed to use the criterion in order to decide which existence domain to prefer, in choosing whether to accept a domain that includes or excludes propositions or other intensional objects, or that includes or excludes sets but not universals. In order to apply Quine's criterion that to be is to be the value of a quantifier-bound variable, we must already know the values of bound variables, which is to say that we must already be in firm possession of a preferred existence domain. This again we cannot do unless or until we have applied Quine's criterion as a first step in assessing the advantages and disadvantages of competing existence domains.

Ockham's razor by itself cannot determine which theories are true and which are false. The reason, we should remind ourselves, is that while there could in principle be as many theories as there are ontologies, there are in fact for logical as well as practical reasons more theories than ontologies. There are multiple theories that share the same ontology while making different jointly logically incompatible assertions about exactly the same entities. This can obviously be the case if theory T states that object O is an electron and not a neutron, and theory T^* states that the very same object O is a neutron and not an electron. The two theories, by hypothesis, are ontologically committed to the existence of object O, and to the existence of at least some, or to the scientific category of, electrons and neutrons, or to the extensions of the count nouns or general terms "electrons" and "neutrons". Clearly, Ockham's razor by itself offers nothing positive to decide which, if either, theory T or T^* is true in classifying object O as electron or neutron in a microphysical taxonomy.[25]

There is additionally a problem about correctly discerning the internal ontological content of any of these expressions on Quine's theory. The difficulty arises even in trying to capture the distinctive ontological commitments of theories about, say, objectified unitary rabbits and spatiotemporally sequential undetached rabbit parts. If we cannot accomplish this translation task with any assurance of success, how can we then go on to assess the merits of each such theory according to its specific ontological commitments, in order to decide whether to accept the theory as a part of science by virtue of judging that it better satisfies the aesthetic requirements of Ockham's razor than its competitors? Quine's ontological project again lapses into circularity precisely at this juncture, when we reflect that it is the choice of a preferred science and its particular ontological commitments that in Quine's view of the insensible grading off of philosophy into natural science is supposed to play a substantial role in selecting a preferred existence domain for all of philosophy, logic, mathematics, and science.

Combinatorial criterion of ontological commitment

It may thus be time to ask whether a syntactical criterion of ontological commitment in any form is likely to succeed, or whether we ought now to begin considering alternatives to syntactical criteria of any type.

There is much to admire in Quine's work on ontology. Quine sets applied scientific ontology on the right track, even if the account he offers requires revision as a whole in order to arrive, first, at a correct criterion of ontological commitment, and then to put the criterion to good use in identifying a preferred existence domain with a strong presumption of its according with the extant domain of actually existent entities. The counter-proposal to be defended below places applied scientific ontology on a more definite foundation, based on the combinatorial answer to the question of being in pure philosophical ontology, by explaining intensionally what it means for something to exist in terms of predicational maximal consistency.

The definition of being as maximal consistency can be applied to the problem of articulating a preferred existence domain. We proceed more informally and positively on this crucial front now that we have in hand a tested definition of the concept of being to fill in the blanks in a complete account of applied scientific ontology. Let us turn again to Quine's trenchant questions. What, first, must I do in accepting a scientific theory to commit myself ontologically to a physical object like a chair or a mitochondrion or an electron or the entire physical universe? What must I do to commit myself ontologically to an abstract object like a number or set or property, relation, proposition or state of affairs? What must I do to commit myself ontologically to the existence of persons or minds, God or the gods, demons, angels or spirits, destiny, moira or kharma? Quine claims one need only assert "There are chairs" or "There are mitochondria" or "God exists". If we choose, we can write these commitment sentences more perspicuously in a logical symbolism, from which we can then read off ontological commitments from the occurrences of bound variables within the scope of existential quantifiers. We have seen that Quine's answer is both viciously circular and counter-intuitive, however, if, with Quine, we also try to interpret the meaning of such formalizations, as opposed to the meaningfulness of the quantifiers they contain, extensionally, in terms of a pre-established extant domain of actually existent entities.

As an alternative to Quine's extensional criterion of ontological commitment, we recommend an intensional criterion based on the combinatorial analysis of being as maximal consistency. We can offer, instead of Quine's syntactical criterion of ontological commitment, a more substantive criterion based on the combinatorial analysis of being as maximal consistency. We can apply then the definition directly in deciding what things or kinds of things exist, depending on whether they satisfy or fail to satisfy the combinatorial analysis, without invoking Ockham's razor to include or exclude putative entities according to the vicissitudes of variably and culturally unstable perceived theoretical needs.

We say that to be is after all to be the value of a quantifier-bound variable, but only provided that the variables in question range over all logically possible objects in an ontically neutral semantics. Onto-logical commitment is then achieved by the intensions of property combinations, rather than whatever predetermined existent objects belong to the extension of a corresponding predicate. Quine refers to the objects that would need to exist in order for the propositions of a theory to be true. What objects are these, we must ask, if they are not intensionally characterizable logically possible objects? Are they such objects as Quine elsewhere in his essay disparages as the possible fat man in the doorway and the possible bald fat man in the doorway?

Again, Quine maintains, speaking of the more ontologically generous of his composite philosophical foils, benighted advocate of unactualized particulars, the wily Wyman:

> Wyman's overpopulated universe is in many ways unlovely. It offends against the aesthetic sense of us who have a taste for desert landscapes, but this is not the worst of it. Wyman's slum of possibles is a breeding ground for disorderly elements. Take, for instance, the possible fat man in that doorway; and, again, the possible bald man in that doorway. Are they the same possible man, or two possible men? How do we decide? How many possible men are there in that doorway? Are there more possible thin ones than fat ones? How many of them are alike? Or would their being alike make them one? Are no *two* possible things alike? Is this the same as saying that it is impossible for two things to be alike? Or, finally, is the concept of identity simply inapplicable to unactualized possibles? But what sense can be found in talking of entities which cannot meaningfully be said to be identical with themselves and distinct from one another? These elements are well-nigh incorrigible. By a Fregean therapy of individual concepts, some effort might be made at rehabilitation; but I feel we'd do better simply to clear Wyman's slum and be done with it.[26]

A theory on a combinatorial criterion of ontological commitment, by contrast, is ontologically committed to the existence of the logical objects that would exist if the theory were true. Unlike Quine, we are not limited to quantifying only over existent entities in the extensions of predicates, but freely refer to logically possible objects, regardless of their ontic status. Quine is concerned about the identity conditions for the possible fat men in the doorway. On the present theory, these are distinct nonentities by virtue of having distinct submaximal property combinations. The possible fat man is not the same as the possible bald fat man, because their properties are different. Curiously, Quine seems to have no trouble maintaining his grip on the identity conditions for his distinct but presumably nonexistent albeit logically possible fictional entities Wyman and McX.

Quine's objection appears to misunderstand the concept of unactualized possibilities, treating them as though they had actual physical properties. If this were correct, then it would obviously be absurd for several fat men, hirsute or otherwise, to crowd together bumping shoulders, hips and elbows in the same narrow doorway. The picture of unactualized possibilities that Quine's criticism suggests, if taken literally, is deeply problematic; but there is no reason to think of nonexistent possible entities, intensionally constituted in their identity conditions by submaximal property combinations, in anything like this way. More importantly, the combinatorial criterion of ontological commitment, essentially Wyman's position, avoids the difficulty attributed to Quine's bound-variable criterion, whereby the ontological relativity of a theorist's ontological commitments entering into the investigation of another theory's ontological commitments inevitably results in the kind of distortions of existence domain characterizations through the limitations of the indeterminacy of radical translation. Limiting concern to the ontically neutral logically possible objects of pure logic, we do not need to survey another theory's ontology through the coloured lenses of our own attachments to a preferred existence domain, even if our theoretical domain should happen to be extant.

If, on the other hand, we turn from quantifier-bound variables in pure logic to the commitment-ridden bound variables of applied logic as it is used, not externally by us from a metatheoretical perspective in discussing another theory's ontological commitments, but internally by proponents of the theory in a way that is not intended to be ontically neutral but committal, then we can say more substantively that a theory is ontologically committed to whatever entities are required by the theory to be maximally consistent, or that would need to be maximally consistent, regardless of how they are designated, in order for the propositions of the theory to be true. Appealing to a syntactical bound-variable criterion of ontological commitment that is at the same time wed to an extensional interpretation of propositional truth for predications, and that presupposes the actual existence of the entities in a preferred existence domain in philosophical semantics, as Quine does, is certain to run into avoidable difficulties of ontological relativity and indeterminacy of radical translation.

These implications are paraded as important discoveries in Quine's philosophy, but they should more properly be regarded as theoretical embarrassments – signs of trouble in his syntactical criterion and extensional interpretation of ontological commitment. Epistemic inconveniences of such magnitude are symptoms of things having gone drastically wrong in ontology, particularly when they are permitted, as in Quine, to affect the shape of ontological commitment assessments and do not merely subtend the quest for a preferred existence domain. They are a further indication of Quine's mixing-up applied scientific ontology with pure philosophical ontology that follows inevitably from Quine's semantic extensionalism, and is preventable only by adopting an intensional combinatorial criterion.

Appearance, reality, substance,
7 transcendence

Scientific ontology

We now consider the first of a series of ontological commitments in four traditional subcategories of applied scientific ontology. Shall we follow the lead of other ontologists by distinguishing between *appearance* and *reality* in a strong metaphysical sense? What shall we say about the ontology of *substance*? Is there an argument to be made for the *transcendence* of a certain part of the preferred existence domain that is, in some sense, above and beyond, or in any case outside, the actual world? What light does the combinatorial analysis of being as maximal consistency shed on any of these time-honoured distinctions in metaphysics and applied scientific ontology?

Applied scientific ontology is not the pure philosophical ontology of being *qua* being but, so to speak, an annotated inventory of entities, in which we offer good reasons for saying yes or no to including contested entities in a preferred existence domain. It is here that we try to identify the ultimate kinds or categories of existent entities that we need, not only for science but for all meaningful thought. In contrast with physical objects and physical states of affairs, we may find it necessary to require convincing philosophical arguments to satisfy natural scepticism about the existence of putative entities that we do not directly experience in sensation, such as abstract entities, especially numbers and universals, propositions, minds and God. The same might also be true for the concepts of imperceptible substance and transcendent entities.

Appearance, reality and substance sometimes go together in metaphysics. In other theories, a sharp appearance–reality division is maintained independently of the concept of substance. Yet other doctrines develop a complex concept of substance without taking special notice of the appearance–reality distinction beyond its mundane occurrence in optical and other kinds of perceptual illusions, artificial versus real flowers, and like phenomena, whose appearance and reality, so construed, can be distinguished experientially through more patient or acute observation of whatever is presented to sensation. Different philosophies have used these terms in different ways, attaching distinct and often incompatible meanings to the vocabulary. Although we shall not try to sort out all of these ambiguities through the history of philosophy in quite the detail or with the thoroughness they deserve, we remain mindful of the alternative concepts that have sometimes been advanced in applied ontology under the banners of these common but often slippery concepts. The point holds with respect to all four of these categories, with appearance arguably being the least variable, and substance, transcendence and finally reality itself occupying the most hotly contested philosophical territory.

Reality and the ontological status of appearance

We first explicate and briefly defend a particular interpretation of these concepts, and consider arguments about the implications of the combinatorial analysis of being as maximal consistency for inclusion in or exclusion from a preferred existence domain of these four putative applied ontological subcategories.

To speak of a distinction between appearance and reality in metaphysics as opposed to epistemology is already to discredit appearances ontologically. This is true in the philosophy of Plato, Descartes, Kant, Schopenhauer, J. M. E. McTaggart and many other ontologists. Plato, interestingly, does not try to argue for the distinction, but leans heavily on Parmenides' separation between the way of seeming and the way of truth, the many appearances and the One reality in Parmenides' monistic ontology, and the otherwise unsupported intuition that the realm of being and truth must coincide for a domain of eternal unchanging entities, appearances in the world as we experience them notwithstanding, so that knowledge can only be of what is eternal and unchanging in order to be itself also eternal and unchanging.

Why anyone should accept without further justification such a concept of knowledge is unexplored in Plato and the surviving fragments of Parmenides.[1] We either share their insight in this fundamental matter or we do not; we either agree and require no persuading that knowledge must be eternal and unchanging or we do not. For present purposes, subject to reconsideration, in lieu of powerful reasons to the contrary, we shall not throw in our lot with Plato and Parmenides, but remain open-minded about other considerations that might uphold a sharp metaphysical distinction between appearance and reality. As we shall see, reasons of this type have from time to time been advanced in connection with the sometimes related concepts of substance and transcendence. We as yet do not take account of any compelling motivation to relegate true relevantly justified beliefs about the world of experience as Plato does to the secondary status of right opinion or mere belief in a likely story concerning the changing face of phenomena, but stand behind the possibility of obtaining genuine knowledge about the empirical world encountered in sensation.

Descartes, who in his famous motto claims to enter philosophical disputes masked, *Larvatus prodeo*, raises the appearance–reality distinction disguised as a deep metaphysical division.[2] Descartes's real interest is in the epistemology of clear and distinct perceptions as a way of overcoming uncertainty about the actual state of the external world, and in establishing rules for the guidance of empirical enquiry in natural science based on purely rational foundations. The foundations of knowledge for Descartes are supposed to be unshakeable even when they concern the changing phenomenal world, and even under the greatest imaginable threat to the veridicality of clear and distinct ideas. Descartes envisions this threat to knowledge as taking the form of a malignant demon, a fictional evil spirit that, for all we know, conspires to deceive us when we exercise our senses in trying to gather knowledge about the external world.

Descartes sees our only hope of epistemic salvation in a rational demonstration of the existence and perfect benevolence of an omnipotent all-knowing God, as the unfailingly veracious architect of human cognition. Descartes thus holds up the spectre of a metaphysical division between appearance and reality merely as a dramatic ploy, which he overcomes by philosophical–theological devices of a rather unusual sort, in order to restore the distinction to its proper epistemic application. In this way, he hopes to secure metaphysical gains in other sectors of his philosophy, concerning the existence of God, the nature of matter and the distinction between the body and soul. He argues that if God vouchsafes clear and distinct perception, and if sensation and inductive inference are appropriately chastened as to their limitations within a special set of principles for avoiding error, then all of science can enjoy the same high degree of epistemic certainty as mathematics. The appearance–reality distinction, epistemically prominent as it is in Descartes's methodology, never assumes a permanent place in his applied scientific ontology. It serves instead only provisionally as a caution to unwarranted inferences, helping us to avoid the equivalent of perceptual illusions throughout our scientific reasoning. By recognizing the distinction between appearance and reality, we can prevent unwarrantedly jumping from the infallible data of immediate sense experience considered only as such to inadequately justified conclusions about the nature and actual state of the external world through hasty insufficiently self-critical attention to the evidentiary requirements of science.[3]

Kant is another historical figure who, like Plato but in different ways, is committed to a metaphysical distinction between appearance and reality in his applied ontology. Kant does not separate the world of appearance from the world of reality in the manner of Plato and Parmenides, but identifies two incongruent aspects of a single unified world: the phenomenal and the noumenal or thing-in-itself (*Ding an sich*). Schopenhauer follows Kant more closely in this crucial respect than in other areas of Kant's philosophy. Although Schopenhauer forgoes reference to noumena in deference to the Kantian thing-in-itself, he also distinguishes between *the* world *as* Will (*Wille*) and *as* idea or representation (*Vorstellung*). Kant's and Schopenhauer's division between appearance and reality thus has real applied ontological bite. While Schopenhauer credits Kant's distinction as among the greatest contributions to the history of philosophy, he faults Kant for not remaining true to the dichotomy between phenomena and noumena.[4] Schopenhauer denies that the *principium individuationis* for identifying, individuating or discriminating among distinct things can possibly apply to thing-in-itself, which he argues is altogether beyond the reach of any explanation of its number, condition, origin or the like, under the four-fold root of the principle of sufficient reason, consisting, as he characterizes it, of laws for understanding the logical, mathematical, causal and moral properties exclusively of phenomena in *die Welt als Vorstellung* (appearance, presentation or idea).[5]

All this leaves us with more unsaid than said, and more that should be said in order to appreciate the history of these philosophers in the ontology and epistemology of appearance and reality. To proceed, let us turn to the relevant applied ontological issues, taking our brief introduction to philosophical treatments of the appearance–reality distinction as background to an ontological investigation of appearance, reality, substance and transcendence. We shall concentrate on what can justifiably be concluded about the meaning and usefulness of each of these applied ontological subcategories.

Appearance and reality in combinatorial ontology

What should we think about the alleged distinction between appearance and reality? Are there good reasons based on the combinatorial analysis of being as maximal consistency to distinguish between the way the world appears to sensation and the way it is in reality? Should we try to restore a sense of the metaphysical distinction that is more in the spirit of Plato, Kant and Schopenhauer? Or should we think of the appearance–reality distinction as more superficially epistemic, merely a matter of avoiding illusion and certifying veridical perceptions, in the manner of Descartes?

One consideration is that without the distinction it may be impossible to avoid the consequences of ontic *idealism*. As with Plato's commitment to the idea that knowledge can only be of what is eternal and unchanging, we need to recall what it is that is supposed to be so bad about idealism. Critics of idealism sometimes assume that there is a slippery slope from any type of idealism to wilful subjectivity, as though to be an idealist of any stripe is automatically to accept the fantastic thesis that individual thinking subjects can will the world or the exact state of the world into existence. Idealism, even of more objective ambitions, is often said to offend against a robust sense of reality, without which ontology is cut adrift from science. There are idealisms, like Berkeley's, that have defied this objection. Let us nevertheless assume that the criticism is correct, and that idealism is objectionable, if for no other reason than because of its inherent subjectivity. It is argued that idealism is the unwelcome result if we do not distinguish between appearance and reality by allowing appearance to occur within the mind, as a sequence of sense impressions and stream of ideas or psychological contents, reserving for reality the existence and state of substances outside the mind in external reality, or, alternatively, in the Kantian thing-in-itself or Schopenhaurian world as Will.

The crux of the argument is that if we limit applied ontology to the way the world appears to thought, especially in immediate sensation and memory, if there is no reality beyond appearance in the content of thought, then the world is nothing but a series of ideas in the mind. This is a conclusion that philosophers, like Berkeley, who have warmly embraced idealism want not to avoid but to enthusiastically accept. To prevent reality from collapsing into appearance in the sense of purely mental occurrences is to require applied ontology to posit a mind-independent reality or substance, the real matter of the external world. The substance of the world as opposed to our sensation and thought about it can then be said to possess *primary qualities* like size, weight and the other properties of physical substances, as studied by physics. The objective properties of substance are further opposed to *secondary qualities* like colour, taste, smell and the like, as studied by psychology, that seem to belong to thought, to the mind of the perceiver. If applied ontology does not posit such a realm of substance, then we seem driven to some version of idealism, which is often assumed to be a worse fate.[6]

The dilemma is that if, in order to escape idealism, we try to establish a metaphysical appearance–reality distinction in this way, then we seem forced to accept an equally if not more unwanted conclusion, that there exists something that is essentially unknowable, but is supposed to possess definite properties and stand in relations to other things. This something, an unperceivable philosophical or metaphysical substance, if we are consistent, must then be acknowledged as transcending all experience. It will be, as John Locke, who was attracted to this kind of solution, and who adduced a version of Galileo's distinction between primary and secondary qualities in its defence, notoriously described in *An Essay Concerning Human Understanding*, in the French adage, a *Je ne sais quoi*: a *something* I know not what.[7] Otherwise, we might be tempted, like Kant, despite the threat of idealism, to adopt a concept of the noumenal thing-in-itself, or Schopenhauerian aspect of the world as Will, existing independently of thought and the mind's pure forms of intuition or sensation, beyond all concepts and categories of the understanding.

By embracing the appearance–reality distinction in this form, we are driven from idealism to a kind of mysticism. We are then obliged to accept the existence of something for which we have no evidence and which we cannot come to know in any meaningful way. Schopenhauer in this vein appears in his own way to go too far by declaring the thing-in-itself to be Will, thus imposing a kind of character on what is supposed, even by Schopenhauer, to be descriptively unknowable, by virtue of falling outside the scope of the four-fold root of the principle of sufficient reason. To attribute a nature of any kind on the world in reality or thing-in-itself even metaphorically, for Schopenhauer, should be the height of treason to his own philosophical principles. For in the Vedic myth that Schopenhauer adapts to his purpose it is only to drape another fold of the veil of Maya over the empirical inscrutability of reality.[8]

We are just as hard-pressed by the demands of a robust sense of reality in the train of modern science to maintain that something exists for which we have no experiential evidence as we would be to accept the idealist conclusion that everything exists within the mind. This would be a regrettable consequence even or especially in the case of a supposedly objective idealism, as in Berkeley's ontology, where sensible things exist *archetypally* in the infinite all-knowing mind of God, and *ectypally* in their parts, aspects and fleeting moments in the finite minds of human perceivers.[9] From the standpoint of the combinatorial analysis of being as maximal consistency, it might be said that the idealist side of the dispute at least has the advantage of not giving up epistemic access to the existence and constitutive properties of real entities. The combinatorial analysis construes these as a combination of ideas of an object's properties, whereas substance theory, in the sense being considered in contrast, posits the existence of an entity that has no knowable properties. Substance in that sense amounts to understanding all existence as a logical object of pure logic, a bare particular or individual predication subject lacking any properties whatsoever, about which we cannot possibly know anything. Far from satisfying the requirements of maximal consistency, such a concept deprives reality of properties. The category of substance should presumably be rejected from applied scientific ontology as failing to satisfy the combinatorial requirements of predicational maximal consistency for an existent entity. The only exception could be if we are willing to accept a sense of predicational maximal consistency that is inherently concealed from epistemic access behind the phenomena–noumena distinction or Schopenhauer's veil of Maya. If such a conclusion is intolerable in the metaphysics of science, then we should find the implication logically incompatible with the combinatorial analysis of being as maximal consistency.

Does this mean that we should instead swing over to some version of idealism in order to remain true to the maximal consistency analysis of being? To avoid both idealism and mysticism in applied scientific ontology it must suffice to deny the existence of substance in the Lockean sense that Berkeley rejects or as Kantian or Schopenhauerian thing-in-itself on the grounds of denying all logically possible epistemic access to an entity's maximally consistent property or states-of-affairs combination. The assumption that we cannot immediately say which of these choices is right already indicates difficulties in the concept of Lockean substance or Kantian thing-in-itself. The Lockean concept of substance or Kantian thing-in-itself does not fit the combinatorial concept of being neatly, if at all, for we do not know what to say about it. If substance or thing-in-itself is a *world*, then we are back to Plato's two worlds conception, and we must deny the reality of the perceived world in order to preserve the unique actuality of an intelligible world of abstract entities. If substance or thing-in-itself is only a part or aspect of the actual world, then its ontological or epistemic predicational incompleteness threatens the completeness of the actual world, and as such is excluded by the combinatorial analysis of being.

Idealism is avoided by denying the questionable assumption that entities are constituted by particular appearances rather than by the actual properties themselves. Such properties, in the case of physical entities, are always logically possibly or, in principle, epistemically accessible to perception, but do not need to be identified with corresponding appearances. The identification of constitutive properties with perceptions or ideas is the core of Berkeley's radical empiricism, phenomenalism and idealism. Why, in the first place, should anyone have ever supposed that they were identical? It is too important and controversial a thesis to be taken for granted, but it is difficult and may finally be impossible to argue with anyone who does not already share the intuition. We have now considered several reasons not to accept its truth, regardless of how reasonable it is made to seem. If we disapprove the thesis, then we avoid idealism and are free to accept some form of nobly naive realism sufficiently robust for the metaphysical underpinnings of empirical science. The appearance–reality bifurcation in that case endures as in Descartes only as an epistemological distinction between the way things under certain conditions can sometimes misleadingly appear, and the way we judge them on more careful inspection or sober reflection to be in reality. Thus, we learn to see through the *fata morgana*, to judge true and false friends, as phenomena here before us in the publicly accessible empirical world.

It is not only the appearance–reality duality that is displaced in this way as an epistemic rather than metaphysical concept, but, more importantly, the concept of an unperceivable substance. Instead of thinking of substance as existing outside thought, a more plausible idea, that is in some ways more traditional, going back to Aristotle's definition of *ousia* as informed matter, or of substance as we ordinarily think of it in the sense of material or physical stuff, can be advanced in an empirical scientific framework. Substance in this more familiar less philosophical sense is equally influential in the history of philosophy, but belongs more properly to the topic of physical entities or material constituents of the actual world. The advantage of the empirical Aristotelian concept of substance as perceivable informed matter is its immediate compatibility with the combinatorial analysis of being.

Transcendence of the physical world

We are left only, in this category, after our evaluation of appearance, reality and substance, with the concept of transcendence. What is meant by transcendence? Should we consider transcendent entities to be included in or excluded from a preferred existence domain? Does the combinatorial analysis of being as maximal consistency encourage, discourage, permit or exclude transcendence?

Intuitively, the idea of transcendence is the idea of something that is beyond the world of appearance or experience. Lockean substance with its primary qualities measurable by science does not transcend the world, but the Kantian thing-in-itself or Schopenhauerian Will is a transcendent aspect of the phenomenal world. Thing-in-itself stands outside the world as it appears to thought, and, as the term suggests, transcends the cognitively available world. The Kantian or Schopenhauerian thing-in-itself is only an example of the only kind of thing some philosophers have claimed to transcend the world of experience. Thinkers as diverse in their methodologies and ontological commitments as Kant, Schopenhauer, Husserl and Wittgenstein have held that the self or metaphysical subject of thought and experience transcends the actual world. In the *Tractatus*, Wittgenstein further maintains that logical form, pictorial form, form of representation, the sense of the mystical or grasp of the world as a whole *sub specie aeterni*, and especially ethics and aesthetics, which in his early philosophy he considers as one along with other kinds of value, transcend any logically conceivable world construed as a structure of states of affairs in logical space. In many religious traditions and philosophies of religion, God is also often claimed to be transcendent, to transcend the world of experience or physical spatiotemporal order that God may be believed to have created or over which God is sometimes believed to rule and judge.

The concept of transcendence is appealing for a variety of reasons. We shall begin, for simplicity's sake, by considering transcendence in the case of aesthetic or moral value. The conclusions we reach for these examples should nevertheless be sufficiently general, having to do with the concept of transcendence. If the implications are correct, then they apply to any theory of transcendence, including thing-in-itself, value, form, God or any other theoretical *transcendentalia*. The combinatorial argument against transcendence is that the analysis of being as maximal consistency precludes transcendence even as a logical possibility. According to combinatorial pure philosophical ontology, the actual world is maximally consistent, leaving no possibility for truths or facts or states of affairs involving true predications other than those already contained in the actual world's states-of-affairs combination. The conclusion may count against combinatorial ontology for those who are firmly committed to the transcendence of value or other entities or factors, but we should not be dissuaded by such considerations unless they are backed by sound arguments.

The intuitive case for the transcendence of value is, in large measure, the desire to strike a philosophical compromise between eliminating value altogether from the preferred existence domain as simply nothing, and recognizing that value is not an ordinary perceivable physical or spatiotemporal property of physical things. We do not ordinarily believe that we perceive the beauty of a painting or the evil of a murder when we see the pigment on canvas or a murderous act being perpetrated. Value seems to be something that is superadded to these physical entities and real-world states of affairs. *Where* is value? Except in the most philosophically inexact colloquial sense, the question does not really have an answer, which may be equivalent to saying that the question is unintelligible. If value literally has no place in the actual world, then it might reasonably be said, in so far as value has being, to be transcendent, and as such to transcend actual existence or to exist in a transcendent ontological order, like the non-spatiotemporal realm of abstract Platonic entities. It is in something like this sense that Kant's thing-in-itself or Schopenhauer's world as Will is supposed to transcend the phenomenal world of appearance. Although not itself part of the world, a transcendent entity is metaphorically, but not of course literally, above and beyond the actual world – in some sense outside the physical spatiotemporal framework of the actual world. Do we have a clear concept of such a thing?

The actual world contains all and only existent entities and states of affairs. If to exist is to be maximally consistent, then the maximality, the predicational completeness of the uniquely actual world, precludes anything existent, anything actual or partaking of being to exist above, beyond or outside the actual world. There could only be transcendence, presumably, but also paradoxically, if the transcendent entities in question were nonexistent nonentities, or if transcendent entities, despite themselves, were nevertheless a part of the actual world. We are confounded if we try to pursue this line of thought, the only relief from which seems to be to deny that there are transcendent entities possessing any mode of being if they are not physically integrated into the actual world. If, on the other hand, we try to include transcendent objects in the preferred existence domain, then they can no longer be described as transcending the actual world, which consists of all and only actually existent facts and objects. From the standpoint of the combinatorial analysis of being, the idea of the transcendence of the actual world by transcendent entities is logically incoherent. Transcendent entities cannot exist, for either they are not transcendent, or they are not entities of the actual world interpreted as a maximally consistent states-of-affairs combination. As with the non-actuality of merely logically possible worlds that are predicationally consistent but incomplete, the predicational maximality of the actual world logically uses up all of the logically possible predicational completeness, leaving only submaximally consistent property and states-of-affairs combinations left over for non-actual merely logically possible entities that by definition are incomplete, allowing no logical space to be occupied by non-physical non-spatiotemporal transcendent entities.

What, then, of the ontology of value? There are several kinds of explanation that avoid commitment to the existence of transcendent entities. We can understand the value of a painting or murder as a psychological projection of attitude by persons reacting in some sort of causal relation with a valued object. Or we can think of value as an abstract and hence imperceptible entity or property of perceivable things, if there should turn out to be abstract entities. We might, finally, think of value as an individual rather than universal but *supervenient* property that in some sense arises or emerges from or supervenes on an object's ordinary properties, as a consequence of their coinstantiation.[10] If we have a variety of options for interpreting aesthetic and moral value non-transcendentally, then we can admit that we are not forced by the facts for which an adequate theory of value must account into concluding that there must be transcendent entities. At least we need not be ontologically committed to the existence of transcendent entities on the grounds that there are values or valuable things, and that values are not experienced as ordinary spatiotemporal physical properties. We are not yet compelled by any argument we have considered to accept transcendent existence, or a realm of transcendent entities, of transcendence as a positive applied scientific ontological category of genuine being. We have as yet no good reason to extend applied scientific ontology to include transcendent entities, and we have stronger philosophical justification in combinatorial ontology for rejecting the category of transcendence and the concept of a transcendent entity as logically incoherent.

Physical entities: space, time, matter and causation, physical states of affairs and events,
8 natural laws

A material–physical world

The category of physical entities is usually supposed to be the least metaphysically problematic in applied ontology. The question for a preferred existence domain is not whether physical entities exist. Their existence can be assumed as established by combinatorial pure philosophical ontology, on the assumption that there are non-actual logical possibilities, and hence distinct logically possible worlds, that all states of affairs logically must either be spatiotemporal or non-spatiotemporal, and that only physical or spatiotemporal entities can distinguish one logically possible world from another.

The existence of physical entities is further confirmed by empirical experience of the actual world in sense perception. To begin with, scientific knowledge of the actual world, impermissible in pure philosophical ontology, is unobjectionable and in many ways indispensable in applied scientific ontology. As we turn to pure logic to get started in pure philosophical ontology, so we turn to empirical science to get started in understanding the nature of physical entities in applied scientific ontology. As a result of our experience of the world we know that there are real existent external physical entities and states of affairs, and we can make progress towards the development of an appropriate applied scientific ontology of physical entities by looking to what are judged to be the most successful natural sciences as a starting place for articulating an applied ontology of physical entities from the standpoint of the things and kinds of things such theories need to posit in their respective preferred existence domains in order to sustain the truth of their principles, assumptions and conclusions.

Combinatorial ontology of space and time

The main task of an applied ontology of physical entities is to identify a structure of ontic subcategories for all philosophically interesting types of physical things. *Space* and *time* can be classified as physical entities, even though they are not generally thought to be perceivable as such, when physical entities are perceived *in* space and time or spacetime.

Space and time are physical preconditions for the existence of perceivable physical substances. Kant's transcendental aesthetic holds that space and time are *pure forms of intuition*, which is to say sensation or perception. As pure forms of intuition, space and time must be brought by a subject to experience, because they are impossible to derive from or discover within experience by a subject who is not so pre-equipped a priori. Without space and time as pure forms of intuition, Kant argues, physical entities could not be experienced as a distribution of cognitively distinct and discrete spatiotemporal objects in what Kant calls the sensible manifold. The world that would appear to us in that case when we opened our eyes would not be objectified, but would be nothing but a sheer chaos without definite shape or patterns of colour, and with no possibility of mentally keeping track of whatever passes through consciousness from moment to moment in time.

What would that be like? It is surely unthinkable, unintelligible for us even to imagine anything we would be prepared to recognize as *experience*, just as Kant says, without definite shape or colour, and unaccompanied by any sense of the passing of time in which we ordinarily live through the flow of thoughts and images. The experienceability of things in space and time, and in particular places in space, is a function of the perception of extended sensibles and of sensibles as extended. The temporal properties of things similarly presuppose time as a pure form of intuition by which things are experienceable as enduring and remaining the same while undergoing accidental changes, as Aristotle says. If we were not already pre-equipped with space and time as pure forms of intuition, our minds would never be capable of discovering them in the flux of experience for which no sense of change, no shape or coloured places or the like, could possibly be discerned.[1]

Space and time in Kant's technical terminology are part of the transcendental ground or ultimate metaphysical presuppositions of intuition. Space and time are nevertheless entities that have many properties, and are involved in innumerable relations. Kant's absolutist Newtonian conception of space and time entails overlapping infinitely extensive and infinitely divisible rectilinear spatial grids suffused with an infinite unidirectional flow of time that marks the changes of state of physical entities within a causal matrix in the mind's experience of objectified external reality. All these facts depend on the physical properties of space and time or spacetime as physical entities. Moments of time, like regions of space, are logical objects with physical properties. As such, they are entities like any others, if, as it seems unobjectionable to assume, they are predicationally consistent and complete, and relationally interwoven with the physical properties of physical entities like particles of matter, macrophysical complex objects and fields of force that make up the physical universe. If it seems odd to count space and time as physical *entities* more or less on a par with physical entities *in* time and space or relativistic spacetime, it is likely to be because space and time or spacetime are intuitively understood as something more like a medium in which physical entities exist, rather than physical entities themselves.

Such a distinction will not stand scrutiny. There is no sound basis for distinguishing a medium of other physical entities as itself something other than a physical entity. Space and time or spacetime evidently have properties like other entities, although they are not like spatiotemporal entities in other ways, and there is no immediate cause to suppose that they are logically inconsistent or predicationally incomplete, arguments of sceptical metaphysicians like Parmenides, Zeno of Elea and McTaggart notwithstanding.[2] Space and time or spacetime are perhaps an unusual kind of physical entity, but an entity that is presupposed by the existence of objectified micro- and macrophysical entities nonetheless. Without space and time, the ordinary objects of experience that we think of more paradigmatically as physical entities would be relationally incomplete, with predicational gaps, contrary to our usual understanding of the external physical spatiotemporal world.

Even if spacetime is the special medium in which the causal matrix of physically interrelated spatiotemporal physical entities have their being, as in Galileo, Descartes, Newton, Leibniz, Locke and Kant, that is no reason to discount the existence of space and time or (hereafter) spacetime as real physical entities. Many types of physical media also exist in the same sense as, even if in a different way than, the physical entities in which they exist. As examples, we may think of the sea and its creatures, a culture broth and its multiplying microorganisms, a radio wave and the information it transmits, a line of ink and the thoughts it expresses. We have grown accustomed to the idea that many different kinds of physical entities exist, not all of which by virtue of being physical are necessarily physical entities belonging to a single unified subcategory.

If spacetime is maximally consistent in its property combination, then it satisfies the combinatorial analysis of the concept of being; according to the combinatorial analysis, therefore, spacetime exists. It is a physical entity, moreover, in the required sense, rather than abstract. It would be untenable to consider spacetime to be non-spatiotemporal, which is sufficient to classify spacetime as physical rather than non-physical or abstract. To include spacetime as an existent physical entity is not to begin to consider its physical and metaphysical complexities. That is a topic that remains for science and philosophy to explore beyond the mere ontological commitment to spacetime's existence as a physical entity.

Matter as the substance of physical entities

We have already considered substance in the eighteenth-century sense, where, idiosyncratically from a contemporary perspective, it is synonymous in the writings of philosophers like Locke and Berkeley with insensible mind-independent matter. We have also suggested that this is a problematic and to that degree uninteresting concept in contrast with the idea of substance or matter as experienceable physical stuff.

Matter, in the physical spatiotemporal sense, is clearly existent according to the combinatorial analysis of being. To confirm that this is true we need only identify good reasons to believe that physical substances in the material universe are predicationally maximally consistent. Physical objects in this sense are paradigmatically maximally consistent, whether we think of matter generally as the ultimate physical stuff, the chemical molecular and atomic constituents of all other relatively more complex physical entities, or specifically as the particular physical entities themselves, regardless of their respective levels of complexity or constitution out of simpler substances.

Our senses, even hearing and taste, are three-dimensional in the sense that they provide spatial information about physical entities. We never, and certainly never simultaneously, experience all the aspects of a physical entity. At most we see one side of an apple, one part, and from one perspective of its external surface. No matter how finely we slice and dice a material entity, we can only experience even the most transparent object from the outside. We thereby confront a fundamental opposition between subjectivity and the objective world. We know that there exists more than we immediately or through the course of human history will ever experience of even the most closely studied physical entity.

The dynamic object, C. S. Peirce has said, is phenomenally inexhaustible. Nicholas Rescher has recently reaffirmed this first vital truth of any understanding of the concept of a physical entity in the context of explaining the multiplicity of perspectives that differently situated objective observers of the same physical phenomena can experience. A similar concept enlivens Husserl's theory of the endlessly receding phenomenological horizons presented to thought in the transcendental *epoché*. We find much the same idea again if we go back to Johann Wolfgang von Goethe and Jean-Jacques Rousseau, who marvelled poetically at the inexhaustible riches of a single blade of grass.[3] We know, as a result, that there is more to the existence of the physical world than will ever meet the eye, as a blade of grass representing any and all physical entities serves to remind ontology.

Physical states of affairs as events

We do not question the actuality of physical states of affairs. We have in fact already acknowledged the combinatorial necessity that transworld-variant physical states of affairs exist in order to prevent all logically possible worlds from collapsing into the actual world. It is only physical states of affairs, different in distinct logically possible worlds, that can possibly distinguish one logically possible world from another. Abstract entities, putatively speaking, including abstract states of affairs, either do not exist at all or exist alike in every logically possible world.

This is the right way for things to turn out. It is not a choice we make in order to obtain a desired philosophical outcome, but one that logically must occur within the totality of all logically possible states-of-affairs or object–property combinations. It is a conclusion we could not prevent even if we wanted to had we found it metaphysically unpalatable. As it is, the combinatorial implication gives us just the expected result. We have, and combinatorially we must have, logically contingent physical objects and physical states of affairs, which is at once to say also that we have, and combinatorially must have, logically contingent physical entities at all descriptive levels of the ontic hierarchy. It is gratifying to see that this is precisely what we demand from an adequate concept of the actual world, and that the combinatorial analysis of the concept of being delivers the account without heroics. We identify physical states of affairs with physical events, if by a physical event we mean a physical state of affairs that occurs in and at a particular region of spacetime. By speaking of a physical event we only emphasize the spatiotemporality of a physical state of affairs, where combinatorially there are no physical states of affairs that are not physical events, and conversely.

Causation and causal connections

Causation falls somewhere between spacetime and material substance. It is not itself a physical entity, but more relational like spacetime, and is itself a spatiotemporal phenomenon. Where spacetime seems to be more entity-like in sustaining predications that have a strong presumption of maximal consistency, causation, as Hume taught, is nominal – merely the name we give to our idea of certain types of regular sequences of physical events. We call an event a cause of another event when, according to Hume, the two types of events exhibit constant conjunction, temporal succession, in which causes always precede effects in time, and spatial propinquity. The propinquity condition requires that physical entities in causal connections physically touch or otherwise come into direct contact, disallowing action at a distance. Modern science hypothesizes causal connections occurring by way of the respective fields of several types of attraction and force, themselves evidently causal concepts, surrounding material entities.

If Hume's enquiry is limited only to the origin of our idea of causation, can anything more definite be said about causation to indicate that it might be a physical entity according to the combinatorial analysis of the concept of being? If we think of physical states of affairs or physical events as physical entities, and of causes and effects as physical events, then we cannot avoid classifying causes and effects as physical entities. This is a relatively uninteresting, even trivial, sense in which causation is construable as a physical entity. What about causation itself? Is there also a physical entity, or any other type of entity, that links together events when one is the cause of the other? Some philosophers have thought of causation in something like this way: as a real force or binding energy, the cement of the universe, in Hume's phrase, holding all things in relation and stringing them together in the complex spatiotemporal world of the physical universe considered as a vast interconnected causal matrix.[4] Such speculative meta-physicians cannot understand causation as something so watered-down as to involve nothing more than Hume's three-part analysis appears to imply. They object to the idea of causation as no more than a certain pattern of relations among existent events in the actual world, a sequence of events that could be disconnected and logically altogether different than it actually is, even totally random, with no identifiable cause-and-effect relations as real physical entities.

Causation seems to many philosophers to be something more; we can count on it so reliably. To flip a light switch or boil an egg, to make or do any of the things we do, to pilot the space shuttle or perform successful brain surgery, is to know that certain types of events that we can try deliberately to produce will undoubtedly be followed by certain other types of events. We generally know what we are doing when we take hold of things, until mishap indicates that we must refine our understanding of causal connections and how and where causation obtains. We never, on the contrary, find ourselves obligated to soften our concept of the necessity with which an effect follows its correlated cause. Technical specialists who exercise control over an aspect of the physical world, to the limited extent that human decision and skill make this possible, can judge with remarkable accuracy precisely how the world will behave when we do this or that. As for things that we have not encountered before, we have relatively well-refined but open-ended flexible ways of proceeding to find out about unknown physical substances and causal relations among physical events, that enable us to venture confidently also, armed with the tried and tested procedures of scientific method, into the unknown.

These are commonplace facts not to be despised but to be appreciated and understood. They presuppose a specific concept of causal relation that we would do as well to explicate. Should this concept be thought of as that of a physical entity? We have already argued that spacetime is a special type of physical entity, an actual thing in the actual world. Although this goes against several prominent philosophical traditions, our purpose is not to fall in line with other metaphysical systems, but to think these things through for ourselves. Why, then, should we not say basically the same about causation, and recommend reifying causation and causal connections in the great network of physical events as itself an existent physical entity? Why not regard causal connections as real physical entities in their own right? If space and time and matter all have being, why not causation?

The answer is that causation already has being by virtue of relating real physical entities and states of affairs in the actual world. There is nothing further for the being of causation to consist in anyway, and no other basis for the existence of causation that would need to be invoked in order to construe causation as a separate entity. It is, after all, not so weak or watery a fact for actually existent events to be so related as to exhibit regular reliable patterns of *constant* conjunction, temporal order and spatial propinquity. It is sufficient in any case to account for the confidence with which technical experts in engineering and the applied sciences causally manipulate the world, reaching out with their *Zuhandenheit*, if they so choose, as non-experts also do in acts of everyday causally efficacious agency, using a hammer or a telephone, or doing anything at all. We do not need to consider anything more than Hume's three conditions to establish the existence of causal connections in the actual world – a rather different situation than that involved in positing spacetime as a physical entity.

Causation does not *need* to be anything else, other than the actual events of the world falling out in such a way as to constitute regular patterns of the sort identified by causal principles and formulated as natural laws for purposes of inductive reasoning. We do not need to suppose that anything more or over and above and in addition to existent events in the actual world exists in order to explain the reality of causal connections as existent physical entities. It is not a question of affirming or denying the reality of causal connections. Causation in that sense is as real as any actually existent entity or state of affairs. It is a question only of understanding what it means for a causal connection or causation considered as such to be real. If Hume is on the right track, then it need be no more than to say that physical events causally related one to another by Hume's three conditions are actual. This is not to deny or affirm the modal status of causal connections as logically necessary or contingent. If the previous argument concerning the logical contingency of constitutive physical states of affairs in the actual world in pure philosophical ontology is correct, then every causal connection, causation as such in the actual world, is equally logically contingent, and ultimately a matter of the same logical random probability or pure chance that we have previously described as combinatorial roulette.

Within a framework of combinatorial analysis in pure philosophical ontology, we say that the being of causation or of particular causal connections is explained by the three conditions of Hume's account of the origin of the idea of causation. For causation to be a real physical entity over and above the real physical events that are causally related to one another by the conditions of Hume's theory on the combinatorial analysis would be for it to be, as it presumably is, a maximally consistent predication subject. We are correct, in that case, to consider causation as something real, an existent entity possessing being at the level of relations among physical states of affairs in the actual world, as real as the entities it relates. We are not, on the other hand, required to suppose that the being of causation or causal connection consists in something over and above the real being of causally related physical events, nor that there is real causation in non-actual merely logically possible worlds.

Causal inefficacy of natural laws
We have said that natural laws codify causal connections between physical events at a higher level of abstraction. It is strange and unnecessary

to reify natural laws, particularly if we have not made distinct applied ontological provision for causation or causal connections. We can think of natural laws as convenient formulations of causal regularities that by chance prevail throughout the physical universe. Natural laws thus take on whatever causal necessity obtains among the regularities themselves. This modality, while not as strong, or, in another way, as weak, as logical necessity, is still strong enough to instil confidence or dread in the law-like causal stability of the actual world, and in our continuing ability to influence events in the physical universe.

To refer to a natural law is to invoke the authority of whatever causal regularities occur throughout the actual world. Alternatively, to mention a natural law is to speak of a principle or proposition, often thought to be an abstract entity or a meaningful sentence or set of sentences, that does not seem to be a likely candidate for causal efficacy or actually making things happen in the physical realm of real physical entities and events. If we are to take a stand for a preferred existence domain in this part of applied scientific ontology, then we might be inclined to argue that a natural law is best understood as a useful description of the causal regularities that happen to hold among existent physical events in the actual world, and that natural laws are expressed by means of principles or propositions that by themselves do not need to be thought of as in any way causally efficacious, except indirectly in so far as they influence thought and action. It is among causally related real existent physical events that the causal efficacy of natural laws is to be found, rather than in their linguistic and mathematical formulation as natural laws.

The truth of a natural law that applies to real existent physical events in the actual world is at most logically contingent, actual and presumably causally, but not logically, necessary. If natural laws exist in any other, third, sense, beyond representing actual relations among existent entities and existent physical events, superseding the existence conditions for natural laws construed only linguistically–mathematically as principles expressing these relations, then, according to the combinatorial analysis of being, natural laws like any other physical entities must be maximally consistent. Such an interpretation does not seem to be either well motivated or intrinsically plausible. It costs us nothing to say that there *are* natural laws in both senses of the word we have now considered. This is true if only because there are causal regularities, and because there may also be principles and propositions if not as existent abstract entities, then at least as concrete particulars or types thereof whose property combinations are maximally consistent. As with causation and causal connections, we have no justification for going beyond these harmless admissions to the preferred existence domain of an applied scientific ontology by maintaining that causation, causal connections and natural laws are actually existent physical entities over and above the regularities by which physical states of affairs or physical events that happen to exist in the actual world are related.

The same style of reasoning must apply to the consideration of any other category of putative physical entity. We must in every case evaluate the merits of a candidate entity according to the combinatorial analysis of being. We must try to determine whether or not the putative entity in question can be considered first and foremost as a purely logically possible object with a maximally consistent property or states-of-affairs combination. If so, then we can justify the introduction of a new entity or type of existent physical entity in a new category to add to the preferred existence domain; if not, then we are not entitled to include the discredited would-be entity. We have seen no good reason to pursue either of these directions here, but conclude our inventory of the types of physical entities in the existence domain with the above-mentioned entities: material substances, space, time or spacetime, physical states of affairs or events and, derivatively, causation in the sense of causal connections holding between actually existent physical events.

Incompleteness in quantum phenomena

There is a peculiar problem that stems from the quantum indeterminacy thesis in contemporary microparticle physics. As it may appear to affect the predicational completeness of physical entities, it is a topic that we should finally address. What are we to say about a physical entity like a tiny quark, or, say, an electron composed of quarks, if the judgement of modern physics is that these particles are indeterminate in their constitutive spatiotemporal properties?

Quantum indeterminacy, realistically interpreted, entails that no quantum-sized particle can have both determinate position and determinate momentum. To discover one of these paired properties we must physically interact with the particle in such a way as to disturb the object, thereby changing the complementary property. Determine a particle's position and we alter its momentum; determine its momentum and we alter its position. If position and momentum can never be simultaneously determined for quantum phenomena, then quantum particles appear to be inherently predicationally incomplete.[5] A quantum particle subject to quantum indeterminacy seems to have either one predicational gap in its property cluster or the other, lacking either a specific physical spatiotemporal location or a specific instantaneous momentum. If so, it is hard to see how we could consider quantum physical entities as maximally consistent, predicationally consistent and complete, for by virtue of being subject to quantum indeterminacy they appear to be inherently incomplete.

The ultimate metaphysical as well as scientific interpretation of quantum indeterminacy is contested, and its applied ontological implications, whatever may be at stake for a preferred existence domain, should be obvious even if the argument is inconclusive. If quantum indeterminacy were deemed to involve a predicational incompleteness in a physical entity, and hence to entail the entity's submaximal consistency, then it is not the existence of quantum phenomena that would have to go, but rather the combinatorial analysis of existence as maximal consistency. We consider the problem of the ontology of quantum phenomena and hence of physical entities generally in light of the quantum indeterminacy principle as a topic for the concept of being as maximal consistency and not as a threat to the ontological status of the microphysical and by extension macrophysical world. What should we say about quantum indeterminacy in connection with the combinatorial analysis of being as maximal consistency?

Suppose that we do not interpret quantum indeterminacy idealistically as a mere epistemic limitation that prevents the simultaneous determination of quantum position and momentum. If quantum indeterminacy is not only a limitation of knowledge, but a deep metaphysical incompleteness in microphysical reality, then we might be faced with the prospect of having to disavow the definition of being as maximal consistency at least of (quantum) physical entities. The potential force of the problem is evident, but how serious is the difficulty? The answer depends on how we understand the predicational completeness requirements of quantum phenomena considered as a specific subcategory of physical entity.

If we think of quantum phenomena as having the same kind of existence conditions as macrophysical entities, such as tables and chairs and galaxies, and if, again, we adopt a realistic non-epistemic interpretation of quantum indeterminacy, then there may be no avoiding the conclusion that, according to the combinatorial analysis of being as maximal consistency, quantum phenomena do not, and perhaps causally or even logically cannot, exist. This is evidently a counterintuitive result to be avoided if at all possible. We are not inevitably saddled with such a conclusion, if we think of the existence conditions for predicational completeness of quantum phenomena somewhat differently than in the case of ordinary macrophysical physical entities. We can do so with good conscience, for example, if we regard quantum physical entities as predicationally complete if either but not both their position and momentum are precisely determinable at any instant of real time. We can say, in other words, that quantum physical entities are predicationally complete, in the only way that spatiotemporal entities of their kind can possibly be complete, when either their position or momentum is determinable.

The problem of human choice and intervention in the verification of a quantum particle's properties is a widely discussed aspect of quantum indeterminacy. It seems to make the propertyhood of a quantum entity a function of what cognitive agents choose to do. Shall we test a quantum particle for its position rather than its momentum, or alternatively try to establish its momentum rather than its position? We can readily imagine, prior to either decision on the part of a quantum physicist investigating the properties of a quantum particle, that if it were decided to check the particle's position then it would indeed have a position to be discovered, while if alternatively it were decided, counterfactually under the circumstances, to check the particle's momentum, then equally the particle would have a momentum to be discerned. The joint determinability of position and momentum of a quantum physical entity prior to the successful effort even in theory to determine one or the other property should be sufficient, other things being equal, on the combinatorial analysis of being as maximal consistency, to maintain that a quantum particle exists at least until a physically interactive intervention is undertaken to assess alternatively its position or momentum.

What happens, then, at the fatal moment, when an investigator chooses to determine a particle's position rather than momentum, or its momentum rather than its position? What difference can it make to the ontological integrity (or lack thereof) of the particle, based on its predicational completeness (or lack thereof), regardless of what a scientific enquirer might choose to do or not do? One scenario is that in which a quantum particle is spinning merrily along, predicationally as complete and maximally consistent in all its property combinations as you please until a meddling researcher intervenes with a procedure to verify alternatively the particle's position or momentum, at the precise instant of the consummation of which the particle becomes predicationally incomplete and hence submaximally consistent, and so passes instantly from existence into nonexistence. The trouble with this interpretation is that it ignores the apparent scientific conviction that a particle persists through the operation, albeit a particle that did not at the moment of enquiry have both position and momentum as equideterminables, and that consequently cannot be precisely reidentified, but whose spatiotemporal career is at most statistical.[6]

Without applying these conclusions to the problem of whether the realistic versus idealistic or epistemic interpretation of quantum indeterminacy is correct, we can draw further conclusions about the nature of quantum phenomena in applied scientific ontology. We can reasonably speculate within a combinatorial framework that the quantum particle does not disappear from existence the instant its position or momentum is verified, because, as we have already suggested, a quantum particle, unlike a macrophysical physical entity, might not simultaneously need to have both position and momentum in order to be predicationally complete. Analogously, a macrophysical entity does not need to be simultaneously solid and liquid in order to be predicationally complete, provided, depending on the physical nature of the entity, it is one or the other, and has generally the potential for either possibility, even if some entities by comparison are simultaneously both solid and liquid at different times or in different proper physical parts. If quantum particles do not simultaneously have determinate position and momentum, then quantum phenomena are not physically determined, just as quantum theory maintains.

The situation is not so different with respect to the particle–wave duality exhibited by quantum phenomena and other microphysical entities. If a quantum particle, unlike other types of physical entities, is not supposed to be simultaneously determinable in position and momentum in order to be predicationally complete, then it can hardly be faulted as predicationally incomplete when a probe of its position makes its momentum inaccessible or even indeterminable, or the reverse. If a quantum particle, given the kind of physical entity it is, is not supposed to have simultaneously both determinable position and momentum, then it cannot responsibly be judged predicationally incomplete when by virtue of quantum indeterminacy it turns out only to have one property or the other, but never both at the same time. Macrophysical entities, in contrast, appear to be a totally different kettle of fish, although their macrophysical properties and ontic status presumably depend in some way on their microphysical properties. They might need to be predicationally complete by virtue of always possessing simultaneously determinable position or centre of mass and momentum. That discrepancy, however, should perhaps be understood metaphysically in the end as testimony to the differences in the physical properties of quantum and macrophysical entities.

Abstract entities, particular and universal: numbers, sets, properties, qualities, relations, propositions and possibilities, logical, mathematical and metaphysical laws

9

Abstract entities

More ink has been spilled on the question of the existence of abstract entities than on any other topic in ontology. Do universals exist? What about sets and numbers, properties, qualities, relations, propositions and laws? What light can we shed on these controversies from the standpoint of a combinatorial analysis of being?

We have already touched on several categories of abstract entities. Looking forward to what might be said or what others have said about non-spatiotemporal particulars and universals, we have provisionally considered the possibility of their existence. We must now put our cards on the table and examine whether in fact there are abstract entities, whether abstract non-spatiotemporal things in addition to physical spatiotemporal things exist, and whether or not abstract entities should be included in the extant or preferred theoretical existence domain.

The fact that the combinatorial analysis provides a definition of what it means for something to exist gives us an important advantage over most of the history of metaphysics in which the ontic status of abstract entities has been debated. Without a clear-cut positive concept of being, applied scientific ontology can only fumble in the dark, relying on Ockham's razor to determine whether or not a purported unperceivable entity exists according to perceived minimal explanatory needs. As we noted in our critique of Quine's criterion of ontological commitment, Ockham's razor is an uncertain basis for deciding what actually exists. We must decide what we think we need to explain or not explain, and whether we can offer good enough explanations that do or do not presuppose the existence of a certain category of putative entities. If we think we need to posit such entities, then, presto, they exist. If, upon due consideration, we conclude that we do not absolutely need such putative entities after all, then, supposedly, they do not exist. This, one might say, is enormous onto-logical largesse, depending for its conclusions on potentially conten-tious conceptions of what needs to be explained and what is to count as an adequate explanation. Are these the kinds of considerations that ought to make or break the existence of an entity?

In our reflections on the requirements of a preferred existence domain thus far, we have followed a different method. We have thematized and brought forward for more self-conscious philosophi-cal examination the problem of what it means for something to exist, just as Heidegger, our beacon in his statement of the fundamental problems if not the solutions of pure philosophical ontology, says we should. In the end, we have arrived at radically different conclusions than Heidegger's, substituting an Aristotelian (early) Wittgensteinian combinatorial theory of being based on pure logic for Heidegger's Kantian (later) Husserlian existential theory of being based on transcendental phenomenology.

We can still go astray in trying to apply the combinatorial analysis of being to the unique problems posed by existence claims and counter-claims for abstract entities, as we can at any step along the way in trying to determine the ontic status of other kinds of other candidate entities. The availability of a positive concept of existence, which the combina-torial analysis affords, nevertheless makes it possible to adjudicate disputes about the extant domain in specific terms according to the requirements of the definition, to decide whether or not abstract enti-ties exist on the basis of whether or not they are maximally consistent, rather than in the more slippery contentious terms of Ockham's razor. At the same time, the enquiry provides an opportunity to test and if necessary correct the proposal that being generally and in the case of putative abstract entities is predicational maximal consistency.

Ockham's razor versus combinatorial ontology

An excellent place to begin considering the problem of abstract entities is with the question of their usefulness and explanatory convenience in mathematics, science, philosophy and other fields of discourse. The utility of being able to appeal to abstract entities is virtually unchallenged even by the most staunch opponents of their existence. Honing Ockham's razor to eliminate them from applied ontology, these critics have held that despite their usefulness abstract entities are not strictly needed for the kinds of explanations we strictly need.

Since we have already found reason to doubt the universal applicability of Ockham's razor, we shall not try to make this strong condition a general requirement for the existence of *abstracta*. The decisive issue for our purposes is instead the question of whether or not putative abstract entities satisfy the combinatorial analysis of the concept of being; whether or not, that is, putative abstract entities are predicationally maximally consistent. If so, then irrespective of current impressions of their explanatory necessity or superfluity, we shall conclude that they exist. If not, if putative abstract entities are either predicationally inconsistent or predicationally incomplete, then, despite the most convincing considerations in support of their explanatory indispensability, we shall provisionally conclude from the current state of argument that they do not exist. If necessary, we will at least provisionally leave some kinds of explanations we may think we require bereft of the corresponding entities we may think the explanations require.

We thereby avoid assumptions about the status of contemporary expectations for good explanations involving putative abstract particulars or universals. If abstract entities satisfy the requirements of the combinatorial analysis of being, and are judged to exist, but are not thought to be necessary for any of the kinds of explanations we now believe ourselves obligated to provide, then we shall hold open the possibility for their future explanatory use. If abstract entities fail to satisfy the requirements of the combinatorial analysis of being, and are judged not to exist, but are believed to be explanatorily necessary, then we hold out the prospect of rethinking our current evaluation of what we need to explain, or of what should count as an adequate explanation, leaving the issue of whether the explanations we are truly obligated to give truly need to make reference to abstract entities.

We observe that assessments of whether or not abstract entities are needed for explanations have varied historically according to the kinds of explanations that have been favoured at different times and in different cultural contexts, and in the future will undoubtedly continue to vacillate. Perceptions of explanatory obligations are subject to what Thomas Kuhn in *The Structure of Scientific Revolutions* portrays in the ongoing sociology of scientific explanation as *paradigm shifts*. Abstract entities, if they exist, must be eternal, changeless, timeless, by virtue of being non-spatiotemporal. We note that putative abstract entities have generally been dismissed from the preferred theoretical existence domain of an applied scientific ontology whenever they could be shown either to be predicationally inconsistent or incomplete, or both, but that many other putative abstract entities have stood the test of time and emerged as *prima facie* maximally consistent, as having or being constituted by maximally consistent property or states-of-affairs combinations, and hence, according to the combinatorial analysis, actually existing.

Particular and universal *abstracta*

It is worth taking stock of a subdivision in applied ontologies that countenance abstract entities. This is the distinction between particular and universal *abstracta*. Roughly, numbers, sets and propositions are assumed to be abstract particulars, even if they admit of universal applications, while properties, including qualities and relations, are usually thought to be universals, despite the fact that each considered in its own right is also in a clear sense a particular entity, distinct from other abstract things.

The number π, for example, seems as much an individual entity, if it is one at all, as the Eiffel Tower or the lucky arrowhead in my pocket, albeit of an ontologically different kind. It is a particular number along the number line with a host of distinguishing properties, including being irrational, involving an indefinite decimal expansion of digits beginning 3.14159 . . ., and many others besides. The putative abstract universal entity red or redness, if there is such an existent abstract entity, in contrast, is commonly characterized as a universal, a quality that all particular red things alike exemplify, instantiate, or in which they participate, or that can hold true of indefinitely many particular red things. Red or redness is also in another sense itself a particular thing, a particular universal, for it is not blue or bashful or triangular or any other distinct quality or relation; it is a particular colour, redness or red, and not another universal. The same is true on reflection, even if we ascend to the top of the universals hierarchy and consider just the universal *universal*.[1]

The fact that some of these entities include spatiotemporal properties in their maximally consistent property combinations and others do not, does not ontologically privilege one category of existent entity over any other in a combinatorial ontology. If putative abstract entities are maximally consistent, then they exist; for in that case they as fully satisfy the logical combinatorial requirements of being as any actual physical entities existing in real spacetime. We may have a soft spot in our hearts for spatiotemporal entities, since we are such entities ourselves and we ordinarily have immediate sensations of them whenever we are conscious. In a combinatorial pure philosophical ontology, on the other hand, there is no justification for ontological prejudice in favour of physical over abstract entities.

The only relevant question is whether the putative entities under consideration are or are not maximally consistent. Then whether their property combinations include or fail to include spatiotemporal properties is no more decisive than whether their property combinations include or fail to include any other category of property or property complements. Being in a combinatorial analysis is one thing, as Parmenides rightly believed. Contrary to Parmenides, however, as Aristotle rightly believed, being is made up of many different kinds of beings, of real existent physical and abstract entities in complicated interrelations of real existent physical and abstract states of affairs in the actual world. It is as much a fact about triangles that their interior angles sum to exactly 180° as it is that you can boil water at sea level at 100° on the surface of the Earth, even though water is a spatiotemporal physical substance, and triangles are not, and the degrees of angles in geometry are not the same kind of thing as the degrees of a physical entity's temperature.

The burden of proof in such an analysis shifts to opponents of the existence of abstract entities either to refute the combinatorial analysis of being, or to argue convincingly that putative abstract entities are logically inconsistent or predicationally incomplete. It remains an open possibility, at this stage of our deliberations, whether a strong philosophical argument can be raised against the maximal consistency of abstract entities. If abstract entities, especially numbers, sets, properties, qualities, relations, propositions and any others that lubricate our explanations of phenomena, in combination with physical entities, play a useful role in discourse, then why not theorize that they exist – unless or until a good reason surfaces to question their consistency or completeness? Why not give them the ontic benefit of the doubt?

Third man argument

A celebrated objection to the existence of universals is the so-called *third man argument*. Universals are supposed to be real existent properties corresponding to the predicates by which the condition of an object is qualified. In Plato's theory of Forms, universals are posited as the abstract archetypes of particular perceivable things. If Joe and Mary and Jill are human, then Joe and Mary and Jill can all be said to exemplify or instantiate or participate in the universal humanity or Platonic Form of the ideal man.

The third man objection states that positing the existence of universals or Platonic Forms runs foul of Ockham's razor. If we suppose that individual flesh and blood human beings (the first man or multiple men) instantiate the Form of man or universal humanity by virtue of the universal being itself a human being (second man), then there must be another higher order Form or universal instantiated by all individual flesh and blood human beings *and* the universal they instantiate (third man). And so on to infinity. Presumably, however, the objection continues, we have no explanatory use for any of these higher universals beginning with the third man, beyond at most the lowest level universal of humanity or Form of man in the series, which is to say the second man.[2]

Ockham advises us to shave Plato's unruly growth of beard right from the start by disallowing even the first universal ideal man, and adopting instead a nominalistic account of multiply instantiated properties. Aristotle forestalls the infinite regress of the third man without giving up at least such universals as inhere in existent particulars, in effect by denying that the ideal man is a man, or that whiteness is itself white. This is enough to block the regress, which cannot get off the ground without the assumption that universals themselves have the property exemplified by their instances. If we are not uncritically committed to Ockham's razor, then the explanatory inutility of higher orders of universals may not matter to us anyway. Finally, combinatorial ontology does not guarantee the existence of a universal instantiated by the members of every random collection of entities. If the ideal man is not itself a man, then, as in Aristotle's solution, the regress cannot get started. Since universals are supposed to be abstract entities, they do not constitute additional instances of the particular individuals that instantiate them. Thus, there is no argument for extending their inclusion in higher and higher orders of greater more comprehensive universality. If we do not apply Ockham's razor uncritically, then the third man argument does not offer a good reason for excluding abstract entities from a preferred existence domain.

Berkeley's objection to abstract ideas

It is significant for the truth of the combinatorial analysis that challenges to specific subcategories of abstract entities or to the very idea of a non-spatiotemporal non-physical entity generally be conducted on the grounds that the entities in question are either predicationally inconsistent or incomplete. If there is a presumption of both the usefulness and maximal consistency of abstract entities, then we can begin to consider criticisms of their existence. Such an attack against the idea of an abstract general object that goes beyond facile appeals to Ockham's razor is mounted by Berkeley and approved by Hume as discrediting the possibility of abstract general entities.

Berkeley's argument offers phenomenological evidence, perfectly appropriate in applied scientific as opposed to pure philosophical ontology, for the conclusion that the concept of an abstract entity precludes its existence, on the grounds that an abstract general object is inherently predicationally incomplete. Thus, in *A Treatise on the Principles of Human Knowledge* (1710), Berkeley states:

> If any man has the faculty of framing in his mind such an idea of a triangle as is here described, it is in vain to pretend to dispute him out of it, nor would I go about it. All I desire is, that the reader would fully and certainly inform himself whether he has such an idea or no. And this, methinks, can be no hard task for any one to perform. What more easy than for any one to look a little into his own thoughts, and there try whether he has, or can attain to have, an idea that shall correspond with the description that is here given of the general idea of a triangle, which is, *neither oblique, nor rectangle, equilateral, equicrural, nor scalenon, but all and none of these at once?*[3]

It may appear that Berkeley's thought experiment concerns only abstract individuals, represented here by "the triangle" as a specific particular abstract entity. The context and its usual interpretation and application by other critics makes it clear that the same argument is supposed to apply with equal force to such universals as triangularity, or any other type of properties, qualities or relations.

Berkeley's criticism of abstract general ideas and his counterproposal for the interpretation of what is called abstract reasoning without ontological commitment to abstract entities prompts Hume in *A Treatise of Human Nature* (1739–40) to proclaim Berkeley's refutation as "one of the greatest and most valuable discoveries that has been made of late in the republic of letters".[4] In *An Enquiry Concerning Human Understanding* (1748), Hume further offers his own version of Berkeley's refutation of abstract general ideas in connection with his objections to the possibility of the infinite divisibility of extension:

> An extension, that is neither tangible nor visible, cannot possibly be conceived: and a tangible or visible extension, which is neither hard nor soft, black nor white, is equally beyond the reach of human conception. Let any man try to conceive a triangle in general, which is neither *Isoceles* nor *Scalenum*, nor has any

particular length or proportion of sides; and he will soon perceive the absurdity of all the scholastic notions with regard to abstraction and general ideas.[5]

Berkeley's argument has convinced many a sceptic of the impossibility of there existing abstract general ideas that could possibly satisfy the predicational completeness required of an actually existent entity. If, as Berkeley contends and Hume applauds, abstract general entities are inherently predicationally incomplete, then they do not exist according to the combinatorial analysis of the concept of being.

Berkeley's refutation of abstract general ideas is inconclusive, and does not show that abstract entities are inherently predicationally incomplete. The failure of Berkeley's argument, supposing the objection convincing, by itself does not establish the maximal consistency of abstract entities, or their existence. It can at best remove one major and historically influential obstacle to the possibility that abstract general objects exist, and to that extent militate against the realist view that some and perhaps even all abstract entities belonging to traditional categories actually exist. The solution to Berkeley's objection must be similar to the distinctions drawn in order to rescue microphysical entities from the charge of predicational incompleteness extrapolated from dilemmas about the position-or-momentum indeterminacy of quantum phenomena. The suggestion is that abstract entities are not predicationally incomplete in the way that Berkeley maintains because entities of the relevant kind are not supposed to have any of the properties or their contraries that Berkeley mentions in order to be predicationally complete.

Where perceivable properties are concerned, it is easy to defend the concept of the triangle as an abstract general entity lacking any colour. The argument is that mathematical entities like the triangle, if they exist, are non-spatiotemporal, and as such cannot enter causally into the chromatic absorption and reflection of light waves of any frequency that constitute colour, nor can they be perceived by colour-sensitive subjects. The triangle is no more supposed to have colour than the number 2. Similarly, then, an adequate idea of the triangle should not be expected to have any colour. The abstract mathematical properties Berkeley lists are less obviously irrelevant to the predicational completeness or maximality of a mathematical entity like the triangle, but the problem there is no different. It is no more incumbent on the abstract entity the triangle to be either isosceles or scalene than it is for the abstract number 2, or than it is for the triangle or for an isosceles or scalene triangle to be even or odd, or prime or divisible without remainder by numbers other than 1 or itself. The number 2 is just not that kind of thing. Nor is the triangle that kind of thing. The predicational completeness or incompleteness of these entities does not depend on their having any of these particular properties or their contraries. To imagine otherwise amounts to what Gilbert Ryle calls a *category mistake* in Berkeley's argument.[6]

There is also an important logical distinction that Berkeley's objection overlooks. It is no mark against the predicational completeness, and hence no detraction from the existence, of an inanimate physical entity like my bicycle that it is neither happy nor unhappy. A bicycle, lacking any psychology, is just not the sort of thing to support either of these properties or their contraries. The bicycle is predicationally complete even if it is neither happy nor unhappy, miserable nor joyful, nor capable of experiencing any other emotion. A physical entity, on the other hand, in order to exist, according to the combinatorial analysis of being, must either be happy or non-happy. My bicycle is non-happy, but not unhappy. In order to be unhappy, my bicycle would have to be capable also of being happy, which I sincerely doubt. A nonexistent bicycle in a work of fiction, on the other hand, would be incomplete in one among innumerable ways were it not specified as being either happy or non-happy, neither unhappy nor non-unhappy, neither having nor failing to have a humanlike internal emotional psychology, as inanimate real-world objects in fairy tales are sometimes described as possessing.

The distinction between un- (contrary) and non- (contradictory or complementary) properties is not unique to modern symbolic logic. It is incorporated already in propositional form in the more classical Aristotelian syllogistic logic with which Berkeley and Hume would have been familiar. We find it explicitly in the difference between contraries and contradictories, as between contrary and contradictory categorical predications, in the traditional square of opposition. Berkeley is right to insist that abstract entities are often not the true predication subjects of many choices of contrary properties. More significantly, though, Berkeley is wrong in thinking that abstract general entities are not the true predication subjects of any chosen pairs of contradictory or complementary properties, and, equally importantly, he would be utterly mistaken in assuming that an entity is predicationally incomplete merely by virtue of lacking all contrarily as opposed to contradictorily or complementarily opposed properties within their respective constitutive property combinations.

The same considerations apply with respect to the predicational completeness or incompleteness of the property combinations that are supposed to constitute the putative abstract entities whose ontic status Berkeley considers. It is no detriment to the predicational completeness of the triangle that it is neither black nor white nor red nor blue nor green nor yellow, or that it is neither isosceles nor scalene nor of any other specific triangular shape, beyond consisting of three angles joined by three line segment sides. It would, on the other hand, very much undermine the predicational completeness and hence the existence of the triangle on the combinatorial analysis of being, if Berkeley were to show that the triangle is neither black nor non-black, neither white nor non-white, and so on; or, in general, that it is neither coloured nor non-coloured. The triangle as an abstract mathematical non-spatiotemporal entity is definitely non-black, definitely non-white and so on, because it is definitely non-coloured. It is the same, although perhaps less obvious, with respect to the properties of having a specific shape, such as being isosceles or scalene. The triangle, as the particular kind of abstract entity it is supposed to be, would be altogether nonexistent if it were neither isosceles nor non-isosceles, neither scalene nor non-scalene, or having neither any specific shape nor its contradictory or complementary property. The counter-objection to Berkeley is that the triangle is definitely non-isosceles, non-scalene and so on, and thus suffers no predicational incompleteness.

As to ideas or mental images of abstract entities, Berkeley is right that they can only be particular in their predicationally complete properties, like a physical representation such as a drawing or painting or model, and hence an inadequate ideational depiction of an abstract universal entity. Berkeley is therefore correct to say that, if we are going to think of a triangle in the sense of holding a corresponding image in mind, then phenomenologically we can only do so by conjuring up a particular triangle with a definite shape, and, what is more, a definite colour, among other definite features, before the mind's eye. The particular triangle image, as Berkeley argues, is at least momentarily delegated to represent the class of all triangles. The particular choice of a type of triangle to be held up to the imagination for these very reasons is thereby guaranteed inadequately to picture the concept of the triangle in general as an abstract entity. The inference to draw from this fact, however, is not that abstract entities do not exist, but that they cannot be adequately imagined. Berkeley and Hume regard this limitation of mental imagery as sufficient proof that the triangle does not exist, and that by implication all putative abstract general entities do not exist. The consequence, nevertheless, follows only for thinkers like Berkeley and Hume who assume that an entity exists only if we can have an adequate idea of it, phenomenologically in the sense that the idea is ultimately related to originating sensations. In Hume's terminology, the idea of an existent entity must originate as an impression of sensation or reflection. Overlooking crucial differences for the sake of emphasizing something they hold in common, Berkeley's and Hume's self-consciously humanized empiricism in this respect more closely resembles Heidegger's dependence on phenomenology in existentialist ontology. We have made no such assumption, and so we are not bound by its limitations. We are not committed to empirical introspective or phenomenological methods in trying to determine the existence of entities, but are relying instead on logical foundations in a combinatorial ontology.

Numbers and sets

We can, accordingly, deal briefly but decisively with what is otherwise a vexed question in applied ontology concerning the ontic status of mathematical entities. The problems here notably concern the existence or nonexistence of numbers and sets, but also geometrical objects like the triangle, considered as abstract particulars. The combinatorial analysis of being implies that mathematical objects exist, not if and only if they are needed in order to explain something else whose existence in another context might equally be subject to doubt, but, instead, if and only if they are predicationally maximally consistent.

Mathematical entities, although they seem in some sense to be things, cannot be directly perceived in order to verify their existence as entities. That, naturally enough, is why philosophical controversies about the existence or nonexistence of abstract objects, especially mathematical entities that seem to be so indispensable to our understanding and application of the sciences, continue to rage. It is also why the philosophy of mathematics is so persistently preoccupied with heated arguments for and against the ontological reduction of numbers to sets or sets to numbers or other mathematical particulars. If we could simply see abstract entities, we would not need to dispute their existence or nonexistence.[7]

Without trying to prove that mathematical entities are absolutely required for explanatory purposes, having relaxed the demands of Ockham's razor, we can rely on the evident usefulness of numbers and sets and other mathematical particulars and universals in accounting for truth in mathematics and the sciences. Additionally, formal mathematical metatheory proves the consistency and completeness of many specific mathematical languages. Typically it does so by applying methods of mathematical induction to establish the possibility of a model for the systems, in which all the axioms and theorems of the language are interpreted as true. Although consistency and completeness cannot be jointly proved in the case of some of the most interesting formalisms, such results, at least where available, provide further partial evidence of the maximal consistency of the abstract mathematical entities posited by the propositions of demonstrably consistent and complete mathematical theories. The effort to certify mathematical systems as syntactically consistent and deductively complete in turn signifies a recognition in metamathematics of the equivalent of the combinatorial analysis of being as maximal consistency with respect to the existence conditions of abstract mathematical entities defined by the axioms and theorems of a mathematical system.

We can say all that needs to be said under the circumstances by maintaining provisionally that there is a strong presumption in favour of the maximal consistency, and hence existence, of numbers and sets, according to the combinatorial analysis of being, unless or until a sound objection to their predicational consistency or completeness is produced. We have already considered two criticisms of the existence of abstract entities, that, if successful, would have had immediate negative implications for the existence of mathematical entities. The third man argument invokes Ockham's razor in an effort to eliminate universals from the ontology, while Berkeley's thought experiment concerning the triangle as an abstract mathematical particular purports to show that there can exist no abstract general ideas. If our counter-arguments are correct, then both of these objections fail. If the third man and Berkeley's thought experiment are the most powerful but still indecisive criticisms to be considered, then the presumed maximal consistency of mathematical entities can at least tentatively be upheld. We thereby satisfy the combinatorial requirements for conditionally including mathematical objects as existent abstract entities, shifting the burden of proof to deny their existence to the opposite side of the controversy, to be met if possible by sceptics and nominalistically minded opponents of the existence of numbers, sets and other abstract mathematical entities.

We shall later engage the problem of ontological reductions of numbers to sets or sets to numbers, or to other mathematical, abstract, or even non-abstract, spatiotemporal entities, in more depth. For the moment, it suffices to remark that if numbers and sets are useful, even if not absolutely explanatorily indispensable, and if there are no knockdown objections to the predicational consistency or completeness of abstract mathematical entities, then we shall consider ourselves entitled in the interim to consider both numbers and sets, along with related abstract mathematical particulars and universals with the same qualifications, to exist as truly and fully and in the same sense of the combinatorial concept of being as any existent physical spatiotemporal entity.

Properties, qualities, relations

The situation is much the same with respect to the ontic status of properties, qualities and relations as with mathematical entities. There is a presumption in favour of the existence of useful even if not absolutely indispensable putative abstract entities in this category. There is also a comparable battery of objections to their existence, which we have already tried to answer, and which are generally variations on the themes of the third man or other applications of Ockham's razor or Berkeley's thought experiment. There is an extensive philosophical tradition of efforts to reduce one subcategory of abstract entities to another, usually offered in league with appeals to Ockham's razor.

Such similarities justify extending the same basic argument in support of the existence of abstract properties, qualities and relations that was previously considered in trying to establish the ontic status of mathematical particulars. We locate the burden of proof with those who want to challenge the existence of universals, acknowledging that we have yet to entertain a convincing objection to their predicational maximal consistency. An interesting twist for this category of putative abstract entity is that we now finally have the opportunity to address the problem of the ontology of the properties, which we previously regarded as ontically neutral logically possible properties in the combinatorial analysis of being. In a sense, this question is no different than that of the ontic status of logically possible objects as the bearers of logically possible properties in logically possible states of affairs. We have already made partial progress concerning their existence in understanding the ontology of physical and abstract entities in the subcategory of abstract particulars. All these issues are intimately interconnected, since logically possible objects can be understood as property combinations, and properties can be understood as objects that themselves have higher-order property combinations by which they are defined.

It is standard to regard properties as the more general category subsuming qualities and relations, and to equate properties of either subcategory as abstract entities with universals. The difference between qualities and relations is at least superficially that qualities are one-place properties, like the property of being red or being happy, and relations are more-than-one-place properties, like being the sister of someone, or being taller than the father of the President of the United States. It is sometimes proposed as an obvious simplification of these distinctions that properties be thought of as limiting cases of relations, or that relations be construed as relational properties. To reduce qualities to relations, a variety of devices for abstracting properties from relations are proposed in symbolic logic, all of which amount more or less to the intuitive idea that we can concatenate the terms of the relation, such as being the sister of May, into the one-place property form, being-the-sister-of-May, and predicate that property, say, of June, so that June then has the one-place relational property of being-the-sister-of-May. We shall follow only the first of these conventions here, recognizing that properties subsume qualities and relations. In contrast, we will no more consider ourselves obligated to reduce qualities to relations or relations to qualities than we are to reduce numbers to sets or sets to numbers.

The ontic status of properties should now be clear. We provisionally accept them as existent entities on the grounds of their extraordinary usefulness in explaining a large variety of phenomena, in lieu of serious objections to the presumption that they are predicationally maximally consistent. The properties in property combinations we have previously spoken of only in an ontically neutral way, as logically possible properties, can now be considered to exist as truly and fully and in the same combinatorial sense as the existent objects we have already commended as physical or abstract individuals. We conclude, in other words, that universals exist, provided they are themselves predicationally consistent and complete. This is not to say that all putative universals exist, since many candidates for inclusion in the preferred existence domain, like many nonexistent objects, will need to be excluded on grounds of predicational incompleteness or inconsistency. In particular, putative universals, properties, qualities or relations that give rise to logical paradoxes must be eliminated from the ontology on grounds of predicational inconsistency. An obvious representative example is the nonexistent property postulated by the so-called barber paradox, of being a barber who shaves all and only those persons who do not shave themselves, $\lambda x[\forall y[Sxy \leftrightarrow \neg Syy]]$.[8] A large part of the importance of trying to uncover logical and other types of conceptual paradoxes in philosophy and logic has as its motivation the testing of putative universals to see if they stand the test of predicational maximal consistency. We ask, in effect, whether a theory gives correct necessary and sufficient conditions for the concept of an abstract object or property. A sustainable antinomy concerning a putative abstract entity is a bad mark against it. If the candidate cannot be defended against objections to its consistency or completeness, then its proponents should in all honesty give up their commitment to its existence and admit that there is no such entity. Maximal consistency is a requirement that not all putative properties can satisfy, even among those that have otherwise been thought to be highly useful in philosophy, mathematics and the sciences.

Do we not, finally, face a vicious circle or infinite regress in this treatment of the ontology of universals? We say that a property has being if and only if its property combination is predicationally maximally consistent. To answer this question affirmatively, we must presumably ask whether the properties in a property's property combination are themselves existent, which requires in turn that their higher-order property combinations be predicationally maximally consistent. We may reel at the dizzying prospect of these seemingly endless ramifications of the combinatorial analysis of being. Can the existence requirements of properties, and hence of logical objects, ever be resolved or come to a definite conclusion? Can the existence of anything whatsoever be grounded firmly in pure philosophical or applied scientific ontology? Are we doomed to going round and round in yet another version of Heidegger's circle?

The situation, luckily, is not so desperate. The problem is important and must not be evaded, but there is a straightforward solution. An infinite regress or vicious circle does not arise if there are properties that do not happen to involve any internal predicational inconsistency or incompleteness. How we are to know whether and which particular properties meet these intuitive qualifications is a topic for epistemology rather than metaphysics. We do not need to guarantee that there are maximally consistent properties at ground level in ontology. We need not posit, as philosophers for other reasons have sometimes done, that there must ultimately be basic, primitive or irreducible indefinable properties. Such properties at the foundations of our conceptual scheme are supposed to be logically and conceptually so elementary that they afford no occasion for internal predicational inconsistency or incompleteness. It is instead a logically necessary consequence of the combinatorial analysis of being that there must be predicationally maximally consistent properties, because among all the logical possibilities there must be at least some maximally consistent combination of the logically possible properties of logically possible properties. With these building blocks, whatever they turn out to be, we can then in principle explain the existence of all other existent properties and all other existent entities. If it is true that universals are existent abstract entities, then the properties that intrinsically satisfy the combinatorial existence requirements are not merely logically contingent, but must be identically constituted and hence exist alike in every logically possible world.[9]

The combinatorial analysis of being also decides the historical dispute between Plato's realism and Aristotle's inherentism. The main distinction between Plato's and Aristotle's theories of universals is that Plato regards Forms or Ideas as existing independently of the ontic status of any of their instances, whereas Aristotle argues that his corresponding definitions and secondary substances exist dependently only in so far as they inhere in actually existent physical spatiotemporal things or primary substances. A combinatorial applied scientific ontology of abstract entities implies that universals actually exist, much as Plato in contrast with Aristotle holds, provided that they are maximally consistent in their constitutive property combinations. This, moreover, is a matter that can be decided defeasibly in practice when there is good reason to believe and no good reason to disbelieve that a putative universal property, quality or relation, is maximally consistent. The question of whether or not a putative abstract entity is maximally consistent considered in itself appears to be logically independent of whether or not there happen to exist any physical spatiotemporal entities instantiating the properties, thereby, other things being equal in choosing between these theories, favouring a Platonistic realism over an Aristotelian inherentist metaphysics of universals.

Propositions as truth-valued sentences

The ontic status of propositions raises special problems for applied scientific ontology. The extreme ontological alternatives with respect to the metaphysics of propositions are a Fregean Platonism on the one hand, and on the other a radical nominalism or inscriptionalism, in which propositions are said to be nothing more than physical marks in a physical medium that are causally related to language users via what Quine, in *Word and Object*, describes as "stimulus-meanings" in a behaviouristic referential semantics.[10]

The advantage of construing propositions along the lines of Frege's *Gedanken*, literally "thoughts", is that abstract entities provide a convenient way to explain the common meanings expressed in different languages, and hence by means of radically different sentences and radically different inscription types. We thereby explain why a sentence written in English can be translated, sometimes with virtually no loss of even the most subtle connotations, into other natural languages like German or Russian or Japanese or Hindi. We can say that these distinct languages have evolved different conventions for expressing an identical proposition as the thought or abstract meaning of the sentences.[11] The existence of propositions has nevertheless often been perceived as a threat to an austere nominalistically inclined applied ontology that seeks to minimize ontological commitments beyond perceivable spatiotemporal physical entities, and that looks with suspicion on putative non-physical entities unless they prove to be absolutely indispensable to the metaphysics of the absolutely indispensable explanations of contemporary science.

An argument against including propositions in the domain depends on the possibility of explaining relevant psychological and linguistic phenomena without appealing to the existence of the universal abstract meanings of sentences. There have been several types of proposals for eliminating propositions by positing another type of non-abstract entity to accomplish the same theoretical purpose. The theory that we shall examine involves a philosophical semantics in which propositions are understood as nothing more than a special category of sentence that proposes the existence of a state of affairs. Not all sentences are propositions, on this account. We exclude questions, commands and requests, expletives, many types of exclamations, and other non-propositional sentences. All propositions are nevertheless sentences. Sentences are conventional expressions of thoughts in the psychological sense, rather than in Frege's Platonistic abstract entity sense of *Gedanken*. Propositions, then, are true or false sentences.

The meanings of sentences, in contrast both with a Fregean Platonistic semantics and a Quinean nominalistic–behaviouristic semantics of stimulus meanings, can be explained in another way. In later chapters we propose an alternative intentional semantics that connects thoughts as psychological episodes with the expression of the meanings of thoughts in sentences considered as existent spatiotemporal physical entities in a way that is neither Fregean–Platonistic nor Quinean–behaviouristic. The explanation requires a more detailed scientific ontology of mind, from which standpoint the expression of thoughts in language can be understood without the excessive ontological riches of a Platonistic concept of proposition nor the poverty of an eliminativist behaviourism or other radically nominalistic theory of sentence meaning. This background will prepare us to recognize meaning in language as a phenomenon related to the expression of meaning in art and the manufacture and use of artefacts, including all technologies.

The meaning of language is a function of thought and of the interpersonal social reality in which linguistic among other expressive phenomena evolve. The theory has as an immediate consequence that there is no justification for including propositions as a special category of abstract entities among others in a preferred existence domain. If the theory succeeds, we can eliminate propositions as special abstract entities by reducing them to true or false sentences that expressively propose the existence or nonexistence of a certain physical or abstract state of affairs. We can explain the meaning of sentences in another way without appealing to the existence of propositions as abstract entities that constitute the meanings of sentences. It is no accident that we have no choice, even in formal semantics, when we are trying to explicate the content of a proposition as the abstract meaning of concrete sentences, including those from different languages equivalent in meaning, than to choose a particular language in which to present the supposedly abstract general meaning the sentences convey. Thus, in the most hackneyed example in semantic philosophy, we say that the English sentence "It is raining", the German sentence "Es regnet" and the French "Il pleut" all mean (reverting now to English, in this context) that it is raining. The philosophical situation is not improved by shifting to German or French, or to another language altogether, say, Turkish, Mandarin or Swahili.

There is no abstract language of abstract propositions in philosophical semantics. The only languages are those we thinkers contrive and into which we are in one way or another linguistically socialized. In the *Tractatus*, Wittgenstein sought to demonstrate the necessity of a transcendent language of propositional symbols that would picture the meanings of corresponding logically isomorphic states of affairs conventionally expressed in a system of natural language signs. We cannot avail ourselves of such a distinction, because we have argued that there are no transcendent entities in combinatorial ontology. In his later philosophy, Wittgenstein also gave up the concept of a transcendent order of fact-picturing linguistic symbols. We shall, therefore, not try to wedge in propositions as a special subcategory of abstract entities along with sets, numbers, properties, qualities and relations. The reason is not, significantly, that we can reduce propositions to another category of abstract entities, for all abstract *entities* exist, but because we can eliminate them from the existence subdomain of abstract entities altogether, and compensate for their explanatory service in other ways, by invoking already established subcategories of entities, such as sentences and types or categories of sentences.

If we do not have a clearly established need to include propositions as existent abstract entities, and if we do not have good reasons to believe that putative abstract propositions are maximally consistent, then we should not include them in the ontology. The merits of this policy in applied scientific ontology cannot be fully assessed until we have set an alternative explanation in place and compared their respective advantages and disadvantages. The point is that the combinatorial analysis of being does not require us to accept the existence of any and all putative abstract entities that have been introduced on grounds of their usefulness in scientific explanation. We can pick and choose those we believe are justified as maximally consistent and relatively more useful than their competitors, even if not indispensable, by applying a more refined version of Ockham's razor, relegating others where possible to another ontological category of non-abstract existent entities. In the same way, we are not obligated to provide a place in the preferred existence domain for such contested putative entities as witches, ghosts or supernatural forces.

Ontic status of abstract laws

The final topic concerning the ontic status of abstract entities is that of laws, especially logical, mathematical and, if there are any, metaphysical laws. These exhibit the same ambiguity as natural laws. In speaking of laws for abstract entities, we can refer alternatively, as in the case of laws for physical entities, either to patterns and regularities among the appropriate types of states of affairs, actual or abstract, or to the linguistic entities, sentences or propositions, by which they are expressed.

Abstract relations seem to be real enough in combinatorial ontology, while propositions have already been shown the door. If logical, mathematical and metaphysical laws are relations of special kinds themselves, structural patterns or regularities among abstract entities in logic, mathematics and metaphysics, then there is good reason to conclude that they exist. If we mean by laws the propositions that express these relations, and if propositions do not need to constitute a distinct subcategory of existent abstract entities, but are only true or false sentences, then in this sense there is even better reason to conclude that all laws, including causal or natural physical laws, as well as logical, mathematical, metaphysical and any others besides, over and above the sentences by which they are expressed, do not exist. As such, laws can have no causal or other necessitating influence of their own on the course of events in the world, but serve at most a descriptive and predictive function in metaphysics and the exact sciences.

It is the ontic status of abstract relations themselves with which we are and ought to be concerned, and not directly with the ontic status of their linguistic expression. The relations in question, the patterns and regularities among abstract entities to which we have referred, can be said actually to exist, provided the laws in question are true. The laws in any case merely summarize the relations that obtain, logically contingently but causally necessarily in the case of natural laws, logically necessarily in the case of logical and perhaps also mathematical and metaphysical laws, or else by appropriate modalities of their own. The laws construed as representing a choice of relations among physical or abstract states of affairs considered only in themselves have no agency or compulsion to make things happen in a certain way. They only describe the fact that physical events happen or abstract entities for different reasons are abstractly interrelated as the laws prescribe.

Against wholesale ontological reduction

We have previously remarked the legerdemain by which entities are made alternatively to exist or not exist according to whether they are judged explanatorily necessary or unnecessary under Ockham's razor. The method does not appear intuitively to be a sound basis for judging whether or not a putative abstract entity exists.

The problem is particularly difficult when we consider that whether or not there is an explanatory need to include a putative entity in the preferred existence domain is often a matter of the purpose of the explanation, the intellectual historical and cultural context in which the explanation is to be given, and the variable analytic, paraphrastic and reductive ingenuity of individuals engaged in explanation. Whether we really need or do not need universals or sets or classes or numbers in order to secure the truths of logic, mathematics and the sciences is not a simple question, but one with many subtleties. There have been and will undoubtedly continue to be substantive philosophical disagreements about whether or not abstract entities are required for different types of explanations. We can only hope to settle limited aspects of the problem in piecemeal fashion by looking closely at some of the particular proposals for doing away with or reducing one subcategory of abstract entities in favour of another.[12]

We can ask in this way whether numbers are sets or sets are numbers, whether qualities are a limiting case of relations, or whether relations are just a special subcategory of relational properties. If we succeed at any of these reductions, then we might be said to have trimmed-down the applied ontology of abstract entities, perhaps from four subcategories to two, and thereby accomplished an ontological economy in the preferred theoretical existence domain. These are all worthwhile efforts, if for no other reason than because of the clarity they bring to the concepts of whatever entities are finally included in a recommended applied scientific ontology. Apparent progress in these reductive programmes notwithstanding, attempts to reduce putative abstract entities in applied ontology are largely a waste of time, and give the false appearance of proceeding with a philosophical or scientific methodology in applied ontology only in the absence of being able to implement a more positive analysis of what it means for something to exist. The idea of reducing sets to numbers or numbers to sets, or any of the other proposals for reduction of any subcategory of abstract entities to any other within the general category of abstract entities, lacks real ontological significance, because it does not give us a good reason, even when the reductions succeed perfectly well on their own terms, for concluding that the reduced abstract entity (or subcategory thereof) does not really exist, in deference to the abstract or concrete entity (or subcategory thereof) to which it is reduced.

The limitations of ontological reduction can partly be seen in the fact that in many cases alternative reduction schemes are advanced with comparable intuitive plausibility, but in opposite directions. The prospect of reducing numbers to sets or sets to numbers is typical. If both of these projects succeed by their own lights, what can we possibly conclude about whether sets really exist and numbers do not, or numbers really exist and sets do not? The same problem extends to proposals to reduce abstract entities generally to non-abstract concrete physical entities, in which the futility and irrelevance of efforts at ontological reduction are even more transparent.

What we should do instead is obvious from the standpoint of a combinatorial analysis of the concept of being. We should include or exclude putative abstract entities from the preferred existence domain solely on the basis of whether or not a good argument can be made for their maximal consistency. In doing so, we gain a new perspective on the futility of the ancient metaphysical deadlock of realism versus nominalism and all the variations in between. We discover in the process that it is as pointless as a general strategy in applied ontology to reduce abstract to concrete entities, whether instances, tokens of types, or tropes or modes, parts or moments, of existent particulars. It is especially futile in contexts of scientific explanation that rely uncritically on the principle of Ockham's razor. We accomplish nothing of ontic significance by trying to decide whether numbers can be reduced to sets or properties or propositions, or propositions to properties or sets or numbers.

It is no more ontically revealing to discover that such reductions can be achieved than to decide that pions and muons can be reduced to quarks, or that, on a gross scale, chairs and tables can be reduced to smaller physical constituents, and ultimately to molecules and atoms and subatomic particles and quarks and energy fields. If we agree that all these physical entities can be reduced to or are actually made up of quarks, do we then want to say that among physical entities only quarks really exist? If quarks exist, however, then, presumably, so do all of the things that are made out of quarks and can in that sense be reduced to quarks. If the parts of my bicycle exist, then so does my bicycle, even if only as a scattered object when I have taken it apart. On the proposed combinatorial analysis of the concept of being, all of these things fully deserve to be considered existent on the assumption that all alike equally satisfy the combinatorial requirement of maximal consistency, predicational consistency and completeness.

The same is true, *pari passu*, of putative abstract entities in their part of the preferred existence domain. Again, we proceed on the assumption that sets, as well as numbers, propositions and the like, are each and all in their respective subcategories and in the relevant appropriate ways maximally consistent. If it is ontologically unexciting to learn that properties are really relations of various kinds, or the opposite, it is nevertheless potentially very instructive with respect to our understanding the conceptual networks to which the ideas of such putative abstract entities appear to belong. Then it is not a matter even of applied scientific ontology, but of higher-order metaphysics and conceptual analysis of the meanings of these terms and concepts, which it is not a trivial matter to work out correctly. If all of these putative abstract entities are maximally consistent in their respective property combinations, then they exist. In that case, they have as much reality, as much being, as the Eiffel Tower or the arrowhead I am turning over in my fingers as I write, or your thoughts just at this moment, or your favourite actually existent entity or physical state of affairs, an event you cannot be made to deny exists. If all of these putative entities are maximally consistent, then, according to the combinatorial analysis of being, they are real actually existent entities.

There is no more need to choose one type over another as actually existent than there is in the case of quarks and muons and gluons and electrons and atoms and molecules and rocks and roses and rhinoceri, planets, solar systems, galaxies and the existent states of affairs that constitute the entire physical universe, all of which with due qualifications can rightly be said to exist. They exist, according to the combinatorial analysis of being, not because we believe we need them in order to make sense of prized scientific theories and because we have thus far failed to reduce them to another more encompassing sub-category of abstract entities or something non-abstract, but because, in more positive terms, they are believed on the basis of reasonable arguments to be predicationally maximally consistent, logically coherent in their descriptions of the entities in question with no legitimate property or property-complement gaps. What more could we possibly want, especially of putatively abstract entities in a preferred existence domain? This should be all that is required, provided we are satisfied in the first place with the combinatorial analysis of being as maximal consistency, and are prepared to have it tested in this way in applied scientific ontology.

Combinatorial ontology of the abstract

While applied scientific ontology remains a work in progress, we can provisionally declare our preference for an abstract subdomain of the ontology that includes sets and numbers, properties, qualities and relations, but not propositions. An alternative theoretical applied ontology could obviously manage these potential metaphysical properties in a different way, resulting in a different preferred theoretical existence domain. Why sets and numbers? Why qualities and relations? The answer is simply that each can plausibly be regarded as maximally consistent, in the absence of contrary argument or solid evidence of their predicational inconsistency or incompleteness.

What about an effort to eliminate properties from the ontology in something like the manner proposed for propositions, taking up the explanatory slack in other ways? This, after all, has been the storm centre of philosophical disagreement about the ontological status of universals in the hoary dispute between realism or Platonism versus nominalism. We refer again to the unmet burden of proof to demonstrate inconsistency or incompleteness generally among universals on the part of opponents of the existence of abstract entities. We need not regard logically possible objects and logically possible properties as real existent entities considered only in themselves, if we can make a good case against their predicational consistency or completeness, as with the discovery of a deep conceptual paradox in their property combinations, as with the property of being a barber who shaves all and only those persons who do not shave themselves. If a sound argument to this effect could be advanced, it would provide a strong reason for eliminating properties, qualities and relations as abstract entities from the preferred existence domain, leaving others like numbers and sets to occupy that niche.

The trouble is, without entering into all the necessary details, that efforts to make particulars only do the work of universals have not succeeded. To offer only a fleeting sense of the difficulties, consider the implications of trying to reconstruct the fact that snow is white without admitting white as a universal to the preferred existence domain. When we argue that the condition of all past, present and future particular instances of snow are individually considered sufficiently similar with respect to their effect on normal colour perception as to be collected together nominalistically under a single term, and that their common shared whiteness amounts to nothing more than this, we overlook the fact that, at least in combinatorial ontology, objects do not stand free and independently of, but are constituted by, their properties. A special combination of properties constitutes a particular object or at least serves to distinguish it logically from others. Combinatorially, properties, even if not existent, are undeniably universal, at least in the sense that the very same properties go into the constitutive, identifying and uniquely individuating property combinations of distinct objects, including the actually existent physical entities encountered in sense experience. We cannot reasonably appeal to stipulative nominalizations of similarities observed between multiple objects as a way of doing without universals in the case of abstract particulars like sets and numbers, if the objects themselves are intensionally defined in terms of particular property combinations. Applied ontologists like Quine, enamoured of a desert landscape nominalism, often see all of these issues as more or less on a par, and strive to eliminate abstract entities of any sort from the existence domains they prefer. If sets and numbers are reduced to properties (or propositions) and these are eliminated, then sets and numbers are also eliminated in one fell swoop.

What about the idea of taking only abstract particular properties as elements of property combinations? This would be a rough but presumably not impossible way to proceed. The difficulty is that when we consider the property combinations [red, ball] and [red, cube], we seem more naturally to be combining the same abstract universal property red with a different second property in each case, thereby providing distinct intensional identity conditions for these logically possible objects, and explaining the truth of predications of properties to the object in unlimitedly many unexemplified states of affairs. If we turn to abstract particular properties, then we must speak instead of specially object-indexed property combinations, such as $[red^a, ball^a]$ and $[red^b, cube^b]$, where a and b are the red ball and red cube, respectively. We can follow this course if we choose, but then we enter unnecessarily into the explicit circularity of identifying object *a* intensionally with [red^a, ball^a] and *b* with [red^b, cube^b]. At this point, we do perhaps finally begin illegitimately to multiply abstract entities beyond explanatory necessity. We do so, moreover, at the risk of making all object–property predications, and hence all states of affairs, logically necessary, since object *a* cannot fail to have all and only the *a*-indexed properties belonging to its uniquely identifying property combination. For similar reasons, it will not do to allow abstract entities with few exceptions to be included only in the actual world. In that case, we cannot begin with such logical possibilities as the combinatorial analysis of being requires, including logically possible objects, logically possible properties and logically possible states of affairs, nor with transworld logical and mathematical truths, which we seem to require to be available universally for the constitution of every logically possible world.

It is interesting in this regard that Quine and other formal ontologists who have tried to eliminate abstract entities have concluded after strenuous efforts that classes in any case must minimally remain in the domain in order to make sense of the propositions of mathematics and science. If classes alone cannot be eliminated from ontology on Quine's terms, and if classes are defined as property combinations, then neither are all properties, universals in the traditional sense, entirely eliminable. If we use Ockham's razor only selectively, and abandon the ideal of wholesale ontological reduction, then we may no longer see it as an important step forward in applied ontology to commit ourselves with Quine to classes exclusively as the only abstract entities. We might then just as well open the floodgates to any putative abstract entities that prove themselves useful, and against which there is no unanswered charge of predicational incompleteness or inconsistency.

The unbearable lightness of logically possible being

We have approached the problems of pure philosophical ontology intensionally, beginning with logically possible properties, and considering their logically possible combinations with logically possible objects. Do these terms of the combinatorial theory have any deep ontic freight of their own? One immediate reaction is to ask, how could they not? To make an informed answer, we must explore the consequences of whatever propositions in the pure classical logic on which we have leaned appear to be ontologically committal.

What, finally, is the ontic status of logical possibilities, on which all else in a combinatorial theory of ontology logically depends? We say that logic is ontologically committed to logical possibilities and their logical relations in all logically possible combinations involving all logically possible objects and all logically possible properties. Are logical possibilities themselves abstract entities, or are they the constituents of all entities, including abstract ones? If logical possibilities are abstract objects, then we may be ontologically committed to them by any use of classical logic, and certainly in combinatorial pure philosophical ontology. We have not only not been particularly forthcoming about the ontic status of purely logical possibilities, but we have argued that, like Wittgenstein in the *Tractatus*, we should not try to specify the ontic status of logical possibilities in combinatorial pure philosophical ontology. In the most important sense, in answering the question of being, the ontic status of logical possibilities does not make any difference.

Is combinatorial ontology committed to a realm of abstract entities? The answer is yes, if we think that logical possibilities must exist, have being in a strong sense, in order to constitute the being of the actual world in any of its parts or moments. We should bear in mind that the possibilities in question are not all merely logical possibilities, since exactly one of them must turn out to be the logically contingent actual world. It would be odd in that case, if not logically incoherent, to regard the ontic status of logical possibilities as actually existent abstract entities. The ontological weight of logical possibilities considered only as such is of negligible importance until their implications are explained in the combinatorial analysis of being. It is logic that is ontologically committed to logical possibilities, and only derivatively the combinatorial analysis of being in so far as it makes use of the presuppositions of pure classical logic as part of its method. Combinatorial pure philosophical ontology produces the same answers to the fundamental problems of ontology no matter what the ontic status of the logical possibilities the logic combines. The possibilities in question are only the possibilities of combining elements, where the exact nature and ontic status of the elements is secondary even when relevant.

Pure classical logic's ontological commitment to logical possibilities is at most a light charge. Logical possibilities are equally the constituents of the actual world and every non-actual merely logically possible world. They are themselves not existent entities, with the single interesting exception of the actual world, but only logically possibly existent entities. Considered as such, even if they are in some sense universal, logical possibilities are still only logical possibilities. Logic cannot do without logically possible objects and logically possible properties in logically possible states-of-affairs combinations. It needs them in order to be able to formalize the internal logical structure of a sentence as it relates expressively to logically possible inferences in reasoning. Logic is a formal theory of all logical possibilities, of predications at the linguistic and symbolic order, and of the possession of properties by objects in states of affairs in the ontic or metaphysical order. If we want to do without logical possibilities, even in whatever form we introduce them into the machinery of combinatorial pure philosophical ontology, then we will also have to do without logic. Combinatorial ontology asks only for whatever logical possibilities are available generally to a logic favoured for the expression and inference of meaningful sentences, and from these modest materials answers fundamental questions about the nature of being.

We begin intensionally with properties. Properties are only the logically possible qualifications of logically possible objects, and the states of affairs in which a logically possible object possesses a logically possible property are only logically possible states of affairs. Logical possibilities, of objects, properties, states of affairs and worlds, have at the outset only whatever ontic status we eventually want to extend to logical possibilities generally, knowing that only one logically possible world consisting of one choice of logically possible objects and logically possible states of affairs is actual. It is not asking much for logic to admit logical possibilities, but logic is nothing without them. Logically possible objects, properties, states of affairs and worlds are minimally sufficient on a combinatorial analysis of the concept of being to deduce the necessary existence of the uniquely existent logically contingent actual world. We start out intensionally with properties, with meanings, as conceived in pure logic, and end up with the actual world, with abstract and spatio-temporal and subjective psychological entities.

The existence of some actual world or other is logically necessitated, although the actual world, its condition and constitution, is logically contingent in all its physical objects and states of affairs. A combinatorial theory of being begins with and depends throughout on the lightest of ontological foundations, the logical possibility of a logically possible object having a logically possible property. All logical possibilities are entities on the combinatorial analysis of being if and only if their constitutive extraontological property combinations are predicationally maximally consistent. If a mere logical possibility is an abstract entity, it is the ontologically most important of all abstract entities.

Subjectivity of mind in the world of objective physical facts

Ontology of mind

The occurrence of thought raises difficult issues in applied ontology. The mind–body problem challenges our understanding of how thought relates to the established existence subdomains of physical and abstract entities.

What is a thought and what is the mind? If the mind and its contents are simply physical entities, if thoughts are simply physical events in the brain and nervous system of a living organism, then the ontic status of the mind can be classified without further ado as a special type of physical entity among others in the universe. The distinction between internal thought and the external world in that case is an illusion that collapses entirely into the world of objective facts about exclusively physical phenomena. If, on the other hand, thoughts are ineliminable and ontologically irreducible to physical events, then we must find a way to expand the existence domain to accommodate the mind and psychological events as something altogether different from physical and abstract entities.

Physicalism or *materialism* in the philosophy of mind proposes to explain mental phenomena reductively as physical occurrences, primarily in the brain and neurophysiological network. The elimination or reduction of mental to physical events is sometimes said to be mediated by environmentally conditioned behaviour or behavioural dispositions in a variation of physicalism known as *behaviourism*. *Functionalism* is a third type of eliminative or reductive physicalist theory, according to which psychological events can be discounted in favour of the mechanical information-processing subroutines performed by the brain as a living machine, a purely physical entity, functioning according to abstract rules much like the number-crunching algorithms of a computer program. We have already established the outlines of an existence domain of physical entities, states of affairs and events. If thoughts are just neurophysiological events, then no new ontic categories are required to subsume psychological states. If we can agree that there is nothing more to mind than a complex physical phenomenon considered in neurophysiological, behavioural or functional terms, then we can solve the mind–body problem in favour of the body.

Whether mental events are reducible to physical events, as many scientists and philosophers have assumed, is by no means easy to decide. Although many theorists are encouraged by the impressive successes of the natural sciences in explaining and predicting other types of previously mysterious and apparently physically recalcitrant phenomena, there are good reasons for being sceptical about the prospects of doing away with or ontologically reducing psychological events to purely physical events. We must consider the best arguments reflecting the most important positions on opposing sides in the mind–body subjectivity–objectivity controversy, and try to sift through the conclusions that emerge for clues to a correct ontology of mind.

Eliminativism and reductivism

A significant ontological economy is achieved by eliminativism and reductivism in the philosophy of mind. Eliminativists argue that there really is no such thing as mind, that there are at best misleading appearances of consciousness and mental content. Reductivists similarly hold that while psychological phenomena are real, they do not belong to a special ontic category of their own, but can be satisfactorily explained by reference to exclusively physical phenomena and their abstract properties.

There are as many forms of eliminativism as of reductivism. Both "isms" begin with scientific findings about the brain and nervous system and externally verifiable facts about the behaviour, including verbal behaviour, of a psychological subject. Thus, they stand in stark opposition to any form of phenomenology that does not allow itself to be fully explained and its conclusions fully recovered only from an external impersonal or third-person standpoint. We have already mentioned materialism, behaviourism, and functionalism as physicalist theories of mind, to which we now add the qualification that there can be either eliminativist or reductivist versions of these three types of theory. It should be clear that if any of these six versions of physicalist theories is true, then there is no need at all to tack on another category to the preferred existence domain as we have characterized it up to this point, or even to establish a separate subcategory of psychical entities for psychological phenomena. If thought does not really exist, or if we can manage to say whatever can legitimately be said about the mind in an explanatory reduction in which no mental or psychological concepts occur, then there is no need to expand the ontology of physical and abstract entities that we already have in place in order to take adequate account of the nature of thought.[1]

In their rejection of first-person subjectivity as unscientific, both eliminativism and reductivism are opposed to any theory of mind that maintains a difference between the externally verifiable properties of the psychological subject, and any supposedly internal aspect of mind. They are particularly interested in disputing what common sense and phenomenology refer to as the *qualia* and *intentionality* of thought. These are the properties of lived-through psychological content, or what it is like to experience a certain thought or type of thought, and the "aboutness" or direction of a thought towards an object, by which a thought refers to, intends or is about this or that existent entity or nonexistent object.[2]

By rejecting the qualia and intentionality of thought as real properties or as ontologically distinct from physical or abstract properties, eliminativism and reductivism propose more or less radically to streamline the preferred existence domain to what we have thus far characterized as the applied scientific ontology of existent physical and abstract entities. The question of whether such an elimination or reduction of psychological phenomena can be accomplished by materialism, behaviourism, functionalism or any other imaginable theory of mind has become the major bone of contention among disputing philosophical factions in their efforts to address the mind–body problem. The undecided ontic status of thought, consciousness and the mind thus boils down in theoretical terms to the undecided ontic status of qualia and intentionality.

Although eliminativists are still very much a force in contemporary philosophical psychology, their efforts to deny the obvious first-person facts of consciousness need not be taken as definitive. Some philosophers have claimed that eliminativism is so blatantly false and counter-intuitive that it can be discounted without further argument. They defy the eliminativist to deny the existence of a howling toothache or the sensation of colour in a field of flowers.[3] This complaint might be justified, but it does not go to the heart of the eliminativist stance, which attempts to acknowledge these reported counter-examples as false appearances. A more powerful objection to eliminativism is that the approach is logically incoherent, for in acknowledging that there are appearances, true or false, of first-person conscious thoughts exhibiting qualia and intentionality, eliminativists thereby admit the existence of consciousness. What is an *appearance*, after all, but a psychological occurrence, a thought or experience, in which there is veridical or illusory mental content that in this case is reflexively about the occurrence itself, whether or not an eliminativist wants to say that it actually exists? If even the appearance of thinking is not itself already a thought, then what is it exactly that eliminativists are supposed to be denying?

If eliminativism is as confused as it appears, we can best proceed by setting aside its implausible refusal to acknowledge the existence of thoughts, and concentrate more profitably on reductivist programmes in behaviourism, materialism and functionalism. We must inquire whether any of these reductivisms satisfactorily answer the mind–body problem, or whether the qualia and intentionality of thought are ultimately explanatorily irreducible, justifying an addition to the preferred existence domain, alongside physical and abstract entities. If so, then we must institute a special new category for ontologically irreducible thoughts, psychological phenomena and states of affairs that is not just a combination of purely physical and purely abstract entities. As the arguments are considered, we discover good reasons for renouncing any form of reductivism, in support of the contrary thesis that qualia and intentionality are explanatorily irreducible. We thereby arrive at an appreciation of the ontologically irreducible subjectivity of mind in the world of objective facts.

Materialism, behaviourism, functionalism

The advantage of any type of reductivism by comparison with eliminativism in the philosophy of mind is supposed to be that it avoids the embarrassment of denying the existence of thought. Anyone can and everyone does experience introspectively psychological states at first hand. At the same time, reductivism allows explanations of psychological phenomena to be given in third-person scientifically respectable causal terms involving publicly verifiable properties of purely physical entities and events and their purely physical and abstract properties. We examine three main types of reductivism, and conclude that none justifies the explanatory or ontological reduction of psychological phenomena to purely physical entities.

Materialism tries to reduce psychological events to facts about a subject's neurophysiological states. These are usually understood to include antecedent conditions and the impact of environment in a general framework of causal connection among physical events governed by natural scientific law. Materialism in that sense is the most basic form of physicalism. It holds that whatever we might otherwise want to say about the qualia and intentionality of internal psychological states can be explained in terms of the external material properties of the brain and nervous system of a psychological subject. A thought is then identical with, nothing other than or over and above, a material neurophysiological occurrence. It is an electrochemical transaction within the complexly connected neural connections in a certain living material entity, the brain and its nervous systems. Thought in principle can then be understood in terms of its material constituents and their physical properties interrelated in a complicated biological system, causally interacting with each other and less immediately with the substances and events of the external material world.[4]

Behaviourism has several forms, but is generally the theory that all psychological phenomena are reducible to occurrent behaviour or conditional counterfactual behavioural dispositions. A classic example is one in which behaviourism, despite, or perhaps because of, its oversimplification, eliminates or reduces references to pain as a mental episode in preference to pain expression, such as moaning, wincing, crying, tending an injured body part, seeking aspirin or the like. A *dispositional* behaviourism, also sometimes known as logical, analytic or philosophical behaviourism, does not require that psychological phenomena be explanatorily and ontologically reduced to concurrent expressions of behaviour, but to the tendency to engage in such behaviours when certain conditions are satisfied. I might have such strong control over my behaviour even when I am in pain that I do not immediately groan out loud. The dispositional behaviourist will argue that I am nevertheless disposed to do so, or probably would do so, if I were by myself or under the relevant disinhibitory circumstances.[5]

Functionalism is similar in some ways to behaviourism. It emphasizes the correlation of inputs and outputs of information to and from a computer. The mind is an information-processing machine, according to functionalism, one specific formulation of which has come to be known as *computationalism*. A functionalist account of psychological processes can be articulated in an information flow and control diagram. The diagram features decision boxes and action modules and arrows indicating how the components of the information-processing device are supposed to relate and interact, along with the direction of information processing, as in the formal description of a computer program. The analogy between computer hardware and software is often exploited by functionalism as part of its solution to the mind–body problem. The body is described as the hardware and the mind as its operating software program, processing information in a rule-governed way in real time. The hardware and software, the neurophysiology of a psychological subject and the information-processing program by which input is converted to multiple modalities of output, requires an intimate connection and exact interaction of neurophysiological information-processing structures. According to functionalism, neither body nor mind can be adequately understood as a separately existing, separately functioning entity. Mind and body must rather be considered as an integrated well-oiled machine that some functionalist philosophers and cognitive scientists prefer to speak of as mind–body.

The standard objections to materialism and behaviourism have emphasized the advantages of functionalism over its rivals as a reductivist theory of mind. Materialism is criticized for its limitation to specific kinds of material entities and events in explaining the nature of thought. We do not know that the only kinds of material substances that can support psychological phenomena are those that happen to be found in terrestrial life forms, in the physical stuff that makes up the thinking things in the particular part of the universe that we inhabit. If, on the other hand, we establish an open-ended list of material substances capable of sustaining thought, then we never arrive at a philosophically satisfactory explanation of the concept of mind, because a list of instances is never a substitute for conceptual analysis. Behaviourism in any of its guises, concurrent or dispositional, in stimulus-response (S-R) or operant conditioning models, is faulted for being too crude to account for the full range of complex psychological occurrences it is meant to explain. An example of the difficulties behaviourism encounters concerns a subject who must be judged behaviourally as thinking about Bach rather than Brubeck or Brubeck rather than Bach. The subject's psychological state arguably cannot be exactly behaviouristically determined, regardless of whatever manifest behaviour or dispositions to behave are evinced, if the subject is honestly mistaken about the conventions for communicating the content of the thought, and intends to express Brubeck by the name "Bach", pointing to pictures of Bach, recordings of Bach's music, and the like, and intends to express Bach by such conventions as uttering or being disposed to utter the name "Brubeck", while indicating pictures and recordings of Brubeck.

Functionalism is thought to enjoy a special advantage over materialism. It is deliberately not limited to any particular material substance, such as the largely carbon-based cytoplasm of human neurophysiology as life happens to have evolved on our planet.

Functionalism can explain psychological states, events and occurrences involving any type of material substances, provided only that they are functionally properly so organized and interrelated as to support equivalent information-processing functions, converting information input to output in identical ways with different types of hardware. Accordingly, once again, we narrow our focus, this time to functionalism, as the most promising, currently popular version of explanatorily and ontologically reductivist philosophy of mind.

Functionalism has philosophically interesting implications that some theorists believe provide additional justification, but that critics of the theory have declared an outrageous *reductio ad absurdum*, of the theory's basic principles. It is supposed to follow, for example, that a sufficiently large number of persons holding cards reading "0" or "1", like the machine language of a digital computer, orchestrated in their movements relative to one another so as to exactly simulate an appropriate information-processing program, would not only formally model the mind's information-processing protocols, but would replicate thought by instantiating self-consciousness. The *danse macabre* of 0's and 1's is supposed to constitute a living intelligence, indistinguishable, since the exact medium of information processing is irrelevant to functionalism, from the natural biological mind whose software program is thereby duplicated.[6]

Philosophical opinion varies diametrically as to whether such results are interesting implications or self-refuting absurdities. Contemporary philosophical psychology is sharply divided over just such issues as these about the existence and nature of the mind. A further, even more intriguing and correspondingly more controversial implication of functionalism is its philosophical underpinning for artificial intelligence, which seeks mechanically to reproduce real psychological occurrences by programming a digital computer with the mind's software of information-processing algorithms. If the exact hardware by means of which strings of 0's and 1's are input to a processor and transformed by the appropriate software into output in a rule-governed way is irrelevant to the explanation of psychological phenomena, then it should be possible in principle to construct a mechanical mind out of any sufficiently complex digital computing machinery. Artificial intelligence thereby at once becomes a computer laboratory in which the functionalist thesis can be tested, and a prospective goal and vindication for functionalism — *if*, that is, functionalism's or computationalism's implications for the possibility of what is sometimes described as strong or mentalistic artificial intelligence should turn out to be feasible, and the opposite if they are not realizable.

The main difficulty with functionalism as an adequate reductive theory of mind is approximately the same as that of behaviourism. The analogy between behaviourism and functionalism is straight-forward if we think of the inputs and outputs that are supposed to be processed algorithmically by the mind or by any material device capable of transforming information by the equivalent of a computer program on the functionalist thesis. We see that these are not so different from the correlation of input environmental stimuli or scheduled operant conditioning and output behaviour or dispositions to behave described by alternative versions of behaviourism. Some behaviourists even speak of the individual psychological subject as a kind of black box, the exact biological and neurophysiological operations of which a behavioural science neither needs to nor can intelligibly investigate. This is just how functions generally are defined, whether in mathematics or functionalist psychology or philosophy of mind. The arithmetical function of addition is just such a black box. There are numerous possible algorithms but no definite answer to the question of how addition converts 2 and 3 into 5. Addition in this elementary calculation really is nothing more than the correlation, among endlessly many other combinations, of the inputs 2 and 3 with the output 5. The problem with functionalism, as with behaviourism, is that we do not have an adequately sensitive way, merely by correlating inputs and outputs of information, in effect, coded strings of 0's and 1's, of distinguishing reductively between a subject's thinking about Bach or Brubeck, based purely on what goes into and what comes out of the information-processing black box.

If functionalism is the best hope for a reductive philosophy of mind that has no need to refer to the ostensible internality and privacy of thought, that avoids speaking of qualia or intentionality, then the prospects for a theory whose applied scientific ontology consists only of physical and abstract entities with no special third category for mental or psychological entities do not seem particularly promising. We now consider two alternatives to mind–body reductivism that have appealed to non-reductivists in the study of mind, known as *substance* and *property dualisms*.

Cartesian substance dualism

A non-reductive philosophy of mind requires significant adjustment in the preferred existence domain, an addition to its previously established categories of physical and abstract entities. It is found in a still more traditional philosophy of mind, often referred to as substance or

Cartesian dualism, named after Descartes, the philosopher with whom this way of understanding the mind is most frequently associated.

According to substance dualism, there are two different kinds of substance – physical and mental or spiritual substance, bodies and minds – that are ontologically distinct but integrated in a living psychological subject. There are several versions of Cartesian dualism, not all of which were explicitly defended by Descartes. Some variations of substance dualism in particular are designed to enable Descartes's distinction between mental and physical substances to meet a variety of philosophical objections. What they have in common is an ontological commitment to the body and mind as separate but interrelated entities. Beyond their shared distinction between the body and mind or soul, substance dualisms disagree in particular on whether or not physical and spiritual substances can causally interact, as Descartes believes, or whether they are related at most only more abstractly. God, also, in Descartes's system, as in that of most other mind–body substance dualists, in contrast, is a purely spiritual entity, and, in Descartes's metaphysics, a pure mind of infinite substance. In some versions of substance dualism, God sustains a divine pre-established harmony between mental and physical events, keeping both synchronically correlated together in parallel tracks.

Substance mind–body dualists, unlike eliminative or reductive materialists, behaviourists or functionalists, add something categorically new and different to the basic ontology of physical and abstract entities. The mind or spirit or soul as a distinct kind of spiritual substance cannot be assimilated in or subsumed under either the physical or abstract realms of a preferred existence domain, but requires its own unique subdomain. Descartes, nevertheless, sees an important gain for religion in his metaphysics of substance dualism, since he believes it implies that the mind, spirit or soul need not perish with the physical body, but might and even must survive its death in a continuing spiritual existence. This is a traditional idea of the soul integral to Descartes's Catholic Christian religious background, that is also taught by many other world religions. The previously described categories of ontology must be expanded if a substance dualist philosophy of mind is accepted, to accommodate physical, mental or spiritual and abstract entities. The minds of psychological subjects, as distinct from their bodies, especially from their brains and nervous systems belonging to the ontology of physical entities, must then be classified as mental or spiritual entities, in a category that might also be adapted to include God as a supreme mind or divine spiritual being.

Substance dualism, despite its implications for the contra-causal freedom of will and the immortality of the soul, has had few adherents in contemporary philosophy of mind, and as a result has had little impact on the choice of a preferred existence domain for the ontology of mind. Objections to substance dualism include the argument that appeals to mental entities as a separate applied ontological category are not needed in order to explain psychological phenomena scientifically for thinkers attracted to some form of eliminative or reductive philosophy of mind, and thus go by the board thanks to Ockham's razor. Another complaint urges the difficulty of accounting for mind–body causal interaction on the substance dualist thesis. We want to be able to do justice to the fact that mental events like decisions, beliefs and desires can cause the body to do certain things, and that physical occurrences of many kinds can in turn bring about specific types of mental events. All perception of the external world needs to be explained in something like this way in a substance dualist framework, as would such mental events as pain experiences occasioned by damage to nerve endings, altered states of consciousness induced by drugs, and many others besides.

By consigning minds to a distinct ontological category different from physical entities, substance dualists like Descartes require the mind and its thoughts to be non-spatiotemporal. The presumption that thoughts while occurring at specific times or during specific intervals of time have no particular spatial location is sometimes considered as good evidence in support of mind–body dualism against any form of eliminativism or reductivism in the philosophy of mind. Such a classification, unfortunately, as critics of the theory are quick to point out, seems metaphysically incompatible with the possibility that the body and mind might causally interact. It implies that while the body and all its parts have definite spatial locations, the mind as a spiritual substance is literally nowhere. Where, in that case, can the body and mind causally interact? Where can they touch one another in space and time to bring about a change of state by transfer of energy, as we expect from our knowledge of all other types of causal interaction? If there is no answer, and no plausible way of discounting the question, then the prospects of substance dualism may be unpromising in the extreme, as critics hostile to the theory on these grounds have concluded.[7] A related objection in modern physics is that while Cartesian dualism entails that the mind as a spiritual substance with its thoughts is non-spatial, as intuitively it sometimes seems to be, thought is nevertheless supposed to be temporal. Descartes and most other theorists, whether or not they are substance dualists, provided only that they are not eliminativists, believe that thinking occurs in real time, which is impossible if space and time are not scientifically distinguishable dimensions, but united in a single relativistic spacetime continuum. If substance dualism is unacceptable on its own terms for any of these reasons, then spiritual substance, distinct from physical and abstract entities, should not be added to a preferred existence domain.

Virtues of property ≠ substance dualism

There is another type of mind–body dualism that is different from Cartesian substance dualism, and that deserves serious mention in the context of exploring an alternative ontology of mind. This is the theory of *property* or *aspect dualism*. Property dualism is not a concept of mind that requires a separate ontological subcategory of mental or spiritual substances, but one that in some formulations necessitates a different kind of revision of the received ontology of physical and abstract entities.

Property dualism does not hold that the mind transcends the body. We have already indicated that there is no room in a combinatorial ontology for transcendent entities. Whereas some philosophers, notably Kant, the later Husserl and the early Wittgenstein, argued that the ego or "noumenal" or "metaphysical" self or "philosophical I" is in some sense transcendent, we have seen that the concept of mind, self, soul or ego transcending the actual world at large is logically incompatible with the combinatorial analysis of being as maximal consistency. If these conclusions are correct, then transcendental mental entities are necessarily excluded from a preferred existence domain in an applied scientific ontology of mind. Property dualism is different from eliminative and reductive philosophy of mind, the metaphysics of substance dualism, and the theory of the mind's transcendence.[8]

There are interesting similarities between property dualism and the theory of the transcendence of mind. The first and most obvious parallelism is that both approaches deny mind–body reductivism and affirm the reality of thought and mental content, in defiance of eliminativism. Property dualism, like substance dualism, rejects the model of mind whereby mental states are identical with physical states. There are various forms of property dualism. The most tenable is perhaps a version of the theory whereby thought is both physical – has a physical neurophysiological aspect – and also a mental non-physical aspect, by virtue of exemplifying qualia and intentional properties that cannot be reduced to or adequately explained in terms of physical qualities and relations. If qualia and intentionality cannot be satisfactorily reduced as proposed by materialism, behaviourism or functionalism, then there are properties of mind that are not purely physical.

We focus for the moment on the intentionality of thought, and return later to the relation between qualia and intentionality. Intentionality or aboutness on some accounts is a primitive irreducible abstract relation holding between thought and its objects. There are good but not unchallenged reasons for thinking that intentionality cannot be explained reductively in terms of non-intentional concepts. One argument is that thought appears phenomenologically to be capable of intending nonexistent objects, and that the intentionality of decision-making in action is directed toward nonexistent as yet unrealized or unactualized states of affairs. A contemplated action is intended to achieve its intended object only thereafter in trying to bring it about as an actual state of affairs, and may or may not succeed in actually doing so. A reductive account of mind must explain or explain away the intentionality of thought in terms of physical properties causally interrelated like other physical occurrences. If intentionality sometimes involves a relation to nonexistent objects, like my as yet merely dreamed-of visit to Sifnos, then such thoughts cannot be adequately explained physically or causally. The reason is that in such explanations only actual physical entities and events involved in actual real-time causal interactions can be mentioned. Here there may also be a clue to understanding the freedom of thought, will and action, all interlinked because of the intentionality of mind, and frequently understood to be an essential presupposition of moral responsibility and moral value.

The intentionality of thought, if it cannot be explained in a physically reductive way or explained away as an illusion and philosophical confusion, superadds a non-physical dimension, a second side or hidden facet concealed from the hard psychological sciences, to the physical neurophysiological properties of mind. The ontology of mind must then make provision for non-physical aspects of thought, and in particular for intentional states that may be different in ontological kind from purely neurophysiological states. Property dualism so conceived does not add any ontologically new entities, if we are literally just counting heads. It does not add any unprecedented non-physical substances to the physical and abstract entities we have already granted or concerning which we may remain sceptical. The theory nevertheless introduces a category of properties that involve the abstract relation of intentionality as a property of appropriately neurophysiologically complex physical entities such as ourselves and notably involving our brains and nervous systems.

The mind, according to property dualism, has two different aspects by virtue of its distinct types of properties. It has physical and non-physical properties, the latter category including qualia and the intentionality of thoughts. The mind has an external side which it shows to the cognitive sciences, and an internal first-person side, which is known only introspectively by the first-person subject in first-person experience. Substance dualism is not implied; only the neurophysiology of a psychological subject in a qualia-bearing intentional state. If we deny this dual aspect of thought, its cognitive scientific third-person outside and its phenomenological first-person inside, or if we fail to look for the right kinds of answers to the right kinds of questions in the appropriate side of the first-person–third-person division of a cognitive subject in a more broadly scientific investigation of the mind, then we are certain to misunderstand the nature of consciousness, to oversimplify psychological faculties, and deny what is obvious to reflection about the content and reference of conscious thought.

Such criticisms are directed only at third-person eliminativism and reductivism as philosophical ideologies, and not against the important scientific discoveries made by cognitive science. When cognitive science fills in another missing piece of the puzzle about how the mind processes information and controls motor activities, we may have significantly increased our knowledge about the mechanics of thought. Why suppose, however, that what even the best third-person science delivers about the workings of the mind gives us a complete picture? Why do so, especially when we have good even if defeasible reasons to believe from the only acceptable source, our own individual first-person introspective or phenomenological experiences, that the mind must be a dual-sided kind of thing, with an outside that others can examine and an inside that only we as first-person subjects can non-inferentially know?

We can freely accept non-reductive materialism, non-reductive behaviourism and non-reductive functionalism in a property dualist philosophy of mind. All such theories make important contributions to our understanding of the concept of mind in its physical aspect. They do not by themselves solve the mind–body problem, if the objections we have raised are correct. Nor as a result do these non-reductive theories determine the ontology of mind. If the mind also has physically irreducible aspects involving the qualia and intentionality of thought, as we have argued, then the preferred existence domain for a correct applied ontology of mind must include a special subcategory of irreducibly subjective psychological phenomena alongside the previously established subdomains of purely physical and abstract entities. The mind in that case is not purely physical or abstract, but something different, by virtue of its physically irreducible qualia and intentionality.

Property dualism interposes a third applied scientific ontological subcategory in the preferred theoretical existence domain, in much the same way that substance dualism, if accepted, would introduce a new subcategory of spiritual entities. The character of the addition to the applied ontology of mind is obviously very different in the case of property dualism than for substance dualism. The mind, according to property dualism, is not altogether a non-physical entity. It has all the physical properties of its neurophysiology, behaviour and information processing that are investigated by the hard psychological and cognitive sciences, together with the non-physical properties that disqualify it as a purely physical entity. Consciousness for property dualism is an episodic succession of qualia-bearing intentional states lived through by a thinking subject in real time. This makes it appropriate to allow phenomenology as well as neurophysiology and behavioural science in the study of mind. We have not objected to phenomenology in philosophy generally, but only to its application in what purports to be pure philosophical ontology, as in Heidegger's metaphysics. Ockham's razor does not legislate against introducing property-dualistic minds into the applied ontology unless the explanatory needs in philosophical psychology for which qualia and the intentionality of thought are emphasized can be satisfied in another way in terms of purely physical and abstract entities alone, levelling the three proposed applied ontological subcategories back to two. It is unclear that there are any immediate prospects for successfully effecting this kind of ontological reduction.

Supervenience in the ontology of qualia and intentionality

The intentionality of mind, as we have urged, is complemented by its qualia or lived-through qualitative content of thought. A quale, in the singular, is what it is like from a thinker's first-person perspective to experience a certain type of thought. Seeing a colour or tasting a claret or feeling grief or lust or joy or the satisfaction that comes from understanding a difficult mathematical proof are sufficiently suggestive examples. The relation between qualia and intentionality is a difficult problem for property dualism.

Qualia and intentionality phenomenologically go together, but thought content evidently underdetermines a thought's intended object. There is no reason why the Taj Mahal could not be intended by a thought whose qualia or content is the equivalent of a mental image of the Statue of Liberty or the Blue Mosque of Istanbul. Like the intentionality of thought, qualia have proven to be resistant to efforts at theoretical elimination or reduction to purely physical non-intentional entities, and equally essential to a complete understanding of the nature of thought and the concept of mind. The stubborn recalcitrance of qualia and intentionality to reductive strategies in philosophical psychology has motivated some philosophers to deny or ignore these properties of mind in order to clear the way for a more traditionally scientific account of psychological phenomena. We cannot satisfactorily solve genuine philosophical problems, however, simply by denying the evidence from which the problems arise.

If it is true that thought possesses both qualia and intentionality, how, if at all, are they related? There is an interesting argument to suggest that qualia and intentionality must be logically independent of one another. Hilary Putnam's *Twin Earth thought experiment* implies that two or more thinkers, neurophysiologically indistinguishable in every way, can have identical qualia, despite intending different objects on Earth and Twin Earth. Twin Earth is exactly like Earth, except that on Earth water is H_2O, whereas on Twin Earth water is XYZ. Putnam assumes that thinkers on Twin Earth are molecule-for-molecule identical with thinkers on Earth, discounting the water in their bodies, apparently, so that everyone on Earth has a Twin Earth doppelgänger. Putnam assumes that mental states supervene on physical states, so that the qualia or thought contents of Earth thinkers and their Twin Earth doppelgängers are identical. If my Twin Earth counterpart and I both think "Water!", then the experience or thought contents of our desires for or beliefs about water are qualitatively identical. If Earth water is H_2O and Twin Earth water is XYZ, then my doppelgänger and I nevertheless referentially intend different objects when we both desire or believe that there is water. The implication is that qualia and intentionality must be different, logically independent from and unrelated to one another, because a thinker on Earth and the thinker's Twin Earth doppelgänger can have identical qualia even when their thoughts intend different objects.[9]

Despite such arguments, there is a sense in which qualia and intentionality are interdependent. Wherever an intentional state occurs, it is accompanied by qualia, and conversely. Qualia, indeed, can be classified as at once the phenomenologically indistinguishable contents and intended objects of certain reflexively intentional psychological states. Conceivably, then, qualia and intentionality need not always if ever be two different things, but rather the same thing considered under two phenomenologically related descriptions, or perhaps as two logically interimplicative properties of a unified mental state. Alternatively, qualia and intentionality might be understood as two distinct aspects of thought, related in such a way that one never occurs without the other. Intentionality, introspection teaches, requires no specific content to determine reference to a particular intended object. If intentionality, as some theorists have argued, is a conceptually primitive logically irreducible abstract relation between thought and its object, then an act of thought intends or is about an object directly without mediation by qualia.

We can think of the connections between neurophysiological physical states and the qualia and intentionality of a thought in terms of a *supervenience* relation. Supervenience is a concept frequently adduced in philosophical psychology to explain how thought is produced by and emerges from its neurophysiological foundations. There are several different theories of supervenience, defining the concept in different ways. Some of these are so weak as to apply to part–whole or mereological relations, in such a way that a whole entity is said to supervene on the sum of its parts.[10] This is a useful model of supervenience for many purposes, but we are looking for something stronger as an adjunct to property dualism. We seek a theory of supervenience according to which the entity that supervenes on its supervenience base is not only different from its base, but has properties that cannot be explained in terms of the properties of its supervenience base.[11] Such an account of supervenience is also sometimes known as a theory of ontological or metaphysical *emergence*.[12] We can informally define supervenience somewhat more precisely in terms of the four conditions indicated below.

An important consequence of conditions (iii) and (iv) is that the analysis establishes an asymmetry or one-way dependence relation by which, if a supervenes on supervenience base b, then b cannot in turn supervene on a. This is what we should expect of the concept of supervenience if it is supposed to reflect the idea that where a supervenes on b, a is emergent from b in the sense that a has properties that cannot be satisfactorily explained in terms of the properties of b.

We shall now describe the connections between a psychological subject's underlying neurophysiology, qualia and intentionality, as involving this sort of one-way dependence type of supervenience in a supervenience hierarchy. Qualia supervene on intentional states,

---

Analysis of supervenience (ontological or metaphysical emergence)

An entity, property or state of affairs *a*, *supervenes* on an entity, property or state of affairs *b*, just in case (logically or nomically, etc.) necessarily, for every object *x* and every property *F* in *a*:

(i) if *x* has *F*, then there is a property *G* in *b* such that *x* has *G*;
(ii) if any object *y* has property *G*, then it also has property *F* (thus, having property *G* is sufficient for something to have property *F*);
(iii) it is not necessarily the case that if any object *y* has property *F*, then it also has property *G* (having property *F* is not sufficient for having property *G*);
(iv) *a* intrinsically possesses at least one property *H* that is not intrinsically a property of *b*.

---

which in turn supervene on neurophysiological states, but not conversely, in either case or at either level of supervenience. The transitivity of supervenience, guaranteed by the transitivity of sufficiency relations in condition (ii) (where, intuitively, if *a* is sufficient for *b*, and *b* is sufficient for *c*, then *a* is sufficient for *c*), entails that qualia, by virtue of supervening on intentional states, also supervene on a subject's neurophysiology as the ultimate supervenience base. The relations between qualia, intentional states, and the underlying neurophysiology are depicted in the following configuration, reading the arrow "→" as the asymmetric ontic and explanatory dependence of supervenience, and structured in such a way that: neurophysiological states → intentional states → qualia.

The one-way ontic dependence of supervenience further entails that all properties of a supervenient entity cannot be adequately explained in terms of the intrinsic properties of its supervenience base. The important element is the converse relation that holds between sufficient conditions and the requirements of adequate explainability. If the possession of property *G* is sufficient for something's also possessing property *F*, but not conversely, then *F* or the possession of property *F* by an object can be explained by its possession of property *G*, but not conversely. If property *G* is sufficient for property *F*, then there is no property of *G* that cannot be understood in terms of property *F*. In that case, *F* either already contains all of *G*, perhaps in addition to other properties, or is anyway such that whatever has property F also has property G. In explaining F, under these circumstances, therefore, one automatically also explains the property G. The reverse, however, is not true, where the supervenience relation is instantiated, if the possession by an entity of property F is not sufficient for the possession of property G.

If intentional states supervene on neurophysiological states, then intentional states likewise have properties that cannot adequately be explained in terms of the properties of the neurophysiological states on which intentional states supervene. If qualia supervene directly on intentional states, and hence, by virtue of the transitivity of supervenience, indirectly on neurophysiological states, then qualia will also have properties that cannot be adequately explained in terms of the properties of the intentional or neurophysiological states on which qualia directly, in the case of intentional states, or indirectly, in the case of neurophysiological states, supervene. This is what we should expect, again as an implication of the distinction between knowledge by description in the case of intended reference, and knowledge by acquaintance in the first-person experience of qualia. In both cases, the opposite will not be true. By virtue of the neurophysiological states in question being a sufficient supervenience base for qualia and intentional states, the neurophysiological states in question cannot possess any properties that the supervenient qualia and intentional states to which they give rise do not also possess. The concept of supervenience provides that there is always at least one intrinsic property of the supervenient entity that is not an intrinsic property of its supervenience base, considered only as such. The intrinsic intentionality of intentional states is not shared by the neurophysiological base on which they supervene. The intrinsic lived-through content or raw feeling of qualia in turn is not shared as an intrinsic property of the intentional states or neurophysiological base on which they supervene, again considered only as such.

The ontic dependence of supervenient intentionality on a neurophysiological base has interesting implications. It helps to explain the fact that we cannot give a phenomenologically or folk psychologically adequate account of intentional states purely in terms of neurophysiological states, whereas we can in principle give a perfectly satisfactory hard scientific psychological explanation of neurophysiological states without invoking the intentionality of experience or the thought contents of qualia. It is the same in the case of qualia relative to their supervenience base in intentional states and ultimately in neurophysiological states. Qualia are themselves the phenomenologically indistinguishable objects and lived-through contents of reflexively intentional states. We cannot, accordingly, adequately explain qualia generally without explaining them as the objects of reflexively intentional states. Nor can we adequately explain qualia merely as reflexively intentional states, because they have at least one additional property or belong to at least one natural kind that is not shared by intentional states considered only as such; namely, the way they subjectively feel or what it is like for the first-person subject when they are experienced.

It is by virtue of the transitivity of supervenience that qualia supervening on intentional states can be said indirectly to supervene on the neurophysiological foundation of intentional states. The application of the model to the metaphysics of neurophysiology, intentional states and qualia requires that qualia, like intentional states, supervene ultimately on a psychological subject's neurophysiology. The model also accommodates two major presumed phenomenological or folk psychological data about qualia and intentionality that might be offered as data and criteria of adequacy for any satisfactory theory of the interrelation between qualia and intentionality. We can thereby explain the impression that intentional states and qualia are always found together, without supposing that any particular qualia are definitive indications of any particular intentional state. We can also explain the presumed fact that qualia are themselves also the intended objects of reflexively intentional states, in which the content of experience and its intended object coincide in episodes of reflective self-consciousness.

If qualia can be explained in terms of intentionality, but not conversely, then qualia, despite always being accompanied by some intentional state or other, supervene on intentionality, and not the other way around. If qualia supervene on intentional states, then intentionality is also explanatorily more fundamental than qualia. The hard psychological scientific facts of neurophysiology, or whatever supervenience base an experience happens to have, for the same reason, are also, as we should probably expect, explanatorily more fundamental than any folk psychological facts about qualia or intentionality. The quarrel between folk psychology and eliminative or reductive philosophy of mind, whether in the form of materialism, behaviourism or functionalism, is a dispute about whether adequate explanations of psychological phenomena need to go beyond their neurophysiological supervenience base. The ground-level explanation of the least controversial facts of human psychology on the supervenience model is human neurophysiology and its physical and information-processing substrate. If a certain neurophysiology is duplicated, according to the concept of supervenience, then a certain intentional state and certain qualia are also duplicated. But not conversely. Particular supervenient qualia, as we also know from the Twin Earth problem and related thought experiments, do not reliably indicate any particular associated intentional state, or any particular underlying neurophysiological state.

We can obtain the same intentional state from an unpredetermined number of different neurophysiological states. The transitivity of supervenience further implies that in principle we can obtain the same qualia from an unpredetermined variety of neurophysiological states, and hence from an unpredetermined variety of intentional states. An intentional state, supervening on a neurophysiological state, as a result, is also in part or in one of its aspects a neurophysiological state. But not conversely. A quale, supervening on an intentional state and ultimately on a neurophysiological state, as a further result, is both an intentional state and a neurophysiological state. Again, however, not conversely. It is possible for intentional states to intend, among indefinitely many other things, their own neurophysiological supervenience base or supervenient qualia, or both, as when a thinker reflectively considers the cause of an immediately experienced headache, the neural mechanisms of binocular vision, or a solution to the mind–body problem. It is the occurrence of such reflexively intentional relations that we experience as self-consciousness, and that may ultimately constitute our sense of self.

God, a divine supernatural
11 mind?

Concepts of God

An enquiry in applied scientific ontology into the existence or non-existence of God is not guaranteed to agree with the attitudes of religious faith. We want to know whether God is an individual divine entity, or a host thereof if there are many gods, just as we want to know whether there are numbers, sets or universals. The difference is, among other things, that God is a person, or the gods are supposed to be persons, or at least personifications of natural forces, whereas numbers and everything else in the existence domain other than minds is assumed to be impersonal, non-mental, non-psychological, non-intentional. It is appropriate, therefore, to consider the ontic status of God as a sequel to the ontology of mind.

God is often supposed to be the greatest intelligent entity, an all-powerful creator and wrathful or merciful judge of mankind. The gods in most cultures often seem to outsiders to be open to strange briberies. The faithful in their rapture and desperation often believe that they can propitiate God or the gods by religious ceremonies and sacraments in acts of piety, to influence divine intervention in the course of their lives. Not unexpectedly, the vast variety of devout practices involve projections of human values, attitudes and expectations onto the idea of a divine entity or entities, by which customary modes of tribute to reigning secular authorities in a local power structure, showing honour to family and community members and rulers, are deemed appropriate also for the worship of a divine entity or entities. Whatever the ontic status of polytheistic pantheons, the prevailing monotheistic idea of God as an all-knowing, all-powerful and perfectly benevolent being, whatever its anthropological origins and however satisfying it may be for believers to contemplate the existence and will of God as a centre for their spiritual lives, raises profound philosophical questions in applied scientific ontology.[1]

We shall try to gain some perspective on the problem of whether God, as conceived in monotheistic religious traditions, exists or does not exist. We shall ask, without assuming that our conclusions need detract from the extraphilosophical faith and religious commitment of the adherents of any religion, whether God, along with physical and abstract entities, and the finite minds of intelligent animals such as ourselves with their combined physical and physically irreducible properties, should be included in a preferred existence domain, or whether philosophical reasoning, as far as it takes us, suggests the opposite conclusion instead, that God does not exist. At no disadvantage to the drama of an enquiry in which many persons have a very deep and personal stake, we can preview the outcome of the combinatorial ontology we have been developing as casting grave doubt on the possibility of God's existence.

It may nevertheless be possible to superadd God to a religiously preferred applied non-scientific ontology under a different metaphysically less problematic description of God's property combination as a divine supernatural mind that is not omnipotent, omniscient and perfectly benevolent. The option restores a modified notion of God to the ontology. Such an idea of God is admittedly unlikely to appeal to most believers, even if they are willing philosophically to grasp at such conceptual straws, because it requires significantly watering-down the properties that are often thought to be necessary in order for God to be worthy of worship.

Scientific ontology and religious faith

The prospects for rigorously demonstrating the existence of God have never been encouraging. Many people who believe in God have not reasoned the matter out, but feel in their hearts that God exists and can answer prayer. Others are likely, without attempt at proof, to follow, through their lifetimes, the religion in which they were raised as children, especially if their beliefs are closely connected with their sense of ethnic or other social identity. A religion is first of all a subcommunity of persons associating to worship something divine. There is nothing necessarily wrong with persons of religious faith gathering for meditation and ceremony and renewal of faith. Such elements of religious belief have nothing positive to do with the problem of God's existence as it comes under the scrutiny of applied scientific ontology. Theology is different from faith and scientific ontology, and philosophy of religion is something else yet again.

What is the application of combinatorial ontology to the question of the existence or nonexistence of God? There are two related issues. One is the problem of whether the combinatorial analysis of being offers any special advantage in the effort to provide a good philosophical reason to believe in the existence of God. Should we include or exclude God from the preferred theoretical existence domain? We must, secondly, look at the problem of God from the standpoint of whether the combinatorial analysis of existence as maximal consistency suggests any special reasons not to include God in the preferred existence domain. When the smoke clears, it is evident that there is no good reason to believe that God has a maximally consistent property combination, from which it follows on the combinatorial analysis of being that there are grounds for disbelieving in God's existence. If God is a fictional object, according to the combinatorial analysis, then the concept of God is, inclusively, either predicationally inconsistent or incomplete. There are indications of both of these ontic failings in God's property combination that raise doubts about the existence of God as a divine supernatural mind. The idea that we might need to suppose that God exists in order to account for the existence of the actual world or to satisfy the demands of justice for unrectified wrongs or unrewarded acts of righteousness, incurred during our human lifetimes, are equally discredited in a combinatorial ontology.

What is left for philosophy of religion in applied scientific ontology is philosophical theology. We can cast religious feeling into philosophical language as many writers in this field have done, from ancient times to the medieval church metaphysicians to Søren Kierkegaard, Reinhold Neibuhr, Paul Tillich and many others. We should equally include contemporary prominent hard-minded analytic philosophers of religion who approach the subject with a prior commitment to the truth of religious beliefs before they try to answer even the most basic philosophical questions about the existence or nature of God. If we impose the same standard on God and the gods as we did in the case of other putative entities we have considered for possible inclusion in or exclusion from a preferred existence domain, then we must admit that the best arguments disprove rather than uphold the existence of God, and that there is no reasoning that establishes the existence of God as a likely implication of the combinatorial analysis of being. The deeper trouble in a conscientious application of Ockham's razor is that we need not bring God into the explanation of the existence or any aspect or property of the actual world in combinatorial ontology.

Divinity through an ontological glass, combinatorially

An actual world must actually exist, as we have argued, as a logical combinatorial necessity. Thus, we do not need the existence of God in order to explain why there exists a physical material universe, a something rather than nothing. Nor do we need to assume the existence of God in order to understand why the particular facts of the actual world exist precisely as they do. Partly the answer is combinatorial roulette; partly it is the inexorable effect of cause and effect on the material entities of the physical world, stirred up less predictably by the intervention of human thought and action, and, as we have suggested, by the contra-causal freedom of intention.

If God exists as a mind, and if some divinely modified property dualism is a correct philosophy of mind, if, that is, a mind divine or mundane must be an entity with intrinsically intentional properties, then presumably we must suppose that God has at least the same freedom of intention as ourselves, by virtue of the intentionality of God's divine thought. If not, then either God is not a mind or we have not yet adequately understood the concept of mind. Only the latter alternative can possibly help the philosophical theist. Nobody wants to allow that God could exist merely by virtue of being an abstract entity like the number π, but only as a thinker, a world designer, creator, judge. Whatever else God is or is not, God like ourselves is a conscious being; not a hunk of rock or wood, not even the sun or wind or rain, or whatever people sorely need more or less of wherever they are trying to live.

If God is a divine supernatural mind, does God exist in time, and hence, like all other spatiotemporal entities, is God subject to change? Can God get old? What if God were just as old as the universe and comes into middle age during some part of our occupation of its lifecycle? What if, eventually, after billions and untold billions of years spreading out over billions and untold billions of light-years of intergalactic space, God gets old and dies, like all things with minds presumably do, without ever noticing that the world his infant thoughts created contains advanced primates capable of reasoning about God? On this analogy, even if God exists, God has no idea of our existence as thinkers, despite the assumption that God sees what humans build as great cathedrals and mosques and synagogues, humble neighbourhood houses of prayer and bedside shrines. Does God know that he, she or it is being worshipped? Does God even have anything like the human concept of worship? If God looks down from heaven, can God understand our thoughts any better than we can determine what a friend is thinking in observing her behaviour? If we believe that philosophy of religion depends on the inclusion of God in the preferred existence domain, then philosophy of religion does not have much of a combinatorial leg on which ontically to stand.

God and Ockham's razor

It is worth reflecting on the fact that we have already completed at least in outline a philosophically coherent and in many ways commonsensical ontology without ever having appealed to the existence of God. Logically, as far as classical logic takes us, it is either true that God exists or that God does not exist. If we do not need to include God in the ontology, if we can complete the project of pure and applied ontology without assuming that God exists, then the concept of God from an explanatory standpoint is philosophically bankrupt, however spiritually rewarding.

We cannot say whether or not God has being from the standpoint of either physical or abstract entities. The physical sciences do not reveal the existence of God; theological–metaphysical but philosophically unsupported speculations by justly renowned physical scientists aside. Nor is God included in the subdomain of abstract entities in a minimalist existence domain ruled by Ockham's razor. If we are correct in thinking that a philosophically coherent and commonsensical ontology can be hammered out without presupposing the existence of God, then God fails Ockham's requirement. This does not mean that God does not exist, but that for philosophical and scientific purposes we do not need to suppose that God exists. If we believe in the existence of God, but are trying to avoid epistemically unjustifiable appeals to revelation and faith, then we must find a good previously overlooked reason why we would absolutely need to include God in a preferred existence domain.

Alternatively, we can regard God, defined as something less than all-powerful, all-knowing and perfectly benevolent, as a detachable part of the ontology optionally available for those who choose to believe. Atheists, if they are right to disbelieve in the existence of God, have no need to dispute with believers, who for their part accept an ontology that on top of everything else also includes God. Believers who bring in God as an add-on to the ontology need not offend tolerant disbelievers who accept a more economical preferred existence domain that excludes God, while anthropologists can try to explain the religious activities, rites and rituals of believers whether or not God actually exists.

Many powerful world religions have not always found it necessary for their religious beliefs to include belief in the existence of God or gods. Classical Buddhism does not worship the historical Buddha as a god. Nor need a true Buddhist believe in reincarnation, if the core of Buddhist teaching is the Buddha's struggle to achieve enlightenment in this life. There is a school of Buddhism that interprets the Buddha's awakening to truth as consisting in his compassion toward the suffering of others. The Buddha solves a long-standing religious riddle, without acknowledging the existence of God or gods, by concluding that we escape the wheel of dharma and attain nirvana, ending the perpetual cycle of birth, death and rebirth, by recognizing that the soul can be laid to rest after the death of the body in this world because there is no afterlife with which we need be concerned. This, too, is a religion that offers its adherents peace of mind, of a very different sort from that of worshippers who desire eternal life and dread the annihilation of their personal psychologies.

With respect to other world religions that presuppose the existence of God, questions persist about the relation of ontology to religious beliefs. Is it possible to settle the question of the existence of God philosophically? If not, then we should probably leave matters of religious belief out of consideration in ontology, beyond allowing that believers who so choose can tack on a truncated concept of God to the existence domain of applied ontology, as, for example, a divine very powerful benevolent mind, in defiance of Ockham's razor.

God, as usually conceived, cannot be classified in any of the three established subcategories of physical, abstract or subjective psychological entities. We have defined the concept of mind as a dual-aspect entity, partly physical and partly non-physical, the qualia and intentionality of whose thoughts supervene on a neurophysiology or other appropriately complex physical structure. Even taking into account the emergence of animal minds in terrestrial evolution, we refer only to physically embodied living biological–social organisms capable of producing thoughts with experienceable mental content and reference to intended objects. God could be included in the existence domain as it stands only in a special category of psychological entity, a mind that is first of all pure spirit, not a dual-aspect entity supervening on or emerging from a physical foundation, that additionally has all the remarkable properties required to fulfil worshippers' expectations of a creative sustaining compassionately judging perfect being, a divine entity, incapable, presumably by virtue of possessing all perfections, of undergoing any sort of real-time change.

We can, in principle, make such an exception in applied ontology for a particular type of being, but only with sufficient philosophical justification. That, however, is just the problem in considering the existence of God. Adequate reasons to support a special order of existence for a purely spiritual entity are conspicuously lacking. We do not experience God in sensation, nor can we imagine God as an abstract entity. Up to this point we have equated physical with spatiotemporal entities, and abstract with non-spatiotemporal entities. If God exists, then God apparently must be non-spatiotemporal despite being non-abstract. To invent an entirely new category for the sake of maintaining God's existence in applied ontology seems unwarranted in view of the failure of the concept of God to meet the explanatory necessity criterion of Ockham's razor. This is not to say that even some of the most unpromising lines of argument for the existence of God do not have occasional enthusiastic adherents. Using philosophy to try to bolster pre-established faith in God intellectually is nevertheless quite another thing than open-minded ontological enquiry that looks candidly into the philosophical question of whether God exists and follows only the best arguments wherever they lead. Philosophy of religion, like any other branch of ontology, should be a mode of enquiry rather than a way of dressing-up prejudices about how we hope and want certain answers to come out. If we adopt the attitude toward philosophical reflections on the ontic status of God, then it is hard to see how applied ontology is ever going to offer much aid and comfort to religious believers.

Arguments for and against the existence of God

If God's being could be rigorously demonstrated, then the conclusion that God should be excluded from a preferred existence domain on the strength of Ockham's razor would plainly need to be rethought. However, there is not only a dearth of good arguments to prove the existence of God, but solid reasons for doubting, especially from the standpoint of a combinatorial analysis of the concept of being, even the logical possibility that the God of monotheism could exist.

The combinatorial analysis of being undermines the argument that God must exist in order to explain why there is something rather than nothing. It substitutes a logical combinatorial explanation in place of God as a divine supernatural being that wills the existence of the world. The *cosmological proof* and the *argument from design for the existence of God* are thereby refuted in a single turn. The so-called *ontological proof for the existence of God* also fares badly in combinatorial ontology. To conclude that God exists because God by definition is supposed to be the greatest conceivable being, and that if God did not exist we could conceive of a being greater than God, one that was actually a being or that actually existed, is disallowed by combinatorial pure philosophical ontology.

The identifying properties by which objects are considered as possible candidates for inclusion in a preferred existence domain are limited to constitutive properties that do not entail an object's ontic status as existent or nonexistent. The reason for the requirement is that otherwise we cannot say of the very same object that it exists or does not exist, because we change the identity of the object if we include the properties of existing or not existing in its individuating property combination. This restriction restates Kant's conclusion in the section of the *Critique of Pure Reason* on "The Ideal of Pure Reason", in which he criticizes the ontological argument for its consideration of existence as a perfection, or as any kind of "predicate". The same objection precludes the evaluation of a property combination as predicationally complete or incomplete, consistent or inconsistent, on the basis of whether or not it includes the fact that an object exists or does not exist. If existence and nonexistence are properties but not identity-determining constitutive properties or "predicates" in Kant's sense, then we cannot validly conclude that God as the greatest conceivable being necessarily exists. We cannot in that case rely on the inference that we can conceive of a being greater than God, when we assume for purposes of indirect proof that God does not exist.[2]

We are left with only the so-called *moral argument for the existence of God*. God must exist, according to this way of reasoning, in order to right the wrongs undergone by human beings in their brief lifetimes, in an eternal afterlife of reward or punishment. The argument projects a period of survival of the person after the destruction of the body that endures long enough to sort out whatever earthly injustices have occurred. The demands of justice logically require that God exist in order to manage the meting out of rewards and punishments in a continuation of the mind's existence beyond death.[3]

The moral argument seems to depend more on emotional wishful thinking than good judgement. That there are injustices in this life no one need dispute. Why suppose, however, that injustices will ever be redressed in an afterlife, or that God must exist in order for justice to be dispensed? What if there were an afterlife in which perfect moral harmony and accord were achieved for persons who did wrong and were never punished during their lives, and for persons who did good and were never rewarded, and all the scales evened out and balanced perfectly after a couple of millennia, but there was no God overseeing the process? What if things just happen this way through the playing-out of abstract principles of justice, the moral equivalent of natural laws, or, perhaps as further consequences of natural laws themselves? What reply can then be made on behalf of the moral argument specifically as an effort to prove the existence of God? Then again, why not simply conclude, as a fact of life that all but the most naive among us should eventually with mature vision come to accept, that some people are destined to enjoy the fruits of wrongful gain without ever being punished, while others, usually the innocent inoffensive ones among us, are as often as not cosmically screwed? Why should the actual world not be that way? Not from any reason we can extract from combinatorial pure philosophical or applied scientific ontology. Why suppose that injustices will ever be made right?

The *problem of evil* poses a positive and still unanswered challenge to the possible existence of God. If God is the creator of the actual world in which, as we all too plainly see, natural evil abounds, then, paradoxically on the traditional monotheistic concept, God does not know about the evil, or is insufficiently powerful to prevent it, or lacks the requisite good will to do so. Any of these three possibilities contradicts the definition of God as all-knowing, all-powerful, and perfectly benevolent. If the concept of God harbours such an evident predicational inconsistency, then the combinatorial analysis of being as predicational maximal consistency entails that God not only does not exist, but logically cannot possibly exist. The existence of such a God is tantamount to attempting to gain admission to the preferred existence domain of a more blatantly predicationally inconsistent nonentity like the round square or carnivorous vegetarian. Philosophers and theologians have wrestled with this problem, and introduced the field of *theodicy* as a branch of philosophy of religion to try to solve it. Many critics continue to believe that all efforts to rectify God's existence as a perfect being with the glaring imperfections of the world of God's creation are abysmal failures. The reaction of some philosophically conscientious believers in light of the problem of evil is to relax the three-part definition of the concept of God to allow God as all-knowing and perfectly good, but not necessarily all-powerful in the sense required to prevent all natural evil, or to compromise on some other diminution of the traditional attributes of divinity. The problem of evil is avoided in this way only by abandoning the full majesty of God as it has usually been conceived.[4]

Along with problems about the predicational consistency of God, construed in the first instance as a logically possible object with a property combination containing the properties of being all-knowing, all-powerful, all-good and the creator of a world rife with natural evil, there are concerns also about God's predicational completeness. Some theologians have postulated that, in addition to being omnipotent, omniscient and perfectly benevolent, God must also be omnipresent, existing everywhere at once throughout the universe, while others have argued that God must transcend the actual world. We have already seen that transcendence and transcendent entities are incompatible with the combinatorial theory of being as maximal consistency. If the argument against transcendence in a combinatorial framework is correct, then we cannot expect to make sense of the idea that God is a transcendent entity.

What else can anyone be said to know about God, about God's properties? Do we know enough to suggest both predicational consistency and completeness in God's constitutive property combination? We know at once too little and too much. We know too much, because from the traditional concept we are thrust into the problem of evil, given the prevalence of pain and other imperfections in God's creation. We know too little, because the standard monotheistic concept of God leaves many predicational gaps in God's property combination. We may hope to fill in the blanks in a variety of ways as religious myths and holy texts sometimes try to do, relying on human imagination to the best of its limited abilities. We can also try to console ourselves that if God exists then God's property combination by definition must be complete, any omissions being due entirely to gaps in our faulty finitely limited knowledge. The deeper difficulty is not merely epistemic, involving our ignorance of God, since we do not know the complete set of properties in the property combination of any except perhaps the simplest abstract entities. We are more conceptually constrained by the fact that we may not be able even in principle to make sense of the attributions of additional properties to God that would need to be maintained in order to project a complete property cluster. We do so unproblematically in many matters of ontological dispute, but we have no way of verifying the accuracy of any of these enterprising conjectures about the nature of God. We can raise such an objection in the case of an object like God, given all the other infelicities in the concept of a divine being that we have already mentioned, without committing ourselves generally to an implausible positivistic verification theory of meaning.

Inherent inconsistency of religious beliefs

A combinatorial ontology by itself does not disprove the possibility of extending the preferred existence domain of applied ontology to include God or other divinities. Such a superaddition can be arranged only if God's property combination is reconceived as maximally consistent, any gaps owing entirely to our ignorance of God's full complement of properties, and, despite appearances and even contrary to much of the driving force of religion, free of any and all predicational incompatibilities.

Inconsistency may turn out to be ineliminable from the essential dynamic tensions in religious beliefs by which the mind seeks personhood, growth and fulfilment in and through religion. That God is both three persons and one person, that a virgin should give birth (common to Buddhism, Christianity and other religions), that God is all-powerful and yet engaged in a struggle with the forces of evil, that God is perfect and hence presumably unchanging and yet amenable to petitionary prayer, together with all the credulity-straining miracles that contradict belief in mundane causation and natural law in most religions, in accounts of religiously significant episodes recorded in holy writings, are among the more conspicuous inconsistencies in religion. The inconsistency inherent in religious belief may be vital to the spiritual awakening of the self, but testifies to a concept of God that for better or worse is riddled with contradictions, and hence excluded from the preferred existence domain by the consistency requirement in a combinatorial analysis of being.

The idea that inconsistencies are essential to religious beliefs is familiar in sceptical literature. The emergence and maturation of the self into self-consciousness might actually depend on contradictions. It is perhaps only in this way that thought is supplied with the necessary motivation to sort out conflicting beliefs, riding the conflicts between and working its way through logically inconsistent commitments, to attain a higher perspective in which at least some of the contradictions are resolved and an equilibrium of religious outlook is achieved.

The emphasis especially in evangelical Christianity on the renewal of faith as a kind of spiritual rebirth in which the believer's soul is born again is an explicit but by no means unique instance of a more pervasive aspect of religion, in which the self comes to be more clearly self-consciously defined as a result of its assimilation of inconsistencies within religious doctrine.[5] If the religious self arises as a result of struggling, even if only subconsciously, to incorporate contradictory beliefs into a unified worldview, then the sort of logical inconsistencies often attributed to religion as a criticism and rebuke of its doctrines can be seen instead in a different light. They are not then automatically a sign of the failure of religion, but the source of its strength and influence in a believer's sense of self in relation to the concept of something much greater than the self and its puny methods of reasoning. It is in the effort to resolve inconsistencies in religion, especially as they reflect deeply grounded contradictions in the concept of God, trying to understand the nature of God as good despite the natural evil in the world, among innumerable similar conceptual discords, that the religious self more fully emerges.[6]

To the extent that even one logical inconsistency remains unresolved in the idea of God, despite the value of contradictions in religious life, the combinatorial analysis of being as maximal consistency must deny that God exists. Regardless of how personally fulfilling and emotionally supportive it may be for many persons to accommodate predicationally inconsistent concepts in their belief systems, the judgement of applied scientific ontology is that no such object can possibly exist. The greatest irony of the ontology of religious belief may then be that in order for religion to succeed, for it to offer the satisfactions of personal development, sense of self, mystical separation from the ordinary world of empirical experience and rational scientific and philosophical explanation, and unity with the divine, God not only does not need to exist, but paradoxically cannot exist. The concept of God in that case serves the most fundamental religious needs of believers only by virtue of subsuming predicational inconsistencies that preclude God's existence.

Ontology of culture: language, art and artefacts

12

Cultures and cultural objects

We turn finally to the topic of cultural entities. The world contains not only natural objects like rocks and plants, but objects that would not exist as complexes or in the exact form with the particular properties they have were it not for human intervention. There are artefacts, products of human thought that are touched and transformed in various ways by human hands. The list of such things includes expressions of thought in language and art, and all the results of human invention, manufacture and technology.

It may be significant, in this study of combinatorial ontology, an expressly anti-Heideggerean anti-existentialist theory of being, that we should end up where Heidegger, relying on phenomenology rather than logic as the key to ontology, finds it necessary to begin. We conclude the analysis of applied scientific ontology in effect with a discussion of *Zuhandenheit* and the impact of human intention and activity that shapes and colours the world in a distinctively human way.

The applied ontology of cultural entities that we shall sketch for simplicity is limited to human culture. We should recognize at the same time that other terrestrial non-human animals also have more restricted social cultures, and in less extensive ways also change their environments by making artefacts and assembling composite entities out of available materials to suit their needs. A nest in a tree, damming a river to make a lodge, even a tunnel in the earth, are cultural artefacts of a crude sort. Nor should we discount the possibility, even the statistical likelihood in the turn of combinatorial roulette that has resulted in the realization of the actual world on the present theory, that in the vast distances of space there might exist other life forms, extraterrestrial beings with intelligence, even advanced civilizations very unlike the human cultures we know. The ontology of language, art and artefacts that we require must be fully general with respect to such possibilities, even if the theory is most conveniently illustrated with examples drawn exclusively from human culture, exemplifying what is most near and dear to us, that we are best able to study and comprehend.

As a further provision, we distinguish between language, art and artefacts, even though there are proposals for reducing these three categories to two or even one, and that in different directions. Thus, one might say that language and art are special kinds of artefacts, so that the ontology of culture need only concern itself with the making of things, imposing human design on tools and weapons, shelter, clothing, objects of religious worship, agricultural and other modifications of the environment, including art and language more narrowly understood. Or language and artefacts might be reduced to art, in which we speak of the art of expressing ourselves verbally, the art of war, architecture, body covering and adornment, the art of farming and so on. We might concentrate categories in yet another way again by speaking of art and artefacts as a kind of language, of which verbal expression, spoken and written language in the ordinary sense, is but one subcategory.

Whatever the prospects of these reductive programmes, it is clear that the three types of cultural entities – language, art and artefacts – are the principal subjects of consideration, however they may turn out to be interrelated. We do not want to prejudge refinements of the ontology of culture that may lead to more reductive characterizations of its preferred existence domain. We proceed accordingly as though our cultural data for ontological reflection came prepackaged in discrete categories for language, art and (other kinds of) artefacts, even if these should turn out to be more economically categorizable as expanded subdomains or as a single more expanded domain. We can begin at least by recognizing the fact that the entities to be discovered in the actual world are different because of the activity of intelligent agents, minds, both human and non-human, and that at their most sophisticated adaptations known to us, so-called cultural entities feature prominently at a certain arguably superficial level of analysis, in the form of language, art and artefacts. With these conspicuous phenomena we can begin to uncover the basic principles of an applied scientific ontology of culture.

Ontic status of culture

The first question we confront is why cultural entities should be considered as constituting a special ontic subdivision. The healthy sceptical impulse that restrains metaphysical extravagance by invoking Ockham's razor might naturally want to raise doubts at the outset about the validity of introducing an ontology of culture.

We have seen in general terms that Ockham's razor is not an absolute criterion in ontological investigations, and that the proper use of the principle requires care if it is not to mislead enquiry. Still, every application is a unique case, and it is at least worth wondering whether or not cultural entities are already properly subsumed under the previously established categories of physical, abstract or subjective psychological entities, or whether they require an applied ontological subdomain all their own. A good, but perhaps not very convincing or ultimately satisfying, argument can be made for both the simple inclusion of cultural entities as physical or abstract.

Let us consider an example of a putative cultural entity from each of the three ostensible categories we have introduced, to ask whether there is any justification for classifying such objects as ontologically distinct in any meaningful way from the workhorse ontological divisions we have already recognized for physical, abstract and subjective entities. As specimens, we introduce a spoken or written sentence of a language, a neolithic cave painting of a buffalo pierced by an arrow, and a tool, say, Heidegger's hammer, or a computer, or the space shuttle or International Space Station. These are all things that are made, and in our limited perspective taken for purposes of illustration, made by human beings, either as individuals or in cooperating social teams, using language and other tools and artefacts along the way among other devices to coordinate their complex activities, resulting in the production of cultural entities. We have already remarked that such entities are not natural. The question is, are they simply or purely physical entities, belonging to a subcategory of artificial physical entities alongside and hence not deeply ontologically distinct from natural physical entities? Or are they instead to be classified as or understandable in terms of abstract entities?

When a sentence is uttered or written, whether with pen and ink or chiselled into stone or inscribed by means of a pattern of magnetic traces on the surface of a plastic computer diskette, it is in some obvious sense a physical entity. It might also be said at the same time to represent an abstract meaning, the proposition, as we have encountered the term in our consideration of the subcategories of abstract entities, if we were to include propositions in the ontology. Much the same can be said of the cave painting or the hammer, computer or space station. These entities too, in different ways, can be thought of as embodying abstract relations, particularly in the case of the cave painting and the computer, but even by extension, if we stretch things far enough, in the hammer and the computer-assisted design and operation of the space shuttle and space station. As responsible ontologists, we should not try to maintain that the sentence, painting, hammer, computer or space station are themselves abstract entities, since all of these things are undeniably here with us in real spacetime in the actual world, whereas abstract entities are supposed to be non-spatiotemporal. We might nevertheless try to skate by with our two established categories of physical and abstract entities by classifying cultural entities of any or all three types as physical entities embody-ing or manifesting certain special types of abstract properties, ideas, concepts, formal relations or the like, and thus dispense with the need to go beyond the ontology of physical and abstract things in order to account for the metaphysics of culture. Would such an analysis of the ontology of language, art and artefacts be satisfactory?

There is an argument to suggest that cultural entities cannot simply be subsumed beneath the pure categories of physical and abstract entities, no matter what other explanatory advantages they afford. The objection for good reason is parallel to that offered in attempts to solve the mind–body problem, of which the question of the ontic status of cultural entities can be seen as a particular related instance. The claim is that we cannot fully understand language, art and artefacts, cultural entities generally, except as expressions of the qualia and intentionality of thought. This is perhaps most clear in the case of language used as a vehicle for recording and communicating sensations, emotions and ideas, but equally so in all of art, even the most modern abstract or supposedly non-representational art.

Derivative intentionality of artefacts

Although artefacts other than language and artworks in the narrow sense are not more obviously expressions of propositional meaning, they are nevertheless, as Heidegger among others rightly recognizes, thoroughly intentional. Their design, manufacture, and use are alike directed toward and embued with human purpose.

If I fashion a hammer by selecting a particular river-smoothed stone and fastening it with leather thongs to a wooden heft, I am choosing, shaping, assembling and finally using physical objects in my immediate environment with a certain end in mind. A boulder will not do if the hammer is supposed to be used as a practical tool; that would make it too big and heavy, whereas I must be able to lift it up and swing it down. A chunk of sandstone will also probably not serve (although I might experiment with any variety of substances until I identify appropriate materials for my purposes) because it will too easily shatter if I use the hammer as I am likely to want to in striking harder objects. When the hammer is made, no matter how ineptly, imperfectly or incompletely, it represents, as much as any speech act or artwork, a mind's intentions and the attempt to fulfil those intentions by acting in and locally manipulating aspects of the physical world in the service of an idea, in the partial fulfilment of an intention.

Minds and their concrete expressions in language, art and artefacts can be classified, accordingly, not as purely physical or purely abstract entities, but as qualia-expressive intentional entities, being in every instance about something or directed toward an intended object. The intended object of a use of language, or the production or display of an artwork or other artefact, is often to express the qualia of a thinker's thought. To paint a canvas or write a letter or sing the blues is to clarify for oneself and make available to others a record of the content of one's psychological states. Cultural entities are not themselves minds, naturally, and if they embody or otherwise manifest thoughts they are not themselves mental occurrences. Here an important division between two kinds of intentional entities can be adduced in the applied scientific ontology of cultural entities, based on a distinction first drawn by John R. Searle in his book, *Intentionality: An Essay in the Philosophy of Mind*, between *intrinsic* and *derivative* intentionality.[1]

It is obvious enough, but bears reminding, that were it not for the existence of minds there would and could be no culture. Language, art and artefacts are products of thought, in all instances their direct expression in physical form. The same is true whether we are referring to a single sentence uttered by an early hominid or all of world literature, a cave painting or the *œuvre* of Michelangelo or Salvador Dali, a stone hammer used to crack oyster shells or the International Space Station. If, as we have argued, we cannot solve the mind–body problem except by recognizing the physically ineliminable and irreducible qualia and intentionality of thought, and if qualia and intentionality require a special applied scientific ontological category of minds as qualia-bearing intentional entities in addition to and distinct from physical and abstract entities, then how can we hope to understand the metaphysics of culture and the ontology of language, art and artefacts, except as products of thought, sharing in some way in the qualia and intentionality of thought whose properties uniquely characterize the ontology of mind?

An intentionalist philosophy implies that cultural entities, like the minds that through physical agency produce them, are intentional entities, and as such require a special category of the preferred existence domain distinct from physical and abstract entities. Cultural entities have physical and abstract properties, just as physical entities have abstract properties and enter into abstract relations, like the abstract property of being divisible or atomic. We may accordingly consider the three-part applied scientific ontology that emerges in the discussion of the mind–body problem, consisting of physical, abstract and qualia-bearing intentional entities, to be sufficient also for cultural entities, without interposing yet another, fourth, category of existent things. The explanation of thought in language, art and artefacts is intentional in the correct sense of the word in so far as these cultural entities are about something or directed toward an intended object, and expressive of the content of a state of mind.

The sentence "It is raining" is about a meteorological state of affairs, and ordinarily expresses a belief that the state of affairs obtains. It is true or false, moreover, depending on the actual state of the world, the existence or nonexistence of the corresponding state of affairs the sentence is intended to represent and the belief it is meant to express. The cave painting is about the buffalo depicted, real or imaginary, and the state of affairs, existent or otherwise, of its being struck by an arrow. It may represent the fears of the artist, the hope for a successful hunt, or something of more metaphorical or religious significance as a cult object. The possibilities, thanks to conventional symbolism and psychological association, and the logical detachment of the content of thought from its intended objects, are potentially limitless. The same analysis explains the collective intentionality that stands behind social institutions such as customs, etiquettes, religious and secular observances, mating and marriage, the use of money as a medium of exchange and all other aspects of culture.

Artefacts as embodied purpose

An artefact like a hammer, computer or space station is likewise the expression of purpose, of varying degrees of complexity, but equally a product of thought and concrete embodiment of the idea or ideas of a mind or many minds acting in concert intentionally and for the sake of realizing an intention. We can often grasp shared or imaginable purposes directly from the object, and even when we are wrong in our assumptions, it is significant that we find it irresistible in such cases to see the work of mind in the creation of such things.

Thus, a hammer is about hammering, about the things its makers and users intend to do with it. Similarly for much more complicated and sophisticated instruments like a digital computer or the space station. To such an extent is intentionality inherent in a purposeful artefact that, even when a tool or like object, a hammer or a cup or bowl, becomes so damaged that it is no longer able to fulfil its function, the entity does not simply return to nature, at least not immediately, but, as Heidegger charmingly puts it in *Being and Time*, even on the rubbish heap, it "bids farewell" to we thinkers and makers. Heidegger's remarks on the evidence of care in broken implements are worth considering at length:

> Beings nearest at hand can be met up with in taking care of things as unusable, as improperly adapted for their specific use. Tools turn out to be damaged, their material unsuitable. In any case, *a useful thing* of some sort is at hand here. But we discover the unusability not by looking and ascertaining properties, but rather by paying attention to the associations in which we use it. When we discover its unusability, the thing becomes conspicuous. *Conspicuousness* presents the thing at hand in a certain unhandiness . . . In its conspicuousness, obtrusiveness, and obstinacy, what is at hand loses its character of handiness in a certain sense. But this handiness is itself understood, although not thematically, in associating with what is at hand. It does not just disappear, but bids farewell, so to speak, in the conspicuousness of what is unusable. Handiness shows itself once again, and precisely in doing so the worldly character of what is at hand also shows itself, too.[2]

The cup, dropped on the floor and broken in two, unable to hold tea, still "says" that it was once something useful, something intended for a specific use, capable in its glory days of fulfilling a practical purpose. We can read intentionality even into a ruined artefact, as when we visit the sites of abandoned ancient cities like Macchu Picchu or Aphrodisias. Here we see clearly a large-scale object that is not merely a work of nature, the result of natural forces acting at random, but an artefact first shaped in thought and then fashioned by hand or with the help of other tools or machines by many persons in a relatively advanced state of technology. Against the background of nature, these creations stand out dramatically in what Heidegger calls their conspicuousness (*Auffälligkeit*).

We might also reflect in this connection on how the trained archaeologist and anthropologist is able (fallibly) to distinguish between natural objects and human-made artefacts that to the layperson's unskilled eye seem indistinguishable. A good example is the flint scraping tools that are hard to discern from the flakes of flint that may have splintered from a block through entirely natural processes. An expert can identify flint scrapers from flint flakes occurring without the hand of a human toolmaker deliberately guided by intention and purpose with a certain end and a certain standard in mind. It is not an occult practice, but a rather exact science, to distinguish such tools and tool fragments from naturally occurring shards of identical stone. The tricks of the trade can be taught to virtually any patient novice, so that it becomes possible also to see, as specialists do, the subtle distinctions between natural and early human cultural entities.

We discriminate between multiple subcategories of physical objects. There are physical forces, fields, and micro- and macro-physical entities, particles and complexes, molecules and atoms and the like. We similarly distinguish between multiple subcategories of abstract entities, particulars like numbers and sets, and universals such as properties, qualities and relations. In the third main ontological category of qualia-bearing intentional entities, we may similarly find it expedient, following Searle's valuable distinction, to acknowledge separate subcategories for intrinsically intentional entities, minds as originating sources of qualia and intentionality, and derivatively intentional and qualia-expressive entities, including all cultural entities, language, art and artefacts. Derivatively intentional cultural entities are about something or expressive of qualia only by virtue of having been chosen by thought as a medium for the derivatively intentional expression of intrinsically intentional meaning, thought and purpose, sensation, emotion, desire and will.

All intentional entities, minds and cultural entities alike, are *about* something in different ways. They can intend something by virtue of themselves alone or by virtue of being used by thought as an expression of another intentional entity's intentionality. The main point from an applied scientific ontological perspective is that intrinsically or derivatively intentional entities cannot correctly be ontically classified as purely physical or purely abstract entities in a preferred existence domain, but require a third main category of their own – the category of intrinsically or derivatively intentional qualia-bearing entities, to which minds and cultural entities generally belong. Things that are made by minds, whether in language, art or as other kinds of artefacts, are not simply physical entities with abstract properties, but, like the mind on a property dualist ontology of psychological phenomena, exhibit both a physical and non-physical aspect, expressing the contents and intended objects of thoughts.

Even the broken teacup speaks to discerning eyes as having another, special, kind of property, a former purpose, a former use, ministering to an intention that cannot in turn be adequately understood in terms of its physical or abstract qualities and relations alone. It partakes derivatively of the intrinsic intentionality of thought to which it owes its existence, and as such is not purely and not merely a physical entity. It is for the same reason that the mind itself on the property dualist conception is not purely and not merely the body, the neurophysiology of brain and nervous system integrated into the somatic matrix of a living psychological subject. If cultural artefacts are as much dual aspect entities as the minds that create them, then, like the mind, they require special provision in a third main category of a preferred existence domain. The world of culture, as Karl R. Popper, in *Objective Knowledge: An Evolutionary Approach*, for quite different reasons, has also maintained, is a third distinct ontological realm, a World 3.[3] The subdomain of cultural entities constitutes a third world as a distinct classification within applied scientific ontology. Physical, abstract and intentional entities exist in the combinatorial analysis of the concept of being as maximally consistent property combinations, including physically and abstractly irreducible derivatively intentional and qualia-expressive properties.

Abstract qualities of art

It might be thought that while the plastic arts like painting and sculpture are readily absorbed into the category of physical entities in the existence domain, other so to speak more formal or mathematical arts like music and even poetry and literature might be taken without residue into the category of abstract entities in the preferred existence domain of an ontology of culture.

To consider only music, as offering perhaps the strongest argument for this type of ontological reduction, it is clear that music is not only the abstract relations that it exemplifies but tone qualities, rhythm and tempo in real time, and, more importantly, expression and expressiveness that is evidently an intentional property originating with the intrinsically intentional qualia-bearing thoughts of composers, conductors and performers, intended to be received and to elicit certain qualia and intentional psychological responses in an audience, that cannot be adequately reduced to or explained in terms of the music's abstract mathematical forms. It is an art that speaks expressively from and to the human soul in a way that is not simply a matter of abstract relations of melody and harmony, essential though these are to the ontology of music.

The same can be said, it should be emphasized, of any art form and of any expressive use of language or purposeful design, manufacture or use of any artefact. An extreme example that makes an important point about the comparative insignificance of the physical substance chosen for artistic purposes is in so-called found-object art, in which an artist selects and exhibits a readymade entity of no special aesthetic quality, such as a porcelain bathroom fixture, as an expression of choice within the conventions of an artistic community. We cannot begin to understand the ontology of any of these cultural entities except as expressions of the qualia and intentionality of thought, as creations of mind, and attempts to satisfy an intended purpose. When we recognize the expression of mental content and intention in language, art and artefacts, then we appreciate the need to include cultural entities in a third category of psychological or psychology-related existents distinct from the purely physical and abstract things in which cultural entities are embodied and whose properties they exemplify.[4]

Conclusion: scientific–philosophical ontology

Modality of being

The problem of ontology is to understand the concept of being, of what it means for something to exist. Ontology investigates the fact, nature and modal status of being, in the course of which it proposes a preferred ontology that is supposed to include all and only existent things. To be successful, ontology must combine a correct pure philosophical ontology with a correct applied scientific ontology, grafting an appropriate preferred existence domain onto a satisfactory analysis of the concept of being.

The proposed theoretical domain must correspond exactly with the extant domain of actually existent entities and states of affairs that constitute the actual world in order for the application of a correct concept of being to be judged satisfactory in an integrated philosophical–scientific ontology. The question of precisely how the concept of being should be understood, and whether at any point we can know with epistemic certainty that we have brought about the positive correlation of theory with reality, are among the difficulties that sustain philosophical controversy in the field of ontology.

What, it is often deemed independently interesting to know, is the most economical ontology needed to keep science and extrascientific discourse afloat? If we confine our attention exclusively to questions of scientific ontology, then we will be avoiding rather than helping to answer the conceptually more basic questions of philosophical ontology, and we risk doing so in violation of the more general higher-order principles of philosophical ontology, and trying to answer the question of what particular things and kinds of things exist without first knowing what it means for anything whatsoever to exist. We open the door to unnecessary confusions if we fail to distinguish or properly observe the distinction between philosophical and scientific ontology, as when ontologists try to address a question of pure philosophical ontology as though it were a question of applied scientific ontology, or the reverse.

The answer to fundamental questions of philosophical ontology require rigorous philosophical enquiry into the concepts of objects, states of affairs and worlds, and of actually existent entities, states of affairs and the actual world. We have taken on the difficult questions of ontology, rather than trying to avoid them as unanswerable or even unintelligible. The right answers to these metaphysical puzzles can only appear when philosophical ontology precedes scientific ontology, which as such is prohibited from appealing to any of the merely logically contingent facts or scientific ontology of the actual world. A correct answer to the question why there exists something rather than nothing must in a sense be logically necessary, or, as is more accurate but also more tedious to say, philosophically metalogically necessary. Whatever logically necessary answer we give to the question of being should not imply that the actual world as it happens to exist is itself logically necessary, as we might say, in the specific details of its scientific ontology.

Logic as a window on ontology

We should be reluctant to give up the logical or even physical contingency of the actual world, and of the existent states of affairs that constitute the actual world. It would make logic too important if we were to interpret the facts of the world, beginning with the descriptive facts and laws of natural science, as a matter of metalogical necessity.

To conclude otherwise is to collapse all presumably distinct logically possible worlds into the one and only actual world. This, to say the least, is much at odds with our ordinary assumption that it is minimally logically possible for particular facts of the actual world to be other than they are. I did not have to write the preceding sentence, or I could have edited it out, or it could have been lost at some stage in the publication process. I, for that matter, did not have to exist, and there are plenty of logically possible worlds in which I do not exist. If there are abstract entities, then only their properties are universally distributed in every logically possible world, and all other facts occur irregularly from world to world.

Or so we think. The dilemma in trying to answer the fundamental questions of philosophical ontology as we have approached the topic is that of showing that, as a matter of combinatorial philosophical metalogic, there must actually exist something rather than nothing, while also concluding that the actual world in all its physical states of affairs is not logically necessary but contingent.

The problem we have tried to solve is to attain both of these apparently conflicting objectives by providing a logically necessary answer to the question why an actual world exists in pure philosophical ontology that does not also make the condition and constitutive facts of the actual world logically necessary, preserving their presumptive logical contingency as a subject for proper investigation by applied scientific ontology. It is only by wending our way delicately between these modal requirements that we can hope to satisfy the twin burdens of ontology. We can then try to provide an analysis of the concept of being, of why something rather than nothing exists, and why there is a uniquely existent logically contingent actual world, while specifying more exactly the things and kinds of things, existent entities and states of affairs, that constitute the actual world.

Ontology demands a correct philosophical metalogic. Logic must therefore be as independent as possible in its explicit commitment to the principles of any particular scientific ontology. It is the implicit ontology in logic that lurks below the surface to be excavated by philosophical metalogic where our deepest philosophical presuppositions are to be found. We have seen as a consequence of philosophical metalogic that logically there must exist something rather than nothing, among all the logically possible combinations of logically possible objects with logically possible properties, if to exist is to be predicationally maximally consistent, and that for the same reason there can exist at most only one logically contingent actual world. Logic answers the problems of pure philosophical ontology by formalizing logical possibilities, true or false, of an object or number of objects having a property.

We cannot imagine anything logically more basic than the combination of objects with properties, and hence we need not fear that the logical analysis of being is as deeply anthropocentric in its methodology as phenomenology. Thinking, even for non-humans, logically requires at least implicitly attributing properties to objects, if what we mean by a possibility is a logically consistent state of affairs, and if what we mean by a logically possible state of affairs is the logically possible possession of a logically possible property by a logically possible object. We are immediately involved in the principles of combinatorial ontology when we reflect on the ultimate presuppositions of classical logic even in the most general sense. We have argued that it is at this level of combinatorial possibility that logically necessary answers to the fundamental questions of pure philosophical ontology can and must be found, and we have indicated directions in which metaphysical enquiry into the fact, nature and modality of existence might proceed.

Pure philosophical and applied scientific ontology

The ideal of presenting an integrated philosophical and scientific ontology has been held out from the beginning as the goal of these investigations. It follows as a consequence of recognizing the distinction between pure philosophical enquiry into the question of being, and the task of specifying what particular things and kinds of things exist in applied scientific ontology. We need both parts of the theory to arrive at a complete understanding of ontology, and both components must be correctly interrelated.

The study of ontology belongs squarely to philosophy. Ontology can nevertheless be conducted in accordance with scientific standards of precision and intellectual rigor. There is, as we have assumed throughout, such a thing as scientific–philosophical ontology. Now that we have completed in outline at least the two main components of a fully integrated scientific–philosophical ontology, it is appropriate to step back and reflect on what it means to have undertaken such an analysis, and whether and to what extent the project as a whole can be understood as answering to both scientific and philosophical criteria, by which its relative success or failure can be properly assessed.

There are several respects in which the combinatorial analysis of being in pure philosophical ontology and the applied ontology that it supports are scientific. Among other things, although the pure philosophical component of the ontology is intended as a conceptual analysis that is necessarily correct in essentials, and necessarily false if mistaken, the applied component is revisable in many of the same ways as ordinary empirical science. It is subject to correction in light of new discoveries while preserving an underlying combinatorial framework. If an unanticipated argument surfaces according to which universals are logically inconsistent or less than maximally predicationally complete, then the provisional conclusion of applied scientific ontology in the combinatorial context in which we have presented it might reasonably reverse its endorsement of the existence of abstract entities as belonging to the preferred existence domain, and conclude instead that universals in this subcategory of abstract entities do not exist and are henceforth to be excluded from a preferred existence domain.

Another important sense in which the applied ontology in the combinatorial mode is scientific has to do with the open-ended potentially unlimited expansion of ontological categories and subcategories. As things stand, we have tentatively identified three main types of existent entities in the preferred existence domain of applied scientific ontology, for physical, abstract, and intrinsically intentional qualia-bearing entities and their derivatively intentional expressions in language, art and artefacts, with numerous subdivisions of categories and subcategories specified within their internal ontic structures. The expectation is that the proposed network of ontic categories and subcategories is adequate to our present understanding of the ontological needs of science, the kinds of things that exist given what we now believe ourselves to know about the entities belonging to the actual world, from our limited history and limited access to its constituent facts. There is surely much about the actual world that we do not yet know, that we may never know, and that we cannot infer from experience of the tiny corner of the universe that falls under even our most instrumentally enhanced survey, or from the infancy of our logic, mathematics, natural science and philosophy. We do not know whether physical, abstract and intentional kinds of entities exhaust the main categories of existents in the actual world, or whether there are other kinds of entities as different as these three categories of abstract entities are different from physical entities, and as different as intentional entities are different again from both physical and abstract entities, that have yet to be discovered and assimilated into our conceptual schemes in an appropriately enlarged scientific ontology.

Ontology is scientific in so far as it remains open to such possibilities in theory or in principle. We may not have any informative way to represent potential ontic discoveries even within the lavish resources of the imagination, but which at this stage of human enquiry we have as yet no good reason to exclude. If the future course of mathematics, science and philosophy is even partially uncharted, then so to the same degree and for the same reason is the future course of applied scientific ontology. We do not know what remains to be known and how scientific and philosophical ontology might need to develop. That is part of the excitement, provided that the basic framework of our integrated pure philosophical and applied scientific ontology is sufficiently flexible to accommodate novelties that are not already covered by the ontology at any penultimate stage of its ongoing development.

It would be incompatible with the characteristic features of scientific method to suppose that the work of ontology can ever be the final statement about the absolute meaning and nature of existence. At least these matters must remain open-ended while the project of empirical science and philosophical reflection is incomplete, and while there are still outstanding unanswered questions of science. If the project of ontology continues indefinitely, we can nevertheless hope that we have now correctly sketched the method, scope and limits of pure philosophical ontology with enough care so as to provide an adequate analysis of the concept of being and the outline for a corresponding theory of applied scientific ontology. To the extent that we have succeeded, we will have advanced a structure for the ongoing work of applied scientific ontology that offers a systematic way of approaching the most difficult outstanding questions of existence.

We grasp the concept of being only when we have satisfactorily answered the question why there is something rather than nothing and why there is only one logically contingent actual world. If we arrive at an understanding of the nature of being, of what it means for something to exist, then we can begin to make sense and judge the truth of the proposition that a certain choice of putative entities exist or do not exist. We can then, but only then, take the first steps towards an applied scientific ontology, in which we decide whether to include or exclude any putative entity from a preferred existence domain. It is only at this stage of ontological enquiry that we can meaningfully enquire whether or not there are good reasons to approve the existence of the usual ontological suspects, standardly beginning, as in preceding chapters, with physical entities of various types, and proceeding to abstract objects, minds and persons, God, language, art and cultural artefacts. Whether or not this is the standard sequence of topics for applied scientific ontology, it is by no means universal. It is open to alternative applied ontologies to begin with the ontic status of God, and proceed to universals, and only then take up the ontology of physical entities; or to begin with mind and then introduce good reasons for supporting or rejecting a given category of numbers, sets or propositions; or to begin with propositions and proceed from thence to other applied ontological categories. At that point, pure logic no longer plays a leading role as it does in pure philosophical ontology in justifying a preferred existence domain as a contribution to applied scientific ontology. Applied scientific ontology, unlike the conceptual analysis of the meaning of being in pure philosophical ontology, must inevitably remain a work in progress in scientific philosophy.

Notes

Part I: Pure Philosophical Ontology

Chapter 1: What it is to be (on Heidegger)

1. The distinction between the verb of being and its cognates in existence and predication senses is essential. There is a grammatical difference of philosophical interest in saying that an object *is* or *is not* (*simpliciter*, full stop), as opposed to saying that an object is or is not red or mortal or fascinating, in attribution of a property. The ambiguity in the two senses of "is" or "to be" is illustrated by W. V. O. Quine's syntactical criterion of ontological commitment, discussed at length in Chapter 6. Quine, "On What There Is", in *From a Logical Point of View*, 2nd edn, rev. (New York: Harper & Row, 1963a), pp. 6–7, 15–16, maintains that "To be is to be the value of a [quantifier-bound] variable." Here the first occurrence of the verb phrase "to be" is clearly intended in the existence sense, and the second occurrence in the complete context, "to be the value of a variable", is obviously predicational. If the distinction between the existence and predication senses of being is not observed, then Quine's criterion, whatever its other merits or defects, is viciously circular, saying in effect that to exist is to exist. Verbs of being in the predication sense can also be used to predicate the property of existing or not existing to an object, as when we say that the Taj Mahal is or has the property of being a real existent thing, or that the flying horse is not existent, or does not have the property of being an existent entity. Recognizing the difference between the existence and predication senses of being is the first step toward understanding their logical interrelations in pure philosophical ontology. A fundamental difference in ontology is marked by whether a theory tries to explain existence in terms of predication (intensional), or predication in terms of existence (extensional). See note 3.
2. Aristotle, *Metaphysics* 1003a32–1005a18. F. Brentano, *On the Several Senses of Being in Aristotle*, R. George (ed. and trans.) (Berkeley, CA: University of California Press, 1975) (translation of Brentano's 1862 dissertation, *Von der mannigfachen Bedeutung des Seienden nach Aristoteles*). In 1907 Heidegger received a copy of Brentano's work from a family friend, Conrad Gröber. The book made an enormous impression on Heidegger's ontology, prompting him in the preface to W. J. Richardson (ed.), *Heidegger: Through Phenomenology to Thought* (The Hague: Martinus Nijhoff, 1963) to write of Brentano's study that it had posed "the question that determined the way of my thought: what is the pervasive, simple, unified determination of Being that permeates all of its multiple

meanings?" (p. x). He adds, "The first philosophical text through which I worked my way again and again from 1907 on, was Franz Brentano's *Von der mannigfachen Bedeutung des Seienden nach Aristotles*" (p. xi). See J. Owens, *The Doctrine of Being in the Aristotelian Metaphysics: A Study in the Greek Background of Medieval Thought*, 3rd edn, rev. (Toronto: Pontifical Institute of Mediaeval Studies, 1978) and F. Volpi, "Heideggers Verhaltnis zu Brentanos Aristoteles-Interpretation: Die Frage nach dem Sein des Seienden", *Zeitschrift für philosophische Forschung* 32.

3. The distinction between *intensional* and *extensional* linguistic or logical contexts and theories is characterized in different ways and identified by a variety of criteria. For present purposes, a context or theory is said to be extensional if it defines properties and interprets predicates and the truth-value of predications in terms of the existent entities that belong to the *extension of a predicate* as the set of existent entities possessing the properties represented by a predicate. An intensional context or theory, in contrast, negatively speaking, is one that is not extensional; more positively defined, it is a context or theory that defines objects independently of their ontic status and interprets names and descriptors and the truth-value of predications in terms of particular property combinations. The distinction between intension and extension as we have presented it further entails the applicability of the more familiar criterion by which intensional contexts and theories are distinguished from extensional ones on the basis of intersubstitution failures *salva veritate* of coreferential terms and logically equivalent sentences, restrictions on truth-preserving quantifying-in, existential generalization and related qualifications of intensional contexts.

4. Semantic extensionalism implies that a property can be truly predicated of an object only if the object exists. Against extensionalist presuppositions, we argue that we cannot make sense of the nonexistence of specific nonexistent objects except in terms of their possessing certain combinations of jointly uninstantiated properties. If semantic extensionalism is true, then if God does not exist, we cannot say that our concept of God is the concept of something omnipotent, omniscient and perfectly benevolent, or of an at least imagined object to whom those properties are truly predicated, independently of God's ontic status as existent or nonexistent. This makes it fallacious to infer that God exists from the proposition that God is or has the property of being omnipotent, or any other property correctly attributed to God or the concept of God. We need a certain amount of logical distance between the predication of constitutive properties and the existence or nonexistence of the objects to which properties are predicated. The reason why God does not exist, according to atheists persuaded by the problem of natural evil, for example, is that God or the concept of God is inconsistently defined as being omnipotent, omniscient, perfectly benevolent and the creator of a vastly imperfect world. If God as traditionally understood did not truly have these properties, then there would be no basis for such an atheist correctly or incorrectly to question God's existence. The ontic neutrality of constitutive property predications for the same reason is crucial to understanding the logical failure of Anselm's so-called ontological argument for the existence of God. See Chapter 11 and Chapter 11, note 2.

5. It appears a superficial distinction whether we ostensibly refer to Pegasus by name or to the flying horse by definite description. It should therefore not matter whether we try to attribute the properties of flying and being a horse to Pegasus or to the flying horse, since Pegasus is just a name for the flying horse. According to Bertrand Russell's extensionalist theory of definite descriptions in his 1905 essay "On Denoting", *Mind* 14, the predication of a property to an object designated by a proper name is analysable as a definite description with three clauses, including an existence assertion, a uniqueness assertion and a predication of the property to

the uniquely definitely described existing thing. Symbolically, the analysis of a definite description, "The F is or has property G", on Russell's theory, is formulated as: $G\imath xFx \leftrightarrow \exists x \big[Fx \wedge \forall y [Fy \leftrightarrow x = y] \wedge Gx \big]$. Russell interprets proper names as disguised definite descriptions, so that to say that Pegasus is a flying horse is just as false as to say that the flying horse is a flying horse, both of which predications fail to satisfy Russell's extensionalist existence condition. If we think of logically possible predication objects combinatorially in terms of a distinguishing combination of constitutive properties, then we properly leave open the question of their contingent existence or nonexistence when we assign truth-values to the predications of properties to objects. The ontic neutrality of intensionally defined objects further avoids the long-standing problem about the concept of non-being considered in Plato's dialogues the *Sophist* and *Parmenides*. We do not need to say that Pegasus paradoxically must exist in order to be the predication subject of the true proposition that Pegasus does not exist, if the logical objects of pure philosophical logic and ontology are intensionally rather than extensionally interpreted. A related approach to Plato's problems featuring a complex choice of analyses of the concept of negation is offered by F. J. Pelletier, *Parmenides, Plato, and the Semantics of Not-Being* (Chicago, IL: University of Chicago Press, 1990) and "Plato on Not-Being: Some Interpretations of the 'Symploki Eidon' (259e) and Their Relation to Parmenides' Problem", *Midwest Studies in Philosophy* 8 (1983).

6. Some medieval metaphysicians distinguish between concrete physical spatiotemporal *existence* and abstract non-physical non-spatiotemporal *subsistence* as distinct *modes of being*. A special third category of spiritual being is also added in theological and philosophical contexts to account for souls, angels and even the being of God as neither physical nor abstract. The scholastic distinction between existence and subsistence is adopted by Russell, and appears in various guises in recent and contemporary logical and metaphysical systems. We shall not observe any form of the existence–subsistence distinction, but collapse the concepts into one by equating existence with being and allowing the two terms to be used synonymously, eliminating references to subsistence altogether. We continue to distinguish between concrete physical or spatiotemporal being or existence and abstract non-physical non-spatiotemporal being or existence, as categories of a preferred applied scientific ontology.

7. M. Heidegger, *Being and Time: A Translation of Sein und Zeit*, J. Stambaugh (trans.) (Albany, NY: State University of New York Press, 1996), p. 9.

8. *Ibid.*, p. 31.

9. *Ibid.*, p. 34.

10. Before 1927 Heidegger underwent a dramatic swing away from Husserlian phenomenology, known to Heidegger scholars as *die Kehre* (literally, the "turn"). Husserl's phenomenology nevertheless underlies even Heidegger's later ontology, which Heidegger in obvious ways transforms for his own purposes in articulating the existentialist principles of *Da-Sein*. Although Heidegger is not explicit about this aspect of his methodology, he seems to rely on the fact that Husserl's *epoché*, and especially transcendental *epoché*, is a priori in its bracketing or suspension of any belief about the ontic status of objects presented to thought for internal structural phenomenological analysis. E. Husserl, *Ideas: General Introduction to Pure Phenomenology*, W. R. Boyce Gibson (trans.) (New York: Collier Books, 1962); *Logische Untersuchungen*, 2nd edn, G. Patzig (ed.) (Göttingen: Vandenhoeck & Ruprecht, 1966); *Cartesian Meditations: An Introduction to Phenomenology*, D. Cairns (trans.) (The Hague: Martinus Nijhoff, 1977). See C. F. Gethmann, *Dasein: Erkennen und Handeln: Heidegger im phänomenologischen Kontext* (Berlin: Walter de Gruyter, 1993), J. R. Mensch, *The Question of Being in Husserl's Logical Investigations* (The Hague and Boston: Kluwer, 1981), D. Moran, "Heidegger's

Critique of Husserl's and Brentano's Accounts of Intentionality", *Inquiry* 43 (2000), R. J. Dostal, "Time and Phenomenology in Husserl and Heidegger", in *The Cambridge Companion to Heidegger*, C. B. Guignon (ed.) (Cambridge: Cambridge University Press, 1993) and T. Kisiel, "On the Dimensions of a Phenomenology of Science in Husserl and the Young Dr. Heidegger", *Journal of the British Society for Phenomenology* 4 (1973).

11. Heidegger, *Being and Time*, especially, pp. 132–7, 141–86, on disclosedness (*Erschlossenheit*), and pp. 121–7, 171–230 and *passim*, on care (*Sorge*).

12. M. Merleau-Ponty, *The Phenomenology of Perception*, C. Smith (trans.) (New York: The Humanities Press, 1962), especially pp. 67–199, on the concept of the lived-body. See D. W. Smith, "Bodily Versus Cognitive Intentionality", *Noûs* 22 (1988).

13. The topic is featured in many commentaries on Heidegger's *Being and Time*. An insightful comparison is offered by J. Young, "Schopenhauer, Heidegger, Art, and the Will", in *Schopenhauer, Philosophy, and the Arts*, D. Jacquette (ed.) (Cambridge: Cambridge University Press, 1996).

14. Heidegger, *Being and Time*, p. 6.

15. *Ibid.*

16. *Ibid.*

17. *Ibid.*, p. 290.

18. *Ibid.*, pp. 290–91. See also M. Heidegger, *Existence and Being* (South Bend: Gateway Editions, 1976b), pp. 11–116.

19. R. Descartes, *Meditations on First Philosophy* (1641), in *The Philosophical Works of Descartes* [2 volumes], E. S. Haldane and G. R. T Ross (trans.) (Cambridge: Cambridge University Press, 1975), dedicatory epistle:

> And although it is utterly true that God's existence is to be believed in because it is taught in the Holy Scriptures, and, on the other hand, that the Holy Scriptures are to be believed because they have God as their source (because, since faith is a gift from God, the very same one who gives the grace that is necessary for believing the rest, can also give us grace to believe that he exists); nonetheless, this cannot be proposed to unbelievers because they would judge it to be a circle.   (p. 1)

20. Heidegger, *Being and Time*, p. 291.

21. *Ibid.*

22. See H. Philipse, *Heidegger's Philosophy of Being: A Critical Interpretation* (Princeton, NJ: Princeton University Press, 1998). For a more sympathetic exposition, compare J. Taminiaux, *Heidegger and the Project of Fundamental Ontology*, M. Gendre (trans. and ed.) (Albany, NY: State University of New York Press, 1991) and D. C. Hoy, "Heidegger and the Hermeneutic Turn", in *The Cambridge Companion to Heidegger*, C. B. Guignon (ed.) (Cambridge: Cambridge University Press, 1993), especially pp. 185–9.

23. Heidegger, *Being and Time*, p. 6.

24. *Ibid.*

25. *Ibid.*

26. *Ibid.*, p. 12.

27. *Ibid.*, p. 108.

28. Heidegger, *Being and Time*, especially, pp. 113–30, 161–4, 237–8, 263–4, 270–72, 280–83, on the concept of *Mitda-sein*.

29. *Ibid.*, p. 341.

30. *Ibid.*, p. 342.

Chapter 2: Combinatorial ontology

1. See G. W. Leibniz, *De Arte Combinatoria*, in *Sämtliche Schriften und Briefe*, series

VI [16 volumes], volume 1 (Berlin: Akademi-Verlag) (originally published in 1666 as *Dissertatio*), L. Wittgenstein, *Tractatus Logico-Philosophicus*, C. K. Ogden (ed.) (London: Routledge & Kegan Paul, 1922) and A. Blass, "Infinitary Combinatorics and Modal Logic", *Journal of Symbolic Logic* 55 (1990).

2. Logic is a more appropriate a priori method for ontology than phenomenology. Whereas logic abstracts its normative principles of reasoning from specifically human thinking, Husserl's and certainly Heidegger's existentialist phenomenology makes the thinker an essential part of phenomenological analysis even when the existence of objects thought about are bracketed in an ontically neutral *epoché*. In *The Metaphysical Foundations of Logic*, M. Heim (trans.) (Bloomington, IN: Indiana University Press, 1984), Heidegger has things precisely reversed from this perspective, construing logic and even the concept of truth as a consequence rather than presupposition of the phenomenology of judgement.

3. An important difference between the combinatorial theory of logically possible objects and properties and Wittgenstein's logic in *Tractatus Logico-Philosophicus* is that in the *Tractatus* simple objects exist in every logically possible world. Wittgenstein does not refer to logically possible worlds as such, but maintains that "Objects form the substance of the world. Therefore they cannot be compound" (§2.021). By considering simple objects as the world's substance, Wittgenstein implies that the same objects can be combined into any possible configuration of facts, and therefore into any logically possible world. The objects of combinatorial ontology need not be simple nor, except in the case of abstract objects, if there are any, must they exist in every logically possible world; they are instead logically possible predication subjects, only some of which actually exist only in the actual world.

4. The ontological priority of objects is defended in another way by P. F. Strawson, *Individuals: An Essay in Descriptive Metaphysics* (Garden City, NY: Doubleday, 1963), pp. 136–219. A similar but more elaborate proposal featuring actual events as the basic objects of ontology is advocated by A. N. Whitehead, *Process and Reality: An Essay in Cosmology* (New York: The Free Press, 1929). See J. W. Lango, *Whitehead's Ontology* (Albany, NY: State University of New York Press, 1972). From the standpoint of combinatorial pure philosophical ontology, both Whitehead's and Strawson's projects appear to substitute applied ontology in the form of a list or descriptive inventory of the kinds of things that exist, along with an account of their explanatory usefulness in metaphysics, and are otherwise exercises in applied ontology that do not even attempt to answer fundamental questions about the concept of being.

5. Aristotle, *Metaphysics* 1005b22-34, 1006b19, 1007a20, 1008a29-b2 . A. Code, "Aristotle's Investigation of a Basic Logical Principle: Which Science Investigates the Principle of Non-Contradiction?", *Canadian Journal of Philosophy* 10 (supplement) (1986). I. Kant, *Critique of Pure Reason*, N. Kemp Smith (trans.) (New York: St Martin's Press, 1965), A786/B814–A789/B817, A737/B765. The method of argument in both Aristotle and Kant is related to but more specialized than that of indirect proof or *reductio ad absurdum*. A *reductio* argument proves the negation of any hypothesis that together with other assumptions leads to a contradiction or literally reduces the hypothesis to an absurdity. Aristotle's defence of non-contradiction and Kant's method of transcendental reasoning by contrast uphold the truth of an assumption when any attempt to question or cast doubt on the assumption presupposes that the assumption is true.

6. The central thesis of combinatorial ontology is that objects as logically possible predication subjects are constituted by combinations of properties independently of their ontic status. These in turn can be further combined with properties in logically possible predications expressed by propositions representing logically

possible states of affairs or object–property combinations. This raises questions about just what kinds of things count as objects. The answer is that we can have any combination of properties constituting objects, not all of which belong to any logically possible world. If the semantics is expanded to include logically impossible worlds, then there is no need to observe the consistency restriction on combinations of properties by which objects are constituted for purposes of predication with other properties. Combinatorial pure philosophical ontology, as opposed to a general semantics, requires only logically possible worlds involving the logically possible properties of logically possible objects. We obtain an object for pure ontology in the combination [golden, mountain], which we can name or represent by means of definite descriptions as "a" or "the golden mountain", and to which we can consider predications of other properties in true or false propositions, some of which will be logically or analytically true or false, and others contingently true or false. We can say, for example, as a logical and analytic truth, that the golden mountain is golden, Ga or G[golden, mountain] or golden[golden, mountain], or even $Gıx[Gx \land Mx]$. We do the same for impossible combinations like [golden, nongolden] or [carnivorous, vegetarian], and for predications colloquially expressed as "Every human is a prime number", "Every prime number is divisible by itself, 1, and at least one other number", "Green ideas sleep furiously" and the like. Predicationally inconsistent impossible objects have no place in an ontology understood as a formal theory of being, since, by virtue of their internally metaphysically impossible property combinations, no such things can possibly exist.

7. A concise explanation of Lindenbaum's Lemma is given by E. Mendelson, *Introduction to Mathematical Logic* (New York: D. Van Nostrand, 1964), pp. 64–5. See note 17.

8. The intensional logic presented here as a contribution to pure philosophical ontology involving logically possible objects is a fragment of a complete intensional theory of meaning. A complete intensional semantics is not limited to logically possible objects, states of affairs and worlds, but needs also to include impossible intended objects. Any predication subject is an object, but not every predication subject is a logically possible object relevant to the formalization of a pure philosophical ontology. An obvious example is $ıx[Fx \land \neg Fx]$. Impossible objects are equivalently combinatorially definable by means of abbreviations, taking "F1" as the property of being an animal other than a horse and "F2" as the property of being a horse, it is logically possible to combine the properties in the logically and analytically impossible object, [F1, F2]. Such logically nonexistent objects again are indispensable in a complete semantics of thought and discourse, but fall outside the scope of ontology. For this reason, it is sometimes said that an intensional semantics requires an *extraontology* of intended objects that are not even logically possible, as well as an ontology of existent or at least logically possible objects. On the semantics for logically impossible worlds, see G. Priest's guest-edited issue of *Notre Dame Journal of Formal Logic* 38 (1997), "Impossible Worlds", including contributions by E. D. Mares, "Who's Afraid of Impossible Worlds?", D. Nolan, "Impossible Worlds: A Modest Approach", D. A. Van der Laan, "The Ontology of Impossible Worlds" and J. Hintikka, "Impossible Possible Worlds". See also the distinction between "inconsistent" and "impossible" worlds in N. Rescher and R. Brandom, *The Logic of Inconsistency: A Study in Non-Standard Possible-World Semantics and Ontology* (Totowa: Rowman and Littlefield, 1979).

9. C. I. Lewis, *A Survey of Symbolic Logic* (Berkeley, CA: University of California Press, 1918); "Implication and the Algebra of Logic", *Mind* 21 (1912); "Interesting Theorems in Symbolic Logic", *Journal of Philosophy* 10 (1913); "The Matrix Algebra for Implication", *Journal of Philosophy* 11 (1914); "Strict Implication: An Emendation", *Journal of Philosophy* 17 (1920). C. I. Lewis and C. H. Langford,

Symbolic Logic, 2nd edn (New York: Dover, 1959).

10. S. A. Kripke, "Semantical Considerations on Modal Logics", *Acta Philosophica Fennica* **16** (1963a); "Semantical Analysis of Modal Logic I: Normal Modal Propositional Calculi", *Zeitschrift für mathematische Logik und Grundlagen der Mathematic* **9** (1963b). J. Hintikka, '"The Modes of Modality", *Acta Philosophica Fennica* **16** (1963).

11. See D. K. Lewis, *Counterfactuals* (Oxford: Basil Blackwell, 1973). Some developments of model set-theoretical semantics for modal logic do not refer to the actual world as such, but make passing reference to the fact that the actual world is to be included as one among all logically possible worlds, and consider only generalized accessibility relations relative to any arbitrary world α. An example is B. F. Chellas, in his *Modal Logic: An Introduction* (Cambridge: Cambridge University Press, 1980), who does not define the concept of a logically possible world but treats it as primitive or intuitive. A generalized semantics of the sort Chellas considers must be supplemented with a method of designating the actual world for applications such as the interpretation of counterfactual propositions, in which the facts of the actual world are contrasted with propositions that are supposed to be true in alternative logically possible worlds via some specification of world-to-world modal accessibility relations.

12. S. A. Kripke, *Naming and Necessity* (Cambridge, MA: Harvard University Press, 1980):

> A possible world isn't a distant country that we are coming across, or viewing through a telescope. Generally speaking, another possible world is too far away. Even if we travel faster than light, we won't get to it. A possible world is *given by the descriptive conditions we associate with it* . . . "Possible worlds" are *stipulated*, not *discovered* by powerful telescopes. There is no reason why we cannot *stipulate* that, in talking about what would have happened to Nixon in a certain counterfactual situation, we are talking about what would have happened to *him*.   (p. 44)

See N. Salmon, "Trans-world Identification and Stipulation", *Philosophical Studies* **84** (1996).

13. G. Forbes, *The Metaphysics of Modality* (Oxford: Clarendon Press, 1985):

> The discussion of the previous section should have imparted a general picture of what model theory for quantified S5 is going to look like. As in the sentential case, there will be a set of possible worlds, but in addition, each world will be assigned a set of objects, the things which exist at that world.   (p. 28)

See also G. Forbes, *Languages of Possibility: An Essay in Philosophical Logic* (Oxford: Basil Blackwell, 1989), and D. K. Lewis, *On the Plurality of Worlds* (Oxford: Basil Blackwell, 1986). Additional references on the realism–actualism controversy in the metaphysics of modal logic notably include C. S. Chihara, *The Worlds of Possibility: Modal Realism and the Semantics of Modal Logic* (Oxford: Clarendon Press, 1998), see below, note 20; R. Stalnaker, "On Considering a Possible World as Actual I", *Proceedings of the Aristotelian Society, Supplement* **75** (2001); M. Bergmann, "A New Argument from Actualism to Serious Actualism", *Noûs* **30** (1996); P. Bricker, "'Isolation and Unification: The Realist Analysis of Possible Worlds", *Philosophical Studies* **84** (1996); S. Bringsjord, "Are There Set Theoretic Possible Worlds?", *Analysis* **45** (1985); J. Divers, "Modal Fictionalism Cannot Deliver Possible Worlds Semantics", *Analysis* **55** (1995); P. Grim, "On Sets and Worlds: A Reply to Menzel", *Analysis* **46** (1986); B. Hale, "Modal Fictionalism – A Simple Dilemma", *Analysis* **55** (1995); A. Hazen, "Expressive Incompleteness in Modal Logic", *Journal of Philosophical Logic* **5** (1976) and "Actualism Again", *Philosophical Studies* **84** (1996); T. Jager, "An Actualist Semantics for Quantified

Modal Logic", *Notre Dame Journal of Formal Logic* 23 (1982); M. Jubien, "Actualism and Iterated Modalities", *Philosophical Studies* 84 (1996); J. Kim, "Possible Worlds and Armstrong's Combinatorialism", *Canadian Journal of Philosophy* 16 (1986); A. McMichael, "A New Actualist Modal Semantics", *Journal of Philosophical Logic* 12 (1983a) and "A Problem for Actualism About Possible Worlds", *Philosophical Review* 92 (1983b); C. Menzel, "On Set Theoretic Possible Worlds", *Analysis* 46 (1986) and "Actualism, Ontological Commitment, and Possible Worlds Semantics", *Synthese* 85 (1990); A. Plantinga, "Actualism and Possible Worlds", in *The Possible and the Actual*, M. J. Loux (ed.) (Ithaca, NY: Cornell University Press, 1979); G. Ray, "Ontology-Free Modal Semantics", *Journal of Philosophical Logic* 25 (1996); P. Van Inwagen, "Two Concepts of Possible Worlds", *Midwest Studies in Philosophy* 11 (1986); and S. Yablo, "How in the World?", *Philosophical Topics* 24 (1996).

14. Modal actualist combinatorial possible worlds semantics does not preclude informal reference to the existence of an object or state of affairs in or at a non-actual world. Such language is not to be taken literally even in the case of conventional model set-theoretical semantics. When, for convenience, we say that Sherlock Holmes exists in another world, we mean only that a non-actually merely logically possible world is defined in part by means of constitutive predications of properties to a non-actual merely logically possible object stipulatively designated as Sherlock Holmes. See G. Rosen, "Modal Fictionalism", *Mind* 99 (1990), "A Problem for Fictionalism About Possible Worlds", *Analysis* 53 (1993), and "Modal Fictionalism Fixed", *Analysis* 55 (1995).

15. Conventional modal realist model set-theoretical semantics disconcertingly tries to hold at the same time that logically possible worlds as maximally consistent proposition sets *exist*, and that objects and states of affairs in some sense *exist in or at* even non-actual logically possible worlds, but that only the actual world and the objects and states of affairs it contains *actually exist*. To speak of actual existence and of a thing's actually existing seems unobjectionable for the sake of redundant emphasis, but when actual existence is distinguished from existence or existence in or at a non-actual merely logically possible world, a sound basis for the distinction is required, which conventional modal realist model set-theoretical semantics, with its concept of a logically possible world as a maximally consistent proposition set, does not provide. The modal semantics considered in pure philosophical ontology is itself pure rather than applied. The modal actualism of the combinatorial analysis of alethic modality already has built into it a principled distinction between the one and only existent or actual maximally consistent world and all other non-actual or fictional submaximally consistent merely logically possible worlds as a feature of its pure semantics. The modal realism of conventional model set-theoretical modal semantics by contrast permits it to distinguish and identify the actual world only in its applications. The characterization of the exact content and condition of the actual world remains a practical task for applied rather than pure combinatorial modal semantics, and, of course, for history and the descriptive natural sciences.

16. Even if a correct or most satisfactory semantics for modal logic turns out to be some version of conventional model set-theoretical semantics incorporating the standard concept of a logically possible world as a maximally consistent proposition set, we cannot avail ourselves of the fact that logically possible worlds exist as abstract entities on such a conception while engaged in trying to address the question of being as a problem of pure philosophical ontology. See M. McKeon, "Logical Truth in Modal Logic", *Pacific Philosophical Quarterly* 77 (1996).

17. Lindenbaum's Lemma entails that if Γ is a syntactically consistent proposition set, then Γ is a subset of some maximally consistent proposition set that is an extension of Γ. If proposition p is actually true, then any world in which $\neg p$ is true must be

submaximal, according to the combinatorial account of non-actual merely logically possible worlds. This fact nevertheless does not contradict Lindenbaum's Lemma. The combinatorial analysis does not identify or equate logically possible worlds with proposition sets, whether they are maximally or submaximally consistent. What is true of proposition sets as an implication of Lindenbaum's Lemma does not therefore translate into any consequences for the modal actualist combinatorial concept of a logically possible world as a logically possible states-of-affairs combination.

18. Is it true, as a combinatorial modal actualist semantics entails, that all non-actual merely logically possible worlds are submaximal? Can we not imagine a logically possible world that is just like the actual world in every respect except for the existence or nonexistence of an elementary particle in a remote corner of intergalactic space that is not in causal interaction with any other part of the universe? Such a particle exists or does not exist, but in either case the scenario appears to project a non-actual merely logically possible world that by virtue of its method of description, beginning with the maximally consistent actual world and considering only one small change, is maximally consistent in the constitutive properties of all its constituent objects and states of affairs. It is essential to the counterexample that the logically possible world in question involves a physical and hence logically contingent entity that is causally isolated in every way from every other event in the universe, since otherwise we would not be able to comprehend all of the ramifications of introducing such a change without taking account of the untold alterations that would cascade throughout that world. It need not be problematic to imagine a causally inefficacious physical transformation within the actual world as a mere logical possibility. Even without causal modifications, however, the addition to or deletion from a complete world of one such particle or physical entity of any size introduces unlimitedly many predication gaps in the stipulative projection of a non-actual world. Any such world is sure to be incomplete with respect to innumerable spatiotemporal relations between the imagined particle and every other physical entity in the universe in what is consequently bound to be at best a submaximal specification of the non-actual world's states of affairs. The same is true if we think of spacetime as involving a branching future with no predetermined course, in which only one pathway is ultimately realized. The way the world turns out to be is describable as the actual occurrence of one of the many branching paths open to it any point, in which all as yet unrealized potential routes are projected when and in so far as they are only considered as submaximal logical possibilities, including whatever particular path later turns out to be actual – which is to say, on the combinatorial modal actualist analysis, whatever path turns out to be maximally consistent.

19. The idea of a logically possible world as a maximal structure of facts or propositions is clearly stated in Forbes, *The Metaphysics of Modality*:

> A possible world is a *complete* way things might have been – a total alternative history . . . In terms of our model theory, the requirement that worlds be complete is reflected in the constraint that *every* sentence letter occurring in the argument in question be assigned one or other truth value at each world. (p. 8)

This intuitive statement of the semantic concept of a logically possible world is equivalent to the conventional modal realist definition of a world as a maximally consistent proposition set. Significantly, Forbes adds, "We shall see in §4 of this chapter that we can get by without this sort of completeness, but that we pay a price in terms of simplicity" (*ibid.*).

20. In *The Worlds of Possibility*, Chihara argues that a Cantorian cardinality paradox afflicts A. Plantinga's set-theoretical principles of modal semantics in *The Nature of Necessity* (Oxford: Oxford University Press, 1974). Chihara identifies the follow-

ing assumptions in Plantinga's modal ontology:

> [1] States of affairs exist. [2] Every state of affairs S has a complement S'. [3] If S is a state of affairs, then necessarily either S or S' obtains. [4] Given any possible state of affairs S, there exists a set whose members are all those possible states of affairs whose members are all those possible states of affairs that include S. [5] Given any set β of states of affairs, the conjunction of that set, *all the members of β having obtained*, exists.   (p. 125)

Chihara infers the existence of at least one logically possible world by building up a set β, adding either S or the complement of S, S', for every S, and defining D as the state of affairs of all the states of affairs in β having obtained. (This is a version of the Lindenbaum maximal consistency recursion; see above, notes 7 and 17.) Set D thereby satisfies the conventional model set-theoretical definition of a logically possible world, which Plantinga also accepts, the existence of which, by Plantinga's principles, is set-theoretically guaranteed. Chihara then deduces a Cantorian paradox:

> As shown above, we can conclude from Plantinga's principles that there is a set α whose elements are *all the possible states of affairs that obtain*. Then, according to Cantor's Theorem, the power set of α, 2^α, has cardinality greater than the cardinality of α. Hence, there cannot be a one-one correspondence between 2^α and any subset of α. But, as will be shown below, there is.   (p. 126)

The proposed combinatorial analysis of alethic modality avoids Chihara's Cantorian paradox by detaching the concept of a logically possible world from that of a maximally consistent proposition or states of affairs set like D. Chihara's paradox refutes conventional model set-theoretical concepts of a logically possible world, like Plantinga's. Importantly, the combinatorial model does not accept Plantinga's principle [2], that all states of affairs exist, since not all states of affairs are maximally consistent. Nor does Chihara's proof of the existence of at least one logically possible world on Plantinga's realist assumptions go through in a combinatorial actualist modal ontology and semantics. At most, Chihara establishes a result that is limited in immediate relevance to set theory in the abstract, including conventional set-theoretical models of logical possibility. In proving the existence of set D, Chihara establishes the existence of at least one maximally consistent states-of-affairs set. From a combinatorial modal actualist perspective, however, he does not thereby prove the existence of a logically possible world. The only logically possible world recognized as existent in actualist combinatorial modal semantics is the actual world, and it is not an abstract set but a maximally consistent states-of-affairs combination. Chihara, moreover, does not explain exactly what he means by a state of affairs "obtaining". If by this he means simply existing, then combinatorial ontology in any case cannot rely on Chihara's applied ontological assumptions about the ontic status of abstract entities such as states of affairs and sets of states of affairs, including the state of affairs in which other states of affairs obtain. Assumptions about the ontic status of sets and states of affairs cannot be introduced without falling into Heidegger's circle while the question of being in pure philosophical ontology remains unanswered, and so cannot be appealed to in trying to prove either the existence of at least one logically possible world or of the actual world as the only existent logically possible world. Cantor's diagonalization proof of the generalized power set principle to which Chihara refers appears in G. Cantor, *Contributions to the Founding of the Theory of Transfinite Numbers*, P. E. B. Jourdain (trans.) (New York: Dover, 1952).

Chapter 3: Why there is something rather than nothing

1. G. W. Leibniz, "On the Ultimate Origination of Things", in *Leibniz: Philosophical Writings*, G. H. R. Parkinson (ed.), M. Morris and G. H. R. Parkinson (trans.) (London: J. M. Dent and Sons 1973e), pp. 136–44.

2. Leibniz's concept of an *haecceity* or individuating essence, together with his commitment to the principle of the identity of indiscernibles, that $x = y$ if x and y share all their properties in common, poses difficulties for the common-sense view that the very same objects in the actual world might have different properties in alternative non-actual merely logically possible worlds. The combined force of these positions in Leibniz threatens to collapse all logically possible worlds into the actual world, and render all predications of properties to existent entities logically necessary. Further implications of Leibniz's logic and metaphysics appear to contradict the logical contingency of facts about physical spatiotemporal entities and the freedom of action and the will. Leibniz tries to solve the problem informally by sketching a theory of counterparts belonging to alternative logically possible worlds that by degrees are relatively similar in their characteristic properties to actual entities, and in terms of which logical contingencies and freedom can be interpreted. Leibniz, *Discourse on Metaphysics*; *Correspondence with Arnauld*, G. R. Montgomery (trans.) (La Salle, IL: Open Court, 1902); "Necessary and Contingent Truth", "On Freedom", "A Letter on Freedom" and "On the Principle of Indiscernibles", collected in *Leibniz: Philosophical Writings*. See G. H. R. Parkinson, *Logic and Reality in Leibniz's Metaphysics* (Oxford: Clarendon Press, 1965). A contemporary exposition of counterpart theory for symbolic modal logic is offered by D. K. Lewis, *Counterfactuals* and "Counterpart Theory and Quantified Modal Logic", *Journal of Philosophy* 65 (1968).

3. M. Heidegger, *An Introduction to Metaphysics*, R. Manheim (trans.) (Garden City, NY: Doubleday, 1961), pp. 1–42. A very different probabilistic approach to this fundamental question of ontology is proposed by R. Nozick, *Philosophical Explanations* (Oxford: Clarendon Press, 1981), pp. 115–64. See also N. Fleming, "Why is There Something Rather Than Nothing?", *Analysis* 48 (1988), C. Mortensen, "Explaining Existence", *Canadian Journal of Philosophy* 16 (1986), N. L. Wilson, "The Two Main Problems of Philosophy", *Dialogue* 12 (1973), R. Sylvan, "Toward an Improved Cosmo-Logical Synthesis", *Grazer Philosophische Studien* 25–26 (1985–86) and D. Parfit, "The Puzzle of Reality: Why Does the Universe Exist?", *Times Literary Supplement*, 3 July (1992).

4. Heidegger formulates the fundamental question of metaphysics in slightly different terms. He asks, "Why are there essents rather than nothing?" (*An Introduction to Metaphysics*: p. 1). Heidegger's own asterisk note indicates that "'Essents' = 'existents,' 'things that art [sic]'" (*ibid.*). Presumably, his choice of a special terminology is meant to highlight the distinctive interpretation and solution of the question he proposes. His avenue back to the existential ontology of *Da-sein* takes the following direction. He argues (pp. 19–20) that the question can and should eliminate the qualification "rather than nothing" as inessential. He maintains that the abbreviated question "Why are there essents?" is to be addressed in terms of the question "How is it with being?", by which he means to ask whether being *has* a ground or *is itself* a ground, in a roughly Kantian transcendental sense. His answer is that being is itself a ground, to be understood in terms of *Being and Time*'s phenomenology of *Da-sein*, whereby the original question "Why are there essents?", or "Why are there essents rather than nothing?", is answered by maintaining that being requires no transcendental ground or further explanation, but is rather the ground of every existent thing that might be considered, presupposed even by the fundamental question of metaphysics. Thus, Heidegger writes:

> Out of the fundamental question of metaphysics, "Why are there essents rather than nothing?" we have separated the preliminary question, "How does it stand with being?" . . . Here the preliminary question is not by any means outside of the main question; rather, it is the flame which burns as it were in the asking of the fundamental question; it is the flaming center of all questioning. That is to say: it is crucial for the first asking of the fundamental question that in asking its *preliminary* question we derive the decisive fundamental attitude that is here essential. That is why we have related the question of being to the destiny of Europe, where the destiny of the earth is being decided – while our own historic being-there proves to be the center of Europe itself.   (pp. 34–6)

All this seems a bit deluded; despite Heidegger's efforts (pp. 24–5) to placate concerns that *Da-sein*, as he conceives it, is anthropocentric and even ego-centric, and (pp. 35–6) that his approach historicizes metaphysics, Heidegger explicitly subordinates the question of being and the fundamental question of metaphysics to the historical situation of a particular collection of (European) thinkers (on the brink of world war) asking and trying to answer these questions. The conclusion is further evidence of Heidegger's entanglement in the methodological circle by which his ontology and ontic sciences are snared. In the previous paragraph, Heidegger writes:

> We ask the questions "How does it stand with being?" "What is the meaning of being?" *not* in order to set up an ontology in the traditional style, much less to criticize the past mistakes of ontology. We are concerned with something totally different: to restore man's historical being-there – and that always includes our own future being-there in the totality of the history allotted to us – to the domain of being, which it was originally incumbent on man to open up for himself. All this, to be sure, within the limits within which philosophy can accomplish anything.
> (p. 34)

Thereafter Heidegger adds:

> Our asking the fundamental question of metaphysics is historical because it opens up the process of human being-there in its essential relations – i.e. its relations to the essent as such and as a whole – opens it up to unasked possibilities, futures, and at the same time binds it back to its past beginning, so sharpening it and giving it weight in its present. In this questioning our being-there is summoned to its history in the full sense of the word, called to history and to a decision in history. And this not after the fact, in the sense that we draw ethical, ideological lessons from it. No, the basic attitude of the questioning is in itself historical; it stands and maintains itself in happening, inquiring out of happening for the sake of happening.   (pp. 36–7)

It is tempting, although probably inaccurate, while at the same time virtually impossible to know Heidegger's final intent in his treatment of the fundamental question of metaphysics, to interpret his solution as holding that the question answers itself, because being as *Da-sein* is presupposed by the fact of the question's being asked. We have by now come to expect the extent to which Heidegger is prepared to try to make a virtue out of this type of circularity.

5. C. G. Hempel, "Science Unlimited", *Annals of the Japan Association for Philosophy of Science* 14 (1973), p. 200.

6. *Dasein* in the ordinary non-Heideggerean sense means simply literally "being-there" or "there-being" in German. For philosophical purposes, it is adopted by many non-Heideggerean philosophers to represent the metaphysical category of actual existence or real presence. The concept of *das Modalmoment* of full-

strength factuality and *depotenzierte* or watered-down being in the object theory tradition is introduced by Meinong, *Über Möglichkeit und Wahrscheinlichkeit: Beiträge zur Gegenstandstheorie und Erkenntnistheorie, Gesamtausgabe*, VI, p. 266. See also J. N. Findlay, *Meinong's Theory of Objects and Values* (Aldershot: Ashgate Publishing, 1995), pp. 77, 103–12. Plato in *Sophist* 259e5–6 discusses the blending or interweaving of the Form of Being with other Forms.

7.   The circularity problem in Descartes's *Cogito* is usually attributed only or primarily to his version of the principle in the *Discourse on Method*, where he offers what appears to be an explicitly inferential formulation, *Cogito, ergo sum*, as opposed to the *Meditations on First Philosophy*, where it is simply made a matter of entertaining a thought and recognizing that one must exist in order to think, *Cogito, sum*. The difficulty is that the inflected Latin ending in the single word "*Cogito*" already commits the expression to the proposition that it is specifially an *I* or *ego*, self, soul, subject or first-person thinker that thinks, rather than, say, an impersonal force or non-subjective impersonal occurrence or emanation of thought.

Chapter 4: Why there is only one logically contingent actual world

1.   Leibniz, "On the Ultimate Origination of Things" and *Discourse on Metaphysics*. See G. M. Ross, *Leibniz* (Oxford: Oxford University Press, 1984), pp. 57–60.

2.   See Russell's common-sense refutation of "The First-cause Argument" in *Why I Am Not a Christian and Other Essays on Related Subjects*, P. Edwards (ed.) (New York: Simon and Schuster, 1957), pp. 6–7.

3.   Plato, *Timaeus* 49a, explains the concept of the *chora* or spatial receptacle. I. Newton, *Opticks* (New York: Dover, 1952) writes:

> Does it not appear from phenomena that there is a Being incorporeal, living, intelligent, omnipresent, who in infinite Space, as it were in his Sensory, sees the things themselves intimately, and thoroughly perceives them and comprehends them wholly by their immediate presence to himself . . .?   (Book III, Query 28, p. 370)

See R. H. Hurlbutt, *Hume, Newton, and the Design Argument* (Lincoln, NE: University of Nebraska Press, 1985): "Infinite space is, 'as it were' God's visual field, and the things in this space are known by him in their complete inner nature and complexity" (p. 10).

Chapter 5: Concepts of existence in philosophical logic and the analysis of being *qua* being

1.   The realism versus nominalism debate is discussed in a combinatorial ontology context below in Chapter 8.

2.   Useful standard expositions of modal logic are found in G. E. Hughes and M. J. Cresswell, *An Introduction to Modal Logic* (London: Methuen, 1968) and Chellas, *Modal Logic: An Introduction*. See also the section on "Modal Logic and Semantics" in D. Jacquette (ed.), *A Companion to Philosophical Logic* (Oxford: Basil Blackwell, 2002a).

3.   Even strong modal systems like S_5 do not generally support the inference of logical necessity, $\Box p$, from the iterated logical possibility of logical necessity, $\Box \Diamond p$. By contrast, S_5 characteristically permits the valid inference $\Diamond \Box p \vdash \Box p$.

4.   The proposition in assumption 6 in the proof on page 143, $\Box \Diamond \exists w_i MaxCon.w_i$, expresses the combinatorial implication whereby it must be logically possible for there to exist a maximally consistent logically possible world, which is to say at least one maximally consistent states-of-affairs or object–property combination

among all logical possibilities. The inference is presented in terms of the weakest modal systems; in stronger modal logics, like modal S_5 and the Brouwersche system, the assumption is derivable, relying on combinatorial possibilities for the simpler modally unqualified assumption, $\exists w_i MaxCon.w_i$. (I am grateful to John Divers for pointing out this alternative route to the conclusion in 7, without directly appealing to the iterated modality in the original assumption 6.) The essential modal principle for these stronger logical systems appears in assumption 5c:

5.	$\Box[\Diamond \exists w_i MaxCon.w_i \to \exists x MaxCon.w_i]$	Df $MaxCon$
5a.	$\Box\Diamond \exists w_i MaxCon.w_i \to \Box \exists x MaxCon.w_i$	(5, Modal logic)
5b.	$\Diamond\neg\exists x MaxCon.w_i \to \Diamond\Box\neg\exists w_i MaxCon.w_i$	(6, Modal duality)
5c.	$\Diamond\Box\neg\exists w_i MaxCon.w_i \to \neg\exists w_i MaxCon.w_i$	(S_5 or Brouwersche)
5d.	$\Diamond\neg\exists x MaxCon.w_i \to \neg\exists w_i MaxCon.w_i$	(5b,5c)
5e.	$\exists w_i MaxCon.w_i \to \Box\exists x MaxCon.w_i$	(5d, Modal duality)
6'.	$\exists w_i MaxCon.w_i$	(Combinatorics)
7.	$\Box\exists w_i MaxCon.w_i$	(5e,6)

5. It might appear, in light of the combinatorial analysis of non-actual merely logically possible worlds as submaximally consistent, that it is obligatory to define logically necessary truth, $\Box p$, non-standardly as a proposition p not being false in any logically possible world, rather than being true in every logically possible world. The grounds for such a claim are that in a modal actualist semantics there are countless propositions that will not describe states of affairs in any given non-actual merely logically possible world, for which the worlds are incomplete, submaximal, or for which they have constitutive predicational gaps. Redefining the concept of logical necessity in this way is not required, however, as we see when we reflect hypothetically on a dilemma concerning the applied ontology of abstract entities, whose ontic status is yet to be determined. If there exist abstract entities, then by definition they exist in every logically possible world, including non-actual merely logically possible worlds; in which case, necessary truths concerning only the properties of abstract entities remain true of every logically possible world. If, on the contrary, no abstract entities exist, then there are no logically necessary truths, but only logically contingent truths involving the variably existent objects and states of affairs differentially distributed across some but not all logically possible worlds. This situation again supports the standard definition of logically necessary truth as truth in every logically possible world, where, by hypothesis, there are no logically necessary truths and equally no propositions that are true in every logically possible world.

6. Inference rules for the delta Δ actuality operator are specified as needed for proofs in the text further below.

7. A difference in modal scope is relevant to the argument. *De re* or *wide modal scope* directly qualifies the modality of an *object*, a thing or *res*, as in the sentence, "Object a is necessarily F", whereas *de dicto* or *narrow modal scope* qualifies the modality of a *proposition*, literally a saying or *dictum*, in which the object is mentioned, such as, "Necessarily, object a is F". *De dicto* contexts, furthermore, including modal contexts, are generally intensional, whereas *de re* contexts are extensional.

8. There is no difficulty in obtaining conclusion 20 by Δ inference rules. It might appear that we could advance the following counter-derivation:

[1]	$\Delta w_@ \to w_@$	[Δ rule]
[2]	$\Box[\Delta w_@ \to w_@]$	[[1] Necessitation]
[3]	$\Box\Delta w_@ \to \Box w_@$	[[2] Modal logic]
[4]	$\Box w_@ \wedge \neg\Box w_@$	[[3], 20]

However, the inference is invalid. The term "$w_@$" does not designate a proposition, but a world, which is to say a (maximally consistent) states-of-affairs combination. The actual world $w_@$ has no truth-value, as the consequent of the conditional in assumption [1] requires. The Δ inference rules explicitly apply only to propositions as truth-value vehicles, and not to worlds, thus blocking the first step in the inference at step [1]. A counterpart version of the corresponding Δ rule holds for worlds of the form: $\forall w_i[\Delta w_i \to \exists w_k[w_k = w_i]]$. With this provision, we preserve the ordinary linguistic equivocation between the actuality of the actual world, which is not itself a proposition, even if it is conventionally identified with or described by a set of propositions, and the actual truth of corresponding propositions. The alternative rule for the actual world does not support a version of the respective inference that would otherwise contradict the conclusion in 20. The modified inference states:

[1′] $\Delta w_@ \to \exists w_i[w_i = w_@]$ [Δ Worlds rule]
[2′] $\Box[\Delta w_@ \to \exists w_i[w_i = w_@]]$ [[1′] Necessitation]
[3′] $\Box\Delta w_@ \to \Box\exists w_i[w_i = w_@]$ [[2′] Modal logic]
[4′] $\Box\exists w_i[w_i = w_@]$ [[3′], 20]

Conclusion [4′] is harmless, particularly when we recall that $\forall w_i[\Box w_i \leftrightarrow \forall p[pw_i \to \Box p]]$. The proposition that $\Box\exists w_i[w_i = w_@]$ states only that the actual world is *de dicto* logically necessarily identical to some logically possible world. This is not only not paradoxical, but intuitively true, since it does not entail that the actual world is logically necessary *de re*. To say that necessarily the actual world is identical to some world is not to say that the content or condition or any constitutive proposition of the world is logically necessary or necessarily true – as always, leaving aside propositions about transworld universal abstract entities, if there are any. Thus $\neg[\Box\exists w_i[w_i = w_@] \to \Box w_@]$. Equally, there is no contradiction in the conjunction of the implications of conclusion 20 with [4′]:

[5′] $\neg\Box w_@ \wedge \Box\exists w_i[w_i = w_@]$ [[4′], 20]

Part II: Applied Ontology and the Metaphysics of Science

Chapter 6: Ontological commitment (on Quine)

1. An example is an ontology of events that are explicitly said within the theory not to be objects, or a metaphysics of properties that are objects. Quine's requirement that a theory first be translated into a canonical notation is doomed to distortion in the first case if properties are to be predicated of events, but events are not representable in standard symbolic logic by means of object terms or variables. It is the same in the second case where a theory holds that properties are objects if properties cannot legitimately be represented by predicate terms.
2. Quine, "On What There Is", p. 1.
3. *Ibid.*, pp. 8–9.
4. *Ibid.*, p. 13.
5. *Ibid.*, pp. 15–16.
6. Quine defines the concept of semantic ascent in *Word and Object* (Cambridge, MA: MIT Press, 1960), pp. 271–6.
7. The criticism is developed independently by R. Cartwright, "Ontology and the Theory of Meaning", *Philosophy of Science* 21 (1954); N. Chomsky and I. Scheffler, "What is Said to Be", *Proceedings of the Aristotelian Society* 59 (1958);

M. Jubien, "The Intensionality of Ontological Commitment", *Noûs* 6 (1972). See also M. P. Hodges, "Quine on 'Ontological Commitment'", *Philosophical Studies* 23 (1972).

8. G. Baker and P. M. S. Hacker, *Frege: Logical Excavations* (Oxford: Basil Blackwell, 1984), pp. 63–76, 88, 200–202, 280; C. Thiel, *Sense and Reference in Frege's Logic* (Dordrecht: D. Reidel, 1968) pp. 118–41; M. Dummett, *The Interpretation of Frege's Philosophy* (Cambridge, MA: Harvard University Press, 1981), pp. 323–42 and *Frege: Philosophy of Language* (New York: Harper and Row, 1973), especially pp. 157–9; W. Carl, *Frege's Theory of Sense and Reference: Its Origins and Scope* (Cambridge: Cambridge University Press, 1994), pp. 96–9; M. Hahn, "The Frege Puzzle One More Time", in *Frege: Sense and Reference One Hundred Years Later*, J. Biro and P. Kotatko (eds) (Dordrecht: Kluwer, 1995), pp. 169–83; and J. Weiner, *Frege in Perspective* (Ithaca, NY: Cornell University Press, 1990), pp. 57–9, 157–61, 164–6.

9. See Chapter 1, note 5.

10. Quine, "On What There Is", pp. 6–7.

11. Quine limits his preferred theoretical ontological domain to physical individuals and the minimum abstract classes needed for a quasi-logicist reconstruction of mathematics according to the programme of his "New Foundations for Mathematical Logic", *American Mathematical Monthly* 44 (1937). He explains these commitments in *Word and Object*. Compare also the references indicated below in note 18. Quine, "On Carnap's Views on Ontology", in *The Ways of Paradox and Other Essays* (Cambridge, MA: Harvard University Press, 1976c). See also, M. Alspector-Kelly, "On Quine on Carnap on Ontology", *Philosophical Studies* 102 (2001).

12. Against the reducibility of mathematics to classical first-order logic, see K. Gödel, "On Formally Undecidable Propositions of *Principia Mathematica* and Related Systems I", in *From Frege to Gödel: A Source Book in Mathematical Logic, 1879–1931*, Jen van Heijenoort (ed. and trans.) (Cambridge, MA: Harvard University Press, 1967). A. Church, "An Unsolvable Problem of Elementary Number Theory", *Bulletin of the American Mathematical Society* 41 (1935). J. B. Rosser, "Extensions of Some Theorems of Gödel and Church", *Journal of Symbolic Logic* 1 (1936).

13. Quine, "On What There Is", p. 12.

14. *Ibid.*, p. 10.

15. Quine introduces the problem of "Gavagai" and the indeterminacy of radical translation in *Word and Object*, pp. 27, 54, 72–9. A selection of the extensive secondary literature on this important topic in Quine includes: H. Field, "Some Thoughts on Radical Indeterminacy", *The Monist* 81 (1998); J. Katz, "The Refutation of Indeterminacy", *Journal of Philosophy* 85 (1988); S. Soames, "The Indeterminacy of Translation and the Inscrutability of Reference", *Canadian Journal of Philosophy* 29 (1999); J. Biro, "Meaning, Translation and Interpretation", *Australasian Journal of Philosophy* 59 (1981); H. J. Glock, "The Indispensability of Translation in Quine and Davidson", *Philosophical Quarterly* 43 (1993); J. F. Harris Jr., "Indeterminacy of Translation and Analyticity", *Southern Journal of Philosophy* 14 (1976); D. Hockney, "The Bifurcation of Scientific Theories and Indeterminacy of Translation", *Philosophy of Science* 42 (1975); D. Rothbart, "Propositions and Quine's Indeterminacy of Radical Translation", *Dialogue* 18 (1976); H. Darmstadter, "Indeterminacy of Translation and Indeterminacy of Belief", *Philosophical Studies* 24 (1974); J. Wallace, "A Query on Radical Translation", *Southern Journal of Philosophy* 68 (1971); B. M. Humphries, "Indeterminacy of Translation and Theory", *Southern Journal of Philosophy* 67 (1970); P. L. Peterson, "Translation and Synonymy: Rosenberg on Quine", *Inquiry* 11 (1968); J. Hintikka, "Behavioral Criteria of Radical Translation", *Synthese* 19 (1968); A.

Cutrofello, "Quine and the Inscrutibility of Languages", *International Studies in Philosophy* **24** (1992); S. G. Harding, "Making Sense of Observation Sentences", *Ratio* **17** (1975); C. Boorse, "The Origins of the Indeterminacy Thesis", *Journal of Philosophy* **72** (1975); and J. Margolis, "Behaviorism and Alien Languages", *Philosophia* **3** (1973). Quine's related topic of ontological relativity is introduced in his landmark essay, "Ontological Relativity", in *Ontological Relativity and Other Essays* (New York: Columbia University Press, 1969). See P. Teller, "On Quine's Relativity of Ontology", *Canadian Journal of Philosophy* **3** (1973); J. M. Thomason, "Ontological Relativity and the Inscrutability of Reference", *Philosophical Studies* **22** (1971); and Quine, "On the Reasons for Indeterminacy of Translation", *Journal of Philosophy* **67** (1970).

16. Quine, *Word and Object*, pp. 191–232. See also Quine, "Three Grades of Modal Involvement", in *The Ways of Paradox and Other Essays* and "Reference and Modality", in *From a Logical Point of View*.

17. For a more detailed criticism of Quine's counter-examples to quantified modal logic, see J. Margolis, "The Planets are Nine in Number", *Canadian Journal of Philosophy* **4** (1975). Jacquette, "Intentionality and Intensionality: Quotation Contexts and the Modal Wedge", *The Monist* **59** (1986). A careful explanation of the ambiguities of scope that are relevant to Quine's problem is found in S. A. Kripke, "Speaker's Reference and Semantic Reference", in *Contemporary Perspectives in the Philosophy of Language*, P. A. French *et al.* (eds) (Minneapolis, MN: University of Minnesota Press, 1979).

18. A. N. Whitehead and B. Russell, *Principia Mathematica* (3 volumes) (Cambridge: Cambridge University Press, 1925–27). Quine, "New Foundations for Mathematical Logic"; "On the Consistency of 'New Foundations'", *Proceedings of the National Academy of Sciences of the USA* **37** (1951); and "The Inception of NF", *Builletin de la Socieété Mathématique de Belgique* **45** (1993). J. B. Rosser, "On the Consistency of Quine's New Foundations for Mathematical Logic", *Journal of Symbolic Logic* **4** (1939a); "Definition by Induction in Quine's New Foundations for Mathematical Logic", *Journal of Symbolic Logic* **4** (1939b); and "The Axiom of Infinity in Quine's New Foundations", *Journal of Symbolic Logic* **18** (1952).

19. Quine, *Word and Object*, pp. 266–71; "On What There Is", pp. 17–18; "Logic and the Reification of Universals", in *From a Logical Point of View*, pp. 102–29; "Ontological Reduction and the World of Numbers", in *The Ways of Paradox and Other Essays*; and "A Logistical Approach to the Ontological Problem", in *The Ways of Paradox and Other Essays*. See J. King-Farlow, 'Metaphysics and Choosing: Sets, Quine, and the One'.

20. Quine, "On What There Is", pp. 9–10.

21. *Ibid.*, pp. 13–14.

22. *Ibid.*, p. 17.

23. Sources in phenomenalism and sensationalism include E. B. de Condillac, *An Essay on the Origin of Human Knowledge, Being a Supplement to Mr. Locke's Essay on the Human Understanding*, T. Nugent (trans.) (Gainesville: Scholars Facsimiles and Reprints, 1971) and *Condillac's Treatise on the Sensations*, G. Carr (trans.) (London: The Favil Press, 1930); and E. Mach, *The Analysis of Sensations*, C. M. Williams (trans.) (Chicago, IL: University of Chicago Press, 1914). See J. T. Blackmore *et al.* (eds), *Ernst Mach's Vienna, 1895–1930: Or Phenomenalism as Philosophy of Science* (Dordrecht and Boston: Kluwer, 2001). The ranks of phenomenalists also include Berkeley, Hume, Russell, Wittgenstein, Carnap, Ayer and Broad and adherents of the sense-data movement in early twentieth-century metaphysics.

24. Quine, "On What There Is", pp. 16–17.

25. Critical discussions of Ockham's razor in theory choice are found in E. Sober,

Simplicity (Oxford: Clarendon Press, 1975), "The Principle of Parsimony", *British Journal for the Philosophy of Science* 32 (1981) and "Let's Razor Ockham's Razor", in *Explanation and its Limits*, D. Knowles (ed.) (Cambridge: Cambridge University Press, 1990); J. J. C. Smart, "Ockham's Razor", in *Principles of Philosophical Reasoning*, J. H. Fetzer (ed.) (Totowa: Rowman and Allenheld, 1984); M. Tweedale, "Ockham's Supposed Elimination of Connotative Terms and his Ontological Parsimony", *Dialogue* 31 (1992); P. Abela, "Is Less Always More? An Argument Against the Natural Ontological Attitude", *Philosophical Quarterly* 46 (1996); D. Nolan, "Quantitative Parsimony", *British Journal for the Philosophy of Science* 48 (1997b); and B. Lauth, "New Blades for Ockham's Razor", *Erkenntnis* 46 (1997).
26. Quine, "On What There Is", p. 4.

Chapter 7: Appearance, reality, substance, transcendence

1. Parmenides, *Parmenides of Elea: Fragments* (Toronto: University of Toronto Press, 1984), especially the selections from Parmenides' *Proem*, *The Way of Truth* and *The Way of Seeming*. See C. C. Meinwald, *Plato's Parmenides* (New York: Oxford University Press, 1991).
2. Descartes inscribes this enigmatic Latin motto in a private notebook.
3. Descartes, *Meditations on First Philosophy*, Meditation 3, 4.
4. Kant's slogan that reason without intuition (sense experience) is empty, and intuition without concepts (innate forms of intuition or categories of pure understanding) is blind, succinctly summarizes his (Copernican) revolutionary synthesis of rationalism and empiricism. Kant, *Critique of Pure Reason*, A51/B75. Schopenhauer regards the distinction between *phenomena* (the world as it appears), and *noumena* (the real world as it is in itself) as the most important achievement of Kant's critical idealism. In *The World as Will and Representation*, E. F. J. Payne (trans.) (New York: Dover Publications, 1969), Schopenhauer writes: *"Kant's greatest merit is the distinction of the phenomenon from the thing-in-itself*, based on the proof that between things and us there always stands the *intellect*, and that on this account they cannot be known according to what they may be in themselves" (vol. I, pp. 417–18).
5. A. Schopenhauer, *On the Fourfold Root of the Principle of Sufficient Reason*, E. F. J. Payne (trans.) (La Salle, IL: Open Court Publishing, 1974), pp. 41–2. See F. C. White, *On Schopenhauer's Fourfold Root of the Principle of Sufficient Reason* (Leiden: E. J. Brill, 1992), for a comprehensive exposition of Schopenhauer's application of the principle in its limited application to phenomena or the world as idea.
6. Berkeley avoids subjectivity in idealism only by appealing to the existence of God as a divine infinite mind who continuously perceives all the ideas that constitute sensible things that are only partially and discontinuously perceived by distinct finite human minds. Subjectivity in Berkeley's theo-empirical ontology might nevertheless arise even on the thesis that sensible things are constituted by "congeries" of ideas in the mind of God, if it should turn out to be impossible in Berkeley's philosophy to disprove the possible existence of multiple gods with distinct perspectives on the world of sensible things. See G. Berkeley, *Three Dialogues Between Hylas and Philonous* (1710), in *The Works of George Berkeley Bishop of Cloyne* (9 volumes), A. A. Luce and T. E. Jessop (eds) (London: Thomas Nelson, 1948–57), vol. 2, especially pp. 210–14.
7. Galileo, *The Assayer* [Il Saggiatore, 1623], in *Le Opera de Galileo Galilei*, A. Favaro (ed.) (Florence: S. A. G. Barbèra Editore, 1929–39); Descartes, *Principles of Philosophy*, IV, §§188–203. R. Boyle, *The Origin of Forms and Qualities* (1666);

J. Locke, *An Essay Concerning Human Understanding* [1700], P. H. Nidditch (ed.) (Oxford: Clarendon Press, 1975), Book II, Ch. 8.

8. An excellent exposition of Schopenhauer's fundamental distinction as it relates to the transcendence of the thing-in-itself construed as Will is given by C. Janaway, *Self and World in Schopenhauer's Philosophy* (Oxford: Clarendon Press, 1989).

9. Berkeley, *Three Dialogues Between Hylas and Philonous*, pp. 154–5.

10. Supervenience and emergence are discussed in Chapter 10.

Chapter 8: Physical entities: space, time, matter and causation, physical states of affairs and events, natural laws

1. Kant, *Critique of Pure Reason* A19-B73. See Kant, *Prolegomena to Any Future Metaphysics That Will be Able to Come Forward as Science*, P. Carus (trans.) (Indianapolis, IN: Hackett, 1977):

> But these [idealists], and among them more particularly Berkeley, regarded space as a mere empirical representation that, like the appearances it contains, is, together with its determinations, known to us only by means of experience or perception. I, on the contrary, prove in the first place that space (and also time, which Berkeley did not consider) and all its determinations can be cognized *a priori* by us, because, no less than time, it inheres in us as a pure form of our sensibility before all perception of experience and makes possible all intuition of sensibility, and therefore all appearances. (p. 114)

2. See W. C. Salmon, (ed.), *Zeno's Paradoxes* (Indianapolis, IN: the Bobs-Merrill Company, 1970); A. Grünbaum, *Modern Science and Zeno's Paradoxes* (Middletown: Wesleyan University Press, 1967); R. Ferber, *Zenons Paradoxien der Bewegung und die Struktur von Raum und Zeit* (Munich: C. H. Beck, 1981); H. Hasse *et al.*, *Zeno and the Discovery of Incommensurables in Greek Mathematics* (New York: Arno Press, 1976); G. E. L. Owen, "Zeno and the Mathematicians", *Proceedings of the Aristotelian Society* 58 (1957–58); J. M. E. McTaggart, "The Unreality of Time", *Mind* 17 (1908) and *The Nature of Existence* (Grosse Point, MI: Scholarly Press, 1968), vol. 2, ch. 33. See C. D. Broad, *An Examination of McTaggart's Philosophy* (Cambridge: Cambridge University Press, 1933–38), vol. 2, pts 1–2; G. Schlesinger, "Reconstructing McTaggart's Argument", *Philosophy* 58 (1983); W. L. Craig, "McTaggart's Paradox and Temporal Solipsism", *Australasian Journal of Philosophy* 79 (2001); N. L. Oaklander, "Craig on McTaggart's Paradox and the Problem of Temporary Intrinsics", *Analysis* 59 (1999); Q. Smith, "The Logical Structure of the Debate About McTaggart's Paradox", *Philosophy Research Archives* 14 (1989); and B. V. Nunn, "Differences Between A- and B-Time", *Philosophical Inquiry* 22 (2000).

3. C. S. Peirce, Letter to Welby, 12 October 1904, in *Semiotics and Significs: The Correspondence Between Charles S. Peirce and Victoria, Lady Welby*, C. Hardwick (ed.) (Bloomington, IN: Indiana University Press, 1977), on the "dynamic object"; N. Rescher, *Objectivity: The Obligations of Impersonal Reason* (Notre Dame: Notre Dame University Press, 1997), especially pp. 97–115; Husserl, *Cartesian Meditations*, Third Meditation, §§27–29, pp. 60–64. See J. W. von Goethe, *The Sorrows of Young Werther*, W. Rose (trans.) (London: The Scholastic Press, 1929) Letter of 18 August, and J. J. Rousseau, *The Reveries of the Solitary Walker*, C. Butterworth (trans.) (New York: Harper & Row, 1982) Fifth Walk and Seventh Walk (on the epistemic romance of botany).

4. D. Hume, *A Treatise of Human Nature* [1739–40], L. A. Selby-Bigge (ed.) and P. H. Nidditch (ed., 2nd edn) (Oxford: Clarendon Press, 1978), pp. 73–86. Hume's "cement of the universe" phrase appears in the appended "An Abstract of a Book

Lately Published, Entitled [sic], *A Treatise of Human Nature, &c.*", p. 662. J. L. Mackie, *The Cement of the Universe: A Study of Causation* (Oxford: Clarendon Press, 1982).

5. W. Heisenberg, *The Physical Principles of the Quantum Theory*, C. Eckart and F. C. Hugh (trans.) (New York: Dover Publications, 1930) and *Physics and Philosophy: The Resolution in Modern Science* (London: Allen and Unwin, 1959); D. Z. Albert, *Quantum Mechanics and Experience* (Cambridge, MA: Harvard University Press, 1992); R. I. G. Hughes, *The Structure and Interpretation of Quantum Mechanics* (Cambridge, MA: Harvard University Press, 1989); and K. R. Popper, *Quantum Theory and the Schism in Physics* (Totowa: Rowman and Littlefield, 1982).

6. See D. Bohm and J. Bub, "A Proposed Solution of the Measurement Problem in Quantum Mechanics by a Hidden Variable Theory", *Reviews of Modern Physics* 38 (1966); S. Kochen and E. P. Specker, "The Problem of Hidden Variables in Quantum Mechanics", *Journal of Mathematics and Mechanics* 17 (1967). A survey of controversies surrounding the interpretation of quantum anomalies is found in J. T. Cushing and E. McMullin (eds), *Philosophical Consequences of Quantum Theory: Reflections on Bell's Theorem* (Notre Dame: University of Notre Dame Press, 1989). See also B. S. DeWitt and N. Graham, *The Many-Worlds Interpretation of Quantum Mechanics: A Fundamental Exposition* (Princeton, NJ: Princeton University Press, 1973); M. Kafatos (ed.), *Bell's Theorem, Quantum Theory, and Conceptions of the Universe* (Dordrecht: Kluwer, 1989); and B. C. Van Fraassen, *Quantum Mechanics: An Empiricist View* (Oxford: Clarendon Press, 1991) and "The Charybdis of Realism: Epistemological Implications of Bell's Inequality", *Synthese* 52 (1982).

Chapter 9: Abstract entities, particular and universal: numbers, sets, properties, qualities, relations, propositions, and possibilities, logical, mathematical and metaphysical laws

1. The medieval dispute over the ontology of properties and relations is discussed by M. H. Carré, *Realists and Nominalists* (London: Oxford University Press, 1946) and M. G. Henninger, *Relations: Medieval Theories 1250–1325* (Oxford: Clarendon Press, 1989). More recent treatments of the problem are found in D. M. Armstrong, *A Theory of Universals: Universals and Scientific Realism*, vol. 2 (Cambridge: Cambridge University Press, 1978); M. J. Loux (ed.), *Universals and Particulars: Readings in Ontology* (New York: Doubleday, 1970); N. Wolterstorff, *On Universals: An Essay in Ontology* (Chicago, IL: University of Chicago Press, 1970). A recent classic treatment of the issues is offered by B. Russell, "The World of Universals", Chapter 8 in *The Problems of Philosophy* (Indianapolis, IN: Hackett, 1990), and "On the Relations of Universals and Particulars", Chapter 9 in *The Problems of Philosophy*.

2. Plato, *Parmenides* 132a1–133b2 and Aristotle, *Metaphysics* 990b1–991b9, 1038b31–1039a14. Among the items of secondary literature on this subject see T. Scaltsas, "The Logic of the Dilemma of Participation and of the Third Man Argument", *Apeiron* 22 (1989) and "A Necessary Falsehood in the Third Man Argument", *Phronesis* 37 (1992); R. Diaz, "What is the Third Man Argument?", *Southern Journal of Philosophy* 16 (1978); M. Durrant, "Plato, the Third Man and the Nature of the Forms", *Southern Journal of Philosophy* 17 (1979); C. Strang, "Plato and the Third Man, I", *Proceedings of the Aristotelian Society, Supplement* 37 (1963); D. A. Rees, "Plato and the Third Man, II", *Proceedings of the Aristotelian Society, Supplement* 37 (1963); R. J. Butler, "The Measure and Weight of the Third Man", *Mind* 72 (1963); R. Barford, "The Context of the Third Man Argument in Plato's *Parmenides*", *Journal of the History of Philosophy* 16 (1978);

S. Peterson, "A Reasonable Self-Predication Premise for the Third Man Argument", *Philosophical Review* 82 (1973); H. Teloh and D. J. Louzecky, "Plato's Third Man Argument", *Phronesis* 17 (1972); S. M. Cohen, "The Logic of the Third Man", *Philosophical Review* 80 (1971); R. Shiner, "Self-Predication and the Third Man Argument", *Journal of the History of Philosophy* 8 (1970); K. W. Rankin, "Is the Third Man Argument an Inconsistent Triad?", *Philosophical Quarterly* 20 (1970) and "The Duplicity of Plato's Third Man", *Mind* 78 (1969); G. Vlastos, "Plato's Third Man Argument (*Parm*. 132a1–b2): Text and Logic", *Philosophical Quarterly* 19 (1969); "Addenda to the Third Man Argument: A Reply to Professor Sellars", *Philosophical Review* 64 (1955); and "The Third Man Arguments in the *Parmenides*", *Philosophical Review* 63 (1954); W. Sellars, "Vlastos and the Third Man", *Philosophical Review* 64 (1955); J. M. E. Moravcsik, "The Third Man Argument and Plato's Theory of Forms", *Phronesis* 8 (1963); N. B. Booth, "Assumptions Involved in the Third Man Argument", *Phronesis* 3 (1958); R. S. Bluck, "Forms as Standards", *Phronesis* 2 (1957); R. E. Allen, "Participation and Predication in Plato's Middle Dialogues", *Philosophical Review* 69 (1960); R. Sharvy, "Plato's Causal Logic and the Third Man Argument", *Noûs* 20 (1986); W. J. Prior, "*Timaeus* 48e–52d and the Third Man Argument", *Canadian Journal of Philosophy* 9 (1983); D. P. Hunt, "How (Not) to Exempt Platonic Forms from *Parmenides*' Third Man", *Phronesis* 42 (1997); B. Frances, "Plato's Response to the Third Man Argument in the Paradoxical Exercise of the *Parmenides*", *Ancient Philosophy* 16 (1996); P. Schweizer, "Self-Predication and the Third Man", *Erkenntnis* 40 (1994); D. Davidson, "The Third Man", *Critical Inquiry* 19 (1993); J. F. Malcolm, *Plato on the Self-Predication of Forms: Early and Middle Dialogues* (Oxford: Clarendon Press, 1991); F. R. Pickering, "Plato's Third Man Arguments", *Mind* 90 (1981); J. Kung, "Aristotle on Thises, Suches and the Third Man Argument", *Phronesis* 26 (1981); and R. A. Brinkley, "Plato's Third Man and the Limits of Cognition", *Australasian Journal of Philosophy* 60 (1982).

3. G. Berkeley, *A Treatise on the Principles of Human Knowledge*, in *The Works of George Berkeley*, vol. 2, p. 33. See also Berkeley, *Three Dialogues Between Hylas and Philonous*, pp. 192–4.

4. Hume, *A Treatise of Human Nature*, p. 17.

5. Hume, *An Enquiry Concerning Human Understanding*, in *Enquiries Concerning Human Understanding and Concerning the Principles of Morals*, L. A. Selby-Bigge (ed.), 3rd edn, P. H. Nidditch (ed.) (Oxford: Clarendon Press, 1975), pp. 154–5.

6. G. Ryle, *The Concept of Mind* (New York: Barnes & Noble, 1949), pp. 16–17, 33, 77–9, 94, 152, 168, 206.

7. A realist position on the ontology of mathematical entities is defended by J. R. Brown, *Philosophy of Mathematics: An Introduction to the World of Proofs and Pictures* (London: Routledge, 1999). An opposing nominalistic account is represented by H. Field, *Science Without Numbers: A Defense of Nominalism* (Princeton, NJ: Princeton University Press, 1980); *Realism, Mathematics and Modality* (Oxford: Basil Blackwell, 1989); "Realism and Anti-Realism About Mathematics", *Philosophical Topics* 13 (1982); and "The Conceptual Contingency of Mathematical Objects", *Mind* 102 (1993). See M. Resnick, "Ontology and Logic: Remarks on Hartry Field's Anti-Platonist Philosophy of Mathematics", *History and Philosophy of Logic* 6 (1985); B. Hale & C. Wright, "A Reductio Ad Surdum? Field on the Contingency of Mathematical Objects", *Mind* 103 (1994); and B. Hale, "Is Platonism Epistemologically Bankrupt?", *Philosophical Review* 103 (1994). An attempt to overcome traditional epistemological difficulties by interpreting mathematical entities as perceptible is found in P. Maddy, *Realism in Mathematics* (Oxford: Clarendon Press, 1992) and *Naturalism in Mathematics* (Oxford: Clarendon Press, 1997). See also D. Bonevac, *Reduction in the Abstract*

Sciences (Indianapolis, IN: Hackett, 1982); Quine, "Ontological Reduction and the World of Numbers"; and S. Iwan, "An Analysis of Quine's 'Ontological Reduction and the World of Numbers'", *Erkenntnis* 53 (2000).

8. The logic of abstraction transposes a true or false predication into a truth-value-less property-designating predicate or property term. The standard device for this purpose is *lambda notation*, whereby a predication *Fa* or $\forall x[\ldots x \ldots]$ of any well-formed internal propositional or predicational complexity is converted by *lambda-abstraction* to a truth-value-less predicate term for the respective property indicated within the context of the abstract, in these cases: λxFx or $\lambda x[\ldots x \ldots]$. Whitehead and Russell make use of a similar reductive device in *Principia Mathematica*, Part I, Section D, "The Logic of Relations", in the theory *30 of descriptive functions. A theory of abstraction is offered by A. Church, *The Calculi of Lambda-Conversion* (Princeton, NJ: Princeton University Press, 1941).

9. Valuable sources on the ontology of properties include G. Bealer, *Quality and Concept* (Oxford: Oxford University Press, 1982) and C. McGinn, *Logical Properties: Identity, Existence, Predication, Necessity, Truth* (Oxford: Clarendon Press, 2000). There is an extensive literature on the realism versus nominalism dispute and the ontic status of universals in medieval through contemporary metaphysics. Further references are indicated in notes 1 and 7.

10. Quine, *Word and Object*; pp. 32–51. J. Vuillement, "Quine's Concept of Stimulus Meaning", *Philosophic Exchange* 2 (1975); F. Tersman, "Stimulus Meaning Debunked", *Erkenntnis* 49 (1998); E. Gotlind, "Stimulus Meaning", *Theoria* 29 (1963); P. Ziff, "A Response to 'Stimulus Meaning'", *Philosophical Review* 79 (1970); E. S. Shirley, "Stimulus Meaning and Indeterminacy of Translation", *Southern Journal of Philosophy* 9 (1971).

11. See G. Frege, "Thoughts", in *Logical Investigations*, P. T. Geach and R. H. Stoothoff (trans.) (Oxford: Basil Blackwell, 1977); B. Bolzano, *Theory of Science: Attempt at a Detailed and in the Main Novel Exposition of Logic with Constant Attention to Earlier Authors*, R. George (ed. and trans.) (Berkeley, CA: University of California Press, 1972), especially pp. 20–31, 171–80; C. S. Peirce, *Collected Papers of Charles Sanders Peirce* (8 volumes), C. Hartshorne *et al.* (eds) (Cambridge, MA: Harvard University Press, 1931–35): "The Meaning of a proposition is itself a proposition. Indeed, it is no other than the very proposition which is its meaning: it is a translation of it" (5.411-436). G. Bealer considers objections to the traditional ontology of propositions and proposes new models for the category in his essay, "Propositions", *Mind* 107 (1998). A similar proposal for selectively eliminating propositions as abstract entities in favour of thinkers expressing cognitive attitudes toward states of affairs by using derivatively intentional sentences is defended by Jubien in his essay, "Propositions and the Objects of Thought", *Philosophical Studies* 104 (2001). See also J. King, "Structured Propositions and Complex Predicates", *Noûs* 29 (1995). If we agree with Jubien that propositions do not exist, but we accept the existence of abstract sets in a realist mathematical ontology, then the combined effect of these ontological commitments has surprising implications for the metaphysics of modal logic, the ontology of logically possible worlds, and the controversy over modal realism versus actualism. The trouble is that, if we hold with Jubien that propositions do not exist, then we face an obvious but previously unremarked trilemma. The propositions in a maximally consistent proposition set $\{p_1, p_2, p_3, \ldots\}$ are supposed collectively to represent every state of affairs associated with a corresponding logically possible world, w_i. The same logically possible world w_i can equivalently be identified or characterized by means of the conjunction of all the propositions in the set, $p_1 \wedge p_2 \wedge p_3 \wedge \ldots$. Identifying or describing worlds alternatively as proposition sets or as conjunctions of propositions in the set seems like a superficial logically trivial

difference. A conjunction of propositions, even if infinite in extent, is itself a proposition. If sets exist but propositions do not exist, then whether or not modal realism is true depends on which of two apparently equivalent methods of identifying, representing, or characterizing logically possible worlds we choose to adopt. If logically possible worlds are maximally consistent proposition sets, and if sets exist even if propositions do not exist, then, as with the default mathematical realist commitment to the existence of even the null set, modal realism is true. If, to all intents and purposes, we equivalently define logically possible worlds as conjunctions of the propositions in the maximally consistent proposition sets identified with or representing logically possible worlds, and if propositions do not exist, as Jubien maintains, then modal realism is false. The nonexistence of abstract propositions in spite of the existence of abstract sets requires a new approach to possible worlds semantics and the distinction between the actual world and non-actual merely logically possible worlds. It requires, in the end, a satisfactory effort to explain what is meant by the concept of an actual world, and not merely the indexical designation of this experienced world as the particular logically possible world in which a thinker, semantic theorist or modal logician, happens to exist.

12. Classic sources include J. G. Kemeny and P. Oppenheim, "On Reduction", reprinted in *Readings in the Philosophy of Science*, B. A. Brody (ed.) (Englewood Cliffs, NJ: Prentice Hall, 1970) and E. Nagel, "Mechanistic Explanation and Organismic Biology", reprinted in *Readings in the Philosophy of Science* (1970). A manifesto for reductionism in the positivist unity of science programme is found in the *International Encyclopedia of Unified Science: Foundations of the Unity of Science*. See also M. Bunge, *The Methodological Unity of Science* (Dordrecht: Reidel, 1973); R. Grossmann, *Ontological Reduction* (Bloomington, IN: Indiana University Press, 1973); L. N. Meyer, "Science, Reduction and Natural Kinds", *Philosophy* 64 (1989); C. U. Moulines, "Ontology, Reduction, and the Unity of Science", in *Proceedings of the Twentieth World Congress of Philosophy*, 10, Philosophy of Science, Tian Yu Cao (ed.) (Bowling Green, OH: Philosophy Documentation Center, 2001); D. J. Mossley, "The (Dis)Unity of Science: Some Tensions Between the Physical, Biological and Social Sciences – A Diagnosis", *Philosophical Writings* 3 (1996); J. Dupré, "The Disunity of Science", *Mind* 92 (1983) and *The Disorder of Things: Metaphysical Foundations of the Disunity of Science* (Cambridge, MA: Harvard University Press, 1993); J. R. Lucas, "The Unity of Science Without Reductionism", *Acta Analytica* 15 (1996); D. Davies, "Explanatory Disunities and the Unity of Science", *International Studies in the Philosophy of Science* 10 (1996); J. Margolis, "Nature, Culture and Persons", *Theory and Decision* 13 (1981); R. M. Burian, "Conceptual Change, Cross-Theoretical Explanation, and the Unity of Science", *Synthese* 32 (1975); J. Jorgensen, "Empiricism and the Unity of Science", *Danish Yearbook of Philosophy* 6 (1969); H. A. Morgenau, "Foundations of the Unity of Science", *Philosophical Review* 50 (1941); L. S. Feuer, "Mechanism, Physicalism, and the Unity of Science", *Philosophy and Phenomenological Research* 9 (1949); C. Morris, "The Significance of the Unity of Science Movement", *Philosophy and Phenomenological Research* 6 (1946); D. Gottlieb, "Ontological Reduction", *Journal of Philosophy* 73 (1976); L. H. Tharp, "Ontological Reduction", *Journal of Philosophy* 68 (1971); R. E. Grandy, "On What There Need Not Be", *Journal of Philosophy* 66 (1969); F. W. Kroon, "Against Ontological Reduction", *Erkenntnis* 36 (1992); and M. Jubien, "Two Kinds of Reduction", *Journal of Philosophy* 66 (1969).

Chapter 10: Subjectivity of mind in the world of objective physical facts

1. J. Bickle, *Psychoneural Reduction: The New Wave* (Cambridge, MA: MIT Press/Bradford Books, 1998); E. G. Boring, *The Physical Dimensions of Consciousness* (New York: Appleton, 1933); D. C. Dennett, *Content and Consciousness*, 2nd edn (London: Routledge & Kegan Paul, 1969) and *Consciousness Explained* (Boston: Little, Brown, 1991); S. P. Stich, *From Folk Psychology to Cognitive Science: The Case Against Belief* (Cambridge, MA: MIT Press/Bradford Books, 1983); H. Feigl, *The "Mental" and the "Physical": The Essay and a Postscript* (Minneapolis, MN: University of Minnesota Press, 1967); J. Cornman, "Mental Terms, Theoretical Terms, and Materialism", *Philosophy of Science* 35 (1968); P. Feyerabend, "Explanation, Reduction and Empiricism", in *Scientific Explanation, Space and Time*, H. Feigl and G. Maxwell (eds) (Minneapolis, MN: University of Minnesota Press, 1962); R. Rorty, "In Defense of Eliminative Materialism", *Review of Metaphysics* 19 (1970); W. G. Lycan and G. Pappas, "What is Eliminative Materialism?", *Australasian Journal of Philosophy* 50 (1972); J. M. Jackson, "Why Mental Explanations are Physical Explanations", *South African Journal of Philosophy* 14 (1995)'; and A. Melnyk, "Testament of a Recovering Eliminativist", *Proceedings of the Biennial Meetings of the Philosophy of Science Association* 3 (supplement) (1996).

2. See T. Nagel, "What is it Like to be a Bat?", *Philosophical Review* 83 (1974); F. Jackson, "Epiphenomenal Qualia", *Philosophical Quarterly* 32 (1982); P. M. Churchland, "Reduction, Qualia, and the Direct Inspection of Brain States", *Journal of Philosophy* 82 (1985) and "Knowing Qualia: A Reply to Jackson", in *A Neurocomputational Perspective: The Nature of Mind and the Structure of Science*, P. M. Churchland (ed.) (Cambridge, MA: MIT Press/Bradford Books, 1990a); B. Loar, "Phenomenal Properties", in *Mind and Cognition: A Reader*, W. G. Lycan (ed.) (Oxford: Basil Blackwell, 1990); G. Harman, "The Intrinsic Quality of Experience", in *Philosophical Perspectives, 4: Action Theory and Philosophy of Mind*, J. E. Tomberlin (ed.) (Atascadero, CA: Ridgeview Publishing, 1990). For a sustained discussion of the problems of qualia, including a more detailed bibliography, see D. J. Chalmers, *The Conscious Mind: In Search of a Fundamental Theory* (Oxford: Oxford University Press, 1996).

3. J. R. Searle, *The Rediscovery of the Mind* (Cambridge, MA: MIT Press/Bradford Books, 1992): "On my view, if your theory results in the view that consciousness does not exist, you have simply produced a reductio ad absurdum of the theory, and similarly with many other views in contemporary philosophy of mind" (p. 8). A similar incoherence undermines efforts to discount any higher-order meta-appearances as something that is not really mental or psychological, but only appears to be so. Indeed, to begin with anything plausibly described as an appearance of a mental or psychological state to be explained away as something other than mental or psychological state is logically incoherent.

4. C. V. Borst (ed.), *The Mind–Brain Identity Theory* (New York: St Martin's Press, 1970); S. Christiansen and D. Turner, *Folk Psychology and the Philosophy of Mind* (London: Lawrence Erlbaum, 1993); P. M. Churchland, *A Neurocomputational Perspective: The Nature of Mind and the Structure of Science* (Cambridge, MA: MIT Press/Bradford Books, 1989); U. T. Place, "Is Consciousness a Brain Process?", *British Journal of Psychology* 47 (1956); J. J. C. Smart, "Sensations and Brain Processes", *Philosophical Review* 68 (1959); P. Feyerabend, "Mental Events and the Brain", *Journal of Philosophy* 60 (1963a) and "Materialism and the Mind/Body Problem", *Review of Metaphysics* 17 (1963b); and R. Rorty, "Mind–Body Identity, Privacy and Categories", *Review of Metaphysics* 19 (1970).

5.   The pioneering scientific literature on behaviour includes works by Pavlov, Watson, James, Skinner and their followers. The main philosophical developments of logical behaviourism include Ryle, *The Concept of Mind*, and D. M. Armstrong, *A Materialist Theory of the Mind* (London: Routledge, 1993).

6.   N. Block, "Troubles With Functionalism", in *Perception & Cognition: Issues in the Foundations of Psychology*, C. W. Savage (ed.) (Minneapolis, MN: University of Minnesota Press, 1978); T. Horgan and J. Woodward, "Folk Psychology is Here to Stay", *Philosophical Review* 94 (1985); J. Kim, "Supervenience and Nomological Incommensurables'", *American Philosophical Quarterly* 15 (1978); J. Searle, "Minds, Brains and Programs", *The Behavioral and Brain Sciences* 3 (1980); and S. Horst, "Symbols and Computation: A Critique of the Computational Theory of Mind", *Minds and Machines* 9 (1999).

7.   A concise criticism of Descartes's substance dualism from the standpoint of the causal interaction problem in contemporary metaphysics is offered by P. M. Churchland, *Matter and Consciousness: A Contemporary Introduction to the Philosophy of Mind* (Cambridge, MA: MIT Press/Bradford Books, 1990b), pp. 18–21. See D. Radner, "Is There a Problem of Cartesian Interaction?", *Journal of the History of Philosophy* 23 (1985) and C. Wilson, "Sensation and Explanation: The Problem of Consciousness in Descartes", *Nature and System* 4 (1982).

8.   Chalmers, *The Conscious Mind*; Jacquette, *Philosophy of Mind* (Englewood Cliffs, NJ: Prentice Hall, 1994). Searle vehemently denies being a property dualist, but his books *Intentionality: An Essay in the Philosophy of Mind* (Cambridge: Cambridge University Press, 1983) and *The Rediscovery of the Mind* (Cambridge, MA: MIT Press/Bradford Books, 1992) defend a non-reductive philosophy of mind that is strongly reminiscent of property dualism. See Jacquette, "Searle's Antireductionism", *Facta Philosophica* 4 (2002b).

9.   H. Putnam, "The Meaning of 'Meaning'", in *Mind, Language and Reality* (Cambridge: Cambridge University Press, 1975). See also, *inter alia*, T. Burge, "Individualism and the Mental", in *Studies in Metaphysics*, P. A. French *et al.* (eds) (Minneapolis, MN: University of Minnesota Press, 1979); "Other Bodies", in *Thought and Object*, A. Woodfield (ed.) (New York: Oxford University Press, 1982a); and "Two Thought Experiments Reviewed", *Notre Dame Journal of Formal Logic* 23 (1982b); and J. A. Fodor, "Cognitive Science and the Twin-Earth Problem", *Notre Dame Journal of Formal Logic* 23 (1982).

10. An explicit analysis of supervenience applied to part–whole as well as body–mind relations is found in J. Pollock, *How to Build a Person: A Prolegomenon* (Cambridge, MA: MIT Press/Bradford Books, 1989), pp. 32–3.

11. Essential papers are collected in Kim, *Supervenience and Mind: Selected Philosophical Essays* (Cambridge: Cambridge University Press, 1993); T. R. Grimes, "The Myth of Supervenience", *Pacific Philosophical Quarterly* 69 (1988); T. Horgan, "From Supervenience to Superdupervenience: Meeting the Demands of a Material World", *Mind* 102 (1993); and S. Mumford, "Dispositions, Supervenience and Reduction", *Philosophical Quarterly* 44 (1994). Properties, entities and events, in philosophical psychology as well as ethics and aesthetics, are sometimes judged to be or regarded as supervenient even in the absence of any clear idea of the relevant supervenience base on which they supervene. It is generally assumed in such cases that the limitation is epistemic and that in principle it is possible to determine the foundations of the relevant supervenience relations.

12. J. Margolis, *Persons and Mind: The Prospects of Nonreductive Materialism* (Dordrecht: Reidel, 1978) and *Philosophy of Psychology* (Englewood Cliffs, NJ: Prentice Hall, 1982); D. Davidson, "The Emergence of Thought", *Erkenntnis* 51 (1999); J. L. Diaz, "Mind–Body Unity, Dual Aspect, and the Emergence of Consciousness", *Philosophical Psychology* 13 (2000); D. V. Newman, "Chaos, Emer-

gence, and the Mind–Body Problem", *Australasian Journal of Philosophy* **79** (2001); and M. Weber, "Fitness Made Physical: The Supervenience of Biological Concepts Revisited", *Philosophy of Science* **63** (1996). See the papers collected in A. Beckermann, H. Flohr, and J. Kim (eds), *Emergence or Reduction? Prospects for Nonreductive Materialism* (Berlin: Walter de Gruyter, 1992); C. Emmeche, S. Koppe and F. Stjernfelt, "Explaining Emergence: Towards an Ontology of Levels", *Journal for General Philosophy of Science* **28** (1997); P. Humphreys, "Emergence, Not Supervenience", *Philosophy of Science* **64** (1997a) and "How Properties Emerge", *Philosophy of Science* **64** (1997b); D. H. Jones, "Emergent Properties, Persons, and the Mind–Body Problem", *Southern Journal of Philosophy* **10** (1972); R. L. Klee, "Micro-Determinism, and Concepts of Emergence", *Philosophy of Science* **51** (1984); T. O'Connor, "Emergent Properties", *American Philosophical Quarterly* **31** (1994). M. Silberstein, "Emergence and the Mind–Body Problem", *Journal of Consciousness Studies* **5** (1998); M. Silberstein and J. McGeever, "The Search for Ontological Emergence", *Philosophical Quarterly* **49** (1999); J. J. C. Smart, "Physicalism and Emergence", *Neuroscience* **6** (1981); R. W. Sperry, "In Defense of Mentalism and Emergent Interaction", *Journal of Mind and Behavior* **12** (1991); L. R. Vandevert, "A Measurable and Testable Brain-Based Emergent Interactionism: An Alternative to Sperry's Mentalist Emergent Interactionism", *Journal of Mind and Behavior* **12** (1991); J. G. Taylor, "The Emergence of Mind", *Communion and Cognition* **30** (1997); and P. Teller, "A Contemporary Look at Emergence", in *Emergence or Reduction*, Beckermann *et al.* (eds).

Chapter 11: God, a divine supernatural mind?

1. W. I. Matson, *The Existence of God* (Ithaca, NY: Cornell University Press, 1965); J. Hick, *Arguments for the Existence of God* (New York: Herder and Herder, 1971); R. Swinburne, *The Existence of God* (Oxford: Clarendon Press, 1991); T. C. O'Brien, *Metaphysics and the Existence of God* (Washington: Thomist Press, 1960); J. L. Mackie, *The Miracle of Theism: Arguments for and Against the Existence of God* (Oxford: Clarendon Press, 1982); P. Vjecsner, *On Proof for the Existence of God, and Other Reflective Inquiries* (New York: Penden, 1988); R. M. Gale, *On the Nature and Existence of God* (Cambridge: Cambridge University Press, 1991); D. Braine, *The Reality of Time and the Existence of God: The Project of Proving God's Existence* (Oxford: Clarendon Press, 1988).

2. Kant, *Critique of Pure Reason*, A599/B627–A600/B628; Anselm (of Canterbury), *Opera omnia, ad fidem codicum recensuit Franciscus Salesius Schmitt* (6 volumes) (Edinburgh: Nelson & Sons, 1945–51) and *Anselm of Canterbury* (4 volumes), J. Hopkins and H. Richardson (trans.) (Toronto and New York: Edwin Mellen Press, 1974). See J. Hick and A. C. McGill (eds), *The Many-Faced Argument: Recent Studies on the Ontological Argument for the Existence of God* (New York: Macmillan, 1967); R. Brecher, *Anselm's Argument: The Logic of Divine Existence* (Aldershot: Gower, 1985) and "Hartshorne's Modal Argument for the Existence of God", *Ratio* **17** (1976); C. Hartshorne, *The Logic of Perfection and Other Essays in Neoclassical Metaphysics* (LaSalle, IL: Open Court, 1962), *Anselm's Discovery: A Re-Examination of the Ontological Proof for God's Existence* (LaSalle, IL: Open Court, 1965), and "Necessity", *Review of Metaphysics* **21** (1967); E. Bencivenga, *Logic and Other Nonsense: The Case of Anselm and his God* (Princeton, NJ: Princeton University Press, 1993); D. P. Henry, *The Logic of Saint Anselm* (Oxford: Clarendon Press, 1967); S. M. Engel, "Kant's 'Refutation' of the Ontological Argument", *Philosophy and Phenomenological Research* **24** (1963); N. Malcolm, "Anselm's Ontological Arguments", *Philosophical Review* **69** (1960); A. Plantinga, "A Valid Ontological Argument?", *Philosophical Review* **70** (1961) and "Kant's

Objection to the Ontological Argument", *Journal of Philosophy* **63** (1966); G. Schufreider, *An Introduction to Anselm's Argument* (Philadelphia, PA: Temple University Press, 1978); and J. Shaffer, "Existence, Predication and the Ontological Argument", *Mind* **71** (1962).

3. Kant, *Critique of Practical Reason*, pp. 127–30. See Ed. L. Miller, *God and Reason: An Invitation to Philosophical Theology*, 2nd edn (Englewood Cliffs, NJ: Prentice Hall, 1995), pp. 89–106.

4. C. G. Hunter, *Darwin's God: Evolution and the Problem of Evil* (Grand Rapids: Brazos Press, 2001); R. Swinburne, *Providence and the Problem of Evil* (Oxford: Clarendon Press, 1998); B. L. Whitney, *Theodicy: An Annotated Bibliography on the Problem of Evil, 1960–1990* (New York: Garland Press, 1993); N. Pike (ed.), *God and Evil: Readings on the Theological Problem of Evil* (Englewood Cliffs, NJ: Prentice Hall, 1964); W. L. Rowe (ed.), *God and the Problem of Evil* (Oxford: Basil Blackwell, 2001); M. B. Ahern, *The Problem of Evil* (New York: Schocken Books, 1971); M. McCord Adams and R. M. Adams (eds), *The Problem of Evil* (Oxford: Oxford University Press, 1990); M. Larrimore (ed.), *The Problem of Evil: A Reader* (Oxford: Basil Blackwell, 2001). In *Theodicy* (Indianapolis, IN: Bobbs-Merrill, 1966), Leibniz attempts to solve the problem of evil by arguing that, if God already contains all perfections, then God can only create an imperfect world that nevertheless remains the best of all logically possible worlds, if God's creation is to be something other than God. This is an ingenious proposal, but one that does not account for the high quantity, degree and extent of natural evil that prevails throughout the actual world. Would it not have been a better world still distinct from God if the natural evil were so slight that it would scarcely be noticed because it did not involve physical pain or suffering?

5. The early Church Father Tertullian is reported with this attitude to have declared: *Credo, quia absurdum est* ("I believe because it is absurd").

6. See H. W. Johnstone Jr., *The Problem of the Self* (University Park, PA: The Pennsylvania State University Press, 1970). Johnstone argues that considering, overcoming and working through inconsistent beliefs is a factor in the emergence of the self. He does not propose, however, as suggested here, extending his model more specifically to the kinds of inconsistencies encountered in religious teachings, let alone as an essential ingredient of religious teachings.

Chapter 12: Ontology of culture: language, art and artefacts

1. Searle, *Intentionality*, pp. 5, 22, 27–8, 167–8, 175–6 and "Minds, Brains, and Programs", pp. 422–4; also Searle's reply to critics in the "Author's Response" section under the title, "Intrinsic Intentionality", pp. 450–6 .

2. Heidegger, *Being and Time*, pp. 68–9.

3. The original statement of Popper's concept of World 3 appears in K. R. Popper, *Objective Knowledge: An Evolutionary Approach* (Oxford: Clarendon Press, 1972), especially, pp. 31, 74–5, and 106–28. B. Carr, "Popper's Third World", *Philosophical Quarterly* **27** (1977); W. M. Miller, "Popper's Third World: A Methodological Critique and Alternative", *Dialogue* **24** (1981).

4. A sustained non-reductivist metaphysics of culture is given by Margolis, *Culture and Cultural Entities: Toward a New Unity of Science* (Dordrecht and Boston: Reidel, 1984a); *Persons and Minds*; *Philosophy of Psychology* (Englewood Cliffs, NJ: Prentice Hall, 1984); *The Language of Art and Art Criticism: Analytic Questions in Aesthetics* (Detroit: Wayne State University Press, 1965); *What, After All, Is a Work of Art? Lectures in the Philosophy of Art* (University Park, PA: The Pennsylvania State University Press, 1999); "The Identity of a Work of Art", *Mind* **68** (1959); "Works of Art as Physically Embodied and Culturally Emergent Entities",

British Journal of Aesthetics 14 (1974); "The Ontological Peculiarity of Works of Art", *Journal of Aesthetics and Art Criticism* 36 (1977); "A Strategy for a Philosophy of Art" , *Journal of Aesthetics and Art Criticism* 37 (1979); "Artworks and the History of Production", *Communication and Cognition* 17 (1984c); "Constraints on the Metaphysics of Culture", *Review of Metaphysics* 39 (1986); M. Krausz and R. Shusterman (eds), *Interpretation, Relativism, and the Metaphysics of Culture: Themes in the Philosophy of Joseph Margolis* (Amherst: Humanity Books (Prometheus), 1999). See also Searle's account of interpersonal intentionality in *The Construction of Social Reality* (New York: The Free Press, 1995).

Bibliography

Abela, P. 1996. "Is Less Always More? An Argument Against the Natural Ontological Attitude", *Philosophical Quarterly* **46**.

Adams, M. McCord & R. M. Adams (eds) 1990. *The Problem of Evil*. Oxford: Oxford University Press.

Adams, R. M. 1991. *Leibniz: Idealist, Determinist, Theist*. New Haven, CT: Yale University Press.

Addis, L. & D. Lewis 1965. *Moore and Ryle: Two Ontologists*. The Hague: Martinus Nijhoff.

Ahern, M. B. 1971. *The Problem of Evil*. New York: Schocken Books.

Albert, D. Z. 1992. *Quantum Mechanics and Experience*. Cambridge, MA: Harvard University Press.

Allen, R. E. 1960. "Participation and Predication in Plato's Middle Dialogues", *Philosophical Review* **69**.

Alspector-Kelly, M. 2001. "On Quine on Carnap on Ontology", *Philosophical Studies* **102**.

Anselm (of Canterbury) 1945–51. *Opera omnia, ad fidem codicum recensuit Franciscus Salesius Schmitt* [6 volumes]. Edinburgh: Nelson & Sons.

Anselm (of Canterbury) 1974. *Anselm of Canterbury* [4 volumes], J. Hopkins & H. Richardson (trans.). Toronto and New York: Edwin Mellen Press.

Aquila, R. D. 1977. *Intentionality: A Study of Mental Acts*. University Park, PA: The Pennsylvania State University Press.

Aristotle 1952. *The Works of Aristotle* [12 volumes], W. D. Ross (ed.). Oxford: Clarendon Press.

Armstrong, D. M. 1978. *A Theory of Universals: Universals and Scientific Realism* [2 volumes]. Cambridge: Cambridge University Press.

Armstrong, D. M. 1983. *What is a Law of Nature?* Cambridge: Cambridge University Press.

Armstrong, D. M. 1989a. *Universals: An Opinionated Introduction*. Boulder: Westview Press.

Armstrong, D. M. 1989b. *A Combinatorial Theory of Possibility*. Cambridge: Cambridge University Press.

Armstrong, D. M. 1993. *A Materialist Theory of the Mind*, rev. edn. London: Routledge.

Armstrong, D. M. 1997. *A World of States of Affairs*. Cambridge: Cambridge University Press.

Bacon, J., K. Campbell, L. Reinhardt (eds) 1993. *Ontology, Causality and Mind: Essays in Honour of D. M. Armstrong*. Cambridge: Cambridge University Press.

Baert, E. 1997. *Aufstieg und Untergang der Ontologie: Descartes und die nachthomasische Philosophie*. Osnabrück: Universitätsverlag Rasch.

Baker, G. & P. M. S. Hacker 1984. *Frege: Logical Excavations*. Oxford: Basil Blackwell.

Barford, R. 1978. "The Context of the Third Man Argument in Plato's *Parmenides*", *Journal of the History of Philosophy* 16.

Bealer, G. 1982. *Quality and Concept*. Oxford: Oxford University Press.

Bealer, G. 1998. "Propositions", *Mind* 107.

Beckermann, A., H. Flohr, J. Kim (eds) 1992. *Emergence or Reduction? Prospects for Nonreductive Materialism*. Berlin: Walter de Gruyter.

Bencivenga, E. 1993. *Logic and Other Nonsense: The Case of Anselm and his God*. Princeton, NJ: Princeton University Press.

Benthem, J van 1985. *Modal Logic and Classical Logic*. Napoli: Bibliopolis.

Bergmann, G. 1979. "Sketch of an Ontological Inventory", *Journal of the British Society for Phenomenology* 10.

Bergmann, M. 1996. "A New Argument from Actualism to Serious Actualism", *Noûs* 30.

Berkeley, G. 1710. *A Treatise on the Principles of Human Knowledge*. See Berkeley (1948–57), volume 2.

Berkeley, G. 1713. *Three Dialogues Between Hylas and Philonous*. See Berkeley (1948–57), volume 2.

Berkeley, G. 1948–57. *The Works of George Berkeley Bishop of Cloyne* [9 volumes], A. A. Luce & T. E. Jessop (eds). London: Thomas Nelson & Sons.

Bickle, J. 1998. *Psychoneural Reduction: The New Wave*. Cambridge, MA: MIT Press/Bradford Books.

Biro, J. 1981. "Meaning, Translation and Interpretation", *Australasian Journal of Philosophy* 59.

Blackmore, J. T., R. Itagaki, S. Tanaka (eds) 2001. *Ernst Mach's Vienna, 1895–1930: Or Phenomenalism as Philosophy of Science*. Dordrecht and Boston: Kluwer.

Blass, A. 1990. "Infinitary Combinatorics and Modal Logic", *Journal of Symbolic Logic* 55.

Block, N. 1978. "Troubles With Functionalism". In *Perception & Cognition: Issues in the Foundations of Psychology* [Minnesota Studies in the Philosophy of Science, vol. 9], C. W. Savage (ed.), pp. 261–326. Minneapolis: University of Minnesota Press.

Bluck, R. S. 1957. "Forms as Standards", *Phronesis* 2.

Bohm, D. & J. Bub 1966. "A Proposed Solution of the Measurement Problem in Quantum Mechanics by a Hidden Variable Theory", *Reviews of Modern Physics* 38.

Bolzano, B. 1972. *Theory of Science: Attempt at a Detailed and in the Main Novel Exposition of Logic with Constant Attention to Earlier Authors*. R. George (ed. and trans.). Berkeley, CA: University of California Press.

Bonevac, D. 1982. *Reduction in the Abstract Sciences*. Indianapolis, IN: Hackett.

Boorse, C. 1975. "The Origins of the Indeterminacy Thesis", *Journal of Philosophy* 72.

Booth, N. B. 1958. "Assumptions Involved in the Third Man Argument", *Phronesis* 3.

Boring, E. G. 1933. *The Physical Dimensions of Consciousness*. New York: Appleton.

Borst, C. V. (ed.) 1970. *The Mind-Brain Identity Theory*. New York: St Martin's Press.

Boyle, R. 1666. *The Origin of Forms and Qualities*. In *The Works of the Honourable Robert Boyle* [6 volumes], volume 3. London: J. & F. Rivington (1772).

Bradley, F. H. 1930. *Appearance and Reality: A Metaphysical Essay* (9th impression, corrected). Oxford: Clarendon Press. Originally published 1897.

Bradley, R. 1992. *The Nature of All Being: A Study of Wittgenstein's Modal Atomism*. New York: Oxford University Press.

Braine, D. 1988. *The Reality of Time and the Existence of God: The Project of Proving God's Existence*. Oxford: Clarendon Press.

Brecher, R. 1976. "Hartshorne's Modal Argument for the Existence of God", *Ratio* 17.

Brecher, R. 1985. *Anselm's Argument: The Logic of Divine Existence*. Aldershot: Gower Publishing Company.

Brentano, F. 1874. *Psychologie vom empirischen Standpunkt*. Leipzig: Verlag von Duncker und Humblot.

Brentano, F. 1911. *Von der Klassifikation der psychischen Phänomene*. Leipzig: Verlag von Duncker und Humblot.

Brentano, F. 1924. *Psychologie vom empirischen Standpunkt* [2 volumes], 2nd edn, O. Kraus (ed.). Leipzig: Felix Meiner Verlag.

Brentano, F. 1966. *Die Abkehr vom Nichtrealen*. Edited from the Brentano *Nachlaß* with an introduction by F. Mayer-Hillebrand. Bern: Francke.

Brentano, F. 1973. *Psychology from an Empirical Standpoint*. O. Kraus (ed.), L. L. McAlister (ed. English edn), A. C. Rancurello, D. B. Terrell, L. L. McAlister (trans.). London: Routledge & Kegan Paul. Originally published 1924.

Brentano, F. 1974. *Kategorienlehre*. Edited with an introduction and commentary by A. Kastil. Hamburg: Felix Meiner Verlag.

Brentano, F. 1975. *On the Several Senses of Being in Aristotle*, R. George (ed. and trans.). Berkeley, CA: University of California Press.

Brentano, F. 1976. *Philosophische Untersuchungen zu Raum, Zeit und Kontinuum*. Edited from the Brentano *Nachlaß* by Stephan Körner and Roderick M. Chisholm, with commentary by Alfred Kastil. Hamburg: Felix Meiner Verlag.

Brentano, F. 1988. *Über Ernst Machs 'Erkenntnis und Irrtum': mit zwei Anhängen, Kleine Schriften über Ernst Mach, Der Brentano-Mach-Briefwechsel*. Edited from the Brentano *Nachlaß* with an introduction by R. M. Chisholm and J. C. Marek. Amsterdam: Rodopi.

Bricker, P. 1996. "Isolation and Unification: The Realist Analysis of Possible Worlds", *Philosophical Studies* 84.

Bringsjord, S. 1985. "Are There Set Theoretic Possible Worlds?", *Analysis* 45.

Brinkley, R. A. 1982. "Plato's Third Man and the Limits of Cognition", *Australasian Journal of Philosophy* 60.

Broad, C. D. 1933–38. *An Examination of McTaggart's Philosophy*. Cambridge: Cambridge University Press.

Brown, J. R. 1999. *Philosophy of Mathematics: An Introduction to the World of Proofs and Pictures*. London: Routledge.

Browning, D. 1973. "Quine and the Ontological Enterprise", *Review of Metaphysics* 26.

Browning, D. 1990. *Ontology and the Practical Arena*. University Park, PA: Pennsylvania State University Press.

Bubner, R., C. Cramer, R. Wiehl (eds) 1975. *Semantik und Ontologie*. Göttingen: Vandenhoeck und Ruprecht.

Bunge, M. 1973. *The Methodological Unity of Science*. Dordrecht: D. Reidel.

Bunge, M. 1974. "The Relations of Logic and Semantics to Ontology", *Journal of Philosophical Logic* 3.

Burge, T. 1979. "Individualism and the Mental". In *Studies in Metaphysics* [*Midwest Studies in Philosophy*, vol. 4], P. A. French, T. E. Uehling, Jr, H. K. Wettstein (eds). Minneapolis: University of Minnesota Press.

Burge, T. 1982a. "Other Bodies", *Thought and Object*, A. Woodfield (ed.). New York: Oxford University Press.

Burge, T. 1982b. "Two Thought Experiments Reviewed", *Notre Dame Journal of Formal Logic* 23.

Burian, R. M. 1975. "Conceptual Change, Cross-Theoretical Explanation, and the Unity of Science", *Synthese* 32.

Butler, R. J. 1963. "The Measure and Weight of the Third Man", *Mind* 72.

Campbell, K. 1990. *Abstract Particulars*. Oxford: Basil Blackwell.

Cantor, G. 1952. *Contributions to the Founding of the Theory of Transfinite Numbers*, P. E. B. Jourdain (trans.). New York: Dover.

Carl, W. 1974. *Existenz und Prädikation: Sprachanalytische Untersuchungen zu Existenz-Aussagen*. Munich: Verlag C. H. Beck.

Carl, W. 1994. *Frege's Theory of Sense and Reference: Its Origins and Scope*. Cambridge: Cambridge University Press.

Carr, B. 1977. "Popper's Third World", *Philosophical Quarterly* 27.

Carré, M. H. 1946. *Realists and Nominalists*. London: Oxford University Press.

Cartwright, R. 1954. "Ontology and the Theory of Meaning", *Philosophy of Science* 21.

Chalmers, D. J. 1996. *The Conscious Mind: In Search of a Fundamental Theory*. Oxford: Oxford University Press.

Chellas, B. F. 1980. *Modal Logic: An Introduction*. Cambridge: Cambridge University Press.

Chihara, C. S. 1973. *Ontology and the Vicious Circle Principle*. Ithaca, NY: Cornell University Press.

Chihara, C. S. 1998. *The Worlds of Possibility: Modal Realism and the Semantics of Modal Logic*. Oxford: Clarendon Press.

Chisholm, R. M. 1984. "The Primacy of the Intentional", *Synthese* 61.

Chomsky, N. & I. Scheffler 1958. "What is Said to Be", *Proceedings of the Aristotelian Society* 59.

Christiansen, S. & D. Turner (eds) 1993. *Folk Psychology and Philosophy of Mind*. London: Lawrence Erlbaum.

Church, A. 1935. "An Unsolvable Problem of Elementary Number Theory", *Bulletin of the American Mathematical Society* 41.

Church, A. 1941. *The Calculi of Lambda–Conversion*. Princeton, NJ: Princeton University Press.

Churchland, P. M. 1985. "Reduction, Qualia, and the Direct Inspection of Brain States", *Journal of Philosophy* 82.

Churchland, P. M. 1989. *A Neurocomputational Perspective: The Nature of Mind and the Structure of Science*. Cambridge, MA: MIT Press/Bradford Books.

Churchland, P. M. 1990a. "Knowing Qualia: A Reply to Jackson". In *A Neurocomputational Perspective: The Nature of Mind and the Structure of Science*, P. M. Churchland (ed.). Cambridge, MA: MIT Press/Bradford Books.

Churchland, P. M. 1990b. *Matter and Consciousness: A Contemporary Introduction to the Philosophy of Mind* (rev. edn). Cambridge, MA: MIT Press/Bradford Books.

Code, A. 1986. "Aristotle's Investigation of a Basic Logical Principle: Which Science Investigates the Principle of Non-Contradiction?", *Canadian Journal of Philosophy* 10 (supplement).

Coffey, P. 1938. *Ontology, or the Theory of Being: An Introduction to General Metaphysics*. New York: Peter Smith.

Cohen, S. M. 1971. "The Logic of the Third Man", *Philosophical Review* 80.

Condillac, É. B. de 1930. *Condillac's Treatise on the Sensations*, G. Carr (trans.), preface by H. Wildon Carr. London: The Favil Press.

Condillac, É. B. de 1971. *An Essay on the Origin of Human Knowledge, Being a Supplement to Mr. Locke's Essay on the Human Understanding*, T. Nugent (trans.), introduction by R. G. Weyant. Gainesville: Scholars Facsimiles and Reprints.

Cooper, D. E. 1990. *Existentialism: A Reconstruction*. Oxford: Basil Blackwell.

Cornman, J. 1968. "Mental Terms, Theoretical Terms, and Materialism", *Philosophy of Science* 35.

Craig, W. L. 2001. "McTaggart's Paradox and Temporal Solipsism", *Australasian Journal of Philosophy* 79.

Cresswell, M. J. 1988. *Semantical Essays: Possible Worlds and Their Rivals*. Dordrecht: Kluwer.

Curry, H. B. with R. Feys & R. Craig 1972. *Combinatory Logic*. Amsterdam: North-Holland Publishing Company.

Curry, H. B. 1977. *Foundations of Mathematical Logic*. New York: Dover.

Cushing, J. T. & E. McMullin (eds) 1989. *Philosophical Consequences of Quantum Theory: Reflections on Bell's Theorem*. Notre Dame: University of Notre Dame Press.

Cutrofello, A. 1992. "Quine and the Inscrutability of Languages", *International Studies in Philosophy* 24.

Darmstadter, H. 1974. "Indeterminacy of Translation and Indeterminacy of Belief", *Philosophical Studies* 26.

David, F. N. & D. E. Barton 1962. *Combinatorial Chance*. London: Charles Griffin.

Davidson, D. 1993. "The Third Man", *Critical Inquiry* 19.

Davidson, D. 1999. "The Emergence of Thought", *Erkenntnis* 51.

Davidson, D. & J. Hintikka 1969. *Words and Objections: Essays on the Work of W. V. Quine*. Dordrecht: D. Reidel.

Davies, D. 1996. "Explanatory Disunities and the Unity of Science", *International Studies in the Philosophy of Science* 10.

Dejnozka, J. 1996. *The Ontology of the Analytic Tradition and its Origins: Realism and Identity in Frege, Russell, Wittgenstein, and Quine*. Lanham, MD: Littlefield Adams Books.

Dennett, D. C. 1969.*Content and Consciousness*, 2nd ed. London: Routledge & Kegan Paul.

Dennett, D. C. 1991. *Consciousness Explained*. Boston: Little, Brown and Company.

Descartes, R. 1628. *Rules for the Direction of the Mind*. See Descartes (1975), volume 1.

Descartes, R. 1637. *Discourse on the Method of Rightly Conducting the Reason and Searching for Truth in the Sciences*. See Descartes (1975), volume 1.

Descartes, R. 1641. *Meditations on First Philosophy*. See Descartes (1975), volume 1.

Descartes, R. 1644. *Principles of Philosophy*. See Descartes (1975), volume 1.

Descartes, R. 1975. *The Philosophical Works of Descartes* [2 volumes], E. S. Haldane and G. R. T. Ross (trans.). Cambridge: Cambridge University Press.

Deutsch, E. 1979. *On Truth: An Ontological Theory*. Honolulu, HI: University Press of Hawaii.

DeWitt, B. S. & N. Graham 1973. *The Many-Worlds Interpretation of Quantum Mechanics: A Fundamental Exposition*. Princeton, NJ: Princeton University Press.

Diaz, J. L. 2000. "Mind–Body Unity, Dual Aspect, and the Emergence of Consciousness", *Philosophical Psychology* 13.

Diaz, R. 1978. "What is the Third Man Argument?", *Southern Journal of Philosophy* 16.

Dilman, I. 1984. *Quine on Ontology, Necessity and Experience: A Philosophical Critique*. London: Macmillan.

Divers, J. 1995. "Modal Fictionalism Cannot Deliver Possible Worlds Semantics", *Analysis* 55.

Dostal, R. J. 1993. "Time and Phenomenology in Husserl and Heidegger". In *The Cambridge Companion to Heidegger*, C. B. Guignon (ed.). Cambridge: Cambridge University Press.

Dreyfus, H. L. 1991. *Being-in-the-World: A Commentary on Heidegger's Being and Time, Division I*. Cambridge, MA: MIT Press.

Dummett, M. 1973. *Frege: Philosophy of Language*. New York: Harper & Row.

Dummett, M. 1981. *The Interpretation of Frege's Philosophy*. Cambridge, MA: Harvard University Press.

Dummett, M. 1991. *The Logical Basis of Metaphysics*. Cambridge, MA: Harvard University Press.

Dupré, J. 1983. "The Disunity of Science", *Mind* 92.

Dupré, J. 1993. *The Disorder of Things: Metaphysical Foundations of the Disunity of Science*. Cambridge, MA: Harvard University Press.

Durrant, M. 1979. "Plato, the Third Man and the Nature of the Forms", *Southern Journal of Philosophy* 17.

Emmeche, C., S. Koppe, F. Stjerfelt 1997. "Explaining Emergence: Towards an Ontology of Levels", *Journal for General Philosophy of Science* 28.

Engel, S. M. 1963. "Kant's 'Refutation' of the Ontological Argument", *Philosophy and Phenomenological Research* 24.

Feibleman, J. K. 1968. *Ontology*. New York: Greenwood Press.

Feigl, H. 1967. *The "Mental" and the "Physical": The Essay and a Postscript*. Minneapolis, MN: University of Minnesota Press.

Ferber, R. 1981. *Zenons Paradoxien der Bewegung und die Struktur von Raum und Zeit*. Munich: C. H. Beck.

Feuer, L. S. 1949. "Mechanism, Physicalism, and the Unity of Science", *Philosophy and Phenomenological Research* 9.

Feyerabend, P. 1962. "Explanation, Reduction, and Empiricism". In Scientific Explanation, Space and Time [Minnesota Studies in the Philosophy of Science, vol. 3], H. Feigl & G. Maxwell (eds), pp. 28–97. Minneapolis: University of Minnesota Press.

Feyerabend, P. 1963a. "Mental Events and the Brain", Journal of Philosophy 60.

Feyerabend, P. 1963b. "Materialism and the Mind/Body Problem", Review of Metaphysics 17.

Field, H. 1980. Science Without Numbers: A Defense of Nominalism. Princeton, NJ: Princeton University Press.

Field, H. 1982. "Realism and Anti-Realism About Mathematics", Philosophical Topics 13.

Field, H. 1989. Realism, Mathematics and Modality. Oxford: Basil Blackwell.

Field, H. 1993. "The Conceptual Contingency of Mathematical Objects", Mind 102.

Field, H. 1998. "Some Thoughts on Radical Indeterminacy", The Monist 81.

Findlay, J. N. 1995. Meinong's Theory of Objects and Values, edited with an introduction by D. Jacquette. Aldershot: Ashgate Publishing (Gregg Revivals) (from the 2nd edition, Oxford University Press, 1963).

Fisk, M. 1974. Nature and Necessity: An Essay in Physical Ontology. Bloomington, IN: Indiana University Press.

Fitch, F. B. 1974. Elements of Combinatory Logic. New Haven, CT: Yale University Press.

Fleming, N. 1988. "Why is There Something Rather than Nothing?", Analysis 48.

Fodor, J. A. 1982. "Cognitive Science and the Twin-Earth Problem", Notre Dame Journal of Formal Logic 23.

Forbes, G. 1985. The Metaphysics of Modality. Oxford: Clarendon Press.

Forbes, G. 1989. Languages of Possibility: An Essay in Philosophical Logic (Aristotelian Society Series, vol. 9). Oxford: Basil Blackwell.

Frances, B. 1996. "Plato's Response to the Third Man Argument in the Paradoxical Exercise of the Parmenides", Ancient Philosophy 16.

Fräntzki, E. 1996. Daseinsontologie: erstes Hauptstück. Dettelbach: J. H. Röll.

Frege, G. 1977. "Thoughts". In Logical Investigations, edited with a preface by P. T. Geach; P. T. Geach & R. H. Stoothoff (trans.). Oxford: Basil Blackwell.

Gaita, R. (ed.) 1990. Value and Understanding: Essays for Peter Winch. London: Routledge.

Gale, R. M. 1991. On the Nature and Existence of God. Cambridge: Cambridge University Press.

Galileo 1929–39. "The Assayer" [Il Saggiatore]. In Le Opere de Galileo Galilei [20 volumes], A. Favaro (ed.). Florence: S. A. G. Barbèra Editore.

Gelven, M. 1989. A Commentary on Heidegger's Being and Time. Dekalb, IL: Northern Illinois University Press.

Gethmann, C. F. 1993. Dasein: Erkennen und Handeln: Heidegger im phänomenologischen Kontext. Berlin: Walter de Gruyter.

Gilson, E. 1952. Being and Some Philosophers. Toronto: Pontifical Institute of Mediaeval Studies.

Glock, H. J. 1993. "The Indispensability of Translation in Quine and Davidson", Philosophical Quarterly, 43.

Gödel, K. 1967. "On Formally Undecidable Propositions of Principia Mathematica and Related Systems I". In From Frege to Gödel: A Source Book in Mathematical Logic, 1879–1931, Jean van Heijenoort (ed. and trans.). Cambridge, MA: Harvard University Press. Originally published in 1931 as "Über formal unentscheidbare Sätze der Principia mathematica und verwandter Systeme I", Monatshefte für Mathematik und Physik 38.

Goethe, J. W. von 1929. The Sorrows of Young Werther, W. Rose (trans.). London: The Scholastics Press.

Gosselin, M. 1990. Nominalism and Contemporary Nominalism: Ontological and Epistemological Implications of the Work of W. V. O. Quine and of N. Goodman. Dordrecht: Kluwer.

Gotlind, E. 1963. "Stimulus Meaning", *Theoria* **29**.

Gottlieb, D. 1976. "Ontological Reduction", *Journal of Philosophy* **73**.

Grandy, R. E. 1969. "On What There Need Not Be", *Journal of Philosophy* **66**.

Grim, P. 1986. "On Sets and Worlds: A Reply to Menzel", *Analysis* **46**.

Grimes, T. R. 1988. "The Myth of Supervenience", *Pacific Philosophical Quarterly* **69**.

Grossmann, R. 1973. *Ontological Reduction*. Bloomington, IN: Indiana University Press.

Grossmann, R. 1992. *The Existence of the World: An Introduction to Ontology*. London and New York: Routledge.

Grünbaum, A. 1967. *Modern Science and Zeno's Paradoxes*. Middletown, CT: Wesleyan University Press.

Guignon, C. B. (ed.) 1993. *The Cambridge Companion to Heidegger*. Cambridge: Cambridge University Press.

Hahn, M. 1995. "The Frege Puzzle One More Time". In *Frege: Sense and Reference One Hundred Years Later*, J. Biro & P. Kotatko (eds). Dordrecht: Kluwer.

Hale, B. 1994. "Is Platonism Epistemologically Bankrupt?", *Philosophical Review* **103**.

Hale, B. 1995. "Modal Fictionalism – A Simple Dilemma", *Analysis* **55**.

Hale, B. & C. Wright 1994. "A *Reductio ad Surdum*? Field on the Contingency of Mathematical Objects", *Mind* **103**.

Hanley, C. 2000. *Being and God in Aristotle and Heidegger: The Role of Method in Thinking the Infinite*. Lanham, MD: Rowman & Littlefield.

Harding, S. G. 1975. "Making Sense of Observation Sentences", *Ratio* **17**.

Harman, G. 1990. "The Intrinsic Quality of Experience". In *Philosophical Perspectives, 4: Action Theory and Philosophy of Mind*, J. E. Tomberlin (ed.). Atascadero, CA: Ridgeview Publishing.

Harman, G. 2002. *Tool-Being: Heidegger and the Metaphysics of Objects*. Chicago and LaSalle, IL: Open Court.

Harris, J. F. Jr. 1976. "Indeterminacy of Translation and Analyticity", *Southern Journal of Philosophy* **14**.

Hart, H. 1984. *Understanding our World: An Integral Ontology*. Lanham, MD: University Press of America.

Hartmann, N. 1948. *Zur Grundlegung der Ontologie*. Meisenheim am Glan: A. Hain.

Hartmann, N. 1953. *New Ways of Ontology*, R. C. Kuhn (trans.). Chicago, IL: H. Regnery.

Hartshorne, C. 1962. *The Logic of Perfection and Other Essays in Neoclassical Metaphysics*. LaSalle, IL: Open Court.

Hartshorne, C. 1965. *Anselm's Discovery: A Re-Examination of the Ontological Proof for God's Existence*. LaSalle, IL: Open Court.

Hartshorne, C. 1967. "Necessity", *Review of Metaphysics* **21**.

Hasse, H., H, Scholzm, H. G. Zeuthen 1976. *Zeno and the Discovery of Incommensurables in Greek Mathematics*. New York: Arno Press.

Hazen, A. 1976. "Expressive Incompleteness in Modal Logic", *Journal of Philosophical Logic* **5**.

Hazen, A. 1996. "Actualism Again", *Philosophical Studies* **84**.

Heidegger, M. 1951. *Was ist Metaphysik?* (6th edn). Frankfurt am Main: A. M. V. Klostermann.

Heidegger, M. 1953. *Einführung in die Metaphysik*. Tübingen: Max Niemeyer.

Heidegger, M. 1958. *The Question of Being*, translated with an introduction by W. Kluback & J. T. Wilde. New York: Twayne Publishers.

Heidegger, M. 1961. *An Introduction to Metaphysics*, R. Manheim (trans.). Garden City, NY: Doubleday.

Heidegger, M. 1972. *Frühe Schriften*. Frankfurt am Main: A. M. V. Klostermann.

Heidegger, M. 1975. *Die Frage nach dem Ding: zu Kants Lehre von den transzendentalen Grundsätzen*. Tübingen: Max Niemeyer.

Heidegger, M. 1976a. *Gesamtausgabe* [85 volumes]. Frankfurt am Main: A. M. V. Klostermann.

Heidegger, M. 1976b. *Existence and Being*, introduction and analysis by W. Brock. South Bend, IN: Gateway Editions.

Heidegger, M. 1979. *Sein und Zeit* (15th edn). Tübigen: Max Niemeyer. Originally published 1927.

Heidegger, M. 1984. *The Metaphysical Foundations of Logic*, M. Heim (trans.). Bloomington, IN: Indiana University Press.

Heidegger, M. 1996. *Being and Time: A Translation of Sein und Zeit*, J. Stambaugh (trans.). Albany, NY: State University of New York Press. Originally published in 1953 by Max Niemeyer Verlag, Tübingen.

Heidegger, M. 1999. *Ontology: The Hermeneutics of Facticity*, J. van Buren (trans.). Bloomington, IN: Indiana University Press.

Heine, S. 1985. *Existential and Ontological Dimensions of Time in Heidegger and Dogen*. Albany, NY: State University of New York Press.

Heisenberg, W. 1930. *The Physical Principles of the Quantum Theory*, C. Eckart & F. C. Hugh (trans.). New York: Dover.

Heisenberg, W. 1959. *Physics and Philosophy: The Resolution in Modern Science*. London: Allen and Unwin.

Heller, M. 1990. *The Ontology of Physical Objects: Four-Dimensional Hunks of Matter*. Cambridge: Cambridge University Press.

Hempel, C. G. 1973. "Science Unlimited", *Annals of the Japan Association for Philosophy of Science* 14.

Henninger, M. G. 1989. *Relations: Medieval Theories 1250–1325*. Oxford: Clarendon Press.

Henry, D. P. 1967. *The Logic of Saint Anselm*. Oxford: Clarendon Press.

Hick, J. (ed.) 1964. *The Existence of God*. New York: Macmillan.

Hick, J. 1971. *Arguments for the Existence of God*. New York: Herder and Herder.

Hick, J. & A. C. McGill (eds) 1967. *The Many-Faced Argument: Recent Studies on the Ontological Argument for the Existence of God*. New York: Macmillan.

Hindley, J. R., B. Lercher, J. P. Selden 1972. *Introduction to Combinatory Logic* (London Mathematical Society Lecture Notes, Series 7). Cambridge: Cambridge University Press.

Hintikka, J. 1963. "The Modes of Modality", *Acta Philosophica Fennica* 16.

Hintikka, J. 1968. "Behavioral Criteria of Radical Translation", *Synthese* 19.

Hintikka, J. 1975. "Impossible Possible Worlds", *Journal of Philosophical Logic* 4.

Hockney, D. 1975. "The Bifurcation of Scientific Theories and Indeterminacy of Translation", *Philosophy of Science* 42.

Hodges, M. P. 1972. "Quine on 'Ontological Commitment'", *Philosophical Studies* 23.

Hookway, C. 1988. *Quine: Language, Experience, and Reality*. Stanford, CA: Stanford University Press.

Horgan, T. 1993. "From Supervenience to Superdupervenience: Meeting the Demands of a Material World", *Mind* 102.

Horgan, T. & J. Woodward 1985. "Folk Psychology is Here to Stay", *Philosophical Review* 94.

Horst, S. 1999. "Symbols and Computation: A Critique of the Computational Theory of Mind", *Minds and Machines* 9.

Hoy, D. C. 1993. "Heidegger and the Hermeneutic Turn". In *The Cambridge Companion to Heidegger*, C. B. Guignon (ed.). Cambridge: Cambridge University Press.

Hughes, G. E. & M. J. Cresswell 1968. *An Introduction to Modal Logic*. London: Methuen.

Hughes, R. I. G. 1989. *The Structure and Interpretation of Quantum Mechanics*. Cambridge, MA: Harvard University Press.

Hume, D. 1975. *Enquiries Concerning Human Understanding and Concerning the Principles of Morals*, L. A. Selby-Bigge (ed.); 3rd edn, P. H. Nidditch (ed.). Oxford: Clarendon Press. (Reprint of *Essays and Treatises on Several Subjects*, originally published 1777.

Hume, D. 1978. *A Treatise of Human Nature*, L. A. Selby-Bigge (ed.); 2nd edn, P. H. Nidditch (ed.). Oxford: Clarendon Press. Originally published 1739–40.

Humphreys, P. 1997a. "Emergence, Not Supervenience", *Philosophy of Science* 64.

Humphreys, P. 1997b. "How Properties Emerge", *Philosophy of Science* 64.

Humphries, B. M. 1970. "Indeterminacy of Translation and Theory", *Southern Journal of Philosophy* 67.

Hunt, D. P. 1997. "How (Not) to Exempt Platonic Forms from *Parmenides*' Third Man", *Phronesis* 42.

Hunter, C. G. 2001. *Darwin's God: Evolution and the Problem of Evil*. Grand Rapids, MI: Brazos Press.

Hurlbutt, R. H. 1985. *Hume, Newton, and the Design Argument* (rev. edn). Lincoln, NE: University of Nebraska Press.

Husserl, E. 1962. *Ideas: General Introduction to Pure Phenomenology*, W. R. Boyce Gibson (trans.). New York: Collier Books.

Husserl, E. 1966. *Logische Untersuchungen* (2nd edn), G. Patzig (ed.). Göttingen: Vandenhoeck & Ruprecht.

Husserl, E. 1977. *Cartesian Meditations: An Introduction to Phenomenology*, D. Cairns (trans.). The Hague: Martinus Nijhoff.

Iwan, S. 2000. "An Analysis of Quine's 'Ontological Reduction and the World of Numbers'", *Erkenntnis* 53.

Jackson, F. 1982. "Epiphenomenal Qualia", *Philosophical Quarterly* 32.

Jackson, J. M. 1995. "Why Mental Explanations are Physical Explanations", *South African Journal of Philosophy* 14.

Jacoby, G. 1993. *Allgemeine Ontologie der Wirklichkeit*. Tübingen: Max Niemeyer.

Jacquette, D. 1986. "Intentionality and Intensionality: Quotation Contexts and the Modal Wedge", *The Monist* 59.

Jacquette, D. 1994. *Philosophy of Mind*. Englewood Cliffs, NJ: Prentice Hall.

Jacquette, D. (ed.) 1996. *Schopenhauer, Philosophy, and the Arts*. Cambridge: Cambridge University Press.

Jacquette, D. (ed.) 2002a. *A Companion to Philosophical Logic*. Oxford: Basil Blackwell.

Jacquette, D. 2002b. "Searle's Antireductionism", *Facta Philosophica* 4.

Jager, T. 1982. "An Actualist Semantics for Quantified Modal Logic", *Notre Dame Journal of Formal Logic* 23.

Janaway, C. 1989. *Self and World in Schopenhauer's Philosophy*. Oxford: Clarendon Press.

Johansson, I. 1989. *Ontological Investigations*. London: Routledge.

Johnstone, H. W. Jr. 1970. *The Problem of the Self*. University Park, PA: The Pennsylvania State University Press.

Jones, D. H. 1972. "Emergent Properties, Persons, and the Mind–Body Problem", *Southern Journal of Philosophy* 10.

Jorgensen, J. 1969. "Empiricism and Unity of Science", *Danish Yearbook of Philosophy* 6.

Jubien, M. 1969. "Two Kinds of Reduction", *Journal of Philosophy* 66.

Jubien, M. 1972. "The Intensionality of Ontological Commitment", *Noûs* 6.

Jubien, M. 1988. "Problems With Possible Worlds". In *Philosophical Analysis*, D. F. Austin (ed.). Dordrecht: Kluwer.

Jubien, M. 1993. *Ontology, Modality, and the Fallacy of Reference*. Cambridge: Cambridge University Press.

Jubien, M. 1996. "Actualism and Iterated Modalities", *Philosophical Studies* 84.

Jubien, M. 2001. "Propositions and the Objects of Thought", *Philosophical Studies* 104.

Kafatos, M. (ed.) 1989. *Bell's Theorem, Quantum Theory, and Conceptions of the Universe*. Dordrecht: Kluwer.

Kaminsky, J. 1969. *Language and Ontology*. Carbondale, IL: Southern Illinois University Press.

Kant, I. 1949. *Critique of Practical Reason and Other Writings in Moral Philosophy*, L. White Beck (ed. and trans.). Chicago, IL: University of Chicago Press.

Kant, I. 1965. *Critique of Pure Reason*, N. Kemp Smith (trans.). New York: St Martin's Press.

Kant, I. 1977. *Prolegomena to Any Future Metaphysics That Will be Able to Come Forward as Science*, P. Carus (trans.), J. W. Ellington (rev.). Indianapolis, IN: Hackett.

Kanthack, K. 1962. *Nicolai Hartmann und das Ende der Ontologie*. Berlin: Walter de Gruyter.

Katz, J. 1988. "The Refutation of Indeterminacy", *Journal of Philosophy* 85.

Kemeny, J. G. & P. Oppenheim 1970. "On Reduction". Reprinted in *Readings in the Philosophy of Science*, B. A. Brody (ed.). Englewood Cliffs, NJ: Prentice Hall.

Kim, J. 1978. "Supervenience and Nomological Incommensurables", *American Philosophical Quarterly* 15.

Kim, J. 1984. "Concepts of Supervenience", *Philosophy and Phenomenological Research* 45.

Kim, J. 1986. "Possible Worlds and Armstrong's Combinatorialism", *Canadian Journal of Philosophy* 16.

Kim, J. 1987. "'Strong' and 'Global' Supervenience Revisited", *Philosophy and Phenomenological Research* 48.

Kim, J. 1990. "Supervenience as a Philosophical Concept", *Metaphilosophy* 21.

Kim, J. 1993. *Supervenience and Mind: Selected Philosophical Essays*. Cambridge: Cambridge University Press.

King, J. 1995. "Structured Propositions and Complex Predicates", *Noûs* 29.

King-Farlow, J. 1999. "Metaphysics and Choosing: Sets, Quine, and the One", *Iyyun: The Jerusalem Philosophical Quarterly* 48.

Kisiel, T. 1973. "On the Dimensions of a Phenomenology of Science in Husserl and the Young Dr. Heidegger", *Journal of the British Society for Phenomenology* 4.

Klee, R. L. 1984. "Micro-Determinism and Concepts of Emergence", *Philosophy of Science* 51.

Kochen, S. & E. P. Specker 1967. "The Problem of Hidden Variables in Quantum Mechanics", *Journal of Mathematics and Mechanics* 17.

Kockelmans, J. J. (ed.) 1986. *A Companion to Martin Heidegger's "Being and Time"*. Washington, DC: Center for Advanced Research in Phenomenology and University Press of America.

Kockelmans, J. J. 1989. *Heidegger's "Being and Time": The Analytic of Dasein as Fundamental Ontology*. Lanham, MD: Center for Advanced Research in Phenomenology and University Press of America.

Krausz, M. & R. Shusterman (eds) 1999. *Interpretation, Relativism, and the Metaphysics of Culture: Themes in the Philosophy of Joseph Margolis*. Amherst: Humanity Books (Prometheus).

Kripke, S. A. 1963a. "Semantical Considerations on Modal Logics", *Acta Philosophica Fennica* 16.

Kripke, S. A. 1963b. "Semantical Analysis of Modal Logic I: Normal Modal Propositional Calculi", *Zeitschrift für mathematische Logik und Grundlagen der Mathematik* 9.

Kripke, S. A. 1979. "Speaker's Reference and Semantic Reference". In *Contemporary Perspectives in the Philosophy of Language*, P. A. French, T. E. Uehling Jr., H. K. Wettstein (eds). Minneapolis, MN: University of Minnesota Press.

Kripke, S. A. 1980. *Naming and Necessity*. Cambridge, MA: Harvard University Press.

Kroon, F. W. 1992. "Against Ontological Reduction", *Erkenntnis* 36.

Kuhn, T. 1962. *The Structure of Scientific Revolutions*. Chicago, IL: University of Chicago Press.

Kung, J. 1981. "Aristotle on Thises, Suches and the Third Man Argument", *Phronesis* 26.

Küng, G. 1963. *Ontologie und logistische Analyse der Sprache: Eine Untersuchung zur zeitgenössischen Universaliendiskussion*. Vienna: Springer-Verlag.

Langan, T. 1996. *Being and Truth*. Columbia, MO: University of Missouri Press.

Lango, J. W. 1972. *Whitehead's Ontology*. Albany, NY: State University of New York Press.

Larrimore, M. (ed.) 2001. *The Problem of Evil: A Reader*. Oxford: Basil Blackwell.

Lauth, B. 1997. "New Blades for Occam's Razor", *Erkenntnis* 46.

Leblanc, H. 1973. "'On Dispensing with Things and Worlds". In *Logic and Ontology: Studies in Contemporary Philosophy*, M. K. Munitz (ed.). New York: New York University Press.

Leblanc, H. 1982. *Existence, Truth, and Provability*. Albany, NY: State University of New York Press.

Leibniz, G. W. 1902. *Discourse on Metaphysics; Correspondence With Arnauld, Monadology*, G. R. Montgomery (trans.). LaSalle, IL: Open Court.

Leibniz, G. W. 1966. *Theodicy*, E. M. Huggard (trans.). Indianapolis, IN: Bobbs-Merrill.

Leibniz, G. W. 1973a. "Necessary and Contingent Truth". See Leibniz 1973f.

Leibniz, G. W. 1973b. "On Freedom" . See Leibniz 1973f.

Leibniz, G. W. 1973c. "A Letter on Freedom" . See Leibniz 1973f.

Leibniz, G. W. 1973d. "On the Principle of Indiscernibles" . See Leibniz 1973f.

Leibniz, G. W. 1973e. "On the Ultimate Origination of Things" . See Leibniz 1973f.

Leibniz, G. W. 1973f. *Leibniz: Philosophical Writings*, G. H. R. Parkinson (ed.), M. Morris & G. H. R. Parkinson (trans.). London: J. M. Dent & Son.

Leibniz, G. W. 1989. *De Arte Combinatoria*. In *Sämtliche Schriften und Briefe*, series VI [16 volumes], volume 1. Berlin: Akademie-Verlag. Originally published in 1666 as *Dissertatio*.

Lewis, C. I. 1912. "Implication and the Algebra of Logic", *Mind* 21.

Lewis, C. I. 1913. "Interesting Theorems in Symbolic Logic", *Journal of Philosophy* 10.

Lewis, C. I. 1914. "The Matrix Algebra for Implication", *Journal of Philosophy* 11.

Lewis, C. I. 1918. *A Survey of Symbolic Logic*. Berkeley, CA: University of California Press.

Lewis, C. I. 1920. "Strict Implication: An Emendation", *Journal of Philosophy* 17.

Lewis, C. I. & C. H. Langford 1959. *Symbolic Logic*, 2nd edn. New York: Dover. Orginally published 1932.

Lewis, D. K. 1968. "Counterpart Theory and Quantified Modal Logic", *Journal of Philosophy* 65.

Lewis, D. K. 1973. *Counterfactuals*. Oxford: Basil Blackwell.

Lewis, D. K. 1986. *On the Plurality of Worlds*. Oxford: Basil Blackwell.

Loar, B. 1990. "Phenomenal Properties". In *Mind and Cognition: A Reader*, W. G. Lycan (ed.). Oxford: Basil Blackwell.

Locke, J. 1975. *An Essay Concerning Human Understanding*, P. H. Nidditch (ed.). Oxford: Clarendon Press. Originally published 1700.

Loux, M. J. (ed.) 1970. *Universals and Particulars: Readings in Ontology*. New York: Doubleday.

Loux, M. J. 1978. *Substance and Attribute: A Study in Ontology*. Dordrecht: D. Reidel.

Loux, M. J. (ed.) 1979. *The Possible and the Actual*. Ithaca, NY: Cornell University Press.

Lovejoy, A. O. 1964. *The Great Chain of Being: A Study of the History of an Idea* (The William James Lectures Delivered at Harvard University, 1933). Cambridge: Harvard University Press.

Lucas, J. R. 1996. "The Unity of Science Without Reductionism", *Acta Analytica* 15.

Luijpen, W. 1969. *Existential Phenomenology*. Pittsburgh, PA: Duquesne University Press.

Lycan, W. G. (ed.) 1990. *Mind and Cognition: A Reader*. Oxford: Basil Blackwell.

Lycan, W. G. & G. Pappas 1972. "What is Eliminative Materialism?", *Australasian Journal of Philosophy* 50.

Mach, E. 1914. *The Analysis of Sensations*, C. M. Williams (trans.). Chicago, IL: University of Chicago Press.

Mackie, J. L. 1974. *The Cement of the Universe: A Study of Causation*. Oxford: Clarendon Press.

Mackie, J. L. 1982. *The Miracle of Theism: Arguments For and Against the Existence of God*. Oxford: Clarendon Press.

MacMahon, P. A. 1984. *Combinatory Analysis*. New York: Chelsea.

Maddy, P. 1992. *Realism in Mathematics*. Oxford: Clarendon Press.

Maddy, P. 1997. *Naturalism in Mathematics*. Oxford: Clarendon Press.

Malcolm, J. F. 1991. *Plato on the Self-Predication of Forms: Early and Middle Dialogues*. Oxford: Clarendon Press.

Malcolm, N. 1960. "Anselm's Ontological Arguments", *Philosophical Review* 69.

Marcus, R. B. 1993. *Modalities: Philosophical Essays*. New York: Oxford University Press.

Mares, E. D. 1997. "Who's Afraid of Impossible Worlds?", *Notre Dame Journal of Formal Logic* 38.

Margolis, J. 1959. "The Identity of a Work of Art", *Mind* 68.

Margolis, J. 1965. *The Language of Art and Art Criticism: Analytic Questions in Aesthetics*. Detroit: Wayne State University Press.

Margolis, J. 1973. "Behaviorism and Alien Languages", *Philosophia* 3.

Margolis, J. 1974. "Works of Art as Physically Embodied and Culturally Emergent Entities", *British Journal of Aesthetics* 14.

Margolis, J. 1975. "The Planets are Nine in Number", *Canadian Journal of Philosophy* 4.

Margolis, J. 1977. "The Ontological Peculiarity of Works of Art", *Journal of Aesthetics and Art Criticism* 36.

Margolis, J. 1978. *Persons and Minds: The Prospects of Nonreductive Materialism* (Boston Studies in the Philosophy of Science, 57). Dordrecht: D. Reidel.

Margolis, J. 1979. "A Strategy for a Philosophy of Art", *Journal of Aesthetics and Art Criticism* 37.

Margolis, J. 1980. *Art and Philosophy*. Atlantic Highlands, NJ: Humanities Press.

Margolis, J. 1981. "Nature, Culture and Persons", *Theory and Decision* 13.

Margolis, J. 1984a. *Culture and Cultural Entities: Toward a New Unity of Science*. Dordrecht and Boston: D. Reidel.

Margolis, J. 1984b. *Philosophy of Psychology*. Englewood Cliffs, NJ: Prentice Hall.

Margolis, J. 1984c. "Artworks and the History of Production", *Communication and Cognition* 17.

Margolis, J. 1986. "Constraints on the Metaphysics of Culture", *Review of Metaphysics* 39.

Margolis, J. 1999. *What, After All, Is a Work of Art? Lectures in the Philosophy of Art*. University Park, PA: The Pennsylvania State University Press.

Marx, W. 1954. *The Meaning of Aristotle's "Ontology"*. The Hague: Martinus Nijhoff.

Matson, W. I. 1965. *The Existence of God*. Ithaca, NY: Cornell University Press.

Mayer, R. 1981. *Ontologische Aspekte der Nominalsemantik*. Tübingen: Max Niemeyer.

McGinn, C. 2000. *Logical Properties: Identity, Existence, Predication, Necessity, Truth*. Oxford: Clarendon Press.

McKeon, M. 1996. "Logical Truth in Modal Logic", *Pacific Philosophical Quarterly* 77.

McLaughlin, B. & M. Tye 1998. "Externalism, Twin-Earth, and Self-Knowledge". In *Knowing Our Own Minds*, C. Wright, B. C. Smith & C. MacDonald (eds). Oxford: Oxford University Press.

McMichael, A. 1983a. "A New Actualist Modal Semantics", *Journal of Philosophical Logic* 12.

McMichael, A. 1983b. "A Problem for Actualism About Possible Worlds", *Philosophical Review* 92.

McTaggart, J. M. E. 1908. "The Unreality of Time", *Mind* 17.

McTaggart, J. M. E. 1968. *The Nature of Existence* [2 volumes]. Grosse Pointe, MI: Scholarly Press. (Originally published 1921–27, Cambridge University Press).

Meixner, U. 1997. *Axiomatic Formal Ontology*. Kluwer.

Melcic, D. 1986. *Heideggers Kritik der Metaphysik und das Problem der Ontologie.* Würzburg: Königshausen & Neumann.

Meinong, A. 1969–78. *Alexius Meinong Gesamtausgabe* [8 volumes], R. Haller & R. Kindinger (eds), in collaboration with R. M. Chisholm. Graz: Akademische Druck-u. Verlagsanstalt.

Meinwald, C. C. 1991. *Plato's Parmenides.* New York: Oxford University Press.

Melnyck, A. 1996. "Testament of a Recovering Eliminativist", *Proceedings of the Biennial Meetings of the Philosophy of Science Association* 3 (supplement).

Mendelson, E. 1964. *Introduction to Mathematical Logic.* New York: D. Van Nostrand.

Mensch, J. R. 1981. *The Question of Being in Husserl's Logical Investigations.* The Hague and Boston: Kluwer.

Menzel, C. 1986. "On Set Theoretic Possible Worlds", *Analysis* 46.

Menzel, C. 1990. "Actualism, Ontological Commitment, and Possible Worlds Semantics", *Synthese* 85.

Merleau-Ponty, M. 1962. *The Phenomenology of Perception*, C. Smith (trans.). New York: The Humanities Press.

Meyer, L. N. 1989. "Science, Reduction and Natural Kinds", *Philosophy* 64.

Miller, Ed. L. 1995. *God and Reason: An Invitation to Philosophical Theology*, 2nd edn. Englewood Cliffs, NJ: Prentice Hall.

Miller, W. M. 1981. "Popper's Third World: A Methodological Critique and Alternative", *Dialogue* 24.

Mohanty, J. N. 1972. *The Concept of Intentionality.* St. Louis, MO: Warren H. Green.

Moran, D. 2000. "Heidegger's Critique of Husserl's and Brentano's Accounts of Intentionality", *Inquiry* 43.

Moravcsik, J. M. E. 1963. "The Third Man Argument and Plato's Theory of Forms", *Phronesis* 8.

Moreland, J. P. 1985. *Universals, Qualities, and Quality-Instances: A Defense of Realism.* Lanham, MD: University Press of America.

Morewedge, P. 1982. *Philosophies of Existence, Ancient and Medieval.* New York: Fordham University Press.

Morgenau, H. A. 1941. "Foundations of the Unity of Science", *Philosophical Review* 50.

Morris, C. 1946. "The Significance of the Unity of Science Movement", *Philosophy and Phenomenological Research* 6.

Mortensen, C. 1986. "Explaining Existence", *Canadian Journal of Philosophy* 16.

Mossley, D. J. 1996. "The (Dis)Unity of Science: Some Tensions Between the Physical, Biological and Social Sciences – A Diagnosis", *Philosophical Writings* 3.

Moulines, C. U. 2001. "Ontology, Reduction, and the Unity of Science". In *The Proceedings of the Twentieth World Congress of Philosophy*, 10, Philosophy of Science, Tian Yu Cao (ed.). Bowling Green, OH: Philosophy Documentation Center.

Mulligan, K. (ed.) 1992. *Language, Truth and Ontology.* Dordrecht: Kluwer.

Mumford, S. 1994. "Supervenience and Reduction", *Philosophical Quarterly* 44.

Nagel, E. 1970. "Mechanistic Explanation and Organismic Biology". Reprinted in *Readings in the Philosophy of Science*, B. A. Brody (ed.). Englewood Cliffs, NJ: Prentice Hall.

Nagel, T. 1974. "What is it Like to be a Bat?", *Philosophical Review* 83.

Neurath, O., G. De Santillana, E. Zillsel 1941. *International Encyclopedia of Unified Science: Foundations of the Unity of Science.* Chicago, IL: University of Chicago Press.

Newman, D. V. 2001. "Chaos, Emergence, and the Mind–Body Problem", *Australasian Journal of Philosophy* 79.

Newton, I. 1952. *Opticks*, 4th edn. New York: Dover.

Nolan, D. 1997a. "Impossible Worlds: A Modest Approach", *Notre Dame Journal of Formal Logic* 38.

Nolan, D. 1997b. "Quantitative Parsimony", *British Journal for the Philosophy of Science* 48.

Nozick, R. 1981. *Philosophical Explanations*. Oxford: Clarendon Press.

Nunn, B. V. 2000. "Differences Between A- and B-Time", *Philosophical Inquiry* 22.

Oaklander, N. L. 1999. "Craig on McTaggart's Paradox and the Problem of Temporary Intrinsics", *Analysis* 59.

O'Brien, T. C. 1960. *Metaphysics and the Existence of God*. Washington: Thomist Press.

O'Connor, T. 1994. "Emergent Properties", *American Philosophical Quarterly* 31.

Owen, G. E. L. 1957–58. "Zeno and the Mathematicians", *Proceedings of the Aristotelian Society* 58.

Owens, J. 1978. *The Doctrine of Being in the Aristotelian Metaphysics: A Study in the Greek Background of Mediaeval Thought*, preface by Etienne Gilson, 3rd edn, rev. Toronto: Pontifical Institute of Mediaeval Studies.

Parfit, D. 1992. "The Puzzle of Reality: Why Does the Universe Exist?", *Times Literary Supplement*, 3 July. Expanded version, "Why Anything? Why This?", *London Review of Books* 22 January and 5 February (1998)).

Parkinson, G. H. R. 1965. *Logic and Reality in Leibniz's Metaphysics*. Oxford: Clarendon Press.

Parmenides 1984. *Parmenides of Elea: Fragments*. Text and translation with an introduction by D. Gallop. Toronto: University of Toronto Press.

Peirce, C. S. 1931–35. *Collected Papers of Charles Sanders Peirce* [8 volumes], C. Hartshorne, P. Weiss, A. W. Burks (eds). Cambridge, MA: Harvard University Press.

Peirce, C. S. 1977. *Semiotics and Significs: The Correspondence Between Charles S. Peirce and Victoria, Lady Welby*, C. Hardwick (ed.). Bloomington, IN: Indiana University Press.

Pelletier, F. J. 1983. "Plato on Not-Being: Some Interpretations of the 'Symploki Eidon' (259e) and Their Relation to Parmenides' Problem", *Midwest Studies in Philosophy* 8.

Pelletier, F. J. 1990. *Parmenides, Plato, and the Semantics of Not-Being*. Chicago, IL: University of Chicago Press.

Peterson, P. L. 1968. "Translation and Synonymy: Rosenberg on Quine", *Inquiry* 11.

Peterson, S. 1973. "A Reasonable Self-Predication Premise for the Third Man Argument", *Philosophical Review* 82.

Philipse, H. 1998. *Heidegger's Philosophy of Being: A Critical Interpretation*. Princeton, NJ: Princeton University Press.

Pickering, F. R. 1981. "Plato's Third Man Arguments", *Mind* 90.

Pike, N. (ed.) 1964.. *God and Evil: Readings on the Theological Problem of Evil*. Englewood Cliffs, NJ: Prentice Hall.

Place, U. T. 1956. "Is Consciousness a Brain Process?", *British Journal of Psychology* 47.

Plantinga, A. 1961. "A Valid Ontological Argument?", *Philosophical Review* 70.

Plantinga, A. 1966. "Kant's Objection to the Ontological Argument", *Journal of Philosophy* 63.

Plantinga, A. 1974. *The Nature of Necessity*. Oxford: Oxford University Press.

Plantinga, A. 1979. "Actualism and Possible Worlds". In *The Possible and the Actual*, M. J. Loux (ed.). Ithaca, NY: Cornell University Press.

Plato 1997. *Complete Works*, J. M. Cooper (ed.). Indianapolis, IN: Hackett.

Poli, R. & P. Simons (eds) 1996. *Formal Ontology*. Dordrecht: Kluwer.

Pollock, J. 1989. *How to Build a Person: A Prolegomenon*. Cambridge, MA: MIT Press/ Bradford Books.

Popper, K. R. 1972. *Objective Knowledge: An Evolutionary Approach*. Oxford: Clarendon Press.

Popper, K. R. 1982. *Quantum Theory and the Schism in Physics*. Totowa: Rowman and Littlefield.

Priest, G. (ed.) 1997. "Impossible Worlds", *Notre Dame Journal of Formal Logic* 38 (guest-edited issue).

Prior, W. J. 1983. "*Timaeus* 48e-52d and the Third Man Argument", *Canadian Journal of Philosophy* 9.

Putnam, H. 1975. "The Meaning of 'Meaning'". In *Mind, Language, and Reality*. Cambridge: Cambridge University Press.

Quine, W. V. O. 1937. "New Foundations for Mathematical Logic", *American Mathematical Monthly* 44.

Quine, W. V. O. 1951. "On the Consitency of 'New Foundations'", *Proceedings of the National Academy of Sciences of the USA* 37.

Quine, W. V. O. 1960. *Word and Object*. Cambridge, MA: MIT Press.

Quine, W. V. O. 1963a. "On What There Is". In *From a Logical Point of View*, 2nd edn, rev. New York: Harper & Row.

Quine, W. V. O. 1963b. "Logic and the Reification of Universals". In *From a Logical Point of View*, 2nd edn, rev. New York: Harper & Row.

Quine, W. V. O. 1963c. "Reference and Modality". In *From a Logical Point of View*, 2nd edn, rev. New York: Harper & Row.

Quine, W. V. O. 1969. "Ontological Relativity". In *Ontological Relativity and Other Essays*. New York: Columbia University Press.

Quine, W. V. O. 1970. "On the Reasons for Indeterminacy of Translation", *Journal of Philosophy* 67.

Quine, W. V. O. 1976a. "Three Grades of Modal Involvement". In *The Ways of Paradox and Other Essays*, revised and enlarged edition. Cambridge, MA: Harvard University Press.

Quine, W. V. O. 1976b. "A Logistical Approach to the Ontological Problem". In *The Ways of Paradox and Other Essays*, revised and enlarged edition. Cambridge, MA: Harvard University Press.

Quine, W. V. O. 1976c. "On Carnap's Views on Ontology". In *The Ways of Paradox and Other Essays*, revised and enlarged edition. Cambridge, MA: Harvard University Press.

Quine, W. V. O. 1976d. "Ontological Reduction and the World of Numbers". In *The Ways of Paradox and Other Essays*, revised and enlarged edition. Cambridge, MA: Harvard University Press.

Quine, W. V. O. 1976e. "On Multiplying Entities". In *The Ways of Paradox and Other Essays*, revised and enlarged edition. Cambridge, MA: Harvard University Press.

Quine, W. V. O. 1976f. "Ontological Remarks on the Propositional Calculus". In *The Ways of Paradox and Other Essays*, revised and enlarged edition. Cambridge, MA: Harvard University Press.

Quine, W. V. O. 1993. "The Inception of NF", *Bulletin de la Société Mathématique de Belgique*, serie B, 45.

Radner, D. 1985. "Is There a Problem of Cartesian Interaction?", *Journal of the History of Philosophy* 23.

Rankin, K. W. 1969. "The Duplicity of Plato's Third Man", *Mind* 78.

Rankin, K. W. 1970. "Is the Third Man Argument an Inconsistent Triad?", *Philosophical Quarterly*, 20.

Ray, G. 1996. "Ontology-Free Modal Semantics", *Journal of Philosophical Logic* 25.

Rees, D. A. 1963. "Plato and the Third Man, II", *Proceedings of the Aristotelian Society, Supplement* 37.

Rescher, N. 1997. *Objectivity: The Obligations of Impersonal Reason*. Notre Dame: Notre Dame University Press.

Rescher, N. & R. Brandom 1979. *The Logic of Inconsistency: A Study in Non-Standard Possible-World Semantics and Ontology*. Totowa: Rowman and Littlefield.

Resnick, M. 1985. "Ontology and Logic: Remarks on Hartry Field's Anti-Platonist Philosophy of Mathematics", *History and Philosophy of Logic* 6.

Richardson, W. J. (ed.) 1963. *Heidegger: Through Phenomenology to Thought*. The Hague: Martinus Nijhoff.

Riefstahl, H. 1983. *Ontische Strukturen*. Mannheim: Verlag der Humboldt-Gesellschaft für Wissenschaft, Kunst und Bildung.

Riordan, J. 1958. *An Introduction to Combinatorial Analysis*. New York: Wiley.

Rorty, R. 1965. "Mind–Body Identity, Privacy and Categories", *Review of Metaphysics* 19.

Rorty, R. 1970. "In Defense of Eliminative Materialism", *Review of Metaphysics* **24**.

Rosen, G. 1990. "Modal Fictionalism", *Mind* **99**.

Rosen, G. 1993. "A Problem for Fictionalism About Possible Worlds", *Analysis* **53**.

Rosen, G. 1995. "Modal Fictionalism Fixed", *Analysis* **55**.

Ross, G. M. 1984. *Leibniz*. Oxford: Oxford University Press.

Rosser, J. B. 1936. "Extensions of Some Theorems of Gödel and Church", *Journal of Symbolic Logic* **1**.

Rosser, J. B. 1939a. "On the Consistency of Quine's New Foundations for Mathematical Logic", *Journal of Symbolic Logic* **4**.

Rosser, J. B. 1939b. "Definition by Induction in Quine's New Foundations for Mathematical Logic", *Journal of Symbolic Logic* **4**.

Rosser, J. B. 1952. "The Axiom of Infinity in Quine's New Foundations", *Journal of Symbolic Logic* **18**.

Rothbart, D. 1976. "Propositions and Quine's Indeterminacy of Radical Translation", *Dialogue* **18**.

Rousseau, J. J. 1982. *The Reveries of the Solitary Walker*, C. Butterworth (trans.). New York: Harper & Row.

Rowe, W. L. (ed.) 2001. *God and the Problem of Evil*. Oxford: Basil Blackwell.

Russell, B. 1905. "On Denoting", *Mind* **14**.

Russell, B. 1910–11. "Knowledge by Acquaintance and Knowledge by Description", *Proceedings of the Aristotelian Society* **11**.

Russell, B. 1911–12. "On the Relations of Universals and Particulars", *Proceedings of the Aristotelian Society* **12**.

Russell, B. 1957. *Why I Am Not a Christian and Other Essays on Related Subjects*, edited with an appendix on the "Bertrand Russell Case" by P. Edwards. New York: Simon and Schuster.

Russell, B. 1990. *The Problems of Philosophy*. Indianapolis, IN: Hackett.

Ryle, G. 1949. *The Concept of Mind*. New York: Barnes & Noble.

Ryser, H. J. 1963. *Combinatorial Analysis*. New York: Wiley.

Sacks, M. 1989. *The World We Found: The Limits of Ontological Talk*. London: Duckworth.

Salmon, N. 1996. "Trans-World Identification and Stipulation", *Philosophical Studies* **84**.

Salmon, W. C. (ed.) 1970. *Zeno's Paradoxes*. Indianapolis, IN: The Bobbs-Merrill Company.

Sartre, J.-P. 1957. *The Transcendence of the Ego: An Existentialist Theory of Consciousness*, translated and annotated with an introduction by F. Williams and R. Kirkpatrick. New York: Farrar, Straus and Giroux. Originally published 1937.

Sartre, J.-P. 1992. *Being and Nothingness: A Phenomenological Essay on Ontology*, translated with an introduction by H. Barnes. New York: Washington Square Press.

Scaltsas, T. 1989. "The Logic of the Dilemma of Participation and of the Third Man Argument", *Apeiron* **22**.

Scaltsas, T. 1992. "A Necessary Falsehood in the Third Man Argument", *Phronesis* **37**.

Schlesinger, G. 1983. "Reconstructing McTaggart's Argument", *Philosophy* **58**.

Schopenhauer, A. 1891. *Arthur Schopenhauers Samtliche Werke* [6 volumes], Julius Frauenstädt (ed.). Wiesbaden: E. Brockhaus.

Schopenhauer, A. 1969. *The World as Will and Representation* [2 volumes], E. F. J. Payne (trans.). New York: Dover.

Schopenhauer, A. 1974. *On the Fourfold Root of the Principle of Sufficient Reason*, E. F. J. Payne (trans.). La Salle, IL: Open Court Publishing.

Schufreider, G. 1978. *An Introduction to Anselm's Argument*. Philadelphia, PA: Temple University Press.

Schweizer, P. 1994. "Self-Predication and the Third Man", *Erkenntnis* **40**.

Searle, J. R. 1969. *Speech Acts: An Essay in the Philosophy of Language*. Cambridge: Cambridge University Press.

Searle, J. R. 1979. *Expression and Meaning: Studies in the Theory of Speech Acts*. Cambridge: Cambridge University Press.

Searle, J. R. 1980. "Minds, Brains, and Programs", *The Behavioral and Brain Sciences* 3.
Searle, J. R. 1983. *Intentionality: An Essay in the Philosophy of Mind*. Cambridge: Cambridge University Press.
Searle, J. R. 1984. *Minds, Brains and Science*. Cambridge, MA: Harvard University Press.
Searle, J. R. 1992. *The Rediscovery of the Mind*. Cambridge: MIT Press/Bradford Books.
Searle, J. R. 1995. *The Construction of Social Reality*. New York: The Free Press.
Searle, J. R. 1999. *Mind, Language and Society: Philosophy in the Real World*. New York: Basic Books.
Sellars, W. 1955. "Vlastos and the Third Man", *Philosophical Review* 64.
Shaffer, J. 1962. "Existence, Predication and the Ontological Argument", *Mind* 71.
Sharvy, R. 1986. "Plato's Causal Logic and the Third Man Argument", *Noûs* 20.
Shiner, R. 1970. "Self-Predication and the Third Man Argument", *Journal of the History of Philosophy* 8.
Shirley, E. S. 1971. "Stimulus Meaning and Indeterminacy of Translation", *Southern Journal of Philosophy* 9.
Silberstein, M. 1998. "Emergence and the Mind–Body Problem", *Journal of Consciousness Studies* 5.
Silberstein, M. & J. McGeever 1999. "The Search for Ontological Emergence", *Philosophical Quarterly* 49.
Slenczka, N. 1993. *Realpräsenz und Ontologie: Untersuchung der ontologischen Grundlagen der Transsignifikationslehre*. Göttingen: Vandenhoeck & Ruprecht.
Slesser, H. H. 1919. *The Nature of Being: An Essay in Ontology*. London: Allen & Unwin.
Smart, J. J. C. 1959. "Sensations and Brain Processes", *Philosophical Review* 68.
Smart, J. J. C. 1981. "Physicalism and Emergence", *Neuroscience* 6.
Smart, J. J. C. 1984. "Ockham's Razor". In *Principles of Philosophical Reasoning*, J. H. Fetzer (ed.). Totowa: Rowman and Allenheld.
Smith, B. (ed.) 1982. *Parts and Moments: Studies in Logic and Formal Ontology*. Munich and Vienna: Philosophical Verlag.
Smith, D. W. 1988. "Bodily Versus Cognitive Intentionality", *Noûs* 22.
Smith, Q. 1989. "The Logical Structure of Debate About McTaggart's Paradox", *Philosophy Research Archives* 14.
Smith, Q. 1990. "A Natural Explanation of the Existence and Laws of Our Universe", *Australasian Journal of Philosophy* 68.
Soames, S. 1999. "The Indeterminacy of Translation and the Inscrutability of Reference", *Canadian Journal of Philosophy* 29.
Sober, E. 1975. *Simplicity*. Oxford: Clarendon Press.
Sober, E. 1981. "The Principle of Parsimony", *British Journal for the Philosophy of Science* 32.
Sober, E. 1990. "Let's Razor Ockham's Razor". In *Explanation and its Limits* (Royal Institute of Philosophy, Supplement 27), D. Knowles (ed.). Cambridge: Cambridge University Press.
Sperry, R. W. 1991. "In Defense of Mentalism and Emergent Interaction", *Journal of Mind and Behavior* 12.
Stalnaker, R. 2001. "On Considering a Possible World as Actual I", *Proceedings of the Aristotelian Society, Supplement* 75.
Stich, S. P. 1983. *From Folk Psychology to Cognitive Science: The Case Against Belief*. Cambridge: MIT Press/Bradford Books.
Stock, G. (ed.) 1998. *Appearance Versus Reality: New Essays on Bradley's Metaphysics*. Oxford: Clarendon Press.
Strang, C. 1963. "Plato and the Third Man, I", *Proceedings of the Aristotelian Society, Supplement* 37.
Strawson, P. F. 1963. *Individuals: An Essay in Descriptive Metaphysics*. Garden City, NY: Doubleday.

Swinburne, R. 1991. *The Existence of God*. Oxford: Clarendon Press.
Swinburne, R. 1998. *Providence and the Problem of Evil*. Oxford: Clarendon Press.
Sylvan, R. 1985–86. "Toward an Improved Cosmo–Logical Synthesis", *Grazer Philosophische Studien* 25–6.
Taminiaux, J. 1991. *Heidegger and the Project of Fundamental Ontology*, M. Gendre (trans. and ed.). Albany, NY: State University of New York Press.
Taylor, J. G. 1997. "The Emergence of Mind", *Communication and Cognition* 30.
Teller, P. 1973. "On Quine's Relativity of Ontology", *Canadian Journal of Philosophy* 3.
Teller, P. 1992. "A Contemporary Look at Emergence". In *Emergence or Reduction? Prospects for Nonreductive Materialism*, A. Beckermann, H. Flohr, J. Kim (eds). Berlin: Walter de Gruyter.
Teloh, H. & D. J. Louzecky 1972. "Plato's Third Man Argument", *Phronesis* 17.
Tersman, F, 1998. "Stimulus Meaning Debunked", *Erkenntnis* 49.
Tharp, L. H. 1971. "Ontological Reduction", *Journal of Philosophy* 68.
Thiel, C. 1968. *Sense and Reference in Frege's Logic*. Dordrecht: D. Reidel.
Thomason, J. M. 1971. "Ontological Relativity and the Inscrutability of Reference", *Philosophical Studies* 22.
Toms, E. 1962. *Being, Negation and Logic*. Oxford: Basil Blackwell.
Trapp, R. W. 1976. *Analytische Ontologie: Der Begriff der Existenz in Sprache und Logik*. Frankfurt am Main: A. M. V. Klostermann.
Tweedale, M. 1992. "Ockham's Supposed Elimination of Connotative Terms and his Ontological Parsimony", *Dialogue* 31.
Van der Laan, D. A. 1997. "The Ontology of Impossible Worlds", *Notre Dame Journal of Formal Logic* 38.
Van Fraassen, B. C. 1982. "The Charybdis of Realism: Epistemological Implications of Bell's Inequality", *Synthese* 52.
Van Fraassen, B. C. 1991. *Quantum Mechanics: An Empiricist View*. Oxford: Clarendon Press.
Van Inwagen, P. 1986. "Two Concepts of Possible Worlds", *Midwest Studies in Philosophy* 11.
Vandevert, L. R. 1991. "A Measurable and Testable Brain-Based Emergent Interactionism: An Alternative to Sperry's Mentalist Emergent Interactionism", *Journal of Mind and Behavior* 12.
Vjecsner, P. 1988. *On Proof for the Existence of God, and Other Reflective Inquiries*. New York: Penden.
Vlastos, G. 1954. "The Third Man Argument in the *Parmenides*", *Philosophical Review* 63.
Vlastos, G. 1955. "Addenda to the Third Man Argument: A Reply to Professor Sellars", *Philosophical Review* 64.
Vlastos, G. 1969. "Plato's Third Man Argument (*Parm.* 132a1–b2): Text and Logic", *Philosophical Quarterly* 19.
Volpi, F. 1978. "Heideggers Verhaltnis zu Brentanos Aristoteles-Interpretation: Die Frage nach dem Sein des Seienden", *Zeitschrift für philosophische Forschung* 32.
Vuillement, J. 1975. "Quine's Concept of Stimulus Meaning", *Philosophic Exchange* 2.
Wahl, J. A. 1969. *Philosophies of Existence: An Introduction to the Basic Thought of Kierkegaard, Heidegger, Jaspers, Marcel, Sartre*, F. M. Lory (trans.). New York: Schocken Books.
Wallace, J. 1971. "A Query on Radical Translation", *Southern Journal of Philosophy* 68.
Weber, M. 1996. "Fitness Made Physical: The Supervenience of Biological Concepts Revisited", *Philosophy of Science* 63.
Weiner, J. 1990. *Frege in Perspective*. Ithaca, NY: Cornell University Press.
Weingartner, P. & E. Morscher (eds) 1979. *Ontologie und Logik: Vorträge und Diskussionen eines Internationalen Kolloquiums* (Salzburg 21–24 September 1976). Berlin: Duncker & Humbolt.
White, F. C. 1992. *On Schopenhauer's Fourfold Root of the Principle of Sufficient Reason*. Leiden: E. J. Brill.

Whitehead, A. N. 1929. *Process and Reality: An Essay in Cosmology*, edited and corrected from the 1929 edition by D. R. Griffin and D. W. Sherburne. New York: The Free Press.

Whitehead, A. N. & B. Russell 1925–27. *Principia Mathematica* [3 volumes], 2nd edn. Cambridge: Cambridge University Press.

Whitney, B. L. 1993. *Theodicy: An Annotated Bibliography on the Problem of Evil, 1960–1990*. New York: Garland Press.

Wiggins, D. 1971. *Identity and Spatio-Temporal Continuity*. Oxford: Basil Blackwell.

Wiggins, D. 1976. *Truth, Invention, and the Meaning of Life*. Oxford: British Academy.

Wiggins, D. 1980. *Sameness and Substance*. Cambridge, MA: Harvard University Press.

Williams, C. J. F. 1981. *What is Existence?* Oxford: Clarendon Press.

Williams, C. J. F. 1992. *Being, Identity, and Truth*. Oxford: Clarendon Press.

Wilson, C. 1982. "Sensation and Explanation: The Problem of Consciousness in Descartes", *Nature and System* 4.

Wilson, N. L. 1973. "The Two Main Problems of Philosophy", *Dialogue* 12.

Winch, P. 1958. *The Idea of a Social Science and its Relation to Philosophy*. London: Routledge & Kegan Paul.

Winch, P. (ed.) 1969. *Studies in the Philosophy of Wittgenstein*. New York: Humanities Press.

Winch, P. 1987. *Trying to Make Sense*. Oxford: Blackwell.

Winch, P. (ed.) 1994. *Norman Malcolm – Wittgenstein: A Religious Point of View?* Ithaca, NY: Cornell University Press.

Wittgenstein, L. 1922. *Tractatus Logico-Philosophicus*, C. K. Ogden (ed.). London: Routledge & Kegan Paul.

Wolterstorff, N. 1970. *On Universals: An Essay in Ontology*. Chicago, IL: University of Chicago Press.

Worrall, J. (ed.) 1994. *The Ontology of Science*. Aldershot: Ashgate Publishing.

Yablo, S. 1996. "How in the World?", *Philosophical Topics* 24.

Yablo, S. 1998. "Does Ontology Rest on a Mistake?", *Proceedings of the Aristotelian Society, Supplement* 72.

Yolton, J. W. 2000. *Realism and Appearances: An Essay in Ontology*. Cambridge: Cambridge University Press.

Young, J. 1996. "Schopenhauer, Heidegger, Art, and the Will". In *Schopenhauer, Philosophy, and the Arts*, D. Jacquette (ed.). Cambridge: Cambridge University Press.

Ziff, P. 1970. "A Response to 'Stimulus Meaning'", *Philosophical Review* 79.

Index